Mapping Jewish Identities

THE UNIVERS

7.

l7

c

J8

}

New Perspectives on Jewish Studies

A Series of the Philip and Muriel Berman Center for Jewish Studies
Lehigh University, Bethlehem, Pennsylvania

General Editor: Laurence J. Silberstein

Mapping Jewish Identities

Edited by
Laurence J. Silberstein

NEW YORK UNIVERSITY PRESS
New York & London

Library of Congress Cataloging-in-Publication Data
Mapping Jewish identities / edited by Laurence J. Silberstein.
p.   cm. — (New perspectives on Jewish studies)
Includes bibliographical references and index.
ISBN 0-8147-9768-7 (cloth : alk. paper) — ISBN 0-8147-9769-5
(pbk. : alk. paper)
1. Jews—Identity.   I. Silberstein, Laurence J. (Laurence Jay),
1936– II. Title. III. Series
DS143 .M23 2000
305.892'4—dc21   00-008121

New York University Press books are printed on acid-free paper,
and their binding materials are chosen for strength and durability.

Manufactured in the United States
10 9 8 7 6 5 4 3 2 1

This volume is dedicated to the memory of Philip I. Berman

Contents

Acknowledgments

Earlier versions of all but one of the chapters in this volume were presented at the Berman Center conference "Mapping Jewish Identities," held at Lehigh University in May 1998. The editor thanks Michelle Friedman, Hannan Hever, and Laura Levitt for their valuable assistance in conceptualizing and structuring the conference. The editor and contributors thank Shirley Ratushny for her diligence and meticulous care in overseeing the editorial process and preparing the manuscript for publication. We also thank Carolyn Hudacek for her significant contribution to the preparation of the manuscript.

The Philip and Muriel Berman Center thanks the Lucius N. Littauer Foundation for providing a grant for publication of this volume.

The cooperation of the following artists, authors, publishers, and photographers is gratefully acknowledged:

Frédéric Brenner and the Howard Greenberg Gallery for permission to publish a section of his photograph "Inventory," which appears in *Jews/America/A Representation* (New York: Harry N. Abrams, 1996).

Irena Klepfisz for permission to quote selections from her poem "Bashert," which appears in *A Few Words in the Mother Tongue: Poems Selected and New (1971–1990)* (Portland, Ore.: Eighth Mountain Press, 1990), copyright © 1974, 1977, 1980, 1982, 1985, 1990 by Irena Klepfisz.

New Directions Publishing Corporation for permission to reprint a portion of Robert Duncan's *The Opening of the Field* (New York: New Directions, 1973), copyright © 1960 by Robert Duncan.

Art Spiegelman and Condé Nast Publications for permission to reprint the cover of the February 15, 1993, issue of the *New Yorker*.

Art Spiegelman and Pantheon Books for permission to reprint sections of *Maus I* (New York, 1986), copyright © 1973, 1980, 1981, 1982, 1983, 1984, 1985, and *Maus II* (New York, 1991), copyright © 1986, 1989, 1990, 1991.

Stanford University Press for permission to reprint a chapter from *Dying for God,* by Daniel Boyarin.

Larry Sultan for permission to publish his photograph "My Mother Posing for Me," which appeared in *Pictures from Home,* by Larry Sultan (New York: Harry N. Abrams, 1992).

Chapter 1

Mapping, Not Tracing: Opening Reflection

Laurence J. Silberstein

For several decades, social scientists seeking to represent differences between and similarities within/among individuals and groups have employed the concept of identity as a defining category. Identity, as the cultural critic Paul Gilroy reminds us, has come to be taken as a key to understanding the formation of the pronoun *we:*

> To share an identity is apparently to be bonded on the most funda-
> mental levels: national, "racial," ethnic, regional, local. And yet,
> identity is always particular, as much about difference as about
> shared belonging. It marks out the divisions and sub-sets in our so-
> cial lives and helps to define the boundaries around our uneven,
> local attempts to make sense of the world. (Gilroy 1997, 301)

The concept of identity has been of fundamental importance in recent discussions about Jewish life. Sociologists, psychologists, and
communal policy makers use the concept "Jewish identity" as a fundamental tool for exploring Jewish life, present and future. Repeatedly, they inquire into the Jewish identity of American (and Israeli)
Jews.[1]

The customary discourse of Jewish identity posits certain attitudes, beliefs, or practices as constitutive of or essential to Jewish
identity. Scholars construct questionnaires based on the premise that
Jewish identity "already is." Subjects are queried as to the extent to
which they do or do not adhere to predetermined attitudes, beliefs,
and behavior patterns. The information is then compiled and analyzed, and judgments are rendered as to whether it indicates a

"growth" or "decline" of Jewish identity.[2] At issue, according to these studies, is the survival of a viable Jewish community in the United States.

The conception of identity that informs most studies of American Jewish identity has been succinctly described by cultural critic Stuart Hall as follows:

> [It] defines "cultural identity" in terms of one shared culture, a sort of collective "one true self," hiding inside the many other, more superficial or artificially imposed "selves" which people with a shared history or ancestry hold in common. Within the terms of this definition, cultural identities reflect the common historical experiences and shared cultural codes which provide us, as "one people," with stable, unchanging and continuous frames of reference and meaning, beneath the shifting divisions and vicissitudes of our actual history. (Hall 1990, 223)

According to Hall (1990), conventional modern discourses on identity presuppose a "'oneness' that underlying other, more superficial differences is regarded as the essence of what we mean when we speak of the identity of a group." Scholars who operate with this concept of identity, including historians and social scientists, seek to "discover, excavate, bring to light and express" that which is essential and unchanging in a group's identity (223). Although acknowledging differences among Jews and Jewish communities, most discussions of Jewish identity tend to assume the existence of a core, authentic, or essential "Jewish self," "hiding," as Hall puts it, "inside the many other, more superficial or artificially imposed selves." This self, this "Jewish identity," is what all Jews, as bearers of a shared history, are said to share in common.

In recent decades, however, essentialist conceptions of identity have been increasingly criticized. The awakening of previously silenced or marginalized groups, such as women, ethnic minorities, and previously colonized peoples; the widespread movement of populations; and the contraction of temporal and spatial distances through technology have revealed the inadequacy of essentialist notions of identity.[3] At the same time, critical movements such as poststructuralism and postmodernism have rendered problematic the theoretical foundations of essentialist thinking.

As a result, scholars have formulated alternative, non-essentialist concepts in which identity is seen as a process, a matter of "becoming" rather than of being.

> Perhaps instead of thinking of identity as an already accomplished fact, which the new cultural practices then represent, we should think, instead, of identity as a "production," which is never complete, always in process, and always constituted within, not outside, representation. (Hall 1990, 221)

Instead of preexisting the ways in which we talk or think about it, identity is seen as produced through the discourses we use. The discourses through which people are identified and categorized include ethnicity, religion, gender, sexual orientation, race, nationality, socioeconomic position, intellectual perspective, and geographic location. Rather than unified or singular, identities are considered to be "multiply constructed across different, often intersecting and antagonistic, discourses, practices, and positions" (Hall 1996, 4).

Rather than viewing identities as eternally fixed in some stationary, recoverable past, critics increasingly see them as subject to the continuous "play" of history, culture, and power. So conceived, argues Hall, "identities do not lend themselves to being recovered or brought to light" (Hall 1990, 225). No longer taken as referring to a fixed condition or a defining body of traits or characteristics, identity is considered to be a process of becoming. Rather than describing "who we are" or where we came from, identity has to do with who we might become.

Memory plays a significant role in the production and construction of identity. Hall suggests thinking of identities as "the names we give to the different ways in which we are positioned by, and position ourselves within, the narratives of the past" (Hall 1990, 225). Insofar as they are "always constructed through memory, fantasy, narrative and myth," identities are inherently unstable.

However, rather than being an innate faculty by means of which we recover events of the past, memory is increasingly understood as a product of diverse and complex techniques and discursive practices:[4]

> Memory . . . is itself assembled. One's memory of oneself as a being with a psychological biography, a line of development of emotion,

intellect, will, desire, is produced through family photograph albums, the ritual repetition of stories, the actual or "virtual" dossier of school reports and the like, the accumulation of artifacts, and the attachment of image, sense, and value to them, and so forth. (Rose 1996a, 180)

To speak of identity, as does Hall, in terms of becoming, production, being "always in process," being "multiply constructed," "antagonistic discourses, practices and positions," and "so-called unities" clearly destabilizes the concept of identity, revealing its slippages and fissures.

Although identities "are constantly in process of change and transformation" (Hall 1996, 4), in the view of Hall and others, such as William Connolly (1991), identity, like self, remains a necessary concept in social and cultural discourse. Rather than eliminate the term, they suggest that we rehabilitate it. Notwithstanding the contingency of all identities, there are, Hall argues, moments of temporary closure.[5]

The Spatial Turn in Identity Discourse

A significant development in recent critical theories of identity is a shift in emphasis from the temporal to the spatial. Along with this shift has come an increasing use of concepts like "position" and "becoming." As Hall formulates it:

> Cultural identities are the points of identification, the unstable points of identification or suture, which are made, within the discourses of history and culture. Not an essence, but a "positioning." (Hall 1990, 226)[6]

Rather than objectify or reify a particular identity, individual or collective, and trace its development over time, a spatialized approach to identity treats subjects according to the various sites in which they are located and the various positions that they occupy. As a subject moves among various sites, social, political, or cultural, he or she is positioned in different ways. At different times, gender, class, race, ethnicity, sexual orientation, or religion takes priority as the positioning discourse.[7]

Social theorists advocating this move from a temporal to a spatial discourse of identity utilize the metaphor of "mapping":

> The map—as our allegory of power and knowledge—and the subject—as our allegory of the body and the self—real identity: Its fluidity and fixity, its purity and hybridity, its safety and its terrors, its transparency and its opacity. The map—as allegory of space-time—and the subject—as allegory of place-in-the-world and limit-of-the-world—reveal that "space" is actively constitutive of the practices of authority and resistance, of grounding meaning and replacing meaning. (Pile and Thrift 1995, 49)

Cultural critics Nigel Thrift and Steve Pile argue that in the modern world, experiences previously limited to colonial populations are increasingly relevant to many other groups. Thus, they argue, "more and more people in general—not only ex-colonial or marginalized people—are beginning to think of themselves, of their identities and their relationship to culture and to place," in terms of movement, multiplicity, and hybridity. Such people "have learned to live with, and indeed to speak from difference." Speaking from the in-between of different cultures, repeatedly unsettling the assumptions of one culture from the perspective of another, people find ways

> of being both the same and different from the others amongst whom they live. Of course, such people bear the marks of the particular cultures, languages, histories and traditions which "formed" them, but they do not occupy these as if they were pure, untouched by other influences, or provide a source of fixed identities to which they could ever fully "return." (Pile and Thrift 1995, 47–48)

Uncovering the Operations of Power: A Genealogical Approach to Identity

The relationship of identity and power has been a major concern to those feminists and postcolonial critics who advocate a rethinking of the prevailing essentialist notions of identity. Operating as grids on which people are located in specific subject positions or identities, concepts such as gender, race, ethnicity, class, nation, and religion have distinct power effects. As Hall argues, to speak about or analyze identity requires that we be aware of

> not only how language and representation produce meaning, but how the knowledge which a particular discourse produces connects with power, regulates conducts, makes up or constructs identities and subjectivities, and defines the way certain things are represented, thought about, practiced and studied. (Hall 1997, 6)[8]

The power effects of identity discourse are of particular concern to French philosophers Michel Foucault and Gilles Deleuze, and to Deleuze's coauthor, French psychotherapist Félix Guattari. They regard discourses and practices that seek to contain the individual within particular identities or spaces as controlling or normalizing. Such discourses and practices, insofar as they threaten the freedom of individuals to become, to individuate in new and creative ways, are dangerous.[9]

Foucault, Deleuze, and Guattari have focused on the processes by means of which selves and subjects are produced. Our notions of what it is to be human, argues Foucault, are the products of specific historically situated discourses and practices. To understand what it is to be human, we must analyze the discursive practices that produce and sustain different forms of subjectivities. Of particular concern to Foucault are the power relations that particular identity discourses presuppose, engender, and legitimate.

The distinction Deleuze and Guattari make between mapping and tracing is particularly important to their critique of identity discourse:

> What distinguishes the map from the tracing is that it is entirely oriented towards an experimentation in contact with the real. The map does not reproduce an unconscious closed upon itself; it constructs the unconscious. It fosters connections between fields, the removal of blockages. . . . The map has to do with performance, whereas the tracing always involves an alleged "competence." (Deleuze and Guattari 1989, 12–13)

Since Plato, Western thought has been dominated by an arborescent mode of discourse. Arborescent systems, framed in terms of roots and branches, are hierarchical. In arborescent thinking, an object (in linguistics and psychoanalysis) is "crystallized into codified complexes, laid out along a genetic axis" (Deleuze and Guattari 1989, 12). The goal of such thinking is to trace, on the basis of an overriding structure or supporting axis, something that comes ready-made.

In contrast to the arborescent model, which is bound up with notions of evolution and temporal development, Deleuze and Guattari offer the model of a rhizome, which relates to space and movement:

> Unlike a structure, which is defined by a set of points and positions, the rhizome is made only of lines; lines of segmentarity and stratification as its dimensions; and the line of flight or deterritorialization as the maximum dimension after which the multiplicity undergoes metamorphosis, changes in nature. (1989, 21)

Whereas arborescent discourse speaks in terms of origins, unities, and continuities, the rhizome "operates by variation, expansion, conquest, capture, offshoots" (Deleuze and Guattari 1989, 22). Whereas tracing entails seriality, continuity, and development, a map "must be produced, constructed, a map that is always detachable, connectable, reversible, modifiable, and has multiple entryways and exits and its own lines of flight" (22).[10]

Arborescent discourse is concerned with tracing the origins and development of preexisting subjects; rhizomatic discourse engages in imaginative experimentation. Whereas tracing is a practice that seeks to represent what has been and is, mapping is experimental and future oriented, seeking to imagine what has not yet come into being. A practice of accounting and bureaucracy, tracing blocks free movement and flexibility by "organizing, stabilizing, and neutralizing multiplicities." Rather than opening the way for becoming, it serves to reproduce "only the impasses, blockages, incipient taproots, or points of structuration" (Deleuze and Guattari 1989, 13).

Arborescent thought has had harmful effects on human society and culture: "We should stop believing in trees, roots, and radicles. They've made us suffer too much" (Deleuze and Guattari 1989, 15).

What we conventionally take to be natural identities or essences are the products of practices of categorization and encoding that serve to position bodies. According to one of their major interpreters, for Deleuze and Guattari, identity and identity loss correspond to being in or slipping out of one's assigned category and the paths through the social field associated with it; they are the end effects, not the foundation, of the process of individuation. (Massumi 1992, 84)

To be locked into a subject position, what Deleuze might call a molar identity, is to be blocked from future movement.

Western culture, under the hegemony of arborescent thinking, privileges unity over multiplicity. Rhizomatic thinking and its practice of mapping privilege multiplicity. Multiplicity is the given; unity has to be explained. Rather than stasis and stability being the norm and movement and change having to be explained, becoming is the norm and being has to be explained.

Whereas Foucault approached subjectivity from the perspective of knowledge and power, Deleuze and Guattari prefer to speak in terms of desire. As explained by feminist philosopher Elizabeth Grosz, "desire refers not to a felt need for something that we lack" but rather to a force that "produces, connects, makes machinic alliances . . . a series of practices, bringing things together or separating them . . . [that] does not aim at anything beyond its own proliferation or self expansion." Desire, she continues, "assembles things out of singularities and breaks things, assemblages, down into their singularities. It moves, it does" (Grosz 1994; cited in Thrift 1997, 128).

The shift advocated by Foucault, Deleuze, and Guattari may be seen as a shift from representational to nonrepresentational discourse. Representational discourse attempts to construct a model that adequately represents such things as "identity." Nonrepresentational discourse, by contrast, treats language not in terms of what it signifies, represents, or means but in terms of what it does. Advocates of nonrepresentational thinking, including Foucault, focus on the usage and effects of language:

Concepts would no longer be considered images of things, but things in their own right, which might transmit intensities or provide means of interaction with other events and processes. (Patton 1994, 155)

Rather than talk in terms of the subject, nonrepresentational thinking is concerned with the practices of subjectification—the practices, techniques, machinic assemblages through which subjects are produced/positioned (cf. Rose 1996a, 173–80).

Feminist philosopher and theorist Judith Butler has been at the forefront of those using Foucault's critique of subjectivity to rethink the categories of self, agency, and identity. Butler seeks to subvert the essentialist political meanings of identity categories, "to displace them from the contexts in which they have been deployed as instruments of oppressive power" (Butler 1992, 17). Butler, like Foucault, wishes to transform the discourse of gender and sexuality and produce an alternative form of analysis that contributes to an expanding enfranchisement and democratization of those who have been marginalized, excluded, and subordinated.

> Through what exclusions has the feminist subject been constructed, and how do those excluded domains return to haunt the "integrity" and "unity" of the feminist "we"? And how is it that the very category, the subject, the "we," that is supposed to be presumed for the purpose of solidarity, produces the very factionalization it is supposed to quell? (Butler 1992, 14)

Butler is particularly concerned with revealing the operation of power in the practices that establish the meaning and limits of concepts such as heterosexuality, homosexuality, and bisexuality, as well as the exclusionary apparatus that produces and limits their meanings. The goal of a genealogical critique is not simply to reveal the constricting effects of one form of identity construction but also to open up, to expand the range of other possible forms of identity enactment, to

> release the term into a future of multiple significations, to emancipate it from the maternal or racialist ontologies to which it has been restricted, and to give it play as a site where unanticipated meanings might come to bear. (Butler 1992, 16)

Combining deconstructive and genealogical critiques, Butler argues that, rather than undermining social relations and inhibiting political action, a deconstructive (and, we would add, a genealogical) approach "enables a purposive and significant reconfiguration of cultural and political relations."

> To deconstruct is not to negate or dismiss, but to call into question
> and, perhaps more importantly, to open up a term, like the subject,
> to a reusage or redeployment that previously has not been author-
> ized. (Butler 1992, 15)

Butler further argues that it is not only possible but also necessary to
continue to speak of subjects and of agency.[11] Although discursively
constituted, the self/subject should not, she insists, be regarded as
passive:

> My position is mine to the extent that "I"—and I do not shirk from
> the pronoun—replay and resignify the theoretical positions that
> have constituted me, working the possibilities of their convergence,
> and trying to take account of the possibilities that they systematically
> exclude. (Butler 1992, 9)

Through our actions, the positions that we take, the ways in which we
act and perform, we participate in the process whereby we are constituted as subjects.

British social and political theorist Nikolas Rose, drawing from
Foucault, Deleuze, and Guattari, has also formulated a genealogical
critique of subjectivity. Rose argues that

> human beings are not the unified subjects of some coherent regime
> of domination that produces persons in the form in which it
> dreams. On the contrary, they live their lives in a constant move-
> ment across different practices that address them in different ways.
> Within these practices, persons are addressed as different sorts of
> human being, presupposed to be different sorts of human being,
> acted upon as if they were different sorts of human being. Tech-
> niques of relating to oneself as a subject or unique capacities worthy
> of respect run up against practices of relating to oneself as the tar-
> get of discipline, duty and docility. (Rose 1996b, 140–41)

Rose is particularly concerned with the discursive practices and tech-
nologies of power that have created the conditions wherein we speak
of distinct identities or selves. He thus advocates a shift from "the apparent linearity, unidirectionality and irreversibility of time, to the
multiplicity of places, planes and practices" (Rose 1996b, 143–44).
Rather than speak of the development over time of stable identities,
individual or collective, Rose advocates a spatial discourse in which

the body, shifting between different spaces/sites, serves itself as the site of different forms of subjectification.[12]

Instead of taking "identification" to be a natural process, as does psychoanalysis, Rose treats identification as historically produced and constructed in specific spaces or contexts. Rather than study identities, Rose advocates that we analyze the spaces in which we are called on to "identify" ourselves, the locations in which we are asked to declare our identities. These are the spaces/locations in which we are interpellated/identified through gender, race, religion, nationality, ethnicity, and sexual orientation.

Rather than subjects "bound by the enclosure formed by the human skin or carried in a stable form in the interior of an individual," individuals are better understood as

> webs of tension across space that accord human beings capacities to the extent that they catch them up in hybrid assemblages of knowledges, instruments, vocabularies, systems of judgement and technical artifacts. (Rose 1996b, 143–44)

Rejecting the conventional psychological discourse that, through concepts such as internalization and identification, differentiates between our "inner" and "outer" selves or between that which is internal and external to the self, Rose argues for a more fluid, dynamic, expansive interpretation of experience. Groups, like individuals, become what they become not by identifying with specific others, past and present, but by enfolding elements from the surrounding milieu.[13]

The writings of Foucault, Deleuze, and Guattari have played an important role in the writings of cultural and social critics seeking to rethink the prevailing conceptions of identity. Rejecting the possibilities of extracting essential characteristics of identities—national, cultural, gender, and otherwise—these critics have begun to analyze the processes by means of which identities are produced and disseminated. As explained by Hall:

> Precisely because identities are constructed within, not outside, discourses, we need to understand them as produced in specific historical and institutional sites within specific discursive formations and practices, by specific enunciative strategies. Moreover, they emerge within the play of specific modalities of power. (Hall 1996, 4)

Identity Unraveled: The Implications for Jewish Identity

Genealogical and deconstructive critiques of identity such as those I discussed above can help clear spaces for a purposive and significant reconfiguration of cultural and political relations among Jews, and between Jews and non-Jews. By revealing those sites and processes through which Jewish subject positions have been and are currently being constructed, they provide openings for contemporary Jews wishing to free themselves from the prevailing normalizing discourses and develop alternative modes of Jewish becoming.

Nonetheless, as I indicated at the beginning of this chapter, most students of Jewish identity take little notice of the changing interpretations of identity I have discussed. For the most part, they tend to regard them as inimical to the perpetuation of Jewish identity. Continuing to view identity in exclusively positive terms, they also ignore issues of power. They thus share what anthropologist Virginia Dominguez regards as a general resistance to acknowledge the power effects of identity construction:

> To see ourselves as constituting others is to acknowledge our having more power than we may wish to have or be comfortable having. To see ourselves as constituting ourselves is to leave the door open for calling into question some of the arguments we ourselves frequently use for claiming the "fact" and the legitimacy of our collective identity. (1989, 191)

However, other scholars, including most of the writers in this volume, assert the need for new, non-essentialist definitions of Jewish identity. Desiring to create conditions for change within Jewish life, they posit concepts of identity that emphasize process over product, multiplicity over unity, and becoming rather than being. Recognizing the complex processes that inform identity production, they view conventional approaches to Jewish identity to be simplistic, showing little understanding of the complex processes through which identities are produced and constructed. Another criticism of essentialist Jewish identity discourse is that it constrains and inhibits the development of alternative imaginative ways of thinking and acting Jewish. Finally, essentialist approaches are seen as occluding relations of power within the Jewish community and between Jews and others, particularly

Palestinians. They thus tend to impede efforts to reevaluate and reconfigure these relations.

Intensifying conflicts over Jewish identity among diverse groups
of Jews are most graphically evident in but by no means limited to Israel. As these conflicts reveal, no universally agreed-upon criteria to
support particular views of Jewish identity exist. All efforts to impose
a dominant category such as religious group, race, nation, transna-
tional people, or ethnic group on the heterogeneous world Jewish
population ultimately fail.[14] Moreover, such efforts have the effect of
excluding some Jews. This point has been effectively made by Jewish
feminists in whose writings excluded domains, to use the phrasing of
philosopher Judith Butler, "return to haunt the 'integrity' and 'unity'
of the (Jewish) 'we'" (Butler 1992, 14).

One alternative to fixed, essentialist notions of Jewish identity is
to think of identity, in Butler's formulation, as "an undesignatable
field of difference, one that cannot be totalized or summarized by a
descriptive identity category" (Butler 1992, 16) such as religion, ethnicity, or nationality. One result of this approach is to reconfigure
such essentially contested terms like *Jew, Judaism,* and *Jewish* into a site
of "permanent openness and resignifiability" (Butler 1992, 16). This
would, in turn, free them of the essentialist, sometimes racialist on-
tologies to which they have often been restricted and open the way to
"play at a site where unanticipated meanings might come to bear."[15]

To many critics, such genealogical or deconstructive discourses of
identity have the effect of undermining efforts to perpetuate the collective identity of specific groups, such as Jews, feminists, or African
Americans.[16] To conceive of boundaries between groups as porous
and fluid and the spaces in which identities are configured as multiple, open, and flexible is perceived as weakening a group's integrity
as well as struggles in its behalf.[17]

Butler's response to these critics is, I argue, relevant for those
concerned with Jewish survival but opposed to essentialist identity discourse. In her view, genealogy can serve as a viable "ground" for feminist politics. Such a critique helps expose those sites, those discourses and practices of exclusion, through which the (feminist) subject has been previously constructed and subordinated. It can thus
assist those (like women) seeking to free themselves from controlling
or normalizing discourses and help open the way to alternative

modes of becoming. Rather than eliminating the concept of a subject, individual or collective, the anti-essentialist approach, argues Butler, "enables a purposive and significant reconfiguration of cultural and political relations" (1992, 12).

Unraveling Jewish Nationalist Identity: The Case of Postzionism

One site of a critique of dominant Jewish identity discourse is that of postzionism. Israeli intellectuals who have designated themselves or have been designated by their critics as postzionist have called attention to the problematic effects of essentialist Jewish identity discourse.[18] To these Israeli intellectuals, essentialist conceptions of Jewish identity impede needed changes in the understanding of relations between Israeli Jews and Palestinians, Israeli and non-Israeli alike.[19] Moreover, the zionist discourse embedded in Israeli culture occludes sites of oppression and violence in Israeli society. Convinced that conventional Israeli cultural discourse, framed through the lenses of zionism, occludes those processes through which power relations in Israeli society are constructed and legitimated, they seek alternative ways to frame Israeli national and cultural identity.

Current debates over postzionism erupted in response to efforts by scholars to reframe and revise the dominant representations of Israeli society and history. Throughout the 1980s, two groups of Israeli scholars, commonly known as "critical sociologists" and "new historians," formulated alternative narratives of Israeli history, society, and culture.[20] In their view, the dominant Israeli sociological and historical paradigms legitimate the marginalization and exclusion of such minority populations as Jews of Middle Eastern origin *(mizrahim)*, women, and Palestinians. Challenging prevailing Israeli historical narratives, the so-called new historians rendered problematic the premises of Israeli collective memory.

Another group, whom I have labeled "postmodern postzionists," links the crisis in Israeli culture to the dominant zionist discourse.[21] Embracing postmodern and poststructuralist theories, these were the first Israeli writers to formulate a genealogical critique of Israeli culture and identity.

In contrast to most Israeli historians and social scientists, the postmodern postzionists problematize the discursive and representational practices through which historical and social-scientific interpretations are produced. In the process, they criticize essentialist notions of Israeli identity and culture. One of their basic objectives is to clear space for the production and dissemination of alternative cultural discourses, historical narratives, and forms of Israeli identity. For the most part, they see conventional Israeli public discourse as occluding power relations and networks in Israeli society.

The debates surrounding postzionism are, among other things, conflicts over identity: national, Israeli, and Jewish. At the heart of these debates are such questions as: What kind of a state should Israel be/become? Should Israel remain a Jewish state, dominated by Jewish symbols, calendar, and images? Or should it be a democratic state of all of its citizens, in which cultural diversity, difference, and multiplicity are respected and encouraged? What is the relation of Israeli identity to Jewish identity?

The conditions that have generated these debates reflect problems encountered by many modern states that seek to preserve and perpetuate essentialist concepts of national identity. In the case of Israel, the effort to position Jews in general and Israelis in particular in unified, fixed, enclosed subject positions is grounded in the discourse of zionism.[22] Insofar as zionism has been the most influential Jewish identity discourse in the past century both inside and outside Israel, the postzionist critique has far-reaching implications for all Jews.

Postmodern postzionists reject the essentialist, organic, holistic discourse of identity and culture that characterizes zionist as well as most other modern Jewish discourse. Like other postmodernist thinkers, postmodern postzionists tend to represent identity as constructed, multiple, heterogeneous, and conflicted. More specifically, criticizing conventional efforts to identify Israeli with Jewish and Jewish with European, they emphasize the diverse, conflicted character of Israeli culture and identity. Zionist discourse, they argue, should not be allowed to determine the cultural and physical borders of the state. Accordingly, they seek to produce alternative discourses, alternative knowledge, alternative subject positions through which to talk about and live Israeliness, Israeli culture, the Israeli past, and the

Israeli future. Two of the contributors to this volume, Adi Ophir and Hannan Hever, are prominent advocates of this position.[23]

Many postzionist critics, following Foucault, frame cultural debates in Israel in terms of power relations. For example, Sara Chinski, an art critic and curator, has analyzed the exclusionary effects of zionist aesthetic representations of space. Chinski takes issue with the dominant Israeli notion of space/homeland, taught to all elementary school children (1993, 115–16), that equates Israeli art with Jewish art and Israeli space with Jewish space. Such notions of space, she argues, exclude the Palestinian other and territorialize (artistic/interpretive) texts (115).

Ariella Azoulay, another curator and cultural critic, also criticizes the dominant Israeli discourse on space (1992, 89). In treating spatial divisions as natural and given, nationalist movements like zionism legitimate particular hierarchies of power. This is evident in zionism's representation of the land as the "homeland." The zionist practice of controlling the ways in which the homeland is represented is part of an effort "to make it possible for them to gradually control that space until they achieved control over all or part of it" (Azoulay 1993, 89).

Among the practices that Azoulay singles out as establishing and legitimating zionist control of the land are creating archaeological sites, establishing settlements, setting up road signs, constructing public structures and monuments, carving out urban/rural spaces, and establishing museums (1993, 89). She is particularly concerned with the ways in which public sites and museums are used to legitimate the zionist dream of a Jewish homeland. To Azoulay, these places actually function as sites of a struggle for power.[24]

According to Azoulay, Israeli historical museums standardize and control the representations of the "past," the identities of individuals and groups, and the ways in which they affiliate with the national collective. In displaying or representing the (culture of the) past, historical museums actually participate in managing the present.

Other postzionist critics focus on the ways in which the dominant Israeli discourse, particularly academic discourse, represents the Palestinians and the physical spaces they inhabit. Whereas the concept of the Arab village is regarded in Israeli cultural discourse as a purely descriptive term with no political overtones, Gil Eyal (1993) argues that this concept, grounded in such binaries as modern/traditional and Jew/Arab, functions to objectify and categorize Arab Israeli space from the perspective of the Jewish Israeli majority. Analyzing the official Israeli spatializing discourse that produced the category "Arab village," Eyal has revealed the ways in which such representational practices exclude Arabs from the boundaries of Israeli collective identity. Whereas most Israeli academic discourse treats the cultural and spatial separation between Jew and Arab as given, both natural and necessary, Eyal argues that this separation has been produced by discursive practices. Far from being natural or given, these practices and the separations they enact legitimate and produce specific forms of power relations.

Even the discourse used to identify and label the Palestinian population of Israel is understood by postmodern postzionists in terms of its power effects. Jewish Israeli discourse, eschewing all terms derived from the name *Palestine*, has traditionally used the generic concept "Arab" when speaking of the Palestinian population of Israel. In so doing, they reject the discourse used by the minority Arab group to speak of themselves. Dani Rabinowitz, a Hebrew University anthropologist, argues that this dominant discourse "divert[s] attention from the painful topic of a place that is mired in controversy [and shifts it] to the less threatening topic of cultural difference—[which] in the liberal Israeli discourse of cultural pluralism, is much more legitimate" (1993, 145). According to Rabinowitz, although no more natural, neutral, or precise than other terms, the commonly used term *Israeli Arab* has, over time, become a part of the dominant Israeli discourse and functioned as a political-historical foundation of zionist Israel.[25]

The power effects of Israeli zionist discourse have also been shown to operate in Israeli literature. Hannan Hever, as reflected in his contribution to this volume (chapter 9), analyzes the power effects of conventional notions of cultural identity embedded in Israeli literary discourse. Hever (1990) regards Palestinian Anton Shammas's Hebrew novel *Arabesques* as an example of what Deleuze and Guattari have called "minority literature." Although writing in Hebrew, the language of the majority, Shammas uses that language to problematize and subvert the dominant zionist/Israeli conception of Hebrew literature as Jewish literature and Israeli culture as Jewish culture. Writing from the perspective of the Palestinian minority, Shammas also subverts the notions of time and history that pervade the dominant Jewish discourse (Hever 1990, 273–74). Dramatically portraying the power effects of the State of Israel on Palestinian culture, Shammas seeks to subvert the hegemonic identification of Israeli culture as Jewish culture and the Hebrew language as a Jewish language.[26]

These examples reveal only some of the ways in which the dominant Israeli conceptions of identity and culture have been subjected to critique. Insofar as Israel is the most concentrated population of Jews in the world, and in light of the formative impact of zionist discourse on the identity construction of diaspora Jewry, the postzionist critique has the effect of destabilizing modernist conceptions of Jewish identity both inside and outside Israel.

Mapping Jewish Identities: The Present Volume

As the writings of American Jewish feminists and other cultural critics suggest, the critique of essentialist Jewish identity discourse is by no means limited to Israel. While the debates over postzionism were taking shape in Israel, a small but expanding group of American Jewish scholars and intellectuals have been engaged in formulating their own critique of the prevailing Jewish identity discourse.[27] A number of the contributors to this book have actively participated in these discussions. All of the contributors are part of a select group of Jewish Studies scholars and cultural critics engaged in rethinking the categories of Jewish identity discourse.

Each essay, with one exception, was first presented at a conference, "Mapping Jewish Identities," held at Lehigh University in May 1998.[28] In advance of the conference, the editor asked the writers to consider the following issues and questions:

1. What are the discourses, apparatuses, and representational practices by means of which Jews construct their identity? How do these relate to issues of power?
2. What practices of inclusion/exclusion do these processes of identity construction entail? In what ways is difference inscribed in them?

3. How do contemporary Jews position themselves within, and/
   or how are they positioned by, the narratives of the past?
4. In what ways do recent theoretical discussions of hybridity
   and borders problematize the concept of distinct group
   identities?

These themes and problems are addressed by each of the authors, albeit in different ways and to varying degrees. Each chapter reflects the effects of contemporary critical discussions of identity from fields such as Cultural Studies, Gender Studies, and Postcolonial Studies.

While they problematize conventional Jewish identity discourse, the contributors do not conceive of their enterprise as negative or destructive. Engaging in a critique of contemporary Jewish identity discourse, they seek to remove blockages so as to make possible new ways of theorizing (and enacting) Jewish identity. Unwilling (and perhaps unable) to sever the bonds that connect them to Jewish culture, past and present, they nonetheless find themselves unable to embrace that culture as conventionally represented. Their critiques thus reflect a felt need for a new language, a new discourse in which to carry on the conversation of and about Jewish identity and culture.

Tresa Grauer (chapter 2) challenges those who read American Jewish writers such as Phillip Roth as reflecting a decline in American Jewish cultural identity. To Grauer, such a reading is grounded in a simplistic understanding of both identity and writing. Reading Marge Piercy's novel *He, She, and It*, Grauer argues for a more complex relationship of identity and writing, one that takes identity as discursively produced.

Grauer takes Piercy's rewriting of the Golem tale as an example of "the ongoing process of defining Jewish American identity through intimate conversation with a Jewish textual tradition" (38). In so doing, she challenges Irving Howe's often-repeated claim that discontinuity, "rupture, break, and disassociation" characterize the cultural experience of American Jewish writers. Continuing to work with a canon of "authoritative Jewish texts," American Jewish writers such as Piercy greatly expand the contents of the canon, according to Grauer, "to include cultural narratives that stand outside a sacred tradition but that nevertheless continue to provide meaning in the shaping of contemporary Jewish identity" (41). Grauer situates such efforts within the midrashic tradition of textual interpretation, understood as "a Jewish interpretive tradition of intertextuality and multiple readings" that both continues and breaches Jewish literary tradition (44). Grauer's depiction of American Jewish identity in terms of "multiple lines of continuity" that "are not in conflict" (44) calls to mind Deleuze and Guattari's notion of the rhizome.

Complementing Grauer's focus on literary representations of Jewish life, Laura Levitt (chapter 3) provides a critique of the ways in which American Jewish identity is conventionally represented through photography. Levitt reads identification in terms of our attempts to compensate for loss and remind ourselves of our similarities to/differences from others. In the recent proliferation of photographic collections about Jews, she sees an indication of American Jews' desire to connect with a lost immigrant past.

Levitt is concerned with the ways in which many photographic collections, here represented by Frédéric Brenner's *Jews/America/A Representation*, reinforce attempts by Jews to avoid the complex processes of identity construction. She is particularly critical of the desire to conceal the ambivalences of Jewish life in America. Collections like Brenner's, argues Levitt, remove or conceal these ambivalences, as well as the contradictions and conflicts that mark the life of most American Jews. Larry Sultan's book *Pictures from Home*, in contrast, does not perform such an attempt at concealment.

Critical of Brenner's attempt to provide "a sustaining narrative even in the face of communal trauma," a conflict-free sense of continuity, Levitt seeks "other ways of imaging contemporary Jews" that are more closely approximated in Sultan's book (76). These "other ways" problematize or disrupt stereotypes, reveal conflicts and differences among and between Jews, describe unfulfilled desires, present multiple narratives, and highlight the ambivalences that inform the process of identifying as Jews in America. Rejecting positions in which identification is seen as "a kind of nostalgic reclamation project" (79), works like Sultan's reveal the multiple identity sites of American Jews, in which Jewishness may or may not be at the center.

Drawing, like Levitt, on Diana Fuss's important interrogation of the concept "identification," Michelle Friedman (chapter 4) criticizes the ways in which American Jews, in remembering the Holocaust, eschew the difficulties that memory work entails. Friedman analyzes the work of one child Holocaust survivor and two children of survivors. Herself the daughter of a child survivor, she explores the complexities that inform the processes of remembering and identification.

Objecting to the simplistic, mythological ways in which the Holocaust has been made to function in the identity formation of contemporary Jews, Friedman explores the complex "labor of remembrance." In Art Spiegelman's two-volume cartoon book *Maus*, the writings of Irena Klepfisz, and the stand-up comedy of Deb Filler, Friedman finds cogent representations of the complexities of remembering and identifying.

Marilyn Reizbaum (chapter 5) also reads Spiegelman's *Maus* as revealing the complexities of identity formation, particularly as it relates to the children of Holocaust survivors. Reizbaum positions *Maus* against the background of Adorno's often-cited warning that "after Auschwitz you could no longer write poems" (Adorno 1973, 262). For Reizbaum, *Maus* represents "the perfect teaching tool for a postmodern, post-Holocaust consideration of form and genre" (123). Spiegelman, as she reads him, is particularly concerned with such issues as the limits of authenticity and the burden of history.

Reizbaum contrasts *Maus* with Spiegelman's provocative *New Yorker* cover depicting "a Hasidic Jew embracing and kissing a black woman dressed in a sleeveless shift and wearing large hoop earrings" (125). She sees these as representing two different aspects of the modern construction of the Jewish self. If *Maus* presents an image of a Jewish self that has been internalized from without, forged by those who would render that self unacceptable and inhuman, the image of the Hasid, she argues, represents an internal Jewish critique. Whereas the *Maus* imagery reinforces a stereotype, the Hasid image "undoes the historical type" (128). Arguing that a burdensome concern for authenticity resulting from the Holocaust deters such a critique, Reizbaum finds that Spiegelman strives to overthrow both internal and external resistance to critique and display post-Holocaust legacies.

Anita Norich (chapter 6) also resists efforts to simplify and sentimentalize the complex processes of loss, recovery, and memory relating to the Holocaust. Writing autobiographically, she analyzes her relationship to Yiddish language as central to the construction of her own identity. At home in American and European languages and literatures, she nonetheless opts to focus her academic talents on the Yiddish language and literature that formed the everyday culture of Jewish communities that are no more. Embracing Yiddish as a language of living communication, she resists that position which would ground Jewish identity in mourning or commemoration.

Seemingly well adjusted and happy, Norich is, at the same time, besieged by fears and anxieties common to children of survivors. Deprived of the photographs, stories, and personal memories that connect most of her contemporaries to deceased relatives, she finds solace in her mother's tombstone inscribed with the Yiddish names of murdered relatives, "a place where names were written" (151). Unable to relate to the vast grave that is Poland as home, she embraces Yiddish, "the language spoken in those older homes to which none of us can return," as the home to which she returns. Physically and materially at home in America, her "imagination continues to live elsewhere" (153). In Norich's account, we see mirrored the ironies and tensions, embraced but not resolved, that contribute to the construction of identity.

Ironies and tensions, albeit of very different kinds, also inform the autobiographical reflections of Regina Morantz-Sanchez (chapter 7). Like Norich, a professor at the University of Michigan, Morantz-Sanchez's path to Jewish identity is formed in very different spaces, thus revealing the diversity and multiplicity that inform the identity of American Jews. Whereas Norich is confronted by the memories of the Holocaust and her relation to the rapidly disappearing Yiddish culture, Morantz-Sanchez is confronted by the tensions of American culture in the 1960s.

During her college years, an awakening feminist consciousness led her to resist the constraints she saw imposed on her by the Judaism in which she had been raised. Seeking to integrate her diverse experiences and connect the various sites in which they were shaped, she achieved what she hoped was a successful integration of liberal, feminist, and Jewish values. Her daughter's decision to reject the mother's choices and embrace an ultra-Orthodox life is clearly a challenge to Morantz-Sanchez's identity choices. Rejecting the uncertainties and instabilities that mark the mother's world, the daughter seeks stability, meaning, and assurance in a very different place. Ironically, in the framework adopted by the daughter, the mother's hoped-for solution is seen as a danger. The spaces in which each of them seeks a meaningful Jewish identity remain alien and threatening to the other.

Adi Ophir's essay, like that of Hannan Hever, highlights the impact of space, both geographical and cultural, on the construction of Jewish identity. A clear example is the different function of the memory of the Holocaust in the lives of American Jews and Israeli Jews, and the different ways in which these communities come to terms with it. Ophir's analysis of the ways in which "the Holocaust is used and abused as a means in the construction of Jewish identity" in Israel (chapter 8, 179) contrasts markedly with the chapters by Friedman, Reizbaum, and Norich. Ophir, an Israeli, is particularly concerned with the ways in which representing or remembering the Holocaust has functioned to position Israeli Jews as victims. Of particular concern to Ophir are the power effects of these practices on relations between Israeli Jews and Palestinians both inside and outside Israel.[29]

To Ophir, the subject position of victim that pervades Israeli collective identity is grounded in a sense of irretrievable loss and an inability to represent the lost object. In the dominant Israeli cultural and political discourse, grounded in zionist discourse, the sense of loss connected to the Holocaust is linked to a sense of loss related to the land.

Postzionists, interrogating the hegemonic Israeli identity narrative and the historical premises on which it is based, deprive Israelis of their victim subject position, forcing them to confront their own role as victimizers. In so doing, postzionism opens the way to alternative forms of Israeli collective identity, forms in which the subject position of victim, and its accompanying demonizing of the Palestinian other, is no longer prominent.

Hannan Hever (chapter 9), like Ophir, places the struggle with the Palestinians at the center of Israeli group identity construction. According to Hever, Israeli literature strives to reduce and condense the "conflicted identities arising out of the violent struggle over territory" (205). In Israeli literature, Hever finds a recurring effort to weave a coherent, serial narrative that resolves the contradictions between Israeliness and Jewishness and between discontinuity (zionism) and continuity (Judaism).

Reading space and mapping as fundamental to themes in Israeli literature, Hever analyzes the ways in which these conceal the originary violence inscribed in the formation of the state. In the Hebrew works of the Palestinian Israeli Anton Shammas and the Jewish Israeli Orly Castel-Bloom, Hever sees efforts to subvert the dominant national identity narrative. Both writers represent the disruptions and contradictions in that Israeli narrative and challenge the illusion of a coherent, monolithic national identity.

Deborah Starr (chapter 10) extensively analyzes the ways in which Castel-Bloom subverts attempts by Israeli writers to represent a coherent, hegemonic Israeli national identity. According to Starr, Castel-Bloom subverts the cultural hegemony of male Ashkenazi voices in Israeli culture while recovering the "repressed voices of women and Mizrahim" (Jews of Middle Eastern origin). Desiring to "create space for alternative subject-positions" (222), Castel-Bloom inserts into her narratives the mother tongues of Israeli minority groups, particularly Arabic. The themes of territory, maps, and borders play a major role in Castel-Bloom's writings. Her representation of territorial borders undermines any sense of a fixed, clearly defined national territory, while her use of the map "evokes the violence of the conquests of the territory" (231), ancient as well as modern.

Castel-Bloom also problematizes the function of the Holocaust in Israeli identity construction. Whereas the memory of the Holocaust forms a central component in the identity construction of the dominant population of Ashkenazi (European) Jews, for Mizrahi Jews it serves only to highlight their otherness. The Holocaust's central role in Israeli collective identity serves to remind Jews from Middle Eastern countries, who for the most part were spared its horrors, that they are positioned "outside" the borders of the dominant Israeli cultural identity.[30]

Whereas the chapters discussed thus far engage in critical analysis, Ammiel Alcalay's postmodern collage (chapter 11) provides a dramatic enactment of hybrid, nomadic postmodern Jewish identity. Diverging, like Norich and Morantz-Sanchez, from the academic discourse of the other authors, Alcalay recollects his wanderings across or into different spaces. Recalling "isolated moments from my own specific experience—poetic, personal, textual, and historical," he sees them as providing "very different ways of reading and mapping the kinds of elements that go into making up what we usually consider such an identity to consist of" (251). Rereading favorite texts through the filters of experiences in such places as Phoenicia, Lebanon, and Palestine, Alcalay finds identity markers that "have been made invisible on the charts we have been given" (251). He thus suggests the need for new discourses if we are to grasp the complexities of contemporary individual and collective identity construction and reveal new possibilities for what we "might again become." Traversing spaces and transgressing boundaries and "natural" divisions, Alcalay suggests that a new discourse of identity is required, one that privileges multiplicity, spaces, and becoming over unity, time, and being.

Daniel Boyarin, questioning the conventional representations of Rabbinic Judaism, emphasizes its hybrid character. His analysis of the relationship between Judaism and Christianity in the second through fifth centuries (chapter 12) touches upon issues that are central to the identity construction of modern Jews. Analyzing the attitudes to Christianity of selected rabbis, Boyarin argues that the boundaries separating Jewish and Christian culture in those early centuries were far more flexible and porous than commonly assumed.

Reading these texts as suggesting a far more open attitude to Christianity than is usually thought, Boyarin argues that Judaism and Christianity each enfolded ideas and values regarded by the other as basic. Far from being walled off and separate from each other, the textual evidence reveals a relationship between the two communities that is consistent with contemporary notions of cultural hybridity espoused by Homi Bhabha and others.

In the final two chapters, the mode of inquiry shifts to philosophical analysis. Susan Shapiro's critique of Emmanuel Levinas (chapter 13) and Gordon Bearn's engagement with Deleuze and Guattari (chapter 14) represent efforts to think of the problem of identity differently than it has commonly been thought in Western philosophy. Each writer seeks in philosophical discourse the possibilities for a new discourse of identity, free of the exclusivity and violence that the dominant ways of thinking identity have inspired.

The problem of the other, central to contemporary thinking about identity construction, is the subject of Susan Shapiro's critique of the writings of philosopher Emmanuel Levinas. To Shapiro, Levinas offers what appears to be a powerful and promising example of an effort to think identity otherwise. Criticizing a totalizing logic that, subsuming the part in the whole, negates difference, Levinas seeks to counter the violence that it generates and legitimates.

Notwithstanding his efforts to generate an ethics that privileges difference over sameness and otherness over identity, Levinas's representation of the feminine subverts his effort to make space for the other. For Levinas, Shapiro asserts, woman remains "the eroticized Other," less than human, while man is seen as the one who is more closely related to the Universal and the Divine. Thus, Levinas reinscribes in the heart of his writing "the very pernicious gender ideology" that he wishes to undo (306).

Simone de Beauvoir's *The Second Sex* represents for Shapiro a truly different way of thinking about difference and identity. In her anti-essentialist and situation-dependent critique, de Beauvoir designates the problem of women as a man's problem. Nevertheless, unwilling to abandon Levinas, Shapiro suggests that Levinas's "rethinking of the relation of Hebrew and Greek and of Jewishness/Judaism" may enable us to move "beyond a persistent impasse in Levinas's thought, toward a thinking of identity otherwise" (316–17).

In contrast to Shapiro, Gordon Bearn, following Deleuze and Guattari, urges us to break free of the discourse of identity and unity that has plagued Western philosophy at least since Plato. In an effort to move beyond the conventional notions of identity, authenticity, and representation, Bearn suggests a Deleuzean discourse that privileges nonteleological becoming, a becoming that Bearn describes as informed by pointlessness.

Deleuze and Guattari, attempting to move beyond talking of other selves, speak instead in terms of the other as "a structure of the perceptual field," or faciality. For Bearn, such Deleuzean concepts (tools) as majoritarian/minoritarian, rhizome, and haecceity make it possible to talk about Jewish identity, or any other kind of identity, in a nonrepresentational way. Ultimately, he imagines a life characterized by not representation but pointless repetition, intensities "beyond identity, beyond authenticity and inauthenticity, life as a work of art, an aesthetics of intensified existence" (345). Concepts such as multiplicities that "have no subject, no center, no self-identical core (332)," and individuation without identity suggest an alternative discourse that may make it possible to move us beyond identifying ourselves as Jewish or as anything else.

Concluding Reflections

Although modern thinkers often speak in terms of the breakdown of identities and the fragmentation of the modern subject, many contemporary theorists now speak positively of multiple subject positions or identities. To these critics, the notion of fragmented identities is grounded in an unacceptable privileging of unity and organic coherence. Rejecting this privileging, they view the concept of multiple selves positively. The individual is seen as desiring to connect to multiple others, in multiple ways, along multiple paths.

Arguing for a multiple conception of identity, Chantal Mouffe urges that we discard the notion of a subject as an agent both rational and transparent to itself. She further urges that we relinquish the idea that the ensemble of a subject's positions is unified and homogeneous:

> We can then conceive the social agent as constituted by an ensemble of "subject positions" that can never be totally fixed in a closed system of differences, constructed by a diversity of discourses among which there is no necessary relation, but a constant movement of overdetermination and displacement. The "identity" of such a multiple and contradictory subject is therefore always contingent and precarious, momentarily fixed at the intersections of those subject positions and dependent on specific forms of identification. It is therefore impossible to speak of the social agent as if we were dealing with a unified, homogeneous entity. We have rather to approach it as a plurality, dependent on the various subject positions through which it is constituted within various discursive formations. (Mouffe 1995, 318)

The contributors to this book, through literary criticism, criticism of photographic representation, cultural critique, autobiography, rhizomatic mapping, and philosophical analysis, bring to the surface fundamental problems in contemporary Jewish identity construction.

In the process, they suggest new possibilities in contemporary Jewish discourse, thereby opening the way to rethinking what it means to identify Jewish and to Jewishly identify.

NOTES

1. As I complete the final draft of this article, social scientists, representatives of Jewish social service organizations, and Jewish communal leaders are meeting on the campus of Brandeis University to discuss the upcoming year 2000 Jewish Population Survey. While the objectives of such surveys are many, a main goal is to determine the extent to which Jews are adhering to or abandoning their "Jewish identity." Usually, the concept used to designate the polar opposite of identity is "assimilation."
2. For recent criticism of the concept of assimilation in relation to American Jewish life, see Goldscheider 1986 and Cohen 1988.
3. See, on these processes, Appardurai 1996.
4. On the problems of collective memory, see Huyssen 1995; Bal, Crewe, and Spitzer 1999; and Sturken 1997.
5. "Doesn't the acceptance of the fictional or narrative status of identity in relation to the world also require as a necessity, its opposite—the moment of arbitrary closure? Is it possible for there to be action or identity in the world without arbitrary closure—what one may call the necessity to meaning to the end of the sentence? Potentially, discourse is endless: the infinite semiosis of meaning. . . . So what is this 'ending'? It's a kind of stake, a kind of wager. It says: 'I need to say something, something . . . just now.' It is not forever, not totally universally true. It is not underpinned by any infinite guarantees. But just now, this is what I mean; this is who I am. At a certain point in a certain discourse, we call these unfinished closures 'the self,' 'society,' 'politics,' etc. Full stop. O.K." (Hall 1993, 136–37). See also Laclau and Mouffe 1985 and 1990.
6. Paul Gilroy, highlighting the importance of diaspora to identity formation, argues that rather than being constructed in one particular place, such as a homeland, identity is best understood as constituted in the spaces between. To focus on diaspora, argues Gilroy, is to shift our understanding of identity away from essentialist notions of land, nation, race, and culture and "towards an emphasis on contingency, indeterminacy, and conflict" (Gilroy 1997, 334). This emphasis on diaspora also heightens our awareness of the hybrid, mutable, itinerant character of cultural forms (336).

7. The spatial shift in identity discourse is also evident in recent feminist thought. According to Susan Stanford Friedman (1998, 17), "new positional, locational, spatial—that is geographical concepts of identity" have fostered a major shift in academic feminism, which she refers to as a locational feminism involving

    the move from the allegorization of the self in terms of organicism, stable centers, cores, and wholeness to a discourse of spatialized identities constantly on the move. . . . Instead of the individualistic telos of developmental models, the new geographics figures identity as a historically embedded site, a positionality, a location, a standpoint, a terrain, an intersection, a network, a crossroads of multiply situated knowledges. It articulates not the organic unfolding of identity but rather the mapping of territories and boundaries, the dialectical terrains of inside/outside or center/margin, the axial intersections of different positionalities, and the spaces of dynamic encounter—the "contact zone," the "middle ground," the borderlands, la frontera. Moreover, this geographic discourse often emphasizes not the ordered movement of linear growth but the lack of solid ground, the ceaseless change of fluidity, the nomadic wandering of transnational diaspora. (19)

8. According to Hall, meanings produced through identity discourse

    mobilize powerful feelings and emotions, of both a positive and negative kind. We feel their contradictory pull, their ambivalence. They sometimes call our very identities into question. We struggle over them because they matter—and these are contests from which serious consequences can flow. They define who is "normal," who belongs—and therefore, who is excluded. They are deeply inscribed in relations of power. Think of how profoundly our lives are shaped, depending on which meanings of male/female, black/white, rich/poor, gay/straight, young/old, citizen/alien [Jew/non-Jew] are in play and in which circumstances. (1997, 10)

9. Thus, Jewish identity discourses that exclude or marginalize women or gays ("Jews do not do that!" "That's not Jewish." "That's not a Jewish position!"), treating them as other, have the effect of inhibiting or restricting a subject's becoming. Similarly, the discourses that privilege zionism, positioning it at the center of Jewish life, have the effect of marginalizing or excluding critics of zionism or those who seek to include Palestinians as full partners in the construction of Israeli society and culture. Finally, a discourse of Jewish identity in which the connection to the Holocaust is central marginalizes or excludes those who find such a connection to be problematic or who reject its central position.

10. According to James Corner, rhizomatic mapping "opens reality to a host of new and alternative possibilities" (1999, 245). Rather than being "the indiscriminate, blinkered accumulation and endless array of data," mapping is an extremely shrewd and tactical enterprise, a practice of relational reasoning that intelligently unfolds new realities out of existing constraints, quantities, facts and conditions" (251).

    Whereas traditional practices of mapping have functioned as a vehicle for appropriation or territorialization, the new concept of mapping is liberating. To Corner, "we might begin to see it as a means of emancipation and enablement, liberating phenomena and potential from the encasements of convention and habit" (252).

11. A similar case is cogently argued by Joan Wallach Scott:

    > Subjects are constituted discursively, but there are conflicts among discursive systems, contradictions within any one of them, multiple meanings possible for the concepts they deploy. And subjects have agency. They are not unified, autonomous individuals exercising free will, but rather subjects whose agency is created through situations and statuses conferred on them. Being a subject means being "subject to definite conditions of existence, conditions of endowment of agents and conditions of exercise." (1992, 34)

12. Instead of identity, Elsbeth Probyn (1996) prefers to speak of "belonging," a concept that reveals the force of desire in the process of identity construction. Probyn acknowledges the necessity of what she terms "zones" of belonging and difference, including race, class, sexuality, and gender, i.e., what we conventionally refer to as types of identity. These, she argues, should "by no means be regarded as end points or resting places" (23). Instead, they should be taken as "the points from where we depart in order to live our singular lives." While not denying the importance of "specificities of difference," she warns against allowing them to function so as to constrict our movement and flexibility, becoming "a set of hard and fast rules that police comportment."

13. "What is enfolded is composed of anything that can acquire the status of authority within a particular assemblage. Machinations of learning, of reading, of wanting, of confessing, of fighting, of walking, of dressing, of consuming, of curing enfold a certain voice (that of one's priest, one's doctor or one's father), a certain incantation of hope or fear (you can become what you want to be), a certain way of linking an object with a value, sense, and affect (the 'Italian-ness' that Barthes so wonderfully reveals with Panzani pasta or perhaps the 'self-control' manifested by the sculpted body of the 'postmodern woman'), a certain little habit and technique of thought (bite the bullet, look before you leap, self-control

is everything, it is good to share one's feelings), a certain connection with an authoritative artifact (a diary, a dossier, or a therapist)" (Rose 1996a, 189–90).

14. In the 1950s, it was common for sociologists to speak of Jews as a religious group. By the 1970s, partly in response to the changes in American society and partly in response to the existence of large numbers of American Jews who self-identified as secular, sociologists increasingly spoke of Jews as an ethnic group.

15. For a preliminary, far less developed version of this argument, see Silberstein 1997.

16. For reflections on postmodernism in relation to African American identity, see hooks 1990. On the problems of postmodernism in relation to feminism, see the critiques by Benhabib and Fraser and the response by Judith Butler in Benhabib et al. 1995. See also Nicholson and Seidman 1995.

17. See Benhabib et al. 1995.

18. I discuss the essentially contested nature of Jewish identity and the power effects as they relate to zionism in Silberstein 1999: on early zionist discourse, see chap. 1; on recent debates, see chaps. 4–6.

19. The ways in which conceptions of Jewish identity that treat Israel as a Jewish state conflict with democratizing processes in Israel has been the subject of much discussion among Israeli intellectuals. For recent examples that clearly connect to postzionist themes, see the section edited by Uri Ram with articles by Ram, Sara Helman, Baruch Kimmerling, Oren Yiftachel, and Yossi Yonah in *Constellations: An International Journal of Critical and Democratic Theory* 6, 3 (September 1999): 323–428.

20. See Silberstein 1999, chap. 4.

21. The primary cultural site for the postmodern, poststructuralist, postcolonial critiques of zionism is the journal *Theory and Criticism,* edited by the Tel Aviv University philosopher Adi Ophir. For a discussion of postmodern postzionist critics, see Silberstein 1999, chap. 6.

22. Ironically, zionism itself constituted a break with previously hegemonic notions of Jewish identity. Criticisms of fixed, essentialist zionist conceptions of Jewish identity, already evident in the early years of zionism, can be traced throughout its history. See Silberstein 1999, chaps. 1–3.

23. Hever and Ophir were instrumental in establishing the journal *Theory and Criticism,* edited by Ophir; see above, n. 21.

24. Azoulay further argues (1993, 80–82) that in zionist discourse and in Israeli culture, spatial sites have been represented as passive places that lie around covered by dust. When the dust is removed, "authentic" documents or objects are revealed. Zionism, regarding such sites

as evidence of Jewish continuity in the land, has removed all traces of the power struggles and conflicts that had transformed them into zones of memory. It has, moreover, represented cultural objects, which are the products of willful and intentional power practices, as "natural."

25. Rabinowitz lists six basic terms used in this process: (1) The Arabs of Israel/*Arviei Yisrael*; (2) Israeli Arabs/*Aravim Yisraelim*; (3) Arabs/*Aravim*; (4) Palestinians/*Palestinim*; (5) Palestinians in Israel/*Palestinim baYisrael*; (6) Palestinians who are citizens of Israel/*Palestinim ezrahei Yisrael*.

26. Hever's essay on Shammas, reproduced in *Theory and Criticism*, forms an important part of the postmodern postzionist critique. On other aspects of Hever's critique, and on Shammas's overall contribution to postzionist discourse, see Silberstein 1999, chaps. 5–6.

27. See Klepfisz 1990, Goldberg and Krausz 1993, Silberstein and Cohn 1994, Nochlin and Garb 1995, Kleeblatt 1996, Peskowitz and Levitt 1997, and Boyarin and Boyarin 1998.

28. Susan Shapiro was invited to submit her chapter after the conference.

29. During the conference at Lehigh, after the presentations by Friedman, Norich, and Reizbaum, Ophir criticized what he took to be their failure to draw out the political implications of their analyses. The somewhat-heated discussion that followed, which included contributions by Hever, Levitt, and Silberstein, clearly revealed significant differences in the ways in which the American and Israeli participants interpreted the politics of Holocaust remembering. This discussion reinforced the diverse, often conflicted character of Jewish collective identity construction carried on in different geographical spaces. Although undoubtedly concerned with inequitable or oppressive power relations in Israel, the American Jewish contributors, for the most part, construct their critique of Jewish identity discourse around other issues.

30. Notwithstanding Castel-Bloom's critique of Israeli national identity construction, Hever and Starr both see her efforts as falling short of fully freeing herself of the dominant zionist discourse.

REFERENCES

Adorno, Theodor W. 1973. *Negative Dialectics.* Translated by E. B. Ashton. New York: Seabury.

Appardurai, Arjun. 1996. *Modernity at Large: Cultural Dimensions of Globalization.* Minneapolis: University of Minnesota Press.

Azoulay, Ariella. 1992. "On the Possibility and Situation of Critical Art in Israel." *Theory and Criticism* 2 (Summer): 89–118.

―――. 1993. "Open Doors: Museums of History in Israeli Public Space." *Theory and Criticism* 4 (Fall): 79–95.

Bal, Mieke, Jonathan Crewe, and Leo Spitzer, eds. 1999. *Acts of Memory: Cultural Recall and the Present.* Hanover and London: University Press of New England.

Benhabib, Seyla, Judith Butler, Drucilla Cornell, and Nancy Fraser, eds. 1995. *Feminist Contentions: A Philosophical Debate.* New York and London: Routledge.

Boyarin, Daniel, and Jonathan Boyarin, eds. 1998. *Jews and Other Differences: The New Jewish Cultural Studies.* Minneapolis: University of Minnesota Press.

Biale, David, Michael Galichinsky, and Susannah Heschel, eds. 1998. *Insider/Outsider: American Jews and Multiculturalism.* Berkeley: University of California Press.

Butler, Judith. 1992. "Contingent Foundations." In *Feminists Theorize the Political,* edited by Judith Butler and Joan Scott, 3–21. New York and London: Routledge.

Butler, Judith, and Joan Scott, eds. 1992. *Feminists Theorize the Political.* New York and London: Routledge.

Chinski, Sara. 1993. "Silence of the Fishes: The Local and the Universal in Israeli Discourse on Art" [in Hebrew]. *Theory and Criticism* 4 (Fall): 105–22.

Cohen, Steven M. 1988. *American Assimilation or Jewish Revival.* Bloomington: Indiana University Press.

Connolly, William E. 1991. *Identity/Difference: Democratic Negotiations of Political Paradox.* Ithaca, N.Y.: Cornell University Press.

Corner, James. 1999. "The Agency of Mapping." In *Mappings,* edited by Dennis Cosgrove, 213–52. London: Reaktion Books.

Deleuze, Gilles, and Félix Guattari. 1989. *A Thousand Plateaus: Capitalism and Schizophrenia.* Translated and edited by Brian Massumi. Minneapolis: University of Minnesota Press.

Dominguez, Virginia. 1989. *People as Subject/People as Object: Selfhood and Peoplehood in Contemporary Israel.* Madison: University of Wisconsin Press.

Eyal, Gil. 1993. "Between East and West: The Discourse on the 'Arab Village' in Israel" [in Hebrew]. *Theory and Criticism* 3 (Winter): 39–55.

Friedman, Susan Stanford. 1998. *Mappings: Feminism and the Cultural Geographies of Encounter.* Princeton, N.J.: Princeton University Press.

Gilroy, Paul. 1997. "Diaspora and the Detours of Identity." In *Identity and*

Difference, edited by Kathryn Woodward, 299–346. Thousand Oaks, Calif.: Sage.

Goldberg, David Theo, and Michael Krausz, eds. 1993. *Jewish Identity.* Philadelphia: Temple University Press.

Goldscheider, Calvin. 1986. *The American Jewish Community: Social Science Research and Policy Implications.* Atlanta: Scholars Press.

Grosz, Elizabeth A. 1994. *Volatile Bodies: Toward a Corporeal Feminism.* St. Leonards, N.S.W.: Allen and Unwin.

Hall, Stuart. 1990. "Cultural Identity and Diaspora." In *Identity, Community, Culture,* edited by J. Rutherford, 222–37. London: Lawrence and Wishart.

———. 1993. "Minimal Selves." In *Studying Culture: An Introductory Reader,* edited by Ann Gray and Jim McGuigan, 134–38. London: Edward Arnold.

———. 1996. "Who Needs Identity?" In *Questions of Cultural Identity,* edited by Stuart Hall and Paul Du Gay, 1–17. Thousand Oaks, Calif.: Sage.

———, ed. 1997. *Representation: Cultural Representations and Signifying Practices.* Thousand Oaks, Calif.: Sage.

Hellman, Sara. 1990. "War and Resistance: Israeli Civil Militarism and Its Emergent Crisis." *Constellations: An International Journal of Critical and Democratic Theory* 6, 3 (September): 391–410.

Hever, Hannan. 1990. "Hebrew in an Israeli Hand: Six Miniatures on Anton Shammas's *Arabesques.*" In *The Nature and Context of Minority Discourse,* edited by Abdul R. JanMohammed and David Lloyd, 264–93. New York: Oxford University Press.

hooks, bell. 1990. *Yearnings: Race, Gender, and Cultural Politics.* Boston: South End.

Huyssen, Andreas. 1995. *Twilight Memories.* New York: Routledge.

Kimmerling, Baruch. 1999. "Religion, Nationalism, and Democracy in Israel." *Constellations: An International Journal of Critical and Democratic Theory* 6, 3 (September): 339–63.

Kleeblatt, Norman, ed. 1996. *Too Jewish? Challenging Traditional Identities.* New York and New Brunswick, N.J.: Jewish Museum and Rutgers University Press.

Klepfisz, Irena. 1990. *Dreams of an Insomniac: Jewish Feminist Essays, Speeches, and Diatribes.* Portland, Ore.: Eighth Mountain.

Laclau, Ernesto, and Chantal Mouffe. 1985. *Hegemony and Socialist Strategy.* London: Verso.

———. 1990. "Postmarxism without Apologies." In *New Reflections on the Revolution of Our Time,* edited by Ernest Laclau, 97–134. London: Verso.

Levitt, Laura. 1997. *Jews and Feminism: The Ambivalent Search for Home.* New York and London: Routledge.

Massumi, Brian. 1992. *A User's Guide to* Capitalism and Schizophrenia*: Deviations from Deleuze and Guattari.* Cambridge, Mass., and London: MIT Press.

Mouffe, Chantal. 1995. "Feminism, Citizenship, and Radical Democratic Politics." In *Social Postmodernism: Beyond Identity Politics,* edited by Linda Nicholson and Steven Seidman, 315–31. New York and London: Routledge.

Nicholson, Linda, and Steven Seidman, eds. 1995. *Social Postmodernism: Beyond Identity Politics.* Cambridge: Cambridge University Press.

Nochlin, Linda, and Tamar Garb, eds. 1995. *The Jew in the Text: Modernity and the Construction of Identity.* London: Thames and Hudson.

Patton, Paul. 1994. "Anti-Platonism and Art." In *Gilles Deleuze and the Theater of Philosophy,* edited by Constantin V. Boundas and Dorothea Olkowski, 141–56. New York: Routledge.

Peskowitz, Miriam, and Laura Levitt, eds. 1997. *Judaism since Gender.* New York and London: Routledge.

Pile, Steve, and Nigel Thrift. 1995. "Mapping the Subject." In *Mapping the Subject: Geographies of Cultural Transformation,* edited by Steve Pile and Nigel Thrift, 13–51. New York and London: Routledge.

Probyn, Elsbeth. 1996. *Outside Belongings.* New York and London: Routledge.

Rabinowitz, Dani. 1993. "Oriental Nostalgia: The Transformation of Palestinians to Israeli Arabs" [in Hebrew]. *Theory and Criticism* 4 (Fall): 141–51.

Ram, Uri. 1999. "The State of the Nation: Contemporary Challenges to Zionism in Israel." *Constellations: An International Journal of Critical and Democratic Theory* 6, 3 (September): 325–38.

Rose, Nikolas S. 1996a. *Inventing Our Selves: Psychology, Power, and Personhood.* Cambridge and New York: Cambridge University Press.

———. 1996b. "Identity, Genealogy, History." In *Questions of Cultural Identity,* edited by Stuart Hall and Paul Du Gay, 128–50. Thousand Oaks, Calif.: Sage.

Scott, Joan. 1992. "Experience." In *Feminists Theorize the Political,* edited by Judith Butler and Joan Scott, 22–40. New York and London: Routledge.

Silberstein, Laurence J. 1997. "Toward a Postzionist Discourse." In *Judaism since Gender,* edited by Miriam Peskowitz and Laura Levitt, 95–101. New York: Routledge.

———. 1999. *The Postzionism Debates: Knowledge and Power in Israeli Culture.* New York and London: Routledge.

Silberstein, Laurence J., and Robert Cohn, eds. 1994. *The Other in Jewish Thought and History: Constructions of Jewish Culture and Identity.* New York: New York University Press.

Sturken, Marita. 1997. *Tangled Memories: The Vietnam War, the AIDS Epidemic, and the Politics of Remembering.* Berkeley: University of California Press.

Thrift, Nigel. 1997. "The Still Point." In *Geographies of Resistance,* edited by Steve Pile and Michael Keith, 125–51. New York and London: Routledge.

Yiftachel, Oren. 1991. "'Ethnocracy': The Politics of Judaizing Israel/Palestine." *Constellations: An International Journal of Critical and Democratic Theory* 6, 3 (September): 364–90.

Yonah, Yossi. 1991. "Fifty Years Later: The Scope and Limits of Liberal Democracy in Israel." *Constellations: An International Journal of Critical and Democratic Theory* 6, 3 (September): 411–28.

Chapter 2

"The Changing Same": Narratives of Contemporary Jewish American Identity

Tresa L. Grauer

> The keys a writer has at his disposal—a whole set of them—are those which let him enter his books.
>
> Which of all the keys spread out before me will I use?
>
> I opted for the one which had overcome the greatest number of doors and, by opening them, had itself become open, as if openness were also a key, as if at a given moment, openness could by itself grant passage by opening onto itself.
>
> Once what is to be opened is open, it will open other things in its turn.
>
> Into this opening, into this series of openings, I write my name.
>
> Judaism and writing seem to participate in one and the same openness to a word whose totality we are called to live.
> —Edmond Jabès, "The Key"[1]

This chapter takes the epigraph from Jabès as its metaphoric "master key"—one that grants access, in part, through its own unlocking. For Jabès, Judaism and writing serve simultaneously as hermeneutic tools and as the subjects of interpretation: the means are also an end. Together, they create an "openness" that contains the author's self-inscription, a space that is not only a void but itself a key with the potential and the tradition of providing passage. "In the book, the Jew himself becomes a book," Jabès continues. "In the Jew, the book itself becomes Jewish words. Because for him, the book is more than confirmation, it is the revelation of his Judaism" (Jabès 1986, 352). To argue that Jews are "the People of the Book" is, in itself, a commonplace; the expression frequently stands as uncritical shorthand for the Jews' ostensible essential affinity for text and learning. Yet Jabès invokes it without complacency. Instead of accepting the representation, he rewrites it: as a Jew, his relation to the text is individual before it is collective; his "I" is a writer as well as a reader; his book is multiple rather than singular. Rather than through answers sought in the text, the only certainty comes through perpetual questioning and re-vision. "To discover means, after all, to create," he writes. Judaism may be found in text, but that text is human as well as divine, its authority diffused: "In this perpetual tête-à-tête with writing [the Jew] recognizes himself: his voice in the voice, his chant in the chant, his word in the word" (Jabès 1986, 352).

I turn to Jabès's aphoristic text to introduce the terms and tropes that resonate throughout contemporary Jewish American literature, paying particular attention to his claim that the Jew "recognizes himself" (or herself) in the "perpetual tête-à-tête with writing." The act of authorial self-inscription that he describes is at the heart of Jewish American literature of the 1980s and 1990s: the narrators, whether they be storytellers, golem-makers, cartoonists, historians, or fiction writers, are all authors who define themselves as Jews in the act of reworking the themes and tropes of inherited Jewish narratives. Although Jabès was an Egyptian Jew rather than an American, the dense prose and enigmatic form of "The Key" usefully encapsulate the central tension of this literature: namely, the ongoing process of defining Jewish American identity through intimate conversation with a Jewish textual tradition. This conversation—for Jabès as well as for many contemporary Jewish American authors—is variably conciliatory and oppositional; the text, sacred and secular. As a commentary itself on the act of interpretation, "The Key" posits the exegetical tradition of midrash as one model for such interchange with the text—a tradition that lies as an unspoken subtext or context for much of contemporary Jewish American literature. "Issued from the book," writes Jabès, "questioning is of primary, burning relevance for both Jew and writer, has been for five thousand years for one, and is anchored in the future for both" (1986, 353).

The terms that I am accumulating here—*Judaism, writing, identity, tradition, midrash*—are fraught with difficulty, profoundly contingent on historical and cultural context. Yet they are precisely the issues that most engage contemporary Jewish American authors. My work to date examines the extent to which contemporary Jewish American literature self-consciously rewrites traditional Jewish narratives both to reflect and to revise current conceptions of the self and the Jew. I am particularly interested in exploring what it means to figure contemporary Jewish American identity in relation to traditional texts at a time when each of those terms is being contested—when "Jewish American identity" is dismissed by many as wishful thinking, when "identity" itself is the subject of heated political and theoretical debate, when "tradition" and "text" are being challenged and renegotiated. If tradition is understood not as a static construct but as an ongoing effort to determine the body of rituals and myths to be perpetuated, what is the nature of the tradition preserved? And if the self is depicted as contingency "all the way down,"[2] how can—and why should—traditional narratives be called on to organize it meaningfully?

I begin this chapter with a broad consideration of these questions in relation to contemporary Jewish American literature and then focus on a specific example, Marge Piercy's 1991 novel *He, She, and It*, as the basis of a more applied reading. In *He, She, and It*, Piercy turns to the Jewish legend of the golem—or man-made man—to evoke contemporary but persistent concerns about the role of narrative in the construction of subjectivity. Her version of the story of the famous golem of Prague and her subsequent rewriting of the golem as a cyborg serve both Piercy and the reader as a textual "key"—a tool and a trope with which to examine the nature of identity, the function of textual production, and the place of women within a Jewish narrative tradition. Relying on a familiarity with Mary Shelley's novel *Frankenstein*, Piercy invokes it as a complementary example of the monster as a powerful metaphor for artistic creation. These intertexts function in Piercy's novel to ground philosophical questions of personhood and authorship within what is, for her, the authoritative context of narrative tradition, both Jewish and otherwise. Piercy foregrounds her concerns about the non-being of woman within Jewish tradition by juxtaposing them to the epistemological issues raised by other literary figures of a non-being; in this case, that of the golem, Frankenstein's parthenogenically created monster, and the cyborg.

I.

In his introduction to the 1977 collection *Jewish American Short Stories*, Irving Howe predicted the decline of American Jewish fiction based on his belief that "most American Jewish writers have had only an enfeebled relationship—indeed a torn and deprived relationship—with the Jewish tradition in its fullness" (Howe 1977, 12). Referring to something that he called "*the* Jewish tradition," Howe had in mind not religion or religious texts primarily but rather the literary culture of Yiddish, mediated for Americans through the experiences of immigration and translation. Yet, according to Howe, this culture too was being lost; when found in the work of mid-century writers, it was only as "historical fragments, [or] bits and pieces of memory" (12). "Tradition as discontinuity" he claimed, "this is the central fact in the cultural experience of the American Jewish writers" (13). As Howe was the person perhaps most influential in the construction of an American Jewish literary canon, his definition of tradition has become part of a largely accepted understanding of what is frequently called second-generation American Jewish literature. However, to *continue* to conceive of tradition as Howe did here—as "rupture, break, and disassociation" (12)—as something that may "infiltrate" the work of American Jewish writers without "affecting their consciousness" (13)—is to disregard the wealth of contemporary narratives that explicitly attempt to integrate *inherited* stories with what Philip Roth calls "the storification of everyday life" (Roth 1993, 231).

What I find fascinating today, both outside the literature and within it, are the continued and dynamic cultural resonances of categories such as "Jewish" and "tradition" at a time when they no longer necessarily reflect either faith or practice. Rather than attempting to define an "authentic" Jewish "essence" or Jewish "experience," I have instead been examining the narrative strategies by which contemporary authors represent Jewishness for themselves. In other words, I assume that the idea of a canon of authoritative Jewish texts remains but that its contents are changing, expanding to include cultural narratives that stand outside a sacred tradition but that nevertheless continue to provide meaning in the shaping of contemporary Jewish identity. For contemporary Jewish American writers, authority is grounded in literature as well as liturgy; what Jews once sought in a particular set of laws and commandments many now find in the stories of ancestors—be they biblical stories, spoken text, folktales, family histories, or national myths.

I begin with the presumption that "Jewish" is *not* primarily a religious signifier in the texts that I examine, nor is "tradition" a fixed construct. This perhaps obvious statement is made most necessary by the tendency among critics of Jewish literature to define both the literature under study *and* Jewish identity according to criteria that are simultaneously too particular and too vague. Too often, assumptions about an author's life and literature are elided, whereby Jewish literature becomes defined simply and tautologically as that which is written by Jews. The "Jewishness" of a given text is frequently determined by the beliefs of the individual critic, variously measured by such categories as "blood" (Is the author the child of a Jewish mother?), "language" (Is the text written in Hebrew or in Yiddish?), "religiosity" (Does the author or the character live according to Jewish law?), and "theme" (Does the text reflect, for example, the inheritance of *Yiddishkeit?*).[3]

To measure Jewish literature by its capacity to meet what Robert Alter calls "our test for authentic Jewishness"[4] seems to me anachronistic. Current scholarship in the fields of gender and cultural studies has demonstrated convincingly that identity, in order to serve as a useful category of analysis, "must be continually assumed and immediately called into question," as Jane Gallop has written (1982, xii). As Stuart Hall explains:

> Identities are about questions of using the resources of history, language and culture in the process of becoming rather than being: not "who we are" or "where we came from," so much as what we might become, how we have been represented and how that bears on how we might represent ourselves. (1996, 4)

Elsewhere, Hall adds usefully that "identities are the names we give to the different ways we are positioned by, and position ourselves within, the narratives of the past" (Hall 1990, 225). In her book *Essentially Speaking*, Diana Fuss provides a compelling argument for moving away from a consideration of essences and toward an analysis of the *narratives* of identity. "Fictions of identity, importantly, are no less powerful for being fictions" (Fuss 1989, 104), she explains. In this, she echoes Henry Louis Gates's claim that although "race, as a meaningful criterion within the biological sciences, has long been recognized to be a fiction" (Gates 1985, 5), it nevertheless possesses extraordinary weight as a metaphor. According to these readings, it is possible to challenge both the idea of a static tradition and the notion of essentialism without negating or destroying the value of identity as a useful concept.

In this context, I suggest that "Jewish" functions similarly in contemporary Jewish American literature, operating as a powerful fiction or trope of identity. "It's the stories that purport to be about 'it,' where the make-believe comes in," claims the character of Philip Roth in the novel *Operation Shylock*. Instead, "the representations of 'it' *are* 'it.' They're everything" (Roth 1993, 200). Rather than depicting an "authentic truth" about Jewish existence, whatever is Jewish about the literature that I have been examining—as well as the fictional authors that it represents—lies in its claim to locate Jewishness within a self-conscious re-visioning of a Jewish narrative tradition. To be sure, this position is complicated by the fact that "Jewish," when read strictly as a signifier of religion, does posit an underlying and incontestable authority that determines its "meaning": God. I suggest, however, that contemporary authors may sidestep the issue of religious belief and practice in their fiction by deflecting ultimate authority onto the text—or, more precisely, onto a tradition of receiving and transmitting, interpreting and reinterpreting, a textual tradition.

The title of this chapter comes from a passage in Paul Gilroy's *The Black Atlantic*, which, I believe, provides a nice anchor for a discussion of some of these issues. In this passage, Gilroy provides an alternative framework for understanding tradition as he talks about the function of shared narratives of history and memory for a community of listeners:

> The telling and retelling of these stories plays a special role, organising the consciousness of the . . . group socially and striking the important balance between inside and outside activity—the different practices, cognitive, habitual, and performative, that are required to invent, maintain, and renew identity. . . . Tradition . . . is redefined here as the *living memory of the changing same.* (Gilroy 1993, 198; emphasis mine)

"The living memory of the changing same." In their introduction to a 1989 special issue of the journal *Representations* on memory, the editors write, "Memory is of course a substitute, surrogate, or consolation for something that is missing," and they go on to describe the papers in their volume as "more or less explicitly preoccupied with rupture and loss" (Davis and Starn 1989, 3). Such a definition of memory—which is by no means unique—implies some kind of "past wholeness" that we can recover only inadequately, if at all. But Gilroy's notion of a *living* memory enacted through the repetition of stories makes it possible to conceive of the past as an ongoing part of the present rather than as something to which one can return only with a kind of melancholy nostalgia. Indeed, a tradition defined as living memory insists on the necessary *continuity* between past and present, rather than positioning itself in dialectical opposition to modernity. Moreover, the notion of tradition as a "changing same" asserts, paradoxically, both stability and flux: not only in the stories that are being perpetuated but in the group that retells—or rewrites—those stories.

By working to challenge received notions of tradition and identity, many contemporary Jewish American authors exhibit a shared faith that storytelling functions simultaneously as a metaphor for self-invention and as a means of connecting them to a Jewish narrative past. For these writers, the "kinds of stories" that comprise that narrative tradition are both Jewish according to conventional terms and, more broadly, secular, and it is precisely this intersection that, to my mind, makes this work most interesting.

On the one hand, many contemporary writers see themselves working within a specifically Jewish hermeneutic heritage, which refers here principally to two things: first, to the biblical interpretation of midrash; and second, to the fulfillment of the biblical imperative to remember.[5] Indeed, I believe that, for contemporary authors, the two are linked as self-reflexive linguistic traditions with their own histories, tropes, and patterns of reading and writing. As such, they are also desacralized, drawing more on the metaphorical and metaphysical foundations of a Jewish discursive tradition than on an underlying faith in God.

Grace Paley's story "A Midrash on Happiness" stands as perhaps the most obvious example of a writer conceiving herself within a Jewish interpretive tradition of intertextuality and multiple readings of texts. Such examples make no claim to be sacred, nor do the narratives that they revise always fall within the sanctioned canon of sacred and exegetical texts that has been, indisputably, central to generations of Jewish belief and practice. Instead, they posit midrash as a *model* for re-visioning, or what Daniel Boyarin calls the "continuing and breaching" of a Jewish literary tradition. "One of the tasks of a successful culture is to preserve the old while making it nevertheless new," he writes (Boyarin 1990, 22). "The literary text in its intertextuality both continues and breaches the literary tradition of the culture; it preserves the signifying practices of a culture precisely by transforming them" (24). Rewriting and re-vision are thus fundamental to the process of writing and creation as contemporary authors respond both to the rhetorical strategies at work in the tradition and to the "content" of the inherited narratives.

But on the other hand, contemporary authors write with quite conscious recognition of American literary history, women's literary history, and the Western literary canon. Moreover, their understanding of the role of narrative in normative Judaism is incontestably informed by the language and assumptions of current poststructuralist thought. Ultimately, I think you can trace in contemporary Jewish American writers a real faith that different cultural allegiances can be held together in productive tension, as each of their texts approaches the question of Jewish subjectivity—and Jewish textuality—through the negotiation of other, related boundaries. Each author brings to his or her Jewish narratives models of other traditions; each text recognizes interpretive possibilities that rely on a familiarity with other literatures. Whether they construct their narrative heritages as religious, national, patriarchal, or historical, these authors provide ample evidence that multiple lines of continuity are not in conflict;

rather, they must be read together to best represent what Philip Roth calls the "amassment of mirrored fragments" that make up the manifold identity of the contemporary American Jew (Roth 1993, 334).

II.

> Identities . . . arise from the narrativization of the self, but the necessarily fictional nature of this process in no way undermines its discursive, material or political effectivity, even if the belongingness, the "suturing into the story" through which identities arise is, partly, in the imaginary.
> —Stuart Hall, "Who Needs Identity?"[6]

> Feminists (and others) need continuous cultural reinvention, postmodernist critique, and historical materialism; only a cyborg would have a chance.
> —Donna Haraway, "A Manifesto for Cyborgs"[7]

Stuart Hall's notion of establishing "belongingness, the 'suturing into the story' through which identities arise," is precisely the project that Marge Piercy undertakes in her novel *He, She, and It*, as she simultaneously invokes and subverts the Jewish legend of the golem and Mary Shelley's classic story of Frankenstein's monster. Moreover, in crediting Haraway's article "A Manifesto for Cyborgs" in her acknowledgments, Piercy provides Haraway's "chance" for feminists by turning to yet another monster figure—the cyborg—as a model for mapping the relationship between human identity and constructed artifact, literary production, and parenthood. The golem in particular serves as the prooftext for Piercy's *He, She, and It* and embodies, as both text and monster, the author's inscriptions of gender and authorship within the larger context of Jewish tradition. By refiguring a classic story and reimagining the relationship of the monstrous to the larger community, Piercy suggests that traditional narrative can provide a usefully complex ground for the expression and understanding of what she sees as contemporary feminist Jewish identity.

After setting the scene in the apocalyptic, technologically mediated world of the twenty-first century, *He, She, and It* comes to a sudden stop in order to start anew. "Once upon a time is how stories begin,"[8] declares Piercy's Malkah Shipman, as she introduces a second plot line with the familiar words of folktale. What follows is her account of the legend of the golem, retold expressly for the ears of her newly created cyborg, Yod. From these two very different points of origin, from the alternating perspectives of futuristic fantasy and mythologized past, the novel posits traditional narrative as essential to the contemporary construction of identity. It also, simultaneously, lays the groundwork for a discussion of revisionary storytelling. What Piercy offers in the figure of the cyborg is a radical re-vision of a long-established text, one that reflects a social reality profoundly different from the cultural context of earlier versions of the legend. *He, She, and It* transforms the questions that can be asked of the original story by bringing together feminist interpretation of Jewish tradition and a broad concern for the potential dangers of scientific progress. But it does so, in large part, by preserving and transmitting what Piercy sees as a vital piece of Jewish collective memory.

That Malkah begins her narrative of the golem with "Once upon a time" points to several of the novel's assumptions about the nature and the function of tradition. Her formulaic opening suggests to the reader of English that her story belongs in the realm of the secular folktale and implies an audience of children rather than a community of learned believers. The teller of folktales implicitly promises to deliver a narrative with a familiar form, summoning shared communal beliefs and values as the basis of her authority. Along with the role of such a storyteller, Malkah assumes the responsibility of transmitting and maintaining a cultural link with the past. Although folktales, despite their normative power, are conventionally viewed as whimsical rather than edifying or sacred,[9] the story that Malkah goes on to relay is not simply fantasy; it is based on Jewish mystical texts and designed, in this case, to teach an audience about the cultural norms of a specific historical period.

Both Malkah as storyteller and Piercy as author participate in what Joseph Roach calls "culture as performance," or the enactment of "representations that can be rehearsed, repeated, and above all, recreated" (Roach 1996, 218).[10] Literature, for Roach, can be understood as a kind of "historic archive of restored behavior," and storytelling, by implication, is the ritual expression of "the process[es] wherein cultures understand themselves reflexively and whereby they explain themselves to others" (218). By calling attention to the performative and fictionalizing elements of her account—"Once upon a time is how stories begin"—Malkah underscores the fact that all narrative, whatever its model, is humanly constructed. In *He, She, and It,* the very constructedness of the ritual performance of stories is at the root of tradition.

Treating the golem story as historically contingent allows Piercy to suggest that traditions are eminently adaptable to speak to contemporary needs and desires. More specifically, *He, She, and It* takes a legend that has long raised questions about the nature of man—and I use the word deliberately here—as well as about the relationship of man to artistic creation, and complicates it through a consideration of gender and technology as projected into an unknown future. In keeping with the feminist project of much of her earlier fiction, Piercy here creates an alternative world in which women participate actively and equally in conventionally male ritual. But by transposing the story of the golem into the future in the parallel form of the cyborg, Piercy does more than simply write women into the text in the classic revisionary terms of much of twentieth-century women's literature.[11] Her cyborg—half human organism, half machine; anatomically male but possessing the programmed psyche of both genders— is a composite being who substantially challenges the range of concepts that characterize human identity.

Monsters, broadly speaking, are liminal figures in the literary imagination, blurring the boundaries between the real and the unreal, disrupting conventional definitions of human identity and human generation. Their kinship with the artificial and the supernatural endows them with often contradictory meanings, making them productive sites for a discussion of the nature of subjectivity and the notion of a coherent, organic self. Although monsters may resemble the human, they lack some essential human quality—whether that lack be understood as flesh, soul, or even genealogy. Indeed, what constitutes "essentially human" is relative to the era in which the monster is produced and reveals a great deal about the values, fears, and desires of that cultural moment. By virtue of their ambiguous status on the borders of the human community, monsters challenge normative constructions of personhood and comment directly on the resulting ontological confusion.[12]

Whether the consequence of reproduction gone awry or of creation *ex nihilo,* monsters are often constructed as a kind of "hideous progeny"[13] that equates artistic production with parenthood and text with child. As such, monsters stand not only as creatures of fiction but as fiction itself, the fruit of an author's fertile mind. In these terms, then, denying association with the creation often demonstrates a profound ambivalence toward the act of authorship, refracted through the act of parenting. Consider Frankenstein, for example, who clearly recoils from the "demon" of his own making while still noting with some pride that by creating "a thing such as even Dante could not have conceived," he has managed to surpass the imaginings of the author of one of literature's most vivid representations of hell (Shelley [1818] 1981, 11, 43).

This tension between pride and horror at one's "conception" has had a wide range of significance in the long literary tradition of the monster.[14] Fascination with the monstrous can mean fear not only of the creature but also of the actual act of creation, which is inherently dangerous to the creator. The power to create images and beings is enormous, even divine, and the dangers involve both the perils of giving rise to an autonomous being and the presumption of attempting to rival God. Of course, metaphors of procreation have been used in conjunction with textual production of all kinds—not only monsters—especially in the context of the long-standing aesthetic theory that writers "father" their fictional universes just as God fathered the world.[15] But monstrous invention invariably invokes images of *maternity* as well, either by attributing defective offspring to the transgressive power of female imagination or by equating the poet's labor to the throes of childbearing. The depiction of the artist as the genitor of an imaginative brainchild tends to elide the difference between male artistic production and female creation—or at least to suggest that male parthenogenesis shares equally in both the miracle and the risks of childbirth. Most significant, the choice of images and metaphors evoked in the narrative of the monster's creation profoundly reflects the attitudes of its cultural moment, from the Renaissance fear that women could literally de-form their fetuses with a mental image (and thereby erase the father's imprint) to the Romantic myth that true imaginative creation was the role of the male artist alone.[16]

In this light, the story of the golem can be read as a canonical text of monstrosity that takes shape in the specific context of a Jewish literary tradition, with implications for both contemporary artistic production and the relationship of Jewish women to traditional Jewish belief and practice. Historically, the golem has been understood, in Gershom Scholem's terms, as "a creature, particularly a human being, made in an artificial way by the virtue of a magic art, through the use of holy names" (Scholem 1971, 351). While descriptions of the actual techniques employed in this creation vary according to different periods and different centers of Jewish knowledge, they consistently rely on the precise use of the energy inherent in language. In other words, the golem came into being according to a wide range of "recipes" for human performance, but all involved the recitation of permutations of letters that reflected the combinations with which God created the universe. In his book *Golem: Jewish Magical and Mystical Traditions on the Artificial Anthropoid*, Moshe Idel explains: "The role that the linguistic elements play in the Golem-techniques is not so much to communicate directly some order to the matter that is to be shaped, but rather to demonstrate the powerful effects of the letters of the Hebrew alphabet and the knowledge of their proper combination, which renders them alone creative."[17] While a number of variants of the "Golem-techniques" emerge from rabbinical discussions of the creature, they all emphasize one essential fact: in relation to the golem, the act of creation is fundamentally linguistic. It is a mirroring of the use of language with which God created the world and evidence of the powerful and mysterious properties of the word. In fact, these permutations are often considered to be the articulation of the name of God and yet another way of expressing God's omnipotence.[18] The golem story thus holds a special fascination for contemporary writers interested in poststructuralism; they see it as a useful medium through which to address the role of language in the construction of individual identity and the fictional universe.[19]

While the *reasons* for golem-making also vary over time, the ability to create a golem was understood as evidence of a high level of learning in a righteous and accomplished man. According to Scholem, the performance of such a creation bore witness to the creator's spiritual achievements; it was "an end in itself, a ritual of initiation into the secret of creation" (Scholem 1965, 177). For Idel, in contrast, golem-making was "an attempt of man to know God by the art He uses in order to create man," a way to "attain the experience of the creative moment of God, who also has created man in a similar way" (Idel 1990, xxvii). Whether conceived of as the means or an end, golem-making was traditionally the exclusive province of men, as women were denied access to the religious training and texts necessary for such an endeavor. Although they do not address the issue of gender, classical Jewish texts reflect numerous philosophical discussions about the capacity to create parthenogenically, ranging from the status and function of an artificially created being to the potential transgression of idol-making, the implied hubris of the inventor, and the responsibility of a creator both to and for the creation.[20]

In the context of recent versions of the golem story, what is most striking about these historical discussions of the legend is the number of contemporary moral, spiritual, and political concerns that they anticipate—and that they ignore. From the early nineteenth century, stories of the golem have made their way into popular literature, embodying a wide range of social and symbolic roles and proving a particularly rich source for the literary imagination. The version of the golem story most widely known today—that of the Maharal of Prague, who created a golem to protect the Jewish ghetto from accusations of blood libel—is itself a product of the nineteenth century; and like many later stories, it synthesizes elements of a number of different golem traditions.[21] Some commentators suggest that this particular story may have become popular when it did because it provided a savior figure for the Jewish community at a time when blood libel, in the form of the Beilis trial, was once again becoming a public concern.[22] In the countless literary works inspired by this legend—I. L. Peretz's short story "The Golem" and Cynthia Ozick's novella "Puttermesser and Xanthippe" are just two examples—each author refashions it to bring together his or her particular concerns with the ethical issues evoked by the legend itself.[23] While some scholars deride such popular versions as owing little to Jewish tradition—for example, Scholem calls them "tendentious modern fiction" (1965, 203)—I suggest that for contemporary writers, they perpetuate a culturally resonant Jewish legend that can be simultaneously adapted and interpreted for the present.

In the context of Piercy's *He, She, and It*, the story of the Maharal and the persecuted Jews of Prague is told in counterpart to an imagined future, as the story of the golem is interwoven with the story of the cyborg through alternating chapters. Piercy establishes a kind of futuristic ghetto to parallel Prague's by creating the Jewish town of Tikva as one of the few settlements able to survive independent of the monolithic corporations that rule the planet. In the postnuclear world of the twenty-first century, Tikva is an anachronism: a hope, a haven for individuality and religious freedom far from the specious conformity of the conglomerates. Like the Maharal's golem, the cyborg Yod has been brought into being in part as a security device to protect the town and in part for the pure pleasure of the intellectual achievement that it represents. And like the golem of Prague, Yod is "unmade" by his creator when his mission has been fulfilled.

But Piercy's adaptation, while sharing obvious structural similarities with the legend, makes a number of significant changes. Golem-making in Piercy's imagined future is no longer the androcentric enterprise that it is in her representation of the past. The cyborg instead becomes a joint project of both a man and a woman, the culmination of years of secret study and fierce disagreement over his programming. Yod—whose name identifies him as the tenth in a series of previously failed attempts at creation—is the first *successful* cyborg because Avram, his male creator, finally agrees to balance the "pure reason, pure logic, pure violence" of *his* ideal with Malkah's suggested "gentler side" (148). Gender is of particular significance in the shift from the traditional story to the new, as a woman becomes involved in the creation of what is to become an androgynous being. Like so many others grappling with the tensions of a feminist Judaism, Piercy insists that for tradition to continue to resonate, it must inscribe as part of its truth an equal status for women. Her goal is both to critique the paradigm and to provide a new model—although in doing so, she reproduces other kinds of essentialist paradigms for women.

Putting a female perspective at the center of each of her narratives—past and future—Piercy attempts to offer a feminist corrective to tradition, but she does so by depending on biologically based claims about female creativity. Her version of the traditional golem story highlights the absence of women not only by depicting the Maharal as working only with men but also by inventing a

granddaughter who comments critically on the proceedings surrounding the Maharal. Prevented from studying with her grandfather
and frustrated by her inability to participate fully in all aspects of Jewish practice, Chava chooses to involve herself in the process of creation by working as a midwife in the Jewish community. Piercy's Maharal is thus made to fear Chava's perspective, afraid that she will see
golem-making "as usurping not only the power of the Eternal, but the
power of women, to give birth, to give life" (63).

Like many other creation myths, the legend of the golem itself appropriates female creativity to discuss male generation, borrowing
the language of maternity to represent intellectual achievement and
production and to accord it mystery and power. Gershom Scholem,
for example, warns: "Golem-making is dangerous; like all major creation it endangers the life of the creator" (Scholem 1965, 190). The
activity is rendered all the more noble for its potential physical risks,
but Scholem goes on to make clear that "the source of danger . . . lies
in the tension which the creative process arouses in the creator himself." Scholem's invocation of pregnancy and childbirth is abandoned
in his description of a process that is fundamentally internal, with no
consequence to the body. Piercy undermines this formulation of
golem-making as "natural" by envisioning a golem-maker who is actually a woman—a re-vision that itself would have excluded her from
Scholem's creative tradition altogether. Refiguring the legend allows
Piercy to consider what "natural" means in terms of both gender and
traditional text—by imagining how the narrative changes when gender is inverted; by considering how women will respond when they,
too, assume the powerful role of creator; and by inventing a golem
who "is" an androgynous human-machine.

Piercy's solution is initially to address the issue of gender explicitly by creating a fictional future in which women can be golem-makers because they have access to power under both secular and religious law. Beyond this, however, lies the broader question for her of
what it means to be fully human according to the narratives available
within a given society. While Piercy relies heavily on essentialist constructions of women in her depiction of the process of creation, she
is theoretically more sophisticated in her consideration of the created
being. By shifting her focus away from the golem-maker to the place
of the golem—or the cyborg—in Jewish tradition, Piercy recontextu-

alizes contemporary discussions of identity by making them more "universally" applicable and by simultaneously locating them within a particularly Jewish realm. The debates that surround the legend of the golem thus become especially pertinent for contemporary Jewish women. Is a golem a Jew? Can he be counted in a minyan? Does a golem have a voice and rights?

These are not theoretical questions in *He, She, and It.* As an intermediary boundary figure situated between man and woman, human and machine, Jewish mysticism and science, Yod—like the golem, like the monster—is both outside and within the conventional social order of the novel. He is a conglomeration of subject positions, almost literally. In "A Manifesto for Cyborgs," Donna Haraway makes the case: "By the late twentieth century, our time, a mythic time, we are all . . . theorized and fabricated hybrids of machine and organism; in short, we are all cyborgs. The cyborg is our ontology; it gives us our politics. The cyborg is a condensed image of both imagination and material reality."[24] For Haraway, the cyborg provides a useful site on which to ground a discussion of constructed identity; if we are all composites of different social realities, then the cyborg is the clearest—and maybe the most generic—example of the synthesis of these different realities. The cyborg serves for Haraway as an ideal, a way of subverting essentialist identities "while still constructing a place from which to speak called home" (Haraway 1989, 282).[25]

But Yod also cannot be understood simply as metaphor. In the context of the text, he is a living being who must come to terms with his place in the world, as other characters do. Malkah's narration of the golem story is designed toward precisely this end—to provide him with an ancestry. As a sentient and speaking being, "programmed with general history, forty languages, Torah, Talmud, [and] halakic [*sic*] law," Yod is nonetheless *sui generis*, lacking family, biology, and actual models for behavior (74). The legend of the golem serves for him as an origin story, a way of explaining the world and how he himself has come to be.

Malkah's definition of the golem includes Yod among its kind, as a "being in human form made not by ha-Shem but by another human through esoteric knowledge, particularly by the power of words and letters" (30). While this definition closely echoes Scholem's, Malkah's version is broad enough to enable her to link artificial intelligence to the sacred work of Jewish mysticism, as well as to provide an alternative metaphoric system. Like his literary predecessors, Yod is not "born" into the world; instead, he bursts into consciousness through the infusion of creative power and the proper combination of words and numbers. Like the golem, Yod is, by definition, outside nature. In this realm, gender, among other things, is a matter of "programming," of cultural production rather than bodies and essences.

This is just one category in which the terms of Piercy's novel force us to consider how we constitute and are constituted by language, at the same time recognizing a tradition that binds language with creation to very different ends. The traditional narrative also provides meaning and hope to the future by virtue of what Stephen Knapp calls "analogy" and "historical continuity" (Knapp 1989, 129). To put it differently, the legend of the golem has authority for Tikva both because the situations in which the creation takes place are perceived to be similar, which establishes useful precedence for behavior, and because the participants cast themselves as part of a historically shared consciousness, which accords the traditional narrative *symbolic* power. Of course, the two worlds are also very different, and the cyborg narrative reflects the ways in which the legend is limited for current application. But the notion that people are linked through narrative across time is central to Piercy's text. Yod is linked to the golem not because he is an actual descendant but through story.[26] For Piercy, this position also provides an answer to the question of whether or not a golem, or a woman, can count as a Jew in a minyan. Yod explains, "Sometimes I feel a sense of belonging, that I am doing something that has been done over and over again for three thousand years. . . . Insofar as Judaism insists on deed rather than on being, I can carry out mitzvot as well as a born person. Then I feel at home" (287).

Before Malkah begins to tell her story to Yod, she wonders whether it is fair to present the golem as a model for a cyborg and whether the story should be passed down at all. But she decides that

> as a woman who spends her working days creating fictions and monsters, . . . I believe in the truth of what is perhaps figurative. . . . Myth forms reality and we act out of what we think we are; we know on many levels truths that are irrational as well as reasoned or experimental. Our minds help create the world we think we inhabit. (27)

"We act out of what we think we are" is a clear statement of Piercy's (sometimes contradictory) position that identity is formed largely through narratives. In other words—at least in the context of the cyborg figure in the novel—who one is depends to a large extent on the kinds of stories one hears. In this, Piercy follows Catherine Belsey's explanation that "subjectivity is discursively produced. . . . Utterance—and action—outside the range of meanings in circulation in a society is psychotic. In this sense existing discourses determine not only what can be said and understood, but the nature of subjectivity itself, what is possible to be" (1985, 5). For Yod, the point of the golem story is not whether it is "true" but rather that it represents the range of meanings that shape the community of which he is a part. It makes normative statements about the culture that he is trying to understand and provides him with a model for his own behavior.

The "range of meanings" available to Yod—or what Roach would consider his "tropes of performance"—are suddenly challenged when a spiteful town member refers to him as Frankenstein's monster, and Yod sets out to learn all he can about this alternative role model. His sense of "self" is compromised by his newfound affinity, and he falls into depression. "I am," he mourns, "just such a monster. Something unnatural" (155). In this, he echoes Frankenstein's monster, who professes despair over his own uncertain identity when he asks:

> And what was I? Of my creation and creator I was absolutely ignorant, but I knew that I possessed no money, no friends, no kind of property. I was, besides, endued with a figure hideously deformed and loathsome; I was not even of the same nature as man. . . . Was I, then, a monster, a blot upon the earth, from which all men fled and whom all men disowned? (Shelley [1818] 1981, 105)

"Nature" here refers explicitly to the physical body; like legions of monsters before him, Frankenstein's creature is most notable for his aberrant form. Although Yod's friends reassure him that he is not "misshapen or monstrous," "not cobbled together out of human garbage" (157), Yod is not appeased. Like Frankenstein's monster, he is also humanized to the extent that he is able to recognize his difference. Endowed with the capacity to think and feel, he is afraid that he, too, will be "cast abroad" by his creator as "an object for the scorn and horror of mankind" (Shelley [1818] 1981, 124). Disenfranchised by his lack of material resources and his strange "nature," Frankenstein's monster is further denied the comforting certainty of place provided by family and origin story. His awareness of the possibility of family relationships only increases his sorrow and exacerbates his existential anguish. "What am I?"—the most fundamental question of being—is provisionally resolved: "a monster, a blot upon the earth," feared by society and ostracized as the quintessential scapegoat.

In the monster's own terms, this ostracism is felt most poignantly when it is most specific: when he realizes that he has been rejected by Frankenstein himself. "From you only could I hope for succour," he cries, "you were my father, my creator; and to whom could I apply with more fitness than to him who had given me life?" (Shelley [1818] 1981, 124). This denial of humanity by the figure of the parent—indeed, the very invocation of the language of parenthood—suggests the greatest kind of betrayal, the most telling indicator of the "child's" subhuman status. Familial loyalty, presumed guaranteed in the "natural" social order, is clearly not applicable to monstrous offspring.

In Piercy's novel, the story *Frankenstein* only highlights Yod's anxiety toward Avram, the man whom he, too, addresses as "Father" in a "feeble attempt to establish a bond that may preserve [him]" (98). Malkah's version of the legend of the golem is designed to counteract this anxiety by emphasizing the golem's humanity, for Yod's sake. Part of the lesson of her narrative is that while the Maharal may serve as an example of a powerful creator and artist, he erred in his failure to love his creature, treating him instead only as a means to an end. Ignoring the golem's pleas to "live," the Maharal simply "unmakes" him when the ghetto is out of danger. This perspective helps Yod understand Avram's expectation that Yod will self-destruct on command. However, as Yod's other creator, Malkah is quite clear in her condemnation of the idea that creation can be designed toward a specific end: "As it is wrong to give birth to a child believing that child will fulfill your own inner aspirations . . . so it is equally wrong to create a being subject to your will and control" (433). Here again, women provide a counterperspective to the "original" narrative—in this case, one that accords free will and full personhood to the created being.

It is this gesture, this narrative declaration of allegiance with the traditionally disenfranchised, that insists on Yod's humanity in the text. Although his status has been a secret to the town throughout the novel, the eventual divulgence of his artificial nature sparks a fury of discussion about what defines a person under the laws of their community. The town council ultimately rules in Yod's favor, but not before it's too late. Forced into a battle that he cannot survive, Yod nonetheless does not leave the world willingly. He protests his status as an owned being until the end by killing Avram in the process of his own destruction.

As the cyborg defies the will of his creator and takes on a life of his own, so too, suggests Piercy, does narrative, and so too identity. For the cyborg in the novel *is* a fiction: a fabricated text and a fabrication *of* texts who comes to signify the possibilities for human identity. As living beings cannot be property, neither can texts remain fixed as they were created. The cyborg is a cultural invention that is also a reinvention of a traditional narrative; in other words, the cyborg is an act of interpretation. For Piercy, the legend of the golem becomes part of a dynamic process by which narrative evolves to reflect a given cultural moment, and identity of the golem and of the contemporary American Jewish woman is both provisionally established and nonetheless changeable. The story of the golem provides Yod with possibilities and, by extension, allows Piercy to imagine a contemporary Jewish feminist identity that is informed by what she, as well as many other contemporary Jewish American writers, still call "tradition."

NOTES

1. Jabès 1986, 349–50. The gender-specific language of the original should be read as inclusive.
2. The phrase is Richard Rorty's (1989); see esp. 23–43 and 96–121.
3. See Wirth-Nesher 1994, where she describes these categories more fully. Howe 1977 is the source of the most frequently cited compilation of Jewish American literary themes; Solotaroff and Rapoport 1992 provide a more recent overview.

4. Alter 1982. For Alter, this is a test that "most Jewish American fiction . . . cannot meet."

5. For a fuller discussion, see Grauer 1995, esp. chaps. 1 and 4.

6. Hall 1990, 4.

7. Haraway 1989, 177.

8. Piercy 1991, 19. All subsequent references to this novel will be noted in parentheses in the body of the text.

9. For a useful discussion of the distinctions between myth, legend, and folklore, see Bascom 1984, 5–29.

10. I owe special thanks to Ann Pellegrini for directing me to Roach's work.

11. As Adrienne Rich writes in her often-quoted essay "When We Dead Awaken": "Revision, the act of looking back, of seeing with fresh eyes, of entering an old text from a new critical direction—is for women more than a chapter in cultural history: it is an act of survival. . . . We need to know the writing of the past, and to know it differently than we have ever known it" ([1971] 1979, 35). This act of revising or reinterpreting traditional texts is a doubly powerful one for Jewish women, who must situate themselves with respect to both a religious and a secular literary tradition. See especially Satlof 1983 and Sokoloff, Lerner, and Norich, eds., 1992.

12. Marie-Hélène Huet points out that "the word *monster* derived from the Latin *monstrare*: to show, to display," or to demonstrate. However, there is "another tradition, the one adopted by current etymological dictionaries, [which] derived the word *monster* from *monere*, to warn, associating even more closely the abnormal birth with the prophetic vision of impending disasters" (Huet 1993, 6). In either case, the etymologies demonstrate the place of the monster as a sign of disorder in the universe.

13. The phrase comes from Mary Shelley's famous preface to *Frankenstein*, which concludes, "And now, once again, I bid my hideous progeny go forth and prosper" ([1818] 1981, xxvi). Much has been written about the parallel between Victor Frankenstein's creation of his monster and Shelley's creation of her book, most of which explores Shelley's perceived ambivalence about motherhood. See, for example, Gilbert and Gubar 1979 and Johnson 1982.

14. Contemporary representations of monsters are no less revealing of the relationship between image production and current politics of identity construction. Kenneth Branagh's 1994 film adaptation of *Frankenstein* stresses the dangers of usurping women's creative power (Dr. Frankenstein brings his creature to life out of a vat of borrowed amniotic fluid) and of mistreating a living being, whose only fault, in this version of the

story, seems to lie in being born unpleasing to an abusive father. (When Frankenstein opens the tank to examine his creation, the accumulated pressure sends both doctor and monster spilling to the floor, where they wrestle in a none-too-subtle struggle for primacy. The creature ends up strung to the rafters and left for dead, only to escape, heroically, to wage his own way toward survival.) Branagh's decision to reproduce *Frankenstein* seems not only to reflect his well-known efforts to bring classic texts to the masses but also to demonstrate that the figure of the monster continues, in Donna Haraway's words, "to define the limits of community in Western imaginations." Despite the fact that this Frankenstein recognizes his hubris and abandons his creation, the sympathy of the audience is expected to lie with the rejected son. In a wonderfully sarcastic review of the movie, Anthony Lane writes that "the film is so full of wounded feelings and buried desires that it could easily be called 'Oprah Winfrey's Frankenstein.' You can imagine the creature sitting there on Oprah's show, with a tag line at the foot of the screen ('Was made from dead people'), and explaining to the audience that he just wants to be recognized for who he truly is. . . . In 'Mary Shelley's Frankenstein' we never encounter the word 'monster.' Branagh thinks of Frankenstein's creation primarily as an unfortunate. . . . The appeal for sympathy becomes embarrassing." The contemporary "community" is—at least theoretically—far more accepting and inclusive than Mary Shelley could have imagined (Haraway 1989, 203; Lane 1994).

15. Gilbert and Gubar provide numerous examples of this trope of paternity in the first chapter of *The Madwoman in the Attic* (1979).

16. Huet explores the relationship between theories of monstrosity and the maternal imagination in *Monstrous Imagination* (1993).

17. The quote continues: "Disclosing this view of language practically is a direct demonstration of the way *Sefer Yezirah* conceived the creation of the world, i.e., by means of the Hebrew alphabet, and hence an indirect demonstration of the superiority of Jewish mystical knowledge" (Idel 1990, 265). For essential discussions of the figure of the golem—in this case, particularly whether the golem was an end in itself or the means of achieving an ecstatic experience—see Idel 1990; and Scholem 1965, 158–204. For a fuller reading of the golem figure in contemporary Jewish American literature, see Grauer 1995, chap. 3.

18. Scholem explains: "All creation—and this is an important principle of most Kabbalists—is, from the point of view of God, nothing but an expression of His hidden self that begins and ends by giving itself a name, the holy name of God, the perpetual act of creation" (1946, 17).

19. Huet provides an interesting Lacanian reading of the golem story,

arguing that giving life through letters is a "*symbolic* birth, entirely determined by the father, in opposition to the rich maternal imagination that had produced the monsters of earlier times" (1993, 244). Her reading emphasizes the invocation of God as "the ultimate symbolic father associated with the power of the word and the omnipresence of the Law. The Name-of-the-Father literally inscribed on the forehead of the inanimate statue brings the human shape to life."

20. Sherwin 1985 is particularly useful in addressing these questions. In one of the earliest talmudic treatments of the golem, such a creation is not a usurpation of God's role but rather a fulfillment of the human potential to become a creator (Sherwin 1985, 2). The implication here is that human beings, created in the divine image, have the potential to imitate God's creative ability—but are prevented from manifesting it fully out of human failure. Compare this, for example, to the Faustian tradition, which aligns artificial creation with the demonic influence.

21. Rosenberg [1909] 1976. Rosenberg could assume that his audience would be familiar with the recurring false accusation that Jews kill Christian children to use their blood in the observation of Passover. This is one of the first systematic treatments of a legend that is similarly corroborated by other authors of the same period. Rosenberg claimed to be presenting material copied from a manuscript subsequently destroyed, although the authenticity of his story is questionable. (And also of note: Idel suggests that this version is perhaps the first time the golem was given a proper name—Yosele Golem [1990, 252].)

22. See, for example, Bilski 1988, 47. The case of Menahem Mendel Beilis, arrested in Russia in 1911 on the indefensible charges of killing a Christian child to use his blood for ritual purposes, received international attention when it went to trial in 1913. The case serves as the basis of Bernard Malamud's novel *The Fixer.*

23. Peretz 1953, Ozick 1983. Ozick's novella provides an especially interesting counterpoint to Piercy's novel, as her revision of the golem story inscribes gender by imagining both a female creator and a female golem. Ozick and Piercy approach the legend from opposite ends of the spectrum of Jewish feminism, however, and their fiction reflects very different concerns about contemporary identity. For a comparative analysis of these two texts, see Grauer 1995.

    Of course, not all the authors of these revisionary works were Jews, nor did their texts confront "Jewish" issues. (See, for example, Meyrink [1915] 1985.) While a discussion of this is beyond the scope of this essay, it is worth considering the story of the golem as part of a cultural exchange between Jewish communities and their surrounding neighbors.

Interestingly, while Scholem claims that Jewish practices of golem-making remained unaffected, or untainted, by the practices of surrounding cultures, Idel argues that they "must be envisioned as a result of the encounter . . . with other types of cultures, which fertilized Jewish thought" (Idel 1988, 16).

24. Haraway 1989, 174. Haraway posits the cyborg as "a kind of disassembled and reassembled . . . collective and personal self" (187).

25. Haraway elaborates on this idea in a 1991 interview with Constance Penley and Andrew Ross: "Politics rests on the possibility of being accountable to each other. . . . It rests on some sense of the way that you come into the historical world encrusted with barnacles. Metaphorically speaking, I imagine a historical person as being somehow like a hermit crab that's encrusted with barnacles. And I see myself and everybody else as sort of switching shells as we grow. But every shell we pick up has its histories, and you certainly don't choose those histories—this is Marx's point about making history, but not any way you choose. You have to account for the encrustations and the inertias, just as you have to remain accountable to each other through learning how to remember, if you will, which barnacles you're carrying. To me, that is a fairly straightforward way of avoiding cynical relativism while still holding on, again, to contingency" (Penley and Ross 1991, 4).

26. Krausz explains: "This discursive view is in contrast to an older ontology that understands persons in terms of fixed essences, be they individual or collective. . . . Accordingly, there is no essence of the Jewish people as such. Rather, there are people in Jewish positions, or positions that are bestowed as Jewish. Jewishness is understood as *a set of characteristic positions in which certain people are cast or ascribed—by themselves and by others*" (1993, 266).

REFERENCES

Alter, Robert. 1982. "The Jew Who Didn't Get Away: On the Possibility of an American Jewish Culture." *Judaism* 31, 3: 274–86.

Bascom, William. 1984. "The Forms of Folklore: Prose Narratives." Reprinted in *Sacred Narrative: Readings in the Theory of Myth*, edited by Alan Dundes, 5–29. Berkeley: University of California Press.

Belsey, Catherine. 1985. *The Subject of Tragedy: Identity and Difference in Renaissance Drama*. London and New York: Methuen.

Bilski, Emily D. 1988. "The Art of the Golem." In *Golem! Danger, Deliverance and Art*, edited by Emily D. Bilski, 44–110. New York: Jewish Museum.

Boyarin, Daniel. 1990. *Intertextuality and the Reading of Midrash.* Bloomington: Indiana University Press.

Davis, Natalie Zemon, and Randolph Starn. 1989. "Introduction." *Representations* 26 (Spring): 1–26.

Fuss, Diana. 1989. *Essentially Speaking: Feminism, Nature, and Difference.* New York: Routledge.

Gallop, Jane. 1982. *The Daughter's Seduction: Feminism and Psychoanalysis.* Ithaca, N.Y.: Cornell University Press.

Gates, Henry Louis Jr. 1985. "Writing 'Race' and the Difference It Makes." *Critical Inquiry* 12, 1 (Autumn): 1–20.

Gilbert, Sandra, and Susan Gubar. 1979. "Horror's Twin: Mary Shelley's Monstrous Eve." In *The Madwoman in the Attic*, 213–47. New Haven: Yale University Press.

Gilroy, Paul. 1993. *The Black Atlantic: Modernity and Double Consciousness.* Cambridge, Mass.: Harvard University Press.

Grauer, Tresa. 1995. "One and the Same Openness: Narrative and Tradition in Contemporary Jewish American Literature." Ph.D. diss., University of Michigan.

Hall, Stuart. 1990. "Cultural Identity and Diaspora." In *Identity: Community, Culture, Difference*, edited by Jonathan Rutherford, 222–37. London: Lawrence and Wishart.

———. 1996. "Introduction: Who Needs 'Identity'?" In *Questions of Cultural Identity*, edited by Stuart Hall and Paul du Gay, 1–17. London: Sage Publications.

Haraway, Donna. 1989. "A Manifesto for Cyborgs." In *Coming to Terms: Feminism, Theory, Politics*, edited by Elizabeth Weed, 173–204 and 279–88. New York and London: Routledge.

Howe, Irving. 1977. "Introduction." In *Jewish American Stories*, 1–17. New York and Scarborough, Ontario: New American Library and Mentor.

Huet, Marie-Hélène. 1993. *Monstrous Imagination.* Cambridge, Mass., and London: Harvard University Press.

Idel, Moshe. 1988. "The Golem in Jewish Magic and Mysticism." In *Golem! Danger, Deliverance, and Art*, edited by Emily D. Bilski, 15–35. New York: Jewish Museum.

———. 1990. *Golem: Jewish Magical and Mystical Traditions on the Artificial Anthropoid.* Albany: State University of New York Press.

Jabès, Edmond. 1986. "The Key." Translated by Rosmarie Waldrop. In *Midrash and Literature*, edited by Geoffrey H. Hartman and Sanford Budick, 349–60. New Haven: Yale University Press.

Johnson, Barbara. 1982. "My Monster/My Self." *Diacritics* 12 (Summer): 2–10.

Knapp, Stephen. 1989. "Collective Memory and the Actual Past." *Representations* 26 (Spring): 123–49.

Krausz, Michael. 1993. "On Being Jewish." In *Jewish Identity*, edited by David Theo Goldberg and Michael Krausz, 264–78. Philadelphia: Temple University Press.

Lane, Anthony. 1994. "Used Parts." *New Yorker* (November 14): 141–42.

Meyrink, Gustav. [1915] 1985. *The Golem.* Translated by M. Pemberton. Reprint. Cambridge: Dedalus.

Ozick, Cynthia. 1983. "Puttermesser and Xanthippe." In *Levitation: Five Fictions.* New York: Dutton.

Penley, Constance, and Andrew Ross. 1991. "Cyborgs at Large: Interview with Donna Haraway." In *Technoculture*, edited by Constance Penley and Andrew Ross. Minneapolis and Oxford: University of Minnesota Press.

Peretz, I. L. 1953. "The Golem." Translated by Irving Howe. In *A Treasury of Yiddish Stories*, edited by Irving Howe and Eliezer Greenberg, 245–46. New York: Penguin Books.

Piercy, Marge. 1991. *He, She, and It.* New York: Knopf.

Rapoport, Nessa. 1992. "Summoned to the Feast." Introduction to *Writing Our Way Home: Contemporary Stories by American Jewish Writers*, edited by Ted Solotaroff and Nessa Rapoport, xxvii-xxx. New York: Schocken Books.

Rich, Adrienne. [1971] 1979. "When We Dead Awaken: Writing as Re-vision." In *On Lies, Secrets, and Silence*, 33–49. Reprint. New York: Norton.

Roach, Joseph. 1996. "Kinship, Intelligence, and Memory as Improvisation: Culture and Performance in New Orleans." In *Performance and Cultural Politics*, edited by Elin Diamond, 217–36. New York and London: Routledge.

Rorty, Richard. 1989. *Contingency, Irony, and Solidarity.* Cambridge: Cambridge University Press.

Rosenberg, Yudl. [1909] 1986. "The Golem or the Miraculous Deeds of Rabbi Liva." In *The Great Works of Jewish Fantasy and the Occult*, compiled, translated, and introduced by J. Neugroschel, 162–225. Reprint. Woodstock, N.Y.: Overlook Press.

Roth, Philip. 1993. *Operation Shylock: A Confession.* New York: Simon and Schuster.

Satlof, Claire R. 1983. "History, Fiction, and the Tradition: Creating a Jewish Feminist Poetic." In *On Being a Jewish Feminist: A Reader*, edited by Susannah Heschel, 186–206. New York: Schocken Books.

Scholem, Gershom. 1946. *Major Trends in Jewish Mysticism.* New York: Schocken Books.

———. 1965. "The Idea of the Golem." In *On the Kabbalah and Its Symbolism,* translated by Ralph Manheim, 158–204. New York: Schocken Books.

———. 1971. "Kabbalah." *Encyclopaedia Judaica,* vol. 7, col. 753, p. 351.

Shelley, Mary. [1818] 1981. *Frankenstein: The Modern Prometheus.* Reprint. New York and Toronto: Bantam Books.

Sherwin, Byron L. 1985. *The Golem Legend: Origins and Implications.* Lanham, Md., and New York: University Press of America.

Sokoloff, Naomi, Anne Lapidus Lerner, and Anita Norich, eds. 1992. *Gender and Text in Modern Hebrew and Yiddish Literature.* New York and Jerusalem: Jewish Theological Seminary of America.

Solotaroff, Ted. 1992. "The Open Community." Introduction to *Writing Our Way Home: Contemporary Stories by American Jewish Writers,* edited by Ted Solotaroff and Nessa Rapoport, xii–xxvi. New York: Schocken Books.

Solotaroff, Ted, and Nessa Rapoport, eds. 1992. *Writing Our Way Home: Contemporary Stories by American Jewish Writers.* New York: Schocken Books.

Wirth-Nesher, Hana. 1994. "Defining the Indefinable." Introduction to *What Is Jewish Literature?* edited by Hana Wirth-Nesher, 3–12. Philadelphia: Jewish Publication Society.

Chapter 3

Photographing American Jews: Identifying American Jewish Life

Laura S. Levitt

Since the vast majority of American Jews have little else to connect them to their families' various immigrant pasts, much less the traumas that mark twentieth-century Jewish history, explicit photographic collections about Jews are increasingly being marketed as identificatory texts. As I read it, this larger situation of loss helps account for the growing market for picture books about American Jews.[1] Taking possession of these texts not only by buying them but by looking at them, showing them to others, and even keeping them out and on display in their homes, American Jews attempt to make visible their relationship to other Jews. In so doing, they try to compensate for some of their losses by possessing the collected images of other Jews. These texts both do and do not offer such compensation precisely because the purchasing of these books also allows us to distance ourselves from the emotions involved in true relationship. By literally keeping our feelings sealed within the pages of these professionally produced texts, American Jews can avoid engaging more directly some of the legacies of loss.[2] In these ways, contemporary American Jews end up enacting some of the ambivalences of identifying as Jews.

This engagement with photographs exemplifies what cultural critic Diana Fuss has described as identification. According to Fuss, "Identification is an embarrassingly ordinary process, a routine, habitual compensation for the everyday loss of our love-objects." She explains, "Compensating for loss may be one of our most familiar

65

psychological experiences, coloring every aspect of our relation to the world outside us." But, she argues, "it is also a profoundly defamiliarizing affair, installing surrogate others to fill the void where we imagine the love-object to have been."[3]

Identification evokes loss and entails the ritualized activities that we employ to compensate for such losses. This psychological process derives from some of the most common meanings of the verb *to identify*: to name, to classify, or to taxonomize. It most often entails our efforts to figure out our relationships with others as a way of dealing with loss. We reinforce our sense of identity by reminding ourselves of either our affiliations with or our distinctions from others. Through these everyday and ordinary processes we take on identities. In so doing, we compensate for past losses as we make our way through an ever-changing present.

Identification engages us in an interplay between sameness and difference. As we acknowledge connections through similarities of dress or comportment or even the familiarity of the tone or content of a narrative, we also simultaneously recall differences between ourselves and others.[4] Something about another captures our attention. Sometimes the initial allure may stem from a certain strangeness or difference. In such cases, something strangely familiar can become apparent in that which at first appeared utterly alien.

Photographs, in particular, offer an alluring means to identification. As positive prints recorded by a camera and reproduced on a photosensitive surface, photographs provide access to the moment of their creation, a time and a place that may no longer be accessible except through memory. Photographs capture these ephemeral moments and make them stand still, allowing us literally to hold them in our hands.

Photographic texts also generate a sense that they offer a form of objective documentation, "some sort of impersonal 'legal proof,' an objective record similar in nature to an official form, a letter, a will, etc."[5] In the face of the traumatic losses of the Holocaust, this verification has been crucial. In this way, photographs have provided evidence of what was lost before the war as well as documentation of the myriad crimes that were committed against European Jews between 1933 and 1945. Despite this desire for photographs to serve as an objective record, however, photographs also offer a highly subjective ac-

count of what is being documented. In the latter sense, "the document's informational value is mediated through the perspective of
the person making it, and it is presented as a mixture of emotion and
information."[6] In other words, photographs are never self-evident.
They do not speak for themselves. As much as we want them to authenticate a lost past or confirm something in the present, their visions are only partial.

Nevertheless, as both objects of and reflections on particular
times, places, or people, photographs encourage us to make connections in the present. In these ways family photographs, even those of
other people's families, can prompt memory even in the less-charged
arena of postwar American Jewish history.

A few years ago I attended a conference on family photography at
Dartmouth College.[7] There were numerous academic papers, film
presentations, and, most important, a photography exhibit. The
works on display on the theme of the familial gaze included a few
photographs from Larry Sultan's *Pictures from Home* (1992). I recognized these shots. Not only had I seen some of them before, on exhibit in the Modern Museum of Art in New York, but I also identified
with his images.

I remembered most vividly a photograph of his parents at
home in one of their suburban houses. In this picture, Sultan's
aging mother stands against a deep-apple-green wall. She is long
and slight. She is posed like a model; "the weight of her poised leg
is awkwardly balanced on the ball of her pointed foot. It is a pose
meant to be graceful and alluring."[8] Her hands are behind her
back. She wears a shimmery pink nylon blouse tucked into white
slacks held up by a large, black leather belt with a big metal buckle.
She barely smiles. In this picture, I noticed her first. To her left, a
man sits in front of a television screen, his back to the camera, his
balding head prominent. He watches a color television set. On the
screen, a pitcher in a blue cap is about to throw the ball. The television set sits on a white wrought-iron shelf that stands against the
same apple-green wall as the woman. The white shelving echoes the
pale colors of her clothing. There are two potted plants on the top
shelf and a single white lamp just above the TV. A tan electrical outlet stands out on the apple-green wall because it is midway between
the woman and the white shelving. Electrical cords link the outlet

"My Mother Posing for Me" (1984), from Larry Sultan's *Pictures from Home,* Harry N. Abrams, 1992.

to the television and the lamp. The overall effect is bright and colorful, but somehow somber.

I remembered this picture because it reminded me of my grandmother who died almost twenty years ago. I identified with the woman in the picture. Her stance was familiar. "I begin to see some of my grandmother's ambivalences in her body."[9] Like my grandmother, this woman is frail, tired, and a bit weary. She is both bored and exhausted. She also shares my grandmother's taste in clothing, circa 1979, as well as her slight frame and gray-white hair. Gazing at Sultan's photograph, I recaptured something of my lost grandmother.

Through Sultan's photograph I reconnected with my grandmother, although the fact that this was *not* my grandmother also made this "a profoundly defamiliarizing affair."[10] I installed this woman as a surrogate other to fill the void where I imagined my grandmother might have been, always aware of the fact that this woman could never be my grandmother.[11] This is a common way of engaging with photographs.

Many of us come to photographs with precisely these kinds of desires for continuity and a sense of connection when and where other forms of intimacy are no longer possible.[12] We are especially attached to our own family pictures, because they make present very specific lost pasts. Ironically, these more intimate images often do this by displacing our memories with the images themselves. We end up remembering the photographs, not our less-tangible experiences. By contrast, in the case of Sultan's photograph, I was well aware that the woman in the picture was not my grandmother. Here, the photograph triggered my memory without usurping its place. There was less confusion. Sultan's photograph helped remind me of these disjunctions, the gap between my memories and the kinds of photographs I assumed might help me hold onto them.

In the case of Sultan's photograph, other clues aided my identification. I not only saw my grandmother in his image; I somehow recognized that this woman was also Jewish.

In what follows, I want to explain these other connections. How did I know that this woman was Jewish? Could I see this in the photograph? What else made these connections apparent? To answer these questions, I go back to Dartmouth.

At the end of his gallery talk, Larry Sultan likened his *Pictures from Home* project to Raymond Carver's short story "Cathedral," which describes a powerful encounter with otherness in the form of blindness.[13] In the story, the narrator allows the blind man to hold onto his hand as he traces the contours of a cathedral. Through this shared act of envisioning, the narrator slowly closes his own eyes so that, like the blind man, he too becomes aware of how another person imagines the world.

Oddly enough, this reference to a Raymond Carver story, a story called "Cathedral," set me thinking about Jewishness. It was Sultan's narrative explanation, rather than anything overt in his photographs, that triggered this connection. As Sultan explained, like the characters in Carver's story, in *Pictures from Home*, Sultan retraces another's vision.[14] Larry Sultan re-envisions his father's photographic legacy of home by taking new pictures of his parents in the present, by rephotographing older images, and by making still prints out of what were once his father's eight-millimeter moving-picture images. Like the blind man in Carver's story, Sultan follows his father's hand and, in the end, offers back to his father another take on a world he thought he already knew.

Despite these formal connections to Carver's story, I found Sultan's reference to Carver, the American writer of Waspy postwar suburban middle-class life, and, more specifically, his reference to a story titled "Cathedral" strange in relation to the photographs before me. This strangeness was due to the fact that I had assumed these photographic images were Jewish. The images I associated with Carver's fiction, let alone with cathedrals, were far removed from what I saw in Sultan's work. This distance was jarring. It was also oddly familiar.

I recognized this ambivalent double move of display and then concealment (showing his parents and then using Carver's narrative to explain these images) as Jewish. In this case, intimate portraits were being explained through a reference to the work of an utterly Waspy writer and, more specifically, to a story named by an overtly Christian edifice, a cathedral. The gap between Carver's fiction and Sultan's images reminded me of my own descriptions of immigrant Jewish efforts to be seen as simply Americans.[15]

At Dartmouth[16] the disjunction between Carver's story, which was supposed to help me better understand Sultan's project, and the familiar images I was looking at prompted me to ask Sultan about the Jewishness of his work. I did this after his formal talk. Only then, in private, was my reading of the images as Jewish confirmed. In retrospect, the ambivalences that marked this entire encounter were themselves deeply familiar. They exemplified the kind of ambivalences that mark many American Jews as Jewish.[17]

As I later learned, part of the allure of Sultan's work stems from the interplay between images and narrative. Unlike the show at Dartmouth, in his text and in his exhibit "Pictures from Home," the photographs never stand alone. They are always accompanied by narratives about those depicted.[18] What I find striking about this whole encounter, however, is how rarely such an ambivalent vision of American Jewish life is ever displayed in picture books about American Jews. Despite the growing market for such books,[19] these explicitly Jewish collections rarely include more complex images or narratives like Sultan's or my own. In these texts there are no questions about the Jewishness of the images. They are clearly marked as such.

Sultan's book has not been viewed as a Jewish book. *Pictures from Home* was neither mass-marketed nor targeted to American Jewish audiences. Instead, this expensively produced art book, with lush color prints on every one of its 127 pages, was marketed as a kind of highly subsidized catalog to Sultan's exhibit.[20] The book sold for only $35. In his acknowledgments at the end of the book, Larry Sultan thanks all of those who made this possible: "This project has been supported by generous assistance from the National Endowment for the Arts, the John Simon Guggenheim Memorial Foundation, the Fleishhaker Foundation, the Englehard Foundation, the Marin Arts Council, and the Louis Comfort Tiffany Foundation" (127). This support helps explain how Abrams was able to produce this expensive artistic text. It also may explain why so few copies of the book were ever printed. Despite a strong review in the *New York Times*, by the time the show "Pictures from Home" reached Queens, New York, its final destination, the book was no longer in print.[21] Sultan's book went out of circulation just as other picture books about American Jews were beginning to be mass-marketed.[22] Ironically, Sultan's subtler text may have more to say to an American Jewish audience than some of these overt texts.

In what follows, I juxtapose Sultan's vision of his family as depicted in *Pictures from Home* (1992) against one of these overtly Jewish texts, Frédéric Brenner's *Jews/America/A Representation* (1996). Through a close reading of these two texts, I address some of the difficulties in identifying American Jewish life through photographs and photographic texts.

Both Brenner and Sultan present readers with pictures of contemporary American Jews, most often assimilated Jews taking on the attitudes, tastes, comportment, dreams, and desires of American culture. Although they both address a certain excess in these efforts to be American, they do so in very different modes. Brenner portrays images that are overtly Jewish: rabbis in prayer shawls; women in phylacteries; people holding menorahs; an image of an elegantly attired group of Jewish men and women, *lulav* and *etrog* in hand, parading around a sukkah on a Manhattan rooftop; a seder table; the facade of a synagogue; and many other visual clues that clearly signal that these are Jewish images.

The title of Brenner's book, *Jews/America/A Representation,* and the captions on each of his photographs explicitly announce a Jewish text. Brenner's book was mass-marketed and heavily promoted to Jewish audiences. The publisher, Harry N. Abrams, sold it to contemporary American Jews as a hip version of themselves, a playful representation of their lives now.

Although expensive (the book was priced at $75), *Jews/America/A Representation* sold reasonably well and was widely distributed. As of this date, it has gone into its second printing, and many of Brenner's individual images have been reproduced in other Jewish contexts.[23] Some of the most effective of these include the cover of the catalog to the exhibit "'Holy Land': American Encounters with the Land of Israel in the Century before Statehood"[24] and the collection *Insider/Outsider: American Jews and Multiculturalism.*[25]

Although Brenner presents an overview of American Jewish life, he never gets too close. Brenner never places himself in his pictures. As an outsider, he covers lots of territory and lots of different individual American Jews and Jewish communities, but there is something cold and distant about his vision. By contrast, Sultan's *Pictures from Home* presents a close-up, a portrait of a single, not necessarily Jewish, American family. In Sultan's text, the photographer is intimately present. Despite the fact that there are no explicit images of Jewish objects and no captions on any of his photographs to signal Jewishness, by using extensive narrative, Sultan brings viewers into his work and shows us a subtler picture of contemporary American Jewish life.

A View from the *New York Times*

My choice of these two books is not without precedent. In 1996 the *New York Times* photography critic juxtaposed these two texts in feature articles in the Sunday "Arts and Leisure" section.[26] These reviews offer a way of examining the popular reception of these works. I find that in so doing, they help clarify why identifying American Jewish life is so difficult and what can and cannot be figured as Jewish in American popular culture.

Take One: Sultan Picturing Home

Not long after the conference at Dartmouth, the *New York Times* reprinted the photograph of Sultan's parents that I described above. It was used to illustrate Vicki Goldberg's review of Sultan's show "Pictures from Home," then on view at the Queens Museum of Art. Tellingly titled "The Snapshot, History's Modest Helper" (*New York Times,* June 16, 1996), the review captured both the intimate familiarity as well as the breadth of Sultan's vision. According to Goldberg, the show included 202 photographs, rephotographs, and text. Queens was the last stop for this show, which was originally organized in 1992 by the San Jose Museum of Art.

In her review, Goldberg stresses the sadness of Sultan's vision. A highlighted blurb reads, "Using photos of his parents, Sultan shows how a dream of success ended in disappointment." The juxtaposition of these words and Sultan's image intrigued me. Here again, I was reminded of the ways in which Sultan's image had captured not only the look of my grandmother but her mood, including the disappointment and sadness that marked her life in this country.[27]

As Goldberg explains, Sultan's work peers into "the gap between the lives his parents expected, devised and posed for—the performances they and their children appeared in—and the actual lives that time, circumstances and the usual insufficiencies forced them to live." Thus, Sultan forces viewers to think about the kinds of desires that shape not only his parent's family photographs and home movies but our own. What was the life these documents were supposed to represent, and what do we see now?[28]

Goldberg goes on to describe Sultan's work as "disturbingly familiar," claiming that this familiarity was its appeal. As she explains, "It almost doesn't matter whose family it is." This statement is intriguing. Like Goldberg, I also read these images as universal. But in this particular context, I argue that it does matter whose family it is. By reading Sultan's work as Jewish, I began to see the ambivalence at the heart of this seemingly more universal vision of Jews. I became aware of the labor required to make specific work universal. Identifying this labor as Jewish helped me recognize other dimensions of the all-too-common American narrative about Jewish success. Because Sultan's work disrupts this story, Goldberg did not read it as Jewish.

Not surprisingly, however, precisely this narrative of Jewish success shapes Goldberg's review of Brenner's text.

In her review, Goldberg goes to great lengths to ignore the Sultan family's Jewishness. She does this by placing Sultan's work within a broader American narrative frame. As she explains, Sultan's images

> are familiar partly because Sultan . . . was on the leading edge of the baby boom. His family moved from Brooklyn to California when he was 3; their story chronicles the post-war dream of life in suburbia, which turned out not to be such a good night's sleep. Many will recognize the stations of *Pilgrim's Progress* through the Vale of Suburbia: Little cowboy. Little Leaguer. Ranch House. New Car. Family Vacations. Such snapshots were the medium in which we wrote our history, or the history we wanted to preserve, or at the very least our dreams, once diaries went out of style.

This is a fascinating reading of Sultan's work, in part because of the audience for whom Goldberg presumes to be writing. Despite the fact that this show was on display in Queens, New York, and its themes are clearly ethnic, if not Jewish, Goldberg does not narrate Sultan's family's story as such. Although the family moves from Brooklyn to California to live out the American dream, Goldberg does not mention narratives of Jewish or urban ethnic upward mobility but refers rather to *Pilgrim's Progress*,[29] the quintessential Protestant American saga, which she ironically recasts in terms of the stations of the cross.[30] Thus, the Christianness of the narrative, presented in both Protestant and Catholic terms, is overdetermined.

In addition, Goldberg suggests that the Sultans are included among those who once wrote diaries and then took snapshots to preserve their family histories. Here again, the gaps between the material legacy of immigrant (Jewish) lives, the lives of various first-generation Americans, and a more universal middle class are effaced. Despite these discrepancies, I believe that Goldberg speaks to a longing at the heart of Sultan's text: the desire to belong, to be seen as really American rather than as hyphenated Americans.[31]

I am struck by Goldberg's efforts to read this as a decidedly not-Jewish story even in the pages of the *New York Times*. Despite the large Jewish readership in the New York metropolitan area, those most likely both to identify with Sultan's image and then go to see the exhibit in Queens, Goldberg insists on reading Sultan's work as all-American. In so doing, she ironically perpetuates Sultan's parents' own explicit desire to be seen as simply American. Like Larry Sultan's reference to Carver, which I described earlier, this, too, is a kind of Jewish gesture. Despite the seemingly inviting setting of the *New York Times*, Jewishness must be read between the lines of Goldberg's review.

Take Two: Frédéric Brenner's American Jews

A few months after her review of Sultan, Vicki Goldberg reviewed Brenner's work in a *New York Times* article titled "The American Chapter of the Jewish Saga."[32] Already figured in this headline is the placement of American Jews within a single grand Jewish narrative. This vision of a unified Jewish story informs both Goldberg's treatment of Brenner's work and Brenner's own text. Goldberg's review not only mimics Brenner's strategy but also reiterates a common tendency to figure Jewishness through an all-too-familiar grand narrative that is taken as confirming Jewishness.

The images that illustrate Goldberg's review are bold; some are even funny. At the top of the full-page article is a reprint of Brenner's powerful image of the people of Billings, Montana, holding menorahs in their hands in solidarity with their Jewish neighbors.[33] The image covers the full width of the page. In addition, Goldberg includes two of Brenner's lighter images on the bottom of the page. The first of these is a series of New York Marxists all wearing prepackaged Groucho Marx eyebrows, glasses, and mustaches: "Marxists, New York City, 1994." The second pictures the Hebrew Academy students of Las Vegas standing in a pyramid alongside the architectural pyramid of the new Luxor Hotel: "The Hebrew Academy, The Luxor, Las Vegas, Nevada, 1994."

In the middle of the page is a more somber photograph. It is not by Brenner. It was taken in Amsterdam during the Second World War. Its caption reads, "**Secret Witness** Broken windows where a Jewish newspaper was printed in Amsterdam, in a 1941 image by Charles Breijer on view at the Jewish Museum." This picture stands midway between the Billings shot and Brenner's more playful images. Across from this photograph, in bold, is a blurb about Brenner the artist and ethnographer: "Frédéric Brenner has tracked the Jewish diaspora for 17 years. The results are stirring and even outright funny." These words attempt to bridge the gaps between all of the works on the page.

The juxtaposition of these very different kinds of photographs and the inclusiveness of the blurb are important. They literally figure the desire of American Jews for a sustaining narrative even in the face of great communal trauma. I am not so sure that Brenner's vision can accomplish this goal. I am not convinced that he can offer a single, sustaining vision of contemporary Jewish life. Nor do I believe that this need be the only approach to telling stories about Jews, Jewishness, and Judaism. Instead, I argue, there are other ways of imagining contemporary Jews; other visions; smaller, less-dramatic stories of contemporary Jewish life.

Although Brenner's work promised a more explicit portrait of American Jewish life than Sultan's, even after purchasing his beautifully produced book, I found myself unable to identify with his vision. This book offered a more distant and less specific account of Jewish life than Sultan's text. But even on these terms, I was uncomfortable with Brenner's text.[34] Even as a distant vision of American Jews, Brenner's text was not compelling.

Reading Brenner

Jews/America/A Representation (1996) poses the question: In what ways is it possible to picture American Jewish life at the end of the twentieth century? Although Brenner's work has been referred to as a form of ethnography, as its critical reception and even the introduction to the book make clear, Brenner is very much an artist. He crafts beautifully executed, carefully orchestrated dramatic images. Photography allows him to capture the results of a kind of theatrical engagement with not only the human subjects of his photographs but the locations, the places, and the times that he attempts to picture. Here architecture (the pyramid in Las Vegas, the Empire State Building), nature, the physical landscape of America (the desert, the coasts), as well as the interior spaces, the homes of American Jews, are all his subjects. Through these images, Brenner explicitly seeks to capture "the distinctiveness" of Jewish life in America.

Ethnography

As an outsider to this American Jewish world, Brenner, a Frenchman, describes his method as akin to a kind of fieldwork. In the first paragraph of his acknowledgments he explains: "During a two-year period I visited thirty-two states, criss-crossing America from New York to Los Angeles, from the Bering Strait to the Mississippi Delta. . . . It was only at the end of a long period of immersion made up of meetings, dialogues, interrogations, debates, and confrontations, that the execution of this portrait became possible" (ii). Although Jewish, Brenner does not focus his camera on himself. He began documenting specific Jewish communities in the early 1980s under the auspices of Beth Hatefusoth, the Nahum Goldmann Museum of the Jewish Diaspora in Tel Aviv. To date, this larger project includes portraits of Israeli Jews, the Jews of India, Italian Jews, and the Jews in the Soviet Union just before the collapse of the Soviet system.[35]

Although, as Jeffrey Shandler argues, Brenner's work combines ethnography and art,[36] I am troubled by the fact that Brenner's artistic vision lays claim to a certain kind of ethnographic authenticity even as he plays with his subjects. Brenner uses the urgency of the documentary to fuel his increasingly artistic ventures. In and of itself this could be an interesting strategy, but in *Jews/America/A Representation,* Brenner fails to follow through on the promise of such an engagement. He does not offer a critical re-evaluation of the stereotypes he reproduces. Instead, here the ethnographic urgency of Jewish continuity after the Holocaust is in conflict with an artistic playfulness. There is no edge to Brenner's play. The painful recognition of complexity that is so crucial to "camp" as a disruptive practice is missing.[37] Given this, I found it difficult to identify with any of his photographs, even the most powerful of these images (such as "Citizens Protesting Anti-Semitic Acts, Billings, Montana 1994," the photograph reproduced in the *New York Times* review), in the context of his book. The staging of one stylized image after another only adds to the distancing that Brenner's ethnographic stance already engenders. In addition, his repetitive use of a kind of theatrical framing of his subjects reinforced my sense of distance.

In his introduction to the text, Simon Schama stresses the artistic merits of Brenner's work and not its ethnographic import. As Schama writes, "Perhaps it's misleading to classify these compositions as photographs at all, if by photography is meant the freeze-framing of a fugitive moment. Brenner has always been more a candid dramaturge, a baroque impresario of cultural encounters" (vii). Building on Schama's metaphor, I find that the imposition of the stage places readers at a distance from those in the pictures. It does not make these photographs compelling works of art.[38]

Brenner's images, relying on familiar clichés, stereotypes, and puns, simply repeat what they are modeled on. There are no new angles. Thus, for example, his image of the Aryeh family of Montclair, New Jersey, an immigrant Jewish family originally from Iran, presents the extended family on a magic Persian carpet. In America, the carpet literally brings the family into the heart of suburbia.[39] Here, as elsewhere, instead of disrupting the production of stereotypes through performance, Brenner simply restages the same old stories. There is no new twist. Unlike more campy performances, in this text Brenner does not use clichés to call attention to their limitations.[40] Instead, time and again, Brenner's text ends up reinforcing the stereotypes he deploys.[41]

Liberal Pluralism

In her critique of liberal pluralism, the cultural critic Janet Jakobsen points out, "The horizontal placement of various 'differences' fails to articulate either power relations or historical conflict among 'different' groups."[42] Through the multiplicity of separate images in the main body of his text, Brenner presents American Jewishness as a form of liberal pluralism. To borrow from Jakobsen: Brenner's text "produces a version of diversity which is made up of multiple 'units' of differences."[43] Thus, although each image is distinct, all units are given equal weight, one image per page. Together they offer a single representation. American Jewish options are laid out one after another, following all too closely Jakobsen's account of liberal pluralism, where "coherent 'units' of difference are placed in horizontal lists, producing clear boundaries." As such, in Brenner's text, as in most representations of American Jewish culture, political and historical struggles among and between Jews, including different legacies of immigration, struggles with particular diseases (e.g., breast cancer), poverty, criminality, and even the trauma of the Holocaust are all presented as "benign variation (diversity) . . . rather than as . . . conflict or struggle, or the threat of disruption."[44] Given the formal structure of the text, each separate position is reduced to a version of the same, as Goldberg describes it, a single chapter in a larger Jewish narrative. As such, trying to find a distinctly familiar image of one's own Jewishness is difficult. Because all differences have been reduced to versions of the same, it is hard to differentiate between various options. In Brenner's text, individual options do not really make much of a difference.

As if somehow cognizant of my lack of recognition, as if already aware of the fact that many American Jews will not find themselves in any of the portraits in his text, Brenner ends his book with three more-condensed, pluralist visions: "Icons"; an installation of "Icons" at Ellis Island, 1996; and "Inventory june 1993–september 1995 (arranged in alphabetical order)." These three compositions at the conclusion of the text together attempt to compensate for the distancing effect of the larger portraits in the main body of the book. They present lots of smaller images of familiar Jewish faces, names, places, and objects. They offer readers the pleasures of the overtly familiar in small doses. Here, identification becomes a kind of nostalgic reclamation project.[45] By recognizing any number of American Jewish celebrities, products, or places, readers can ultimately feel included in Brenner's vision of American Jewish life.

In each of these works, Brenner offers images of well-known American Jews and all-too-familiar American Jewish places and things in a condensed format. "Icons" offers a series of portraits of famous American Jews. Each Jewish "icon" is elaborately "framed"; the subjects literally play with a version of an identical large gold frame. In the first rendition, these images are presented separately, one after the other in alphabetical order in two nearly neat rows. There are thirty-nine images in total, with one extra image on the end of the top row (of Roy Lichtenstein). This collection of portraits takes up four full pages. Underneath the two rows of images, the names and occupations of the icons are clearly labeled.

In the installation, the same icons are all present, but this time they are arranged in random order on a large metal frame literally set up on Ellis Island. The photograph of the installation opens up to a view of the Manhattan skyline. The logic that links these images is a shared promise of American success that marks the immigrant's arrival in New York, the city of dreams. The composition seems to say that not only did all of these people come through Ellis Island to fulfill the legendary American dream but you, too, can become a legend. In this way the installation replicates the mythic narrative of Jews making it in America.[46]

The final piece in the volume offers an alphabetical inventory of Jewish American memorabilia. These pages form a symmetrical grid, with thirty-five 1½-by-1½-inch pictures of a vast array of stuff that cover almost twenty pages. There are 731 numbered images, followed by two full pages of tiny printed explanations identifying each of the numbered pictures. Here, again, difference is obscured as symmetry creates a sense of equality and connection between often disconnected places and things. Although many of these photographs are hard to see, as familiar images they nevertheless appeal to a series of nostalgic desires through a proliferation of familiar Jewish commodities.[47] These images do not have to be read that closely. Readers can find themselves through their connection to at least some of these Jewish objects. The inventory includes: kosher wine and brand-name products; bagels and lox; an AIPAC (American Israel Public Affairs Committee) name tag; explicitly Jewish bumper stickers, books, restaurants, and signs; as well as a menorah, Shabbat candlesticks, and many other mass-produced ritual and decorative objects.[48] The range of things on display offers a kind of relief from the alienation of the text as whole. By providing something—literally a thing or two—to hold onto, the book, attempting to be inclusive, offers something Jewishly familiar to as many American Jews as possible. This time, images of Jewish commodities allow us to buy into a form of liberal inclusion. In this way the inventory objects are not unlike Brenner's text—commercial vehicles for Jewish identification. Here, capitalism and liberal pluralism converge. In the end, Jewishness becomes a kind of consumer choice.

Section of page 69 from "Inventory," Frédéric Brenner, *Jews/America/A Representation*, Harry N. Abrams, 1996.

Reading Sultan

Unlike Brenner, the artist-ethnographer, Sultan is very much a part of his text. In *Pictures from Home,* he offers readers an intimate portrait of his parents and the home(s) in which he grew up. Sultan intersperses words and images. There is no single break between an acknowledgment and introduction (there are none) and the photographic text. The relationship between pictures and words is indirect; there are no captions. Alongside ten years' worth of photographs of his aging parents, old stills from his family's home movies that he had enlarged, and reprints of old family photographs is a series of narratives, three separate voices telling family stories. These include his own voice, as well as the voices of both parents. Each of these distinct narrations is presented visually through the use of a different typeface.[49]

Very much an American portrait, Sultan's text displays the excessiveness that informs the desire to be seen simply as an American. This longing is expressed not only in the accumulation of images but also within the images themselves. As I have argued elsewhere, such excess can be read as a kind of Jewish marker.[50] Much like my own immigrant Jewish family, the Sultans' Americanness can be read as partial, as both incomplete and virtual. Despite how hard they try to present themselves as simply Americans, their desires, like the desires of many assimilated American Jews, betray them. As cultural critic Homi Bhabha explains, we see this almost-but-not-quite status of the liberal or colonial subject expressed in a "proliferation of inappropriate objects."[51] This proliferation is evident in Sultan's images.[52] Just as colonial or liberal mimicry often marks the liberal Jewish subject as almost-but-not-quite American through a kind of exaggerated loyalty, here, too, Jewishness is expressed in terms of an excessive desire to fit in, to not be marked as different.[53] Before turning to Sultan's more explicit Jewish narratives, I offer some examples of how he visualized this form of mimicry.

All the interior spaces, the homes Sultan so vividly portrays, are richly detailed. Inside his parents' homes, excess is evident in the carefully matching wallpapers and fabrics, a kind of self-conscious sense of the importance of the decorative touch. Even his parents are made to participate in these elaborate tableaux. His mother, for example, is always presented in carefully orchestrated color-coordinated outfits that match the rooms in which she is being photographed. In some photographs she echoes the wallpaper or the paint color on the walls; in others she matches particular objects in a room.[54]

Excess, however, is not only about what is placed in a room or on a body. It is not only a kind of set or costume; it is also embodied in Sultan's work. It is seen in his parents' various repeated poses in the family album, as well as in his artistic text. In most of these images his parents are figured as the athlete and the model over and over again.[55] As the text explains, for over fifty-one years, Mrs. Sultan struck the same modeling pose in virtually all of the family's photographs. Not only are we told this in Larry Sultan's text, but we are also offered numerous examples to illustrate the point.

Alongside his wife, or alone more often than not, Mr. Sultan is figured in terms of a kind of self-conscious athleticism. One of the earliest shots of Larry's father is as a strapping young man on the beach. The once-athletic father continues to pose in this way even as he ages. In more recent shots taken by his son, Mr. Sultan is often figured with golf club in hand, about to take a practice stroke inside the house, or bare-chested in a bathing suit at poolside.

Although I read these details as Jewish, I do not doubt that they are also familiar to other upwardly mobile ethnic Americans. But this does not mean that they cannot be viewed as Jewish. Gestures need not be repeated as exclusively Jewish to be viewed as such.

Other dimensions of Sultan's text draw me in and call my attention to its Jewishness. This is clear in the book's narratives, where Larry Sultan's parents explicitly discuss their Jewishness. Although Jewishness is by no means a constant or overarching theme in these narratives, it is an explicit part of the Sultans' family stories. It shows up most often in Jean's (Larry's mother) and Irving's (Larry's father) individual accounts of particular moments in their lives. Thus, *Pictures from Home* conveys how, for some American Jews, Jewishness is present although not necessarily central to family life. Although being Jewish cannot account for all that this text describes, it has a place in this family portrait.

The family's Jewishness figures prominently in Jean Sultan's account of her courtship with her husband. As their relationship becomes serious, Irving is invited to meet Jean's mother to make clear his intentions. As Jean explains:

> Well, after a while he came out to meet my mother in New Jersey. He took the train in because he didn't have a car. Later that night we went to a basketball game and then to Meadowbrook to hear Frank Sinatra. When I asked my mother what she thought she said, "He seems like a nice Gentile boy." (33)

At this moment Jewishness matters. Although he is nice, if her daughter has any intention of marrying this man, he really should be Jewish. In Jean's Jewish family, the stereotype of unattractive Jewish men has been internalized. Here Irving's good looks deceive. Because Irving is handsome, Jean's mother cannot believe that he is actually Jewish. Seeing is not believing. Irving does not look familiar. She needs additional evidence.

As the narrative continues, Irving's Jewish credentials must be verified. Jean arranges for her Jewish mother to meet Irving's Jewish mother. Yet even after this meeting, Jean tells us, her mother is not convinced that Irving is Jewish. As Jean explains, "I said, 'Ma, he's a Jew, really. He's been BarMitzvahed'" (33). The effort it takes for Jean to prove to her mother that Irving is Jewish calls into question the conventional idea that Jews are easy to identify. Even Jews cannot always identify other Jews when they see them. This is true even in the case of pictures. As the text constantly reminds us, pictures cannot speak for themselves. We need narratives to explain them.

Jewishness also appears earlier in the narrative, in Irving's descriptions of his childhood. As he explains, sometime after his father's death, when the family could no longer support itself, Irving's mother appealed to a Jewish relief agency for help. Hence, he and his brother were sent to the Hebrew Sheltering and Guardian Society in Pleasantville, New York. Irving goes on to describe how Jewishness was expressed in this institution. At the home, a meager effort was made to adhere to Jewish customs, especially on the Sabbath, which was distinguished by a special meal for the children. As Irving recalls, "The only relief from [bad food] was on Friday nights, the Sabbath. It was our big night, and as a ritual we would be served hot dogs and sponge cake for dinner. I can still smell those hot dogs" (28).

Jewishness is also revealed in names. The names of Larry's aunts, uncles, and cousins are all common Jewish names of a generation of American Jews.[56] These names include Irving, Ben, Shirley, Bert, Henry, and Sadie, among many others. As Irving makes clear later in the text, names were important Jewish signifiers. Temporarily changing his name while working as a suit salesman in New York City in the 1940s, he became privy to the antisemitic comments of his customers. Wearing a different name on his lapel, Irving passed as a non-Jew and heard all kinds of antisemitic slurs:

> You have no idea about prejudice until you pass yourself off as someone else, as one of them. Irving Sultan was a Jew, but John Sutton wasn't. The stuff I'd hear people say about Jews was hard to believe and even harder to take. I wanted to punch people right in the nose, but where would that get me? I had a wife and two kids. So I had to accept their stupidity. The whole thing made me sick. (44)

In a reversal of the critical story line of the Academy Award–winning motion picture *Gentleman's Agreement*,[57] Irving, the Jew, passes himself off as a non-Jew when he is a soldier returning home after the war. Unlike Gregory Peck's character in the film, Irving does not do this to get a good story; Irving changes his identity in order to keep his job and support his family. Unlike Peck's character, as the non-Jew, "John Sutton," Irving Sultan is made keenly aware of antisemitism. And unlike Peck's character in the movie, he does not feel free to confront those who make antisemitic remarks. Irving must keep quiet in order to keep his job. He is not a successful reporter at a swanky New York magazine.

Finally, the narratives in Sultan's text describe a precise time and place in a specific and complex way. *Pictures from Home* places the Sultans' family stories and images in the context of postwar America. The text chronicles Larry's parents' more or less successful efforts to work their way into the upper ranks of the American middle class.[58]

In *Pictures from Home,* happy images from home-movie stills and family photographs bulge with the promise of suburban success. The book contains numerous images of bigger and better homes and cars, children playing, and family members united in their various suburban houses. Such images are juxtaposed against other stories. The photographs contrast with the various narratives offered in his text.

These are tales of miscommunication and loneliness, as well as more recent accounts of professional disappointment. Thus, in one of its most powerful sections, *Pictures from Home* chronicles Irving Sultan's professional downfall through corporate downsizing.

In Sultan's text, the American dream of upward mobility and westward expansion is simultaneously embraced and questioned. Underlying U.S. society's many happy narratives and images about these times and this place is a more complicated account.[59]

By offering narratives and images of a particular postwar moment, Sultan's text provides access into the familial dreams of a specific era, an era that, although past, remains hauntingly present in contemporary American (Jewish) life. Even within the elaborate interiors of their various homes, the Sultans' lives were never hermetically sealed. In this text, history and culture are figured in terms of both what the Sultans had hoped their lives might be and the more complicated experiences they underwent in seeking to attain their goals. This vision contrasts vividly to Brenner's breezy liberal story of success.

Although Jews are seemingly at home and comfortable in America, there is more to the story. Sultan penetrates some of the subtler and more painful aspects of this legacy. His book puts a more explicitly Jewish face on the narrative of loss Goldberg describes in her review.

Part of what draws me to this book is that Jewishness is not central and defining. It is and it isn't there. While very much a part of Sultan's family story, it's not the book's central motif. I find this stance refreshing. It expands the whole question of what American Jews can look like. Jewishness does not and cannot explain all aspects of this family's collective story or the stories of its individual members. I find that a relief. Nor should we expect Jewishness to carry such an unrealistic burden. *Pictures from Home* tells us that visions of American Jewishness need not be an all-or-nothing proposition. Instead, as in many other American Jewish families—families like my own—while being Jewish is a part of the lives of Larry Sultan and his parents, it is not at the center of their lives.

The ambiguous ways in which this text is and isn't Jewish attract me. I know this form of Jewishness well and do not often see it depicted in either words or images about American Jews. In *Pictures from*

Home, Larry Sultan uses personal images and narratives as a way to explain broader issues in contemporary American life, precisely the issues Goldberg addresses in her review. Although Sultan allows readers to identify with his vision, the specificity of his portraits and narratives is at the heart of his text. These constantly remind us that this is not a bland, generic story.

Some Conclusions

Sometimes that which at first seems strange is actually familiar, and that which purports to be familiar is far more distant and stranger. In this case, a text explicitly about American Jews and marketed to American Jews—a text that uses a familiar liberal pluralist vocabulary to present contemporary American Jewish life—ends up making us feel distant, whereas a text about a single American family—a text that does not overtly present itself as Jewish—is that much more Jewishly familiar.

Instead of critically engaging the excesses and discomforts of American Jewish life, Frédéric Brenner's *Jews/America/A Representation* ends up simply reproducing them. Brenner's text either mocks or avoids painful contradictions in contemporary American Jewish life, thus making it hard for readers like me to identify with his vision. In contrast to the liberal pluralist logic of his text, I argue that the diversity of American Jewish life cannot be reduced to one of many American Jewish consumer options.[60] This is not how American Jews experience being Jewish in the present. Given this, Brenner's Jewish text ends up alienating many readers like me, who had hoped to find ourselves within its pages.

Questioning the limitations of Brenner's all-too-common approach to diversity and differences, I argue for the merits of looking at a more historically specific account of a particular American Jewish family. Precisely these kinds of stories tend to get lost in ostensibly grander Jewish narratives.[61]

Sultan's text offers a much more intimate portrait of the complexity of American Jewish life in the second half of the twentieth century. Because Sultan's text is so specific, it allows readers to make connections between the Sultans' and their own family's stories.

Ironically, what we learn from Sultan's text is that these are not exclusively Jewish stories. Jewish experiences of prejudice reverberate with the experiences of many other Americans.

By telling family tales through multiple narratives and a broad range of images from different times and places, Sultan reminds readers that appearances can deceive. He invites us to look deeper in order to see more than the veneer of success or good looks. In this way, he shows us some of the less overt, less complete, and less than happy sides of postwar American life. He thus offers insight into a non-exclusive and complex vision of contemporary Jewish life.

NOTES

I thank Ruth Ost; Michelle Friedman; and my colleagues in the Young Scholars in American Religion Program, Ava Chamberlain, Tracy Fessenden, Kathleen Joyce, Elisabeth McAllister, Leonard Primiano, Jennifer Rycenga, T. Paul Thigpen, and especially Deborah Dash Moore, for their thoughtful and insightful readings of various versions of this essay. I also thank Larry Silberstein for his help in editing the final version of this chapter.

1. Examples of these texts include Dorothy and Thomas Hoobler, *The Jewish Family Album* (New York: Oxford University Press, 1995), and Rachel Salamander, *The Jewish World of Yesterday 1860–1938* (New York: Rizzoli, 1990). See also Bill Aron's important larger study *From the Corners of the Earth: Contemporary Photographs of the Jewish World* (Philadelphia: Jewish Publication Society, 1985).

2. Here I have in mind the critical role of coffee-table books. See, for example, Jack Kugelmass, "Jewish Icons: Envisioning the Self in Images of the Other," in *Jews and Other Differences: The New Jewish Cultural Studies*, ed. Jonathan Boyarin and Daniel Boyarin (Minneapolis: University of Minnesota Press, 1997), 30–53. See also the various essays in "Going Home," *YIVO Annual* 21 (1993). For a broader reading of identification and its deployment in the realm of commodified culture, see Eric Santner, *Stranded Objects: Mourning, Memory, and Film in Postwar Germany* (Ithaca, N.Y.: Cornell University Press, 1990), esp. chap. 3.

3. Diana Fuss, *Identification Papers* (New York: Routledge, 1995), 1.

4. For more on this issue of difference within identification, see Kaja Silverman, *Threshold of the Visible World* (New York: Routledge, 1996).

5. Stuart Hall, ed., *Representation: Cultural Representations and Signifying Practices* (London: Sage, 1997), 81.

6. Ibid., 83. See also Robert Coles, *Doing Documentary Work* (New York: Oxford University Press, 1997). Also on this point, see James Young, *Writing and Rewriting the Holocaust: Narrative and the Consequences of Interpretation* (Bloomington: Indiana University Press, 1988).

7. The conference, "Family Pictures: Shapes of Memory," was held at Dartmouth College on May 24–26, 1996. It took place in the Arthur M. Loew Auditorium at the Hood Museum of Art at the college. The exhibit at the Hood that was developed in conjunction with the conference was "The Familial Gaze," which ran from May 4 to July 21, 1996. For more on this conference, see Marianne Hirsch, ed., *The Familial Gaze* (Hanover, N.H.: University Press of New England, 1998).

8. Larry Sultan, *Pictures from Home* (New York: Harry N. Abrams, 1992), 31. Further references to this work cite the page numbers in the text.

9. Laura Levitt, *Jews and Feminism: The Ambivalent Search for Home* (New York: Routledge, 1997), 163. Although I wrote these words about a photograph of my grandmother, I could have just as easily written them about Sultan's mother.

10. Fuss, *Identification Papers*, 1.

11. My "reading" of this photograph echoes the kind of ambivalent reading practice I call for in my essay "(The Problem with) Embraces," in *Judaism since Gender*, ed. Miriam Peskowitz and Laura Levitt (New York: Routledge, 1997), 213–23. See also Laura Levitt, "Blurring the Familiar, an Afterword," in Hirsch, ed., *Familial Gaze*, 343–47. I am also working on these issues in *Picturing American Jews: Photography, History, and Memory*, a new book in process.

12. See Roland Barthes, *Camera Lucida: Reflections on Photography* (New York: Hill and Wang, 1981), for a gorgeous exposition of these longings and this way of reading photographs. For a powerful critique of Barthes's argument on the issue of difference—more specifically, the move from an idiosyncratic reading of images of others always in recognition of difference—see Kaja Silverman's reading of Barthes in her *Threshold of the Visible World*, 181–84. For a different but also powerful reading and application of Barthes's text, see Marianne Hirsch, *Family Frames: Photography, Narrative, and Postmemory* (Cambridge: Harvard University Press, 1997).

13. Raymond Carver, *Where I'm Calling From: Stories* (New York: Vintage, 1989), 356–75.

14. I thank Larry Sultan for elaborating on these connections in a telephone conversation, September 1998.

15. More specifically, I was reminded of my account of my grandmother and

the snapshot of her that I included in *Jews and Feminism*, especially the introduction and conclusion.

16. Here, too, the setting was important. Dartmouth was itself a strange site to see all too many unmarked, unaccounted for images of American Jewish families. This was a setting much more in keeping with the kinds of families envisioned in Carver's fiction. For more on the ambivalent and undertheorized Jewishness present in many of the works presented at the conference, see Levitt, "Blurring the Familiar," 343–47.

17. See Levitt, *Jews and Feminism*, especially my discussion of the Jewish position of Nancy K. Miller, chaps. 7, 8, and 9.

18. Unfortunately, I was not able to see the exhibit, but at Dartmouth, Sultan described it to me in terms of the interplay between word and pictures. In the exhibit, words as well as images were "all over the walls." Conversation with Larry Sultan, Dartmouth College, May 1996.

19. Since 1996 there has been a proliferation of exhibits on Jews and photography across the United States. Some of these include the following exhibits at the Jewish Museum in New York: "The Illegal Camera," August 18–December 1, 1996 (the exhibit reviewed alongside Frédéric Brenner's work in September 1996); "A Witness to History: Yevgeny Khaldei, Soviet Photojournalist," January 19–April 13, 1997; "Points of Entry," May 18–August 1997; and, in 1998, "Selections/Contemporary Photography."

20. Unlike Frédéric Brenner's *Jews/America/A Representation* (New York: Harry N. Abrams, 1996), the "Jewish" text I discuss below—another Abrams book, which sold for $75 in hardback—Sultan's text cost $35. Further references to Brenner's book cite the page numbers in the text.

21. For more on the *New York Times* review (June 16, 1996), see my discussion below. After this article appeared, I called the publisher to order a copy of the book and was told at that time that the book was out of print. Telephone conversation with editorial staff at Harry N. Abrams, New York, June 1996.

22. Frédéric Brenner's widely circulated *Jews/America/A Representation*, the other text I discuss, was published in 1996.

23. According to its publisher, as of 1998, this book had just gone into its second printing. The first run was between five and ten thousand books. Telephone conversation with editorial staff at Harry N. Abrams, New York, May 1998.

24. *Encounters with the "Holy Land": Place, Past and Future in American Jewish Culture*, ed. Jeffrey Shandler and Beth S. Wenger (Hanover, N.H.: University Press of New England, 1997). Wenger and Shandler co-curated the exhibit, which was sponsored by and held at the National Museum

of American Jewish History, the Center for Judaic Studies at the University of Pennsylvania, and the University of Pennsylvania Library and ran from January 23 through July 5, 1998. The catalog cover uses Brenner's image of contemporary suburban Jews donning Hasidic garb to pose in front of a photograph of the Western Wall, "International Jewish Arts Festival, Suffolk Y Jewish Community Center, Commack, Long Island, 1995."

25. David Biale, Michael Galchinsky, and Susannah Heschel, eds., *Insider/Outsider: American Jews and Multiculturalism* (Berkeley: University of California Press, 1998). On the cover of this book is a tinted version of Brenner's image "Citizens Protesting Anti-Semitic Acts, Billings, Montana, 1994."

26. It should also be noted that Vicki Goldberg, the critic in question, has written extensively on photography. See, for example, Vicki Goldberg, *The Power of Photography* (New York: Abble Press, 1993).

27. For a somewhat different reading of the quest for the American dream by Jews who went to California, see Deborah Dash Moore, *To the Golden Cities: Pursuing the American Jewish Dream in Miami and L.A.* (Cambridge: Harvard University Press, 1994). Part of what differentiates Moore's account from Sultan's is that Moore addresses those Jews who chose to affiliate with other Jews through synagogues and Jewish communal organizations. As Moore explains, "Jews setting out after the Dream, a new kind of life in Miami and Los Angeles in the postwar era, often succeeded handsomely. Some, of course, merely fled what they considered to be an oppressive past and jettisoned their Jewish identity" (264). Although I would not say that the Sultans stopped being Jewish, their position is much closer to those not depicted in Moore's study.

28. See Richard Chalfen, *Snapshot Versions of Life* (Bowling Green, Ohio: Bowling Green State University Popular Press, 1987).

39. As N. H. Keeble explains in the introduction to the Oxford World's Classics edition of *The Pilgrim's Progress*, "No other seventeenth-century text save the King James Bible, . . . and no other Puritan, or indeed, committed Christian work of any persuasion, has enjoyed such an extensive readership" (introduction to John Bunyan, *The Pilgrim's Progress* [New York: Oxford University Press, 1984], ix).

30. I thank Ann Pellegrini for pointing out to me the additional reference to the stations of the cross and its Catholic resonances.

31. For a powerful reading of young American Jewish women and diaries, see Joan Jacobs Brumberg, "The 'Me' of Me: Voices of Jewish Girls in Adolescent Dairies of the 1920s and 1950s," in *Talking Back, Images of Jewish Women in American Popular Culture*, ed. Joyce Antler (Hanover, N.H.:

Brandeis University Press, 1998), 53–67. Brumberg's essay helps place Jewish women within the matrix of those who kept diaries in America during their adolescence and then gave them up as they began to take family photographs when they started families of their own.

32. The review appeared in the Sunday *New York Times*, September 22, 1996. An old friend sent me an invitation to the opening of Brenner's exhibit at the Howard Greenberg Gallery within days of my ordering the book. I thank William Meyers for his personal account of this exhibit and his disturbing reaction to these images, as related in a telephone conversation, May 1998, and in personal correspondence, June 23, 1998.

33. This photograph was inspired by the community's actual act of solidarity. In response to an antisemitic incident, many non-Jews in the town placed menorahs in the windows of their homes. As in Brenner's portrait, this diverse community expressed support for their Jewish neighbors.

34. For a particularly critical reading of this text, see Leon Wieseltier, "Shooting Jews," *New Republic*, December 9, 1996, 46. I thank William Meyers for sharing this review with me. I also thank him for sharing his own troubled reactions to Brenner's work with me (personal correspondence, June 23, 1998).

35. See Jeffrey Shandler, "Photoethnography as a Performance Art: The Recent Work of Frédéric Brenner" (conference paper presented at the Association for Jewish Studies Annual Meeting, Boston, December 1996), on the development of Brenner's work over time from a more simple ethnographic gaze toward a performative art form, what Shandler refers to as a kind of "photoethnography." According to Shandler, Brenner's latest works, including *Jews/America/A Representation,* are much more collaborative projects than his earlier ones. Although I read these images somewhat differently than Shandler, the development he traces in Brenner's work is important. This project continues. See the *New York Times Magazine,* Sunday, May 3, 1998, which included two prints from what was then Brenner's forthcoming book on Israel's immigrant Jews; and Frédéric Brenner, *Exiles at Home* (New York: Harry N. Abrams, 1998).

36. See Shandler, "Photoethnography." Moreover, as Simon Schama reminds us in his introduction to Brenner's *Jews/America/A Representation,* iv–xiv, although trained as an artist, Brenner also has a master's degree in social anthropology from the Sorbonne (1985). For a different account of this shift in Brenner's work, see Wieseltier, "Shooting Jews," 46, where he argues for the merits of Brenner's earlier ethnographic works: "A few years ago, in a wonderful book called *Marranes*, that appeared in Paris, Brenner published a series of haunting and valuable pictures of

descendants of Marranos in Portugal." Wieseltier continues by noting that this earlier work is in sharp contrast to *Jews/America/A Representation*.

37. I thank Ann Pellegrini for helping me make these connections to camp. For an excellent account of the dynamic potential of camp and its complexity, see Susan Sontag's classic 1964 essay "Notes on Camp," in *Against Interpretation and Other Essays* (New York: Delta Books, 1966), 275–92. For an updated and critical reading of Sontag, especially on "Jewish camp," see Ann Pellegrini, "Notes on Jewish Camp: The Crisis of 'Convertability'" (conference paper presented to the American Studies Association, Washington, D.C., 1997), as well as Ann Pellegrini, "Melancholy Camp: Notes on Jewishness, Gender, and Identification" (conference paper presented at the "Mapping Jewish Identities" conference, Lehigh University, Bethlehem, Pa., May 1998).

38. See Ann Pellegrini's reading of Jewish camp in "Melancholy Camp." As in camp performances, the stage may enable identification. The problem is that in Brenner's work, the stage does not work in this way. Rather, it gets in the way of identification.

39. See Brenner, *Jews/America/A Representation*, 52–53. Although I think it is possible that some of Brenner's individual images might work to produce identificatory effects in other contexts, they do not do so in *Jews/America/A Representation*. They need to be reframed. See the covers of *Encounters with the "Holy Land"* and *Insider/Outsider*.

40. By contrast, see Norman L. Kleeblatt, ed., *Too Jewish? Challenging Traditional Identities* (New Brunswick: Rutgers University Press, 1996).

41. This is part of Wieseltier's frustration with Brenner's more recent works.

42. Janet Jakobsen, *Working Alliances and the Politics of Difference* (Bloomington: Indiana University Press, 1997), 9–10.

43. Ibid.

44. Chandra Mohanty, as cited by Jakobsen, *Working Alliances*, 10. For more on the problematics of diversity management and its relation to liberal pluralism, see Chandra Talpade Mohanty, "On Race and Voice: Challenges for Liberal Education in the 1990s," in *Between Borders: Pedagogy and the Politics of Cultural Studies*, ed. Henry Giroux and Peter McLaren (New York: Routledge, 1994), 145–66.

45. On the problematics of nostalgia, see "Going Home," *YIVO Annual* 21 (1993); Beth Wenger, "Memory and Identity: The Invention of the Lower East Side," *American Jewish History* 85, 1 (1997): 3–27; as well as the various discussions about nostalgia, Jews, and modern visual culture in Linda Nochlin and Tamar Garb, *The Jew in the Text: Modernity and the Construction of Identity* (London: Thames and Hudson, 1995). For a powerful critique of nostalgia, see also the epilogue to Miriam Peskowitz's

Spinning Fantasies: Rabbis, Gender, and History (Berkeley: University of California Press, 1997), 154–71.

46. Barbara Kirshenblatt-Gimblett, "Ellis Island," in *Destination Culture: Tourism, Museums, and Heritage* (Berkeley: University of California Press, 1998), 177–88.

47. At the end of "Inventory," in the condensed explanation that Brenner offers, each numbered photograph is identified. His descriptions of those images included here read as follows:

> **1** "A guide to the direct mail perplexed": A. B. Data; **2** "A Heritage of Perfection"; **3** Ad campaign offices, Jewish Federation, Los Angeles; **8 to 10** AIPAC (American Israel Public Affairs Committee); **15** "All the greatest Yiddish songs"; **16** American Israel Public Affairs Committee Annual Meeting, Sheraton Hotel, Washington, D.C., May 8, 1995; **17** Antiquarian, New Orleans; **22** As advertised in *Jewish Week;* **23** At the Polo Shoppes, Boca Raton, FL; **24** Atlantic Avenue Subway Station, Brooklyn, N.Y.; **29** B'nai B'rith Perlman Camp, Starlight, PA; **30** Babylonian Talmud, bilingual edition; **31** Back to Broadway. (Brenner, *Jews/America/A Representation*, 90)

48. "Inventory" is presented in alphabetical order; for a full listing of all of the images on display, see Brenner, *Jews/America/A Representation*, 91–92. Here, especially, Brenner builds on the legacy of the French artist and photographer Christian Boltanski. See, for example, Boltanski's "Inventaire des objets ayant appartenu à un habitant d'Oxford" (1973). See Jennifer Flay, ed., *Christian Boltanski: Catalogue, Books, Printed Matter, Ephemera, 1966–1991* (Cologne: Walter König, 1992).

49. Sultan's work reminded me very much of my own efforts to tell some of my family stories in *Jews and Feminism*. I began reading his book as I was finishing my manuscript.

50. Again, this echoes my reading of Sultan's gallery talk and Goldberg's article. On Jewishness as excess, see my introduction to *Jews and Feminism*. Also on excess as Jewish in representations of Jews in the modern period, see Nochlin and Garb, *Jew in the Text*.

51. On this process, see Homi Bhabha, "Of Mimicry and Man: The Ambivalence of Colonial Discourse," in *The Location of Culture* (New York and London: Routledge, 1994), 85–92. For my reading of Bhabha's postcolonial work in an American Jewish context, see *Jews and Feminism*. As I read it, many other Americans also find themselves insecure in their status as Americans, based not only on visible difference but often precisely because they can "pass." On this point, see Janet Jakobsen's reading of the video *Gay Rights, Special Rights* in *Working Alliances*, 122–49.

52. Bhabha takes this a step further to show how this not-quite fit is built into

the discourse of colonialism to ensure that the colonial subject remains always in this precarious position. He also suggests that resemblance and menace become linked in this dynamic. Here I am reminded of the kinds of dangers posed by the "internal" threat of communism during the 1950s in the United States. For more on this frightening menace who might look just like us, especially in relation to the threats of homosexuals and Jews, see Janet Jakobsen, "Reproducing the Family: Value, Values, and the Production of American-ness" (conference paper presented to the American Studies Association, Washington, D.C., 1997). For a broader account of these issues of containment and familialism, see Elaine Tyler May, *Homeward Bound: American Families in the Cold War Era* (New York: Basic Books, 1988); and Patricia R. Zimmermann's "Do-It-Yourself: 1950–1962," in *Reel Families: A Social History of Amateur Film* (Bloomington: Indiana University Press, 1995), 112–42. In a different way, this dynamic is well described in relation to explicit representations of Jews in Nochlin and Garb's *Jew in the Text*. It is also a part of the kinds of representations of Jewish bodies that Sander Gilman describes in *The Jew's Body* (New York: Routledge, 1991).

53. As cultural critic Homi Bhabha explains, "The excess or slippage produced by the *ambivalence* of mimicry (almost the same, *but not quite*) . . . becomes transformed into an uncertainty which fixes the colonial subject as a 'partial' presence" ("Of Mimicry and Man," 86). For more on the connection between liberal and colonial mimicry as they relate to Jews and Jewishness, see my introduction to *Jews and Feminism*. On colonial mimicry, see Bhabha, "Of Mimicry and Man," 85–92.

54. For more on interior culture and the display of art in American homes, see David Halle, *Inside Culture: Art and Class in the American Home* (Chicago: University of Chicago Press, 1993).

55. For more on this issue of fashion, dress, and comportment, see Laura Levitt, "American Jews: Passing through the Family Photograph" (conference paper delivered at the Mid-Atlantic Regional Meeting of the American Academy of Religion, New Brunswick, N.J., March 1998).

56. For more on Jewish names, see chap. 11, "What's in a Name?" of my *Jews and Feminism*. See also Melanie Kaye-Kantrowitz, "Some Notes on Jewish Lesbian Identity," in *Nice Jewish Girls: A Lesbian Anthology*, ed. Evelyn Beck (Boston: Beacon Press, 1989), 34–50.

57. Elia Kazan, director, *Gentleman's Agreement* (1947). The movie was based on Laura Z. Hobson's novel *Gentleman's Agreement* (New York: Simon and Schuster, 1946).

58. On this larger context, see May, *Homeward Bound,* as well as Wendy Kozol's careful reading of the vision of this brave new life offered in the

pages of *Life* magazine; see Wendy Kozol, Life *'s America* (Philadelphia: Temple University Press, 1994). For an account of more affiliated American Jews taking on these challenges in Los Angeles and Miami, see Moore, *To the Golden Cities*; and for more on the development of southern California, see Mike Davis, *City of Quartz: Excavating the Future of Los Angeles* (New York: Vintage Books, 1990).

59. For a somewhat different take on the American dream, as an ambivalent legacy, see Levitt, *Jews and Feminism.*

60. For an excellent critique of liberal pluralism, see Jakobsen, *Working Alliances.*

61. Despite this critique, I suspect that Brenner's text may appeal to those who identify as Jews but do so from even more distant and unaffiliated positions. For these Jews, Brenner's ironic vision may create a safe enough distance between legacies of Jewish loss and a more carefree and happy American narrative of choice. This may, in fact, be part of this text's allure for some readers.

Chapter 4

The Labor of Remembrance

Michelle A. Friedman

Irena Klepfisz asks whether there are "moments in history which cannot be escaped or transcended, but which act like time warps permanently trapping all those who are touched by them" (Klepfisz 1990a, 192). Specifically, she poses this question in response to her experience as a child survivor of the Holocaust, but she also addresses broader issues: what it means to live with traumatic memory and the aftereffects of trauma, to live with the past in the present, and to struggle with "the labor of remembrance."[1] The labor of remembrance requires one to wrestle with what it means to remember and how it is possible to remember what has come to be considered an incomprehensible history; it involves articulating oneself in relation to this history without erasing its "messiness" and complexities. The labor of remembrance is also a process intimately connected with the psychical mechanism of identification. Diana Fuss, in *Identification Papers*, asserts: "Identification names the entry of history and culture into the subject . . . [and] names not only the history of the subject but the subject in history" (Fuss 1995, 3 and 165). Identification, according to Fuss, not only delineates the individual history of a subject but positions that subject within the larger history to which she also belongs. Like the labor of remembrance, identification entails articulating oneself in relation to history and is "necessary and difficult, dangerous and effectual, naturalizing and denaturalizing" (10). If we consider Klepfisz's question, then, in relation to this description of identification, it seems apparent that there are indeed moments in history that cannot be escaped or transcended, because history itself leaves a permanent mark and shapes how we know who we are.

In this chapter, I read three texts: Art Spiegelman's *Maus,* Irena Klepfisz's *"Bashert,"* and Deb Filler's *Punch Me in the Stomach.* Each of these texts struggles with the legacy of the Holocaust and the complicated desires and dynamics of remembrance and identification. Each exemplifies what I mean by the "labor of remembrance" and, by contrast, provides one way of understanding how the Holocaust has helped to shape American Jewish identity. And each insists on the ambivalences of history in a way that effectively challenges some of the basic principles of today's American Holocaust culture. In their work, Spiegelman, Klepfisz, and Filler engage with and even embrace the complexities of representing the Holocaust, without simplifying this history or allowing it to destroy them. They put themselves in the place of the ones they remember, for whom they remember, whose stories they inherit and share, and yet they never erase the fact that they cannot fit comfortably in these places, that in some important way these stories and this history cannot fully belong to them. These authors construct texts that provide complicated and effective ways of articulating themselves in relation to what has come to be seen as an ineffable and incomprehensible history.

In comparison with the labor of remembrance, which acknowledges and wrestles with the complexities embedded in historical narratives, much contemporary American Holocaust memory-work seems propelled by a different force: mythologization.[2] To mythologize is to refuse ambivalence by flattening and erasing the specificity, detail, and complexity of history. It responds to the longing for "total" understanding and a totalizing narrative and successfully transforms the past into something familiar and functional. But in so doing, it also effaces the ambiguities and messiness of history and obscures the fact that any knowledges and narratives we possess about history, and the Holocaust in particular, can be only partial.[3]

In *Maus,* Art Spiegelman effectively illustrates what I mean by the partialness of our available knowledges and narratives. In one scene in the second volume, Vladek describes marching to work every morning in Auschwitz. In response to Vladek's narrative, Artie comments that he has recently read about the orchestra that played while the prisoners filed out the gates. Vladek, calling on the authority of his experiences, contests Artie's "factual" knowledge: "No. I remember only MARCHING, not any orchestras. . . . At the gate I heard only guards shouting" (Spiegelman 1991, 54). In Vladek's memory, no orchestras play; despite the weight of documented evidence, then, for him no such orchestra existed.

Spiegelman depicts the conflict between his father's "experiential" knowledge and his own "historically accurate" knowledge not only in the dialogue he writes but in what he draws. In the first frame of this conversation, Spiegelman fills half the space with marching prisoners and half the space with a drawing of prisoners playing instruments, led by a conductor. In the next frame, as Vladek refutes the existence of the orchestra, the line of marching prisoners advances to fill the entire space, effectively concealing all but the smallest traces of the instruments and musicians. We can see that while Spiegelman replaces his father's description of events (the one without the musicians) for his own, he does not erase his original depiction of this scene (the one that portrays the image supported by documentation). By including both versions of the morning march, Spiegelman engages with the problems of representation and remembrance; he articulates the ambivalences of history and the multiplicity of historical knowledges, rather than trying to eliminate them. In addition, by both preserving and failing to preserve history as his father tells it, Spiegelman refuses to grant his father's voice—and the voice of the "survivor" in general—the power of myth.[4]

Spiegelman, importantly, gives prominence to the survivor's voice and perspective in his two volumes of *Maus*. He recognizes that individual survivors' experiences provide invaluable knowledge and information about the Holocaust. At the same time, however, he asserts that there are many levels of knowing. In *Maus*, he presents the vision of one survivor and does not claim it as a totalizing narrative, as the only version of events. Spiegelman communicates the limitations of his father's vision in a number of ways. Among these, two make his point especially clear. First, toward the beginning of the first volume, Spiegelman reveals that Vladek is blind in one eye and has impaired vision in the other. Vladek explains his impairment by reciting his history of glaucoma and cataracts, but Spiegelman pointedly chooses to insert this information immediately after Vladek has explained that "on September 1, 1939, the war came" (Spiegelman

1986, 39). After Vladek makes this statement but before he continues with his narrative about the war, the Holocaust, and his survival, Vladek interrupts himself by pointing to his eyes and saying, "Now I don't see so well" (39). While Vladek tells Artie this in order to explain why he has knocked his bottle of pills over for a second time, Spiegelman includes this statement to provide readers with some insight into the narrative they are about to read.

Like James Young, a highly respected scholar of Holocaust memorials and literature, Spiegelman seems to want the reader to perceive history as constructed from a collection of individual memories and narratives, rather than as singular and monolithic. Young makes it clear that he prefers "to examine 'collected memory'" and that he considers society's memory "as an aggregate collection of its members' many, often competing memories" (1993, xi). Similarly, in emphasizing the deficiencies in Vladek's vision, Spiegelman does not call into question the truth of his particular narrative. Rather, he makes readers see the inaccuracies of Vladek's vision in order to remind them that they are reading only one version of history, only one telling of the truth, and that this narrative belongs to a larger collection of historical narratives. Spiegelman ends *Maus* II with a final warning about the frailties of historical knowledge and representation, as he records Vladek's words: "So . . . Let's stop, please, your tape recorder. . . . I'm *tired* from talking, Richieu, and it's enough stories for now" (1991, 136). In addition to announcing his own exhaustion and requesting an end to the recording of his narrative, Vladek calls Artie "Richieu." Vladek's mistakenly calling Artie by the name of his dead son may reveal several things: Vladek's unfulfilled longing for his dead son, his approval of his living son (in that Vladek now sees Art as Richieu, the "perfect son"), closure for both Vladek and Art (in that Vladek has finished with his stories and finally given Art the approval he desires). Most important for this argument, however, Vladek's misrecognition serves as one more reminder to readers about the messiness of history: For Vladek, there is no simple beginning and ending to his history—it is layered upon the present as much as the present is layered upon the past; and as this scene clearly reveals, the narration of his history is affected powerfully by his desires, both conscious and unconscious.

The Mythologization of the Holocaust

In contrast to Spiegelman's vision and version of the Holocaust, what I see as a contemporary American turn to mythologization can be seen, in part, as a result of discomfort with this messiness. I also see this turn as evidence of the American Jewish community's desire to hold tightly to a "precious" legacy that affects how it sees itself and its history.[5] The ambivalences produced by and illustrated in Spiegelman's text differ from the mythologization that helps American Jews preserve the preciousness of their inheritance and their claims to an event that lies ultimately beyond their, or anyone's, comprehension, and that helps erase or diminish the struggles and tensions of remembrance. Many American Jews have latched onto the myths and limited knowledge that they possess about the Holocaust and let these represent the whole. Taking the position that these events can be known or understood, that the horrors can be contained and limited to the knowledge they have inherited or have learned, has become one way of coping with what has come to be accepted as the incomprehensible nature of the Holocaust.

Indisputably, there are significant reasons for this mythologization. Most notably, reducing the Holocaust to the simplicity of myth enables it to become a central component of an American Jewish social, cultural, and communal identity. Jacob Neusner argues this convincingly, and in such a way that his argument remains convincing nearly twenty years after it was originally published.[6] Neusner contends that the events of 1933–1945 have lost their historical specificity and instead have become an "evocative symbol" or myth that, in this country, has come to be known as "the Holocaust."[7] In this transformation to myth, it is assumed that "the Holocaust" carries "meanings all of us know and none needs to articulate and expatiate upon" (Neusner 1981, 84).[8] Moreover, it means that "the Holocaust" has come to bear "its own, unexamined, self-evident meanings" (Neusner 1981, 86).

In defining "the Holocaust" as such a symbol, Neusner calls attention to the contemporary mythologizing of these events. According to Roland Barthes, mythologization involves a process of naturalizing an image of reality:

> In passing from history to nature, myth acts economically: it abol-
> ishes the complexity of human acts, it gives them the simplicity of
> essences, it does away with all dialectics, with any going back beyond
> what is immediately visible, it organizes a world which is open with-
> out contradictions because it is without depth, a world wide open
> and wallowing in the evident, it establishes a blissful clarity: things
> appear to mean something by themselves. (Barthes 1972, 143)

In other words, myth discards complexities and contradictions; it
does away with all but the visible, removes all that is "messy" and un-
containable, and makes the assumption that the significance of historical events is self-evident and universal. In Neusner's argument, becoming a history stripped of all complexity has allowed "the Holocaust" to become a primary element in the construction of an
American Jewish identity, providing both a simple meaning and mo-
tivation for nonreligious Jews to remain Jewish and a means of distinguishing the same Jews from other American ethnic groups. As
Neusner explains, "the Holocaust" provides nonreligious American
Jews, otherwise lacking in "culturally and socially distinctive characteristics," with a "special thing" that "sets them apart from others
while giving them a claim upon those others" (1981, 89). "The Holocaust" as myth fosters a resistance to engaging with very difficult questions of meaning. By removing the complex realities of the events of
1933–1945, Neusner argues, "a profound inner dilemma and a difficult matter of social differentiation and identification [can] work
themselves out within the myth of 'Holocaust'" (90). "The Holocaust"
as myth helps sustain a fierce commitment to what has been inherited
by concealing the tension between what can and cannot be known.

Like Neusner, Adi Ophir, in his essay "On Sanctifying the Holocaust: An Anti-Theological Treatise," examines the myths that help
configure contemporary Jewish identity.[9] Ophir asserts that because
of mythologization, the Holocaust may become "the core of Jewish
identity in the future, overshadowing the role of traditional Judaism
or of contemporary Zionism" (Ophir 1985, 61). In a satirical critique
of this trend, Ophir argues for the deconstruction of Holocaust myth
by writing and then rewriting what he sees (with an ironic but fright-
eningly prescient vision) as the four basic "commandments" of the
new "religion" of the Holocaust. He drafts these commandments to

illustrate what "a religious consciousness built around the Holocaust" would look like. And he constructs them to echo the Ten Commandments received at Sinai by Moses—especially "You shall have no other gods beside me," "You shall not take the name of God in vain," and "Remember the Sabbath to make it holy"—as well as the prohibition against making graven images or likenesses. What makes Ophir's insights so powerful, however, is that he bases his "commandments" on what have generally been accepted as "truths" about the Holocaust: The Holocaust is unique. The Holocaust cannot be represented. The word *holocaust* may be used to refer only to the destruction of European Jewry. The Holocaust must never be forgotten. Reading these commandments, it is quite possible to conceive of a religion based on the Holocaust. More important, however, is that in devising these commandments Ophir reveals how these accepted truths function as myths.

His fourth commandment, "Remember," serves as a compelling example of the role these truths have come to play in Jewish culture and how they need to be revised. According to Ophir, the original, uncritical commandment "Remember" has been embodied in "institutions of immortalization and documentation," in "Holocaust-priests" and "keepers of the flame," in "rituals of memorial, remembering, and repetition," and in "forms of pilgrimage [which] are taking hold" (Ophir 1985, 63).[10] He proposes that this commandment should be rewritten as "remember in order to understand. To understand the technology of power and the modes of 'excluding' discourse which made the Holocaust possible" (65). In taking apart the mythic commandment "Remember," Ophir explains why it is important to remember and for what purpose. He substitutes specificity and meaning for the vague yet potent imperative to remember that reveals itself so clearly in the omnipresent declaration "Never again."

Ophir also demonstrates and explains that to rewrite these truths means to refuse the lure of myth and "sanctification": to "rewrite means . . . to engage critically with the past in a way that has meaning for the present" (65). He argues against mythologization, which reduces the Holocaust to simple ways of knowing and remembering. Such mythologization discourages finding real meaning in the Holocaust and its consequences, prevents the difficult and necessary labor of remembrance, and resists historical complexity and ambiguity. In rewriting these so-called command-ments, Ophir argues for demythologization, which, among other things, means acknowledging and articulating the complicated re-lationship between past and present.

Identification: A Form of Psychic Memorialization

I read the texts of Irena Klepfisz, Art Spiegelman, and Deb Filler to examine this process of demythologization more closely. These au-thors—the first a child survivor, and the last two children of sur-vivors—are haunted by the legacy of the Holocaust and feel obligated to wrestle with its aftereffects. In their work, they are unavoidably ab-sorbed and consumed by the complicated relationship between past and present. While they narrate the stories of their parents and those who did not survive, they also tell their own stories and what it means to possess and be possessed by these other stories, to be the inheritors of these others' narratives, their lives and losses. In their work, Klep-fisz, Spiegelman, and Filler engage in a complex process of masking and unmasking in order to produce and reproduce these narratives. In many ways, this creative process resembles the psychic mechanism of identification—identification not construed as assimilation, re-semblance, or sameness but as a dynamic fueled by tensions and dif-ferences. Diana Fuss describes identification in the following way:

> Identification is an act of repetition and remembrance. . . . The whole unconscious process functions as a form of psychical memo-rialization. . . . [It] pertains . . . to what can and cannot be digested, to what goes into (and eventually comes out of) the corporeal sub-ject. Freud's story of identification is a tale of interiors and exteri-ors, boundaries and permutations, transgressions and resistances. (Fuss 1995, 34–35)

Though at its simplest identification can be seen as a routine process by which we compensate for the everyday losses of our love-objects (Fuss 1995, 1), Fuss argues that identification can also be understood as a complicated psychic form of remembrance and memorialization. It is a process that operates as a complex dance that renders permeable the boundaries between inside and outside, between past and present, between remembering and forgetting, and between what can and cannot be incorporated into the self. The tensions this dance fosters mirror those located in the struggles of remembrance and history.

To think further about the labor of remembrance and its relationship to identification, it is useful to examine one of Fuss's most striking metaphors for this process: incorporation. One way in which *The American Heritage College Dictionary,* Third Edition, defines the verb *incorporate* is "to give substance or material form to; embody." This definition comes from the Latin root for this verb, which means "to form into a body." In considering identifications and their relations to history, it is valuable to examine narratives in which they literally are given substance and body. Here, I read Klepfisz's *"Bashert,"* Spiegelman's *Maus,* and Filler's *Punch Me in the Stomach* as examples of how the labor of remembrance is rendered explicitly as incorporation and embodiment, performed as a series of identifications that seek to recuperate and assimilate the traumatic losses of history and that, ultimately, cannot do either. These authors desire to know the past and understand their relationship to it. And yet, rather than turning toward myth, the authors conceive of these works as complex and dynamic memorials to both the past and present.

Another Time, Another Place: Repetition and Remembrance

Irena Klepfisz, as a child survivor, offers one strategy for understanding the relationship between the Holocaust and its complicated legacies. Klepfisz was born in the Warsaw Ghetto in 1941, was smuggled out as a young child, and survived the rest of the war in hiding. Because she was so young at the time, she possesses only limited memories of the events of the war. She notes in her essay "Resisting and Surviving in America" that she has had to supplement these scanty memories with knowledge from other sources:

> My sense of danger [about being Jewish] was rooted in a total physical and emotional knowledge of the war. Yet this knowledge was acquired only after I came to America in 1949 at the age of eight. It was in New York—at the annual memorials for the Uprising of the

> Warsaw Ghetto, during conversations among my mother's friends,
> in the books I was encouraged to read—that I absorbed the full hor-
> ror and insanity of the camps and ghettos, absorbed them in such a
> way that they became first-hand knowledge. (Klepfisz 1990b, 61)

Klepfisz must learn about the Holocaust in order to contextualize her
earlier experiences and begin to make sense of them. But she attempts to do more than this. In listening to her mother's friends, in
attending annual memorials, and in reading books, she puts herself
in the place of those who survived and died; and, she claims, in so
doing she manages to absorb "the full horror . . . of the camps and
ghettos" and gain "first-hand knowledge" of them. But Klepfisz was
not in the camps and does not possess a conscious knowledge of the
Warsaw Ghetto. How, then, can she claim that she has gained "first-
hand knowledge" and absorbed "the full horror"? Given the nature
of trauma, it seems impossible ever to possess knowledge of its full
horror, just as it seems impossible to acquire firsthand knowledge of
an event that one has not experienced.[11] For these reasons, Klepfisz's
claims appear logically impossible. At the same time, however, they
reveal a powerful desire for knowledge and understanding. Her assertion that she "absorbed the full horror and insanity of the camps
and ghettos . . . [and] that they became first-hand knowledge" resonates with the desires that motivate children of survivors, such as
Spiegelman and Filler: to know what it would have been like to experience the circumstances of one's survivor-parents, to understand
what they endured.[12]

At various points in *"Bashert,"* a poem that details her efforts to
remember those who survived and died, her efforts to figure out what
it means to remember, Klepfisz metaphorically puts herself in the
place of those who possess what she calls "first-hand knowledge"—her
mother, her father, as well as generations of Jewish women and men
who have experienced persecution. Fuss argues that "Freud's scientific theory of identification is entirely predicated on a logic of
metaphoric exchange and displacement" (1995, 5). These
metaphoric exchanges, for Klepfisz, represent identificatory moments in which she engages in the labor of remembrance. One of the
most powerful of these moments occurs in the second section of her
poem, titled "Chicago, 1964: I am walking home alone at midnight."

Klepfisz's narrator recalls in this section a walk home from the library late one night, during which she traverses the decaying streets of a Chicago ghetto, which are rife with concrete traces of a traumatic history different from the one that has left its marks on her. The narrator begins by explaining that, here, she feels alienated and alone, "isolated, baffled at how to make a place for [herself] in this larger, gentile world which [she has] entered" (1990a, 190). This world, this city, this place is alien to her: American, gentile, black, and poor. And she is alien to it: a foreigner, an immigrant, a displaced, educated Jew who feels she should not have survived the war. The narrator describes an emptiness that emerges from this alienation; it engulfs the rubble-strewn streets and conjures the emptiness within her.

In this moment, empty and without a place, outside of the place in which she walks, Klepfisz's narrator invokes Elza—a Jewish friend who survived the war but not its aftereffects, taking her own life at the age of twenty-five. Thoughts of Elza fill the void through which the narrator passes. She writes: "totally preoccupied with another time, another place . . . I think only of Elza who is dead" (1990a, 190). She thinks about Elza because Elza's fate could have, perhaps should have, been her own, because both of them were "accidental survivors," because she needs to claim the fate that is hers.[13] Not only does Klepfisz's narrator think about Elza; she recalls Elza's narratives and memories almost as though they were her own. In reciting Elza's story, in recalling Elza's memories, the narrator seems to appear before the reader as Elza herself. The narrator incorporates and embodies Elza—as a Jew alone in an alien, gentile world, a place in which she, too, might be eyed sharply as a little Jewess, as a keeper of accounts. Like Elza, the narrator is also in danger, and to make her way through it, she needs to make sense of "a fact about [Elza], a fact which stubbornly resists classification: nothing that happened to her afterwards mattered" (1990a, 190). If nothing afterward matters, then the narrator, too, is trapped in and by history, and the present has no meaning.

But ultimately, Klepfisz's narrator is not Elza. She is alive; she has, thus far, survived the reverberations of a history that killed her friend; she walks alone in a different landscape, one that does not bear the traces of her own persecution. In acknowledging her place in the present, the narrator acknowledges that she is not Elza and cannot take her place. She develops perspective, or at least begins to do so. She realizes that she has been marked not only by Poland 1944 but also by Chicago 1964. She begins to see how she must engage in negotiations with the past. These negotiations involve not just her history and the fate she feels she escaped, not just her desire to know what it would have been not to avoid that fate, but the devastation that surrounds her in the here and now, in this place where she is. Klepfisz's narrator cannot walk through these ravaged streets as Elza because she is rooted in "the rubble of this unbombed landscape [which] is not simply a geographic place, but a time zone" (1990a, 192–93). She can understand the past and claim herself again only by acknowledging that self and her place in the present, in the "time zone" in which she exists now. At the end of this section, Klepfisz returns, it seems, to the emptiness with which she began. Earlier, however, the emptiness was construed as one that could be "filled up, swallowed and forgotten," and that held forth the promise of wholeness and fullness. Here, however, "everything is waiting for the emptiness to be filled up, for the filling-up that *can never replace*, that can only take over" (1990a, 193). This emptiness is offered without the expectations of recuperation it held earlier, signifying that she cannot re/place what has been lost; she cannot re/place Elza, and she no longer hopes to. In her poetry, then, unlike in her prose, Klepfisz acknowledges the impossibility of gaining "first-hand knowledge" and absorbing the "full horror" of that knowledge. And, in allowing her narrator to enact and embody her powerful identification with Elza, Klepfisz reveals both the desires and losses involved in acts of remembrance.

Masking and Unmasking: Boundaries and Permutations

Spiegelman and Filler, even more vividly than Klepfisz, illustrate how the labor of remembrance can be seen as a struggle to sustain the tension between past and present. Working as they do with visual media, they graphically render this labor as a series of identificatory moments in which they seem literally to "give substance" to the past at the same time that it forever eludes their grasp. Spiegelman, in masking himself as a mouse, and Filler, in playing the role of her father, animate and enact this labor of remembrance within and against their own bodies. In doing so, they explicitly define the tension between past and present as that which can and cannot be incorporated into the self, as that which can and cannot be claimed as their own.

In *Punch Me in the Stomach*, Deb Filler (the star and co-writer of this one-woman show) appears to give life and "material form" to history in the space of her body. The film begins with a shot of Filler in white makeup, wearing a dressing gown with her hair pulled up, applying deep-red lipstick with bold, sure strokes. She appears before the camera as a stage actress preparing to put on both her stage makeup and her character. In this film, however, Filler puts on not just one character but many. Using hats, scarves, voices, postures, accents, and gestures, she transforms herself into various members of her extended family—grandparents, parents, aunts, uncles, cousins—in order to tell their histories and stories, in order to tell her own, each of which resonates with a larger history—that of the Holocaust.

Central to this film is Filler's portrayal of her father, which she accomplishes by reconfiguring her own rather substantial body to appear as her small-shouldered, rather diminutive father. Filler's father, and Filler-as-her-father, prompts the film in a number of ways. Filler-as-her-father appears regularly backstage—at the side of the stage entrance—providing Filler-as-herself with directions and instructions.[14] For example, he tells her, "Remember to thank them" (directed to the audience); and he repeatedly urges her to "tell them about Auschwitz" (their trip, not his story), which lies at the heart of this narrative.

Filler also plays her father in more extended sequences. In the first of these, she dramatically interrupts what has been until this point a somewhat lighthearted, humorous film tinged only slightly with traces of melancholy, which only hint at the tragic and incomprehensible history that motivates the film. In this scene, she appears as her father—wearing a conservative gray suit, with gray hair, wrinkles, and a brush mustache—sitting at the anchor desk of a television news station.[15] For the most part, Filler plays the other characters through implication and suggestion: a change of accent or posture, recurring verbal and facial expressions, perhaps a scarf. But here, she wears full makeup and redoes herself to appear as her father. She plays her father so convincingly, in fact, that it takes several seconds for viewers to realize that Filler, not her father, sits behind the anchor desk. It seems as though Filler figuratively and literally must don her father's face and character in order to tell his story: prewar life in Poland, invasion by the Nazis, selections, mass murder, labor camps, and, finally, Auschwitz. Only by transforming herself into a facsimile of her father can she recount his narrative and claim it, in some way, as her own.

In wearing her father's face, Filler calls to mind Art Spiegelman's guise in *Maus*. Like Filler, Spiegelman also must put on a mask in order to tell his father's story. This imperative reveals itself most clearly in the second chapter of the second volume in which he begins to write about his father's most traumatic experiences during the Holocaust. Though Spiegelman begins to describe Auschwitz in the first chapter—with his father's entry into the camp and his experiences in the "quarantine block"—he explains that Vladek felt that he "had it still happy there" (Spiegelman 1991, 35). Here, however, Spiegelman attempts to render the "real" and unspeakable horrors his father experienced. Before embarking on this daunting task, he disrupts the historical narrative to explore what it means for him to try to tell this part of his father's story. He has addressed problems of representation up to this point—raising questions and consciousness about the comic medium, his metaphoric choices, the difficulty of knowing, as well as the problematics of perspective, memory, and narrative construction. At this moment, however, confronted with the enormity of Auschwitz, which, he says, "just seems too scary to think about" (Spiegelman 1991, 44), Spiegelman explicitly reveals the mask he has been wearing from the beginning. Rather than portraying himself, as he has throughout, with an unobtrusive, simply drawn mouse face, here Spiegelman reveals himself sitting at his drawing table wearing a stiff mouse mask. This mask is drawn with darkly visible cross-hatching and a string tying it to the back of his head; his ears protrude; his hair is visible, as is a sliver of his unshaven, human face.

By exposing the contours and edges of this mask, Spiegelman denaturalizes the metaphor that has shaped the narrative and reminds readers of the artificiality of this representational construct. In disclosing the strings, he also questions his claims to this metaphor, this narrative, and this history. He draws himself sitting above a pile of emaciated mouse corpses; flies swarm around the bodies and his own head; readers can see a guard tower and barbed wire fencing through a domestic window framed by curtains. While these images reveal the unquestionable weight and tangibility of his parents' legacy, as well as its persistent presence in his life, at the same time Spiegelman suggests the complicated and difficult relationship he maintains with this legacy and history, both by the artificiality of the mouse mask and by the tensions revealed in the written text. In the dialogue boxes, Spiegelman sets several facts of his life against some that belong to his father and this history. Two are most striking:

> Vladek started working as a tinman in Auschwitz in the spring of 1944 . . . I started working on this page at the very end of February 1987. In May 1987 Françoise and I are expecting a baby . . . Between May 16, 1944, and May 24, 1944 over 100,000 Hungarian Jews were gassed in Auschwitz. (Spiegelman 1991, 41; see also page 134, below)

To juxtapose his father's work in Auschwitz with his own work on this page, to compare the birth of his child with the death of one hundred thousand Jews, seems unavoidable for Spiegelman. This juxtaposition asserts an undeniable truth: the inextricable relationship between past and present, the powerful effects of this history on the events of his own life. At the same time, this juxtaposition underlines the unbridgeable distance that lies between past and present, between his father's survival and Spiegelman's representation of it, between the birth of his daughter and the genocide of his people. The mouse mask perched stiffly on Artie's face reiterates these tensions and reflects the irretrievability of these losses: the difficulties of his work cannot even approximate those of his father; his daughter cannot re/place one hundred thousand Jews.

In the pages that follow this scene, Spiegelman places a visible mask on each character's face (cameramen, reporters, his psychiatrist) until the narrative, once again, returns to his father in Auschwitz. Before this scene, the only perceptible masks exist on the faces of mice/Jews "passing" as pigs/Poles. Vladek, for example, pretends to be Polish when he returns home from the POW camp. Spiegelman draws Vladek wearing a pig mask to emphasize the effectiveness of his disguise and to underline these words: "I still had on my army uniform, and I didn't let *know* I was a Jew" (Spiegelman 1986, 64). Given the previous incidents of masking in *Maus*, Spiegelman clearly wants to suggest in this scene that he, too, is somehow "passing." Through the visibility of his mask, Spiegelman calls attention to the fact that he looks "like" his father, who looks like all the other mice/Jews that populate this text. The discussion Artie has with Françoise about how she should be depicted (as a French convert) suggests that how a character is drawn matters. Being a mouse hence locates Spiegelman in a particular place in this historical narrative.

That the reader should perceive Spiegelman as "passing" is clear; what he is passing *as*, however, is less so. In a conversation with his psychiatrist, a shrunken, child-sized version of Spiegelman wears a mouse mask and remarks: "No matter what I accomplish, it doesn't seem like much compared to surviving Auschwitz" (Spiegelman 1991, 44). This comment betrays how inconsequential his life and accomplishments seem to him in comparison with his father's survival of Auschwitz; and it also intimates that he feels as though he lacks sufficient authority and does not have adequate claims on this history to tell his father's story properly. Perhaps, then, Spiegelman wears this mask to pass as someone properly qualified to construct an "authentic" narrative. In the next frame, however, Spiegelman includes his psychiatrist's suggestion that Artie himself might be the "real" survivor. As his psychiatrist points out, Artie has had to survive the after-effects of his father's survival; though Rego Park was not Auschwitz, it required certain survival strategies as well. Though Spiegelman does not embrace this statement, saying only "um" in response, he does make the choice to include it in his text. This idea insinuates that by wearing this mask, Artie can pass as the survivor and somehow displace his father and his experiences; and, in contrast with what he says above, it affirms Spiegelman's stake in this history.

Spiegelman only looks like his father but continues to speak in his own voice. Deb Filler, by contrast, alternates between speaking as herself and as her father. When she sits at the anchor desk, for example, she speaks in the first person, saying "my brother, my father, my mother"—when these, in reality, are the uncle and grandparents she has never known. She pauses, makes facial expressions and gestures that suggest a struggle to remember and to tell a painful history that is her own. In these moments, Filler becomes her father in order to tell his story. And in these moments, Filler-as-her-father seems to displace him; his memories and histories become hers. In this act of displacement, Filler appears to satisfy the desire found in many children of survivors—a desire to cross the unbridgeable distance, similar to what Spiegelman faces and describes, and to understand fully what their parents experienced and endured during the Holocaust.

Filler enacts this desire for understanding, and its haunting impossibility, in another scene, in which she plays herself as a child. Spiegelman transforms himself into a child—or at least, gives himself childlike proportions—in order to convey how overwhelming the Holocaust feels and how much he wants to understand and claim some part of it as his own, and Filler portrays herself as a child for similar reasons. She creates the illusion of herself as a child in two ways: an enormous, larger-than-life desk laden with enormous, larger-than-life books dwarfs her as she stands in their midst; and she asks for "other books about Europe in the 1930s and '40s that feature girls hiding in attics" with a quiet intensity that suggests innocence and youth. Filler wants to read these books in order to fill in the gaps in her knowledge and try to understand the history that haunts her. While the giant objects promote the illusion of Filler-as-a-child, they also signify the vastness of what she cannot know—then or now—as well as her desire to do so. Deb wants to fill in the gaps of history, to fill in what she cannot know; perhaps to serve as a kind of filler herself by embodying this history.[16]

This scene in the library stands in contrast to the scene in the television station, in which Filler becomes her father and seems to possess his knowledge, history, and memory. The tension between these two moments—which portray Filler's entire lack of knowledge and, conversely, her complete possession of knowledge—is played out most vividly when Filler and her father finally arrive in Poland, where they are about to embark on a "whirlwind tour of the finest death camps in Europe." In this scene, Filler plays herself as the narrator, herself as herself, and herself as her father—both subtly (using hat, gestures, and accent only) and in full makeup. As Filler and her father (played, of course, by Filler-as-her-father) drive along the country roads of Poland, Filler's father's memory reshapes the landscape, revealing things that only he can see but which he wants Deb to see, and which Deb herself wants to see, too. Filler's father points to the fields that they are passing. Being polite, engaging with her father, Filler answers him by mentioning their beautiful color. But that is not what he means at all. He has pointed to the fields not to remark on their beauty but to mar their beauty with the ugliness of the past that lies just below the surface. In response to Deb's comment "Yeah Dad, they're a wonderful color," Filler's father notes that he saw a French girl, who had tried to escape from the back of a truck, shot in those fields. Filler's father uses this memory as an opportunity to tell Deb how lucky she is, "lucky not to see things like that" (*Punch Me in the Stomach* 1995). Though Deb has had the "luck" of never having seen or endured "things like that," at the same time these images have been imprinted on her mind, just as they have been imprinted on the landscape.

At this point, Filler removes the mask of her father and dons a different kind of mask (herself, backstage in white makeup). She provides a commentary on the scene viewers have just witnessed:

> From the time I was four or five, I listened as he told his stories about the camps. I wanted to tell him that, in a way, it was my Holocaust, too. We were driving through a landscape that was filled with his memories. Where I saw a beautiful field, he saw a French girl kneeling for her execution. Where I saw a town square, he saw a group of people being herded into cattle trucks. What could I say about being the child of a survivor? It all seemed so insignificant. (*Punch Me in the Stomach* 1995)

Filler acquires an inheritance that, among other things, prompts her to develop an imaginary landscape dotted with death camps and labor camps. When, later, she and her father visit Thereseinstadt, she comments: "I felt like I've known this place my whole life." And as a child, this legacy prompts Filler to teach her sister self-defense—just in case Hitler should come back to life and head straight for their home in New Zealand. Despite the potency of this inheritance, however, Filler sees only the beautiful fields, whereas her father sees a murderous past etched onto the landscape itself. Though Filler claims some part of this history as hers, she also clearly distinguishes between what she can and can never know, between what she can and can never possess, between what can and can never possess her. This history both belongs to her and does not. As much as it is her Holocaust, it is not. She can never see what her father sees; she can never possess his memories. Filler illustrates, in this scene, the limits of what she can and cannot know, of what she can and cannot be, of what she can and cannot incorporate into her self. In alternately playing her father and herself, Filler plays with the boundaries of history, self, and memory and gives substance and material form to the tensions contained within each of them.

In the final scene of *Punch Me in the Stomach,* the camera moves from the stage to focus on Deb Filler's father, who sits alone, waiting for his daughter to join him. Just as, in an earlier scene, viewers momentarily do not realize that what they see is Filler appearing *as* her father, here viewers momentarily mistake her *father* for Filler-as-her-father. This moment of misrecognition helps viewers realize how effectively Filler has imitated her father and put on "his face"; but this moment also reiterates how, ultimately, she cannot incorporate him, his memories, or his history into her self, that there is always something that eludes her. Filler walks out of the auditorium with her arm around her father's shoulders and his arm around her waist. The way in which they are linked together expresses something essential about the complicated labor of remembrance she engages in so effectively: Filler's present is inextricably intertwined with his past; she shares in his history, and yet it remains alien to her; she has traveled with him through his past, and yet she cannot comfortably inhabit the places he has been.

In the desire and the failure to recover what has been lost, in the powerful rendition of both the desire and the failure, and in the acknowledgment of the value of specificity and place, Filler, like Klepfisz and Spiegelman, articulates a relationship to history and a practice of remembrance that is complex and ambivalent, "necessary and difficult, dangerous and effectual." The practice of remembrance exemplified in each of these narratives stands in contrast to the practice of mythologization evident in so much American Holocaust remembrance. These narratives provide a way of understanding the kind of memory work that can engage with the legacy of the Holocaust more effectively than that allowed for by mythmaking.

The ending of Spiegelman's *Maus* demonstrates the nature of this work and its difficulties. The ending, which can be divided into three parts, acknowledges the desires that motivate mythologization yet also affirms the labor required by the act of remembrance. The image of the first part reduces and transforms this difficult and complicated historical narrative to the simplicity of a romance. Anja and Vladek embrace, backlit by a full moon, and Vladek proclaims: "More I don't need to tell you. We were both very happy, and lived happy, happy ever after" (Spiegelman 1991, 136). This image and statement effectively close off Vladek's narrative and history. The phrase "more I don't need to tell you" implies that Vladek's narrative is fully comprehensible and accessible to Spiegelman and, by extension, to the reader. This part proffers the idea of wholeness and recuperation promised by the Holocaust as myth.

The next two parts, however, complicate the message of the first one. As I discussed earlier, in the second part, Vladek misidentifies Artie as Richieu and halts the day's interview: "I'm *tired* from talking, Richieu, and it's enough stories for now . . . " (Spiegelman 1991, 136). The final ellipses and the words "it's enough . . . for now" indicate that more remains to be said and that this ending is in some way arbitrary, necessitated by human limitations—of memory, fatigue, and age—as well as the limits of what can be known and what can be said. In recognizing these limits, Spiegelman accepts that he cannot contain his father's Holocaust narrative and its meanings within the pages of this text. The final part of the ending, then, comes as a response to this acknowledgment: Spiegelman draws Vladek and Anja's tombstone, with their dates of birth and death, and underneath places his own signature along with the dates of *Maus*'s creation. In the final frames of his narrative, Spiegelman concedes that he cannot represent or comprehend the Holocaust fully, but in an effort to understand this history and how it has helped him know who he is, he can place his story next to that of his parents. This final statement thus reflects on the narrative as a whole and helps explain what it means to engage in the labor of remembrance.

NOTES

1. The title of this chapter, "The Labor of Remembrance," was suggested by a phrase that I encountered in Andreas Huyssen's *Twilight Memories: Marking Time in a Culture of Amnesia*. The phrase appears in the follow-

ing passage: "Post-Holocaust generations can only approach that core by mimetic approximation, a mnemonic strategy which recognizes the event in its otherness and beyond identification or therapeutic empathy, but which physically innervates some of the horror and the pain in a slow and persistent labor of remembrance. Such mimetic approximation can only be achieved if we sustain [this] tension" (Huyssen 1995, 259).

2.   Some examples of contemporary American Holocaust memory-work: the March of the Living, Holocaust education and curricula as these are taught in Hebrew schools, memorial events and activities commemorating the Holocaust in Jewish communities and on college campuses throughout the United States, and the proliferation of Holocaust memorials and museums throughout the country.

3.   Mythologization is not the only strategy of remembrance that conceals the messiness and complexities of history. A German colleague has explained to me that she received an education different from that of many American Jews: rich in "factual knowledge" and devoid of myth. She, for example, "always knew about [such things as] the Wannsee Conference." And yet, she also needed to engage in a "labor of learning" in order "to replace some vague notions about the 'horror of Auschwitz' with knowledge about what [Des Pres] calls the 'real behavior' of survivors, the details, . . . what happened in the camps" (e-mail correspondence with Tania Oldenhage, 16 June 1998). For my German colleague, factual or historical knowledge can be seen as a "partial knowledge," because its attention to historical specificity led to an abstraction of the "actual" horrors of the Holocaust. For her, a legacy that could be considered "historically accurate" resulted in a flattening of this history's complexities similar to the processes of mythologization.

4.   To imply that the voice of the survivor may contribute to mythologization will undoubtedly provoke cries of protest and outrage that will dismiss me as disrespectful, question my integrity as a Jew and a scholar, and worry that I provide fuel for those who would deny the very existence of the Holocaust. But I intend none of these things, and in fact, the protest and outrage contribute to my concerns about mythologization: that in sacralizing the voices and narratives of survivors, we may limit our knowledge of the complexity of this history. Indeed, survivors possess a certain knowledge that those of us who were not there can never know. But if we rely on their narratives alone, the fullness of this history will elude us entirely. As James Young asserts: "Even though a survivor's testimony is 'privileged' insofar as it is authentic, the factuality of his literary testimony is not necessarily so privileged" (Young 1988, 22). Young argues against privileging the factuality or "historical accuracy" of

survivors' testimony because, like all narratives, they are necessarily mediated by the "inevitable variance in perceiving and representing" facts and events. In addition, victims in the ghettos and camps "were at the mercy of their persecutors in all ways—even in their attempts to testify against them," which means that survivors' testimony may, in fact, be flawed and inaccurate because Nazis prevented their victims from knowing and understanding exactly what was happening to them (Young 1988, 32–33).

5. Mary Gordon's memoir *The Shadow Man* has helped me think about the preciousness of memories and legacies. Gordon describes the preciousness of her father's memory (he died when she was only seven) and her desire to preserve the portrait he constructed of himself as a father, a writer, and a religious, philosophical, and political thinker. Gordon's narrative explores what it means for her to challenge these memories and wrestle with the legacy her father has left her, and how this work helps her define and redefine herself as well as him.

6. It is important to note that although Neusner's essay "How the Extermination of European Jewry Became 'The Holocaust'" was published in the early 1980s, and although the forces influencing American Jewish identity have clearly shifted to some degree (the function of Israel in an American Jewish discourse, for example), the observations Neusner makes about what he calls "Holocaustomania" still appear quite relevant. Neusner writes also about Jewish and national identity in Israel, but his primary interests in this essay are focused on the United States.

7. As James Young points out in his essay titled "Names of the Holocaust," the names we assign the events of 1933–1945 "automatically figure and contextualize events, locating them within the continua of particular historical, literary, and interpretive traditions" (1988, 85). I deliberately use the word *Holocaust*, as I assume Neusner does as well, because this word elicits the particular American context I discuss in this chapter. In the United States, *Holocaust* is the most commonly used word for signifying the events of this historical period.

   In addition to *Holocaust*, however, the Hebrew terms *Churban* and *Shoah* refer to the destruction of European Jewry. Each carries different implications and different historical frames of reference. *Churban* has its roots in the Yiddish word *churbm* and in "specific historical disasters like the destructions of the First and Second temple" (Young 1988, 85); it places this contemporary disaster on a continuum that includes other Jewish tragedies. *Shoah* does not possess the same religious implications of divine retribution as does the term *Churban*. The word also emerges from biblical references but suggests a broader sense of disaster. Those

who use it (to begin with, secular and religious Zionists) have emphasized "more its roots of desolation and metaphysical doubt than its more
pious echoes of sin and punishment" (Young 1988, 86).

8. In using the word *myth*, neither Neusner nor I intend to suggest a lie or
something that is not true, which colloquial use of this word might imply
(see, for example, the third definition in *The American Heritage College
Dictionary*, 3d ed.: "a fiction or half-truth, esp. one that forms part of an
ideology"). Rather, Neusner and I use the word *myth* to describe a kind
of speech or language that provides a way of understanding culture. This
language permits History to be confused with Nature. As Barthes explains: "The starting point of these reflections [on myth] was usually a
feeling of impatience at the sight of the 'naturalness' with which news-
papers, art and common sense constantly dress up a reality which . . . is
undoubtedly determined by history" (Barthes 1972, 11).

9. Writing as he does in an Israeli context, Ophir's comments pertain explicitly to the role of the Holocaust in Israeli society. They do, however,
resonate quite clearly with Neusner's observations and are certainly
broad enough to be included in this discussion.

10. In the fall semester of 1997, for example, I had a young man in one of
my classes who has been to nearly every major Holocaust museum numerous times, and who goes to such museums at least four times a year.

11. Theorists have conceptualized trauma as an experience that defies temporal containment and knowledge. Traumatic events, they argue, cannot be assimilated fully in the moment of trauma and therefore return
perpetually as repetition, in repeated suffering of the events. Given the
nature of trauma, it appears that even those who have experienced
trauma cannot absorb or assimilate its "full horror." See, for example:
Cathy Caruth, "Introduction" to "Psychoanalysis, Culture, and Trauma,"
a special issue of *American Imago: Studies in Psychoanalysis and Culture* 48
(Spring 1991): 1–12; Shoshana Felman and Dori Laub, *Testimony: Crises
of Witnessing in Literature, Psychoanalysis, and History* (New York: Routledge, 1992).

12. In his psychological studies of children of survivors, Aaron Hass reveals
powerful identifications between these adult children and their survivor-
parents and an equally powerful desire to understand their survivor-parents' experiences. One way in which these identifications and this desire
manifest themselves is that these "children believe they know about the
Holocaust simply because they have perceived its aftereffects on their
parents" (Hass 1990, 85). Many children of survivors have experienced
in the relationship with their parents the emotional, psychological, and
sometimes even physical aftereffects of the Holocaust. Some confuse

this knowledge and experience with that which they will never own: the knowledge and experience of their survivor-parents.

13. A short poem written by Klepfisz succinctly defines this idea of Jewish children as "accidental survivors": "during the war / germans were known / to pick up infants / by their feet / swing them through the air / and smash their heads / against plaster walls. / somehow / i managed / to escape that fate" (Klepfisz 1990a, 43).

14. When I presented this paper orally, I had substantial difficulties articulating the complexities of this relationship as Filler portrays it. I found myself confused about how to signify Filler-as-herself as distinct from Filler-as-her-father. I stumbled over pronouns, subjects, and indirect objects. In retrospect, I realize that my confusion itself signifies and enacts the complicated dynamic contained in and portrayed by this embodied history.

15. The viewers first see Filler-as-her-father through the lens of the camera that shoots this news broadcast, then on a television screen in the studio, then finally in an unmediated view of the anchor desk (unmediated, that is, within the scene of the film, which itself is a form of mediation). The shots through the camera lens and the television are intended to remind the viewers that, ultimately, this narrative can only re-present the events it describes, distanced as they are by time, space, circumstance, and perspective. This mediated introduction to Filler-as-her-father resembles the scene in which Spiegelman appears for the first time in *Maus* wearing a mouse mask. Though he appears to be at home, the setting is also reminiscent of a sound stage on which he sits spotlighted (and, in fact, cameramen and reporters come swirling onto the scene on the next page), which underlines the representationality of his masking and narration.

16. I thank Ann Pellegrini for supplying me with this insight and for recognizing the wonderful way in which Filler's name resonates with her particular labors.

REFERENCES

Barthes, Roland. 1972. *Mythologies.* Translated by Annette Lavers. New York: Hill and Wang.

Fuss, Diana. 1995. *Identification Papers.* New York: Routledge.

Gordon, Mary. 1997. *The Shadow Man: A Daughter's Search for Her Father.* New York: Vintage Books.

Hass, Aaron. 1990. *In the Shadow of the Holocaust: The Second Generation.* Ithaca, N.Y.: Cornell University Press.

Huyssen, Andreas. 1995. *Twilight Memories: Marking Time in a Culture of Amnesia.* New York: Routledge.

Klepfisz, Irena. 1990a. *"Bashert."* In *A Few Words in the Mother Tongue: Poems Selected and New (1971–1990).* Portland, Ore.: Eighth Mountain Press.

————. 1990b. "Resisting and Surviving in America." In *Dreams of an Insomniac: Jewish Feminist Essays, Speeches, and Diatribes.* Portland, Ore.: Eighth Mountain Press.

Neusner, Jacob. 1981. "How the Extermination of European Jewry Became 'The Holocaust.'" In *Stranger at Home: "The Holocaust," Zionism, and American Judaism.* Chicago: University of Chicago Press.

Ophir, Adi. 1985. "On Sanctifying the Holocaust: An Anti-Theological Treatise." *Tikkun* 2, 1: 61–66.

Peskowitz, Miriam. 1997. "Engendering Jewish Religious History." In *Judaism since Gender,* edited by Miriam Peskowitz and Laura Levitt. New York: Routledge.

Punch Me in the Stomach. 1995. With Deb Filler. Written by Deb Filler and Alison Summers. Directed by Francine Zuckerman. Toronto: Punch Me in the Stomach Productions, Inc.

Spiegelman, Art. 1986. *Maus I: A Survivor's Tale.* New York: Pantheon.

————. 1991. *Maus II: And Here My Troubles Began.* New York: Pantheon, 1991.

Young, James E. 1988. *Writing and Rewriting the Holocaust: Narrative and the Consequences of Interpretation.* Bloomington and Indianapolis: Indiana University Press.

————. 1993. *The Texture of Memory: Holocaust Memorials and Meaning.* New Haven: Yale University Press.

Chapter 5

Surviving on Cat and Maus: Art Spiegelman's Holocaust Tale

Marilyn Reizbaum

When I first encountered Art Spiegelman's *Maus*, this "tailing," you might say, of Spiegelman's survivor parents' lives during the Holocaust and after, where the Jews are figured as mice, the Germans as cats, the Poles as pigs, the French as frogs, and the Americans as dogs, I exploded in response—with some distress and some despair. Somewhere, in between, was a kind of elation. Here was someone who had truly responded to Theodor Adorno's now-famous, or infamous, exhortation (1949) that "after Auschwitz you could no longer write poems" (Adorno 1973, 362). Many have taken a romantic view of that remark, namely, that the specter of the Holocaust has made aesthetics unviable (unconscionable, at least) and banished the lyrical from the realm of possibility. But I had always taken it to be generic in nature: the forms of expression, our generic capabilities and possibilities, had been irrevocably altered by the nature of the subject. Indeed, much of the revolution in our thinking about genre, in both American and other literatures, has instantiated this view, as does, I argue, the essay from which Adorno's remark comes. It is worth mentioning that Adorno's remark has mostly been plucked out of context, and that he himself continued to revise this notion of the "impossibility" of literature after the Holocaust, asking rather, as he put it, "the less cultural question whether after Auschwitz you can go on living" (363).[1] Spiegelman's text had managed to put form literally, graphically, on the table as an issue for consideration, especially in relation to the subject of the Holocaust, about which utterance of any kind other than testimony was being called into question as trivial, ineffectual, unsuitable, "barbaric."

What does it mean, then, to use the comic-book form—what is, in contemporary parlance, the "graphic novel"—to tell the story, or one story, of the Holocaust? Is it the ultimate trivialization or the ultimate in mediation? In every frame, *Maus* asks us to consider this question, as well as whether or not representation of any kind is acceptable, à la Adorno. *Maus* asks us again and again whether the form that is used is being elevated to poetry or whether the subject demands a kind of degraded form. *Maus*, I argue, proffers the perfect teaching tool for a postmodern, post-Holocaust consideration of form and genre, and—it touched my soul.

Yet, despite my excitement about what *Maus* had to offer, I could not avoid the question of degradation, whether of the form, the subject, or my soul. What should we make of the post-Holocaust depiction of Jews as mice in a work that makes a comic book of Holocaust lives? Many have pointed out that Spiegelman is not the first Jewish American writer to use the comic-book form, though he may be the first to use it to depict the Holocaust. And, they ask, why is this American form particularly suitable for Jewish American or self-consciously Jewish American writers? Is it faithful, as one *Tikkun* critic puts it, "to a large if mostly hidden legacy of Jewish comic form" (Buhle 1992, 9)? In fact, many critics have pointed to the hidden as the mark of success of *Maus*, rendering what is unreal in an unreal fashion, distancing the horror through fable. Spiegelman himself has said that

> when one draws this kind of stuff with people it comes out wrong. And the way it comes out wrong, is first of all, I've never lived through anything like that—knock on whatever is around to knock on—and it would be counterfeit to try to pretend that the drawings are representations of something that's actually happening. . . . I'm bound to do something inauthentic. . . . To use these ciphers, cats, mice, it is actually a way to allow you past the cipher at the people who are experiencing it. So it's really a much more direct way of dealing with the material. (Cited in Witek 1989, 102)

Despite his compelling claim for authenticity here, you get the feeling he is hiding something (perhaps from himself), or at least working with something that is hidden—perhaps a historical concept of Jewishness (hidden, dangerous, and representationally impossible except through such distillations, reductions, types).

Other critics and readers are haunted by the sense that these figures, as depictions of post-Holocaust Jewish lives, appear more essentialist than metaphoric. Here is how Hayden White puts it in his contribution to a symposium on the Holocaust called *Probing the Limits of Representation*:

> The manifest contents of both the frame story and the framed story are, as it were, compromised as fact by their allegorization as a game of cat-and-mouse-and-pig in which everyone—perpetrators, victims, and bystanders in the story of the Holocaust and both Spiegelman and his father in the story of *their* relationship—comes out looking more like a beast than a human being. *Maus* presents a particularly ironic and bewildered view of the Holocaust, but it is at the same time one of the most moving narrative accounts of it that I know because it makes the difficulty of discovering and telling the whole truth about even a small part of it as much a part of the story as the events whose meaning it is seeking to discover. (White 1992, 41)

Truth telling, form, and representation—or, to put it another way, the compulsion toward discovery, the burden of history, and the limits of authenticity—are the issues that concern Spiegelman, as they do many writers of and about the Holocaust. What is arguably the uniqueness of his formal vision may seem to raise the ante on Adorno's dictum that there can be no poems after Auschwitz to: there can be no representation of the Holocaust after Spiegelman. At the same time, unique as it seems, Spiegelman's text is conformist in its vision of Jewish self-representation since the Holocaust; it is, finally, more testimony than autobiography (though *Maus* II comes closer to autobiography than the first volume), more radical in expression than in concept.

I do not, however, agree with Spiegelman's detractors (such as Hillel Halkin), some of whom object to the kind of Disney inevitability of cat and mouse in his figures—the cat naturally chases the mouse, the mouse is the resourceful, always potential/imminent victim. I argue that through these ("degraded and degrading") depictions, Spiegelman bears witness to such roles as part of the legacy of the Holocaust. When asked by one interviewer, "Why a mouse?" Spiegelman replied:

> In part because of the rhetoric of extermination, the basic language of the Nazi world. One doesn't exterminate people, one exterminates rodents, insects, subhumans. Note the epigraph by Hitler at the beginning of the book: "The Jews are undoubtedly a race, but they are not human." I had seen the Nazi documentary, "Eternal Jew," that included very effective cross-cutting between Jews huddled together in a ghetto and rats swarming around a sewer. What could be a clearer manifestation of the ways Jews were perceived. A mouse which is a timid animal, reflects what had been until recently the ubiquitous vision of the Jews in the Holocaust, that they were timid, that they didn't fight back. The basic facial structure is an inverted triangle so that the snout is forward, a little bit like the racist caricatures of the Jew, with the long beaky nose. (Hirt-Manheimer 1987, 23)

One might object that to reproduce these images in kind is to rehearse and reinforce them (I will come to the question of objection in a moment); but what can it mean for Spiegelman to reproduce them for himself? He literally illustrates and (re)lives these roles as with the impulse of survivor children to live through/die for their parents' Holocaust experiences. In doing so, Spiegelman displaces and thereby avoids the story of his own life through the rehearsal of his father's; or at least, father and son, both increasingly Art's constructions, are always in contention in these terms, both at risk of becoming guilty for and inconsequential for, as Adorno put it, going on living. One critic has poignantly suggested that Spiegelman creates a kind of "impossible visual text," and this would be in keeping with the problematics of representing the "historically impossible" or missing Jewish body (Rothberg 1994, 675).

Another kind of space that Art Spiegelman occupies or frequents is the cover of the *New Yorker* magazine. On February 15, 1993, he produced what he called a "Valentine Card" for the *New Yorker* cover, in which he depicted a Hasidic Jew embracing and kissing a black woman dressed in a sleeveless shift and wearing large hoop earrings. The cover caused a stir in the general community and an outcry from the Hasidic community. This depiction of a seemingly transgressive

Cover by Art Spiegelman. Copyright © Art Spiegelman, 1993, *The New Yorker* Magazine, Inc. Reprinted by permission.

act was itself a transgressive act. Spiegelman was being a bad Jewish boy in perhaps every resonant sense of that expression. He was acting up and acting out.[2]

But what was the point? The transgressive image? I have not heard Spiegelman address this, but I was struck by the reaction to this image, especially in light of his graphic representations in *Maus*. While there have been some objections along the lines of authenticity and trivialization, the *Maus* works, for the most part, have been more than tolerated; they have been lauded, even receiving the 1992 Pulitzer Prize. I have wondered about this in the context of a half century that has been hard on many of its Jewish writers, such as Philip Roth, who has been roundly criticized for his unflattering semi- or quasi-autobiographical depictions of Jews. It seems to me that what is projected in *Maus*, as I have been suggesting, is a familiar and—however abominably—"acceptable" Jewish self that is internalized from without; a figural legacy. The depiction of the Hasidic Jew, however, represents an internal critique of a certain kind of Jew. That is, the first represents images of a Jewish self that have been forged by those who would render that self unacceptable or *un*human, an internalized image fortified by its subsequent projections on a variety of public screens. In contrast (and to some degree these are historically related), the critique of the Hasidic community emerges from within a Jewish framework. In this framework, such images of Jews have been forged and, ironically, dissociated, becoming figments, for a certain part of the larger community (both Jewish and non-Jewish), of an objectionable or unacceptable representative, an insistent throwback to a susceptible (perhaps dangerous) Jewish type. Spiegelman's cover image is provocative in its playfulness and in its suggestion that the Hasid potentially becomes, for the rest of the Jewish community, an image of dissimulation—an unrecognizable self.[3]

Some might argue that Spiegelman's *New Yorker* Hasid is no less an essentialized view of Jews than is the depiction of them in *Maus*—and no less the product of what might be called a Jewish self-hatred, the kind of charge that regularly is hurled at Philip Roth for his portrayal of Jewish types. Both depictions are types that may be taken or feared to represent the whole body or group (though this was not the reason for the outcry from the Black and Hasidic communities, who either rejected the kiss-and-make-up dictum as irritatingly simplistic or were outraged by the sexual transgressiveness of the image). I argue, instead, that *Maus* reinforces a stereotype, whereas Spiegelman's *New Yorker* image undoes the historical type by localizing it. After all, this was not just any Jew on the cover of the *New Yorker* in the year after the Crown Heights incidents, in which there were a series of violent exchanges between the Black and Hasidic communities after a young black boy was killed by a car driven by a member of the Hasidic community. (One might ask the same question about the image of the Black woman and get a different answer.) But it is—though Spiegelman self-reflexively worries this in the text itself—*any* Jew who is depicted in those mice.

Why is the first degraded image, the finally uncritical self that has been *cate*gorized from without, acceptable to the Jewish American reader as self-text (or any other reader, for that matter), whereas the illuminated critique from within is refused? To put it another way: Why is *Maus* a readable image whereas such an interfacing as that which is imaged on the *New Yorker* cover is not? Aren't they both transgressive acts in which Jews criticize, even defame Jews? It seems that the concern for authenticity in the case of the Holocaust is such a burden that it deters rather than encourages criticism or autobiography. At the very least, this burden of history has produced an autobiographical self that is literally masked, more than revealed; that needs to be hidden to be saved, or to conform to "history's" view. We might expect that bearing witness would satisfy to some degree the search for truth, that testimony would redeem the life—both that of the author and that of the subject—that taling/telling would be a way of surviving. Instead, Spiegelman and his *Maus* texts seem to be responding to both an internal and an external resistance to critique or display, protecting the self from scrutiny and disapprobation despite the sense that the *Maus* texts will lay him open to exactly that. I would say that both responses, both kinds of resistance, external and internal, are post-Holocaust legacies, wherein telling is not saving or surviving.

Spiegelman explains that one of his inspirations for *Maus* was a film class he took at State University of New York at Binghamton, where the instructor was showing racist cartoons and at the same time showing cat-and-mouse chase cartoons. "They conflated for me and originally steered me toward possibly doing something about racism against blacks in America" (cited in Tabachnick 1993, 155). It is interesting, in the light of his *New Yorker* cover, that the analogy with racism toward Blacks led Spiegelman to the subject of his self-text. One can imagine that such historical alignments might serve as displacements from a particular history (another mask or hiding place). The analogy between Blacks and Jews remains salient for Spiegelman, as we can see from the *Maus* books where, in a twist on the potential of such displacement for disguise, hiding from the connection becomes a way of hiding the self (see, for example, *Maus* II; Spiegelman 1991, 98–100).

Nevertheless, the impulse or compulsion to tell, even if originating in an act of displacement, and despite what I have identified as internal and external resistances, is everywhere in Spiegelman's text. We see it in his self-reflexive narrative and in his discussions about the making of *Maus*. The seemingly conflicting needs/aims to tell and disguise, the paradoxically anti-autobiographical impulse to tell, can be illuminated by looking at what Dori Laub and Shoshana Felman identified as a psychic trait of survivors or survivor children around the issue of testimony. Laub, a psychiatrist, and Felman, a literary scholar, collaborated to produce *Testimony: Crises of Witnessing in Literature, Psychoanalysis, and History*. In a chapter titled "An Event without a Witness: Truth Testimony and Survival," Laub discusses what he calls the "imperative to tell" and the "impossibility of telling." Whereas survivors link surviving to telling, the conditions of their post-Holocaust lives are not conducive to satisfying the wish or need to do either. Laub explains this by saying that survivors have lost the ability to bear witness to oneself:

> What I feel is therefore crucial to emphasize is the following: it was not only the reality of the situation and the lack of responsiveness of bystanders or the world that account for the fact that history was taking place with no witness: it was also the circumstance of *being inside the event* that made unthinkable the very notion that a witness could exist, that is, someone who could step outside of the coercively totalitarian and dehumanizing frame of reference in which the event was taking place, and provide an independent frame of reference through which the event could be observed. One might say that there was, thus, historically no witness to the Holocaust, either from outside or inside the event.

What do I mean by the notion of a witness from inside? To understand it one has to conceive of the world of the Holocaust as a world in which the imagination of the *Other* was no longer possible. There was no longer an other to which one could say "Thou" in the hope of being heard, of being recognized as a subject, of being answered. The historical reality of the Holocaust became, thus, a reality which extinguished philosophically the very possibility of address, the possibility of appealing, or of turning to, another. But when one cannot turn to "you" one cannot say "thou" even to oneself. The Holocaust created in this way a world in which one *could not bear witness to oneself.* The Nazi system turned out therefore to be foolproof, not only in the sense there were in theory no outside witnesses but also in the sense that it convinced its victims, the potential witnesses from the inside, that what was affirmed about their "otherness" and their inhumanity was correct and that their experiences were no longer communicable even to themselves, and therefore perhaps never took place. This loss of the capacity to be a witness to oneself and thus to witness from the inside is perhaps the true meaning of annihilation, for when one's history is abolished, one's identity ceases to exist as well. (Felman and Laub 1992, 81–82)

Such theories about the relationship between surviving and telling make us think of Primo Levi, for whom telling was not surviving. But, you might ask, what relevance has this for Spiegelman's text? After all, his father does tell his story before dying, as does the son, Art (a remarkable name in this context), who does so with increasing detail and nuance about the truth of the relationships between father and son, narrator and subject, author and text. In response, I observe that the very telling here portends its own untelling, its lack of success or survival, in the way that the telling of a dream or a nightmare is its undoing. As Laub suggests, no amount of telling ever seems to do justice to the inner compulsion, not only because of the compulsion's incapacity, by definition, to be relieved but because, as Laub points out in relation to Levi's narratives and eventual suicide, "if one talks about the trauma without being truly heard or truly listened to, the telling itself might be lived as a return of the trauma" (Felman and Laub 1992, 67). At almost the conclusion of the first volume, *Maus*, at the point where the father arrives in Auschwitz in his telling, the frame has the father saying, "And we came here to the concentration camp Auschwitz, and we knew from here we will not come out anymore" (Spiegelman 1986, 157). The way in which he states this negates the very context in which it appears, that of a story of a survivor who did just that—"come out of here." And yet the way it is phrased gives it a kind of metaphoric power that lingers over the section and the books, even though we know there is to be a sequel, since, for one thing, it is indicated on the back cover.

In the final pages of the first volume of *Maus*, after representing the arrival of his father to Auschwitz in this language that suggests that he was in some way murdered there, Art calls his father a murderer for having destroyed what he thought were his mother's *lost* notebooks; his mother, Anja, committed suicide in 1968. On the one hand, it seems as though he is addressing the death of narrative (back to Adorno)—both his mother's and the potential for his own—by aligning narrative and history, personal and public, in this way. His father becomes the agent of that death. But to use the word *murderer* in relation to his survivor father, whose story he has been telling, is in one way to align telling with dying (or killing) and to invert his position in relation to his father in order to deal with his own guilt, which he details for us in different ways in both volumes. As I have already suggested, his is a guilt, typical of survivor children, for living and for not suffering as have the parents. In *Maus II*, for example, Art tells his wife about his childhood and adult nightmares, of being dragged out of class by SS men (as happens to the Jewish boy in Louis Malle's *Au revoir, les enfants*) or having Zyklon B rather than water come out of the showerhead: "I know this is insane, but I somehow wish I had been in Auschwitz *with* my parents so I could really know what they lived through!" (Spiegelman 1991, 16). His need to return his father to that time and place is, in part, a wish to live it himself; but for both, it is a kind of dying, a not coming out of there. "Murderer" or murdering, then, ironically conjoins father and son and reunites the family: Art murders the father by telling his story and returning him to the trauma; his father murders the mother in Art's terms by destroying her tale, though he arguably demonstrates by that gesture his resistance to recovery, in both senses of that word (recover her story, recover from his own). The mother, too, as we shall see, is accused of murdering Art through her suicide. Her cessation of life counterpoises his living, and in the accusation we see the same inversion and displacement as that with his father—Art has murdered her—which serves at once to unite them.[4]

I refer here specifically to "The Prisoner on the Hell Planet: A Case History" section of the first book, where for a moment Art is unmasked, if not unmediated (Spiegelman 1986, 101–3; reproduced on pages 141–44, below). As you can see, in this story within a story, the frame narrative comes to a grinding halt, both in the mother's act and in the son's and father's responses. It is the graphic realization of "not coming out of here," the ironic product of "emerging" from the Holocaust. In the mental hospital cell, he is in the prison house of his imagination, getting as close to Auschwitz as he can, and making reparation for the distance between the two. Art's discussion with his therapist in *Maus II* is another instance of unmasking, permitted by the very form of psychoanalysis (the articulation of the hidden; Spiegelman 1991, 43–46). In "Prisoner," he wonders about his role in his mother's death, and in the psychiatrist's chair, he deals with his own agency in his father's undoing, with being, as he depicts himself elsewhere in the books from time to time, a callous and ruthless narrator (like his father), interested more in the telling (surviving) than in the subject. The therapist, himself a survivor, serves to disturb and illuminate Spiegelman's metaphor in a number of ways, as self-consciously marked by Spiegelman: he suggests that Art is feeling remorse for exposing his father to ridicule; he raises the issue about the guilt of survival; he wonders out loud, almost inappropriately given his role as therapist, whether "maybe it's better not to have any more stories." To this Art muses, "Uh-huh. Samuel Beckett once said: 'Every word is like an unnecessary stain on silence and nothingness.'" "Yes," responds the therapist. The frame after this shows a silent therapist and patient, facing each other, the only visible signs of life coming from the (perhaps resonant) smoke of their respective pipe and cigarette. In the frame that begins this sequence at the therapist's office, Art tells us that "his place is overrun with stray dogs and cats" and, in a seeming aside, queries whether he can mention this, "or does it completely louse up my metaphor?" In fact, there are framed photos of dogs and cats everywhere, "really," Art emphasizes (Spiegelman 1991, 43–45). This seems like yet another frame within a frame, continuous in this and other ways with the "Prisoner" sequence. The framing, as it were, of Art's metaphor by his therapist, the survivor, would seem to suggest both a capacity to dissociate and an incapacity for escape, release, survival. At the end of their exchange, they acknowledge the paradoxes that attend telling, as in Beckett's utterance of the need for silence. "He was right. Maybe you can include it in your book" (45).

Finally, Art's guilt about his need or wish to tell the story (produce the book), perhaps at his father's expense, effectively produces a dissociation of telling from surviving. This tale of survival emphatically ends on a note of dying. The survival of the son will perforce preclude the survival of the parent. Yet Spiegelman finds a way of graphically fixing this too: the last frame of *Maus II* pictures his parents' gravestone, with dates of birth and death. Underneath, Spiegelman has signed his name with the dates of the *Maus* volumes—1978–1991. Nancy Miller has suggested that this points "to the fact Art's text keeps his father as well as his mother alive" (Miller 1992, 50). Would it be too gauche in this context to counter with "Art is dead"? After all, the dates of his books signed in this way resonate with the span of a life inscribed on the headstone. At least, one comes away with the sense that Art's signature is imprinted on his parents' life and death.

We might also think of chapter 2 of *Maus II*, which begins with a self-reflexive series of frames in which the author, now visibly wearing a mouse mask, tells us not only of his father's death but of his difficulty in writing this self-text, this tale of survival. (One might ask what he was wearing before; this graphic gesture serves to confirm the sense of inextricability from this historical self-image and unmasks his need to hide.) As he sits at his drafting board, at which—to draw on the title of Nancy Miller's treatment of this work ("Cartoons of the Self")—Spiegelman is literally making a cartoon of himself, he gradually turns to his audience with a running narrative (see page 134).

In the final frame of this first page, we see him keeled over his drafting board in a kind of funk, beneath him the piled bodies of naked mice, and we must ask ourselves what effect his telling has had on this survivor child. If nothing else has compelled us to wonder, here we must: Was *he* the murderer all along for telling—for telling in the way he has, for telling at all? (The subtitle of Miller's essay, by the way, is "Portrait of the Artist as a Young Murderer.") The subsequent frames, in which Art talks some of this through—in dialogue both with the press and with his therapist—do not resolve the questions. At

"Time Flies," from *Maus II*, by Art Spiegelman. Copyright © 1986, 1989, 1990, 1991 by Art Spiegelman. Reprinted by permission of Pantheon Books, a division of Random House, Inc.

the end of her compelling essay "Family Pictures: *Maus,* Mourning, and Post-Memory," Marianne Hirsch addresses these questions and concludes:

> *Maus* is subtitled "My Father Bleeds History" and the book shows us that this bleeding, in Laub's terms, "defies all healing." In the words of the subtitle to the second volume, "And Here My Troubles Began"—his troubles never end. I have tried to argue that the three photographs in *Maus* (that of his father, his brother, and his mother and himself), and the complicated narrative of unassimilable loss that they tell, perpetuate what remains in the two volumes as an incongruity appropriate to the aesthetic of the child of survivors, the aesthetic of post-memory. (Hirsch 1992–93, 27)

This is the effect of the "Mauschwitz," to pick up on Spiegelman's coining of the exchange between his act of representation and the historical site (the title of chapter 1 of *Maus II*), where telling is bleeding, where no one gets out alive, where "happy, happy after," in the last frame of Vladek's narrative, is a graphic lie.[5]

Though it may be a bit overdue, I want to say something about the question of audience here. It may seem that I have been addressing a kind of closed-circuit viewer audience, as though this were a matter for Jewish readers only. Many of the critiques and responses to these texts have been from Jewish readers, many of whom have made their own subjectivity a dynamic part of their critique. I do think that the phenomenology of reading *Maus* posits audiences that are differentiated (at the very least) between the Jewish and non-Jewish communities. Some might argue for further distinctions along national lines; for example, in the section in *Maus II* where Spiegelman is being grilled by reporters, one asks what animal he would have used to depict Israeli rather than American Jews, thereby, albeit briefly, touching on the problematic of "any Jew." His response—"I don't know, porcupines?" (Spiegelman 1991, 42)—is an ironic reference to the *tsabar,* the cactus plant/fruit that has become the metonymic Israeli national symbol (prickly on the outside, sweet on the inside), itself ironic as a national symbol. This passage signals the different myths of self-representation held by and about each—Israeli and American Jews—myths surrounding, for example, the figure of the timid and weak diasporic Jew versus the resistance fighter. It was not surprising to discover in this context that the overall response to the *Maus* texts in Israel was decidedly more negative or indifferent from that in the United States.[6]

Such problems of identification and representation are signaled self-reflexively through the books, as at the beginning of the second book, when Spiegelman's wife—French and a convert to Judaism—depicted throughout as a mouse, queries such depiction. Spiegelman suggests that a frog might be just right, returning us to the idea of type and myth, internalized and externalized, that attends these figures and the notion of identity. In other words, neither Jews nor non-Jews are univocal on any topic. Nevertheless, such bifurcation may signal a sort of emblematic relation between these two however-imagined communities with regard to the subject of the Holocaust, whatever form of expression it may take, each trying to find a place in relation to the event—a complex space in Spiegelman's terms (though not in Spielberg's, let's say), beyond innocence and redemption.

Let me, then, talk along national lines for a moment—more specifically, in Jewish American terms, however elusive a place that may be. Whatever its "dangers," I have always felt enormously drawn by and intimately connected to the *Maus* work, whose quintessential American form reminds us of the role of America in the post-Holocaust imagination as a survivor's domain that has provided, in E. M. Cioran's phrase, "the temptation to exist."[7] I am always somewhat reluctant to participate in the current practice of entering one's subjectivity into the critical debate, taking one's own place in relation to the subject, since, though I mostly applaud the principle, it can be abused along the lines of relevance. Is it, as in the case of many of the other Jewish critics, such as Marianne Hirsch, that Spiegelman's most compelling self-text elicits from us Jewish critics an impulse toward testimony, disguised in form, perhaps, as autobiographical in nature? Or does my reluctance derive from a fear to tell/die/kill?

On the back cover of the first *Maus*, Spiegelman provides a map of the pre–World War II Poland. In the bottom right-hand corner is superimposed a small square in which there is a map of Rego Park, with an arrow pointing to the house and street in which Spiegelman grew up. In the lower left-hand corner, Spiegelman and his father are

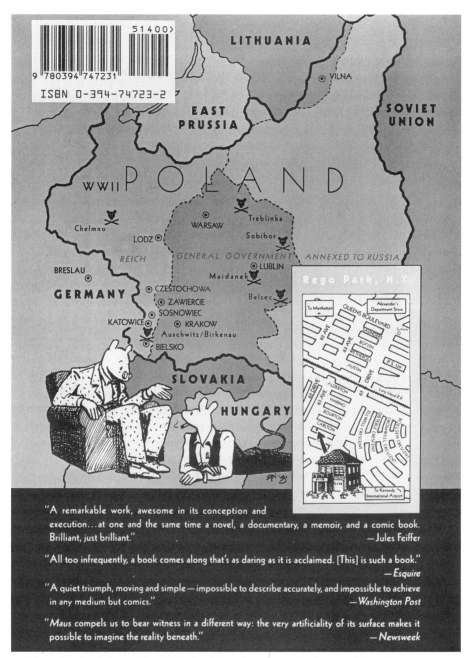

Map of Poland from *Maus I,* by Art Spiegelman. Copyright © 1973, 1980, 1981,
1982, 1983, 1984, 1985, 1986 by Art Spiegelman. Reprinted by permission of Pantheon Books, a division of Random House, Inc.

pictured, his father/mouse in his armchair gesturing in a way that suggests telling, while the son/mouse is stretched out on the floor, head turned toward the father, attentively listening. If you move off that map of Rego Park several blocks to the north and east, you will come to the building I grew up in with my survivor Polish parents, where my mother still lives and where, on occasion, in a rather unsystematic effort, my sister and I, in our own (dis)guises, record laboriously and prosaically my mother's story, our attempt at a survivor's tale, hers and our own.

NOTES

1. Michael Rothberg discusses Adorno's "prescriptions" in terms of Spiegelman's work in "'We Were Talking Jewish': Art Spiegelman's *Maus* as 'Holocaust' Production" (Rothberg 1994, 670–71).

2. Rothberg mentions this *New Yorker* cover, though his aim there is to comment on Spiegelman's neglect of the intersections of race and gender that his depictions produce and draw upon (1994, 677 n. 14).

3. This idea of dissimulation produces a funny play on historical or quasi-historical notions of ethnic authenticity. There has been much discussion about the east-west split within the modern Jewish community, with the *ostjude*, as Sander Gilman has observed, becoming the reification of German anti-Semitism (Gilman 1985, 151) and thereby at once the image of the Jew against which assimilated Jews would draw the self. In one way of reading this relation, then, it is the assimilated Jews who are dissimulated.

4. Nancy Miller discusses this double-murder, as it were:

   > By forcing Vladek to "rebuild" his memory, Art becomes both the "*addressable other*" [as in Laub's theory, to which Miller has a footnote here (Felman and Laub 1992, 68)] necessary to the production of testimony and the subject of his own story. In the end the man in the mouse mask moves beyond his task by fulfilling it, by turning it into art, and replacing it in history. This is not to say that his losses, anymore than those which define the survivor's life during and after Auschwitz, are erased by that gesture: Anja will not return to explain herself. Rather, that by joining the murderers he also rejoins himself. (Miller 1992, 52)

5. Miller comments on this frame too, suggesting that it is the very last frame of the gravestone that "gives the lie to Vladek's 'happy ever

after' since Anja killed herself some twenty years after the war" (1992, 50).

6. I did a quick overview of the Israeli response to the *Maus* books, which I cannot quote or cite here since I have them in the original Hebrew. I will mention one exchange between reviewer Lawrence Weinbaum, an Israeli teaching at the University of Warsaw, and Veronica Lane, whose letter in response to Weinbaum's review appeared in the Israeli journal *Ketiv* (which means "writing," or "orthography"). Weinbaum's review (*Ketiv* 4, 1 [1991]) explains the way in which Spiegelman's work defied his expectations of a "comic" degradation of the Holocaust to produce what he predicts will become a classic text of representation of the Holocaust. In the next issue of this biannual journal there were several responses to Weinbaum. Lane's review stands out, both for rejecting what she identifies as the diasporic image of Jews as mice and for her conclusion that, as she puts it, "the diaspora sickness"—the pathology of self-hatred—"does not skip over Jews who live in their own country" (*Ketiv* 4, 2 [1991]: 85–86). She suggestively uses the verb *pasach* (skip over), which invokes the Passover and the exemption of newborn Jewish males from the mission of the angel of death. It is the covenantal sign of sacrifice, the blood of the lamb, at once the symbol of the people of Israel (and therefore of their self-sacrifice), that staves off the angel. Modern Israelis have almost programmatically eschewed the symbolic equations of rescue and self-sacrifice as integral to Jewish identity.

7. This phrase is the title of a book by E. M. Cioran, *The Temptation to Exist* (Chicago, Quadrangle Books, 1968).

REFERENCES

Adorno, Theodor W. 1973. *Negative Dialectics*. Translated by E. B. Ashton. New York: Seabury.

Buhle, Paul. 1992. "Of Mice and Menschen: Jewish Comics Come of Age." *Tikkun* 7, 2 (March–April): 9–16.

Felman, Shoshana, and Dori Laub, M.D. 1992. *Testimony: Crises of Witnessing in Literature, Psychoanalysis, and History*. New York and London: Routledge.

Friedlander, Saul, ed. 1992. *Probing the Limits of Representation: Nazism and the "Final Solution."* Cambridge, Mass., and London: Harvard University Press.

Gilman, Sander. 1985. *Difference and Pathology: Stereotypes of Sexuality, Race, and Madness*. Ithaca, N.Y., and London: Cornell University Press.

Halkin, Hillel. 1992. "Inhuman Comedy." *Commentary* (February): 55–56.

Hirsch, Marianne. 1992–93. "Family Pictures: *Maus*, Mourning, and Post-Memory." *Discourse: Journal for Theoretical Studies in Media and Culture* 15, 2 (Winter): 3–29.

Hirt-Manheimer, Aron. 1987. "The Art of Art Spiegelman." *Reform Judaism* (Spring): 23–25.

Miller, Nancy K. 1992. "Cartoons of the Self: Portrait of the Artist as a Young Murderer: Art Spiegelman's *Maus*." *M/E/A/N/I/N/G* 12: 43–54.

Rothberg, Michael. 1994. "'We Were Talking Jewish': Art Spiegelman's *Maus* as 'Holocaust' Production." *Contemporary Literature* 35, 2 (Winter): 661–87.

Spiegelman, Art. 1986. *Maus: A Survivor's Tale: My Father Bleeds History*. New York: Pantheon.

———. 1991. *Maus II: A Survivor's Tale: And Here My Troubles Began*. New York: Pantheon.

Tabachnick, Stephen E. 1993. "Of *Maus* and Memory: The Structure of Art Spiegelman's Graphic Novel of the Holocaust." *Word and Image: A Journal of Verbal/Visual Enquiry* 9, 2 (April–June): 154–62.

White, Hayden. 1992. "Historical Emplotment and the Problem of Truth." In *Probing the Limits of Representation: Nazism and the "Final Solution,"* edited by Saul Friedlander. Cambridge, Mass., and London: Harvard University Press.

Witek, Joseph. 1989. *Comic Books as History: The Narrative Art of Jack Jackson, Art Spiegelman, and Harvey Pekar*. Jackson: University Press ofMississippi.

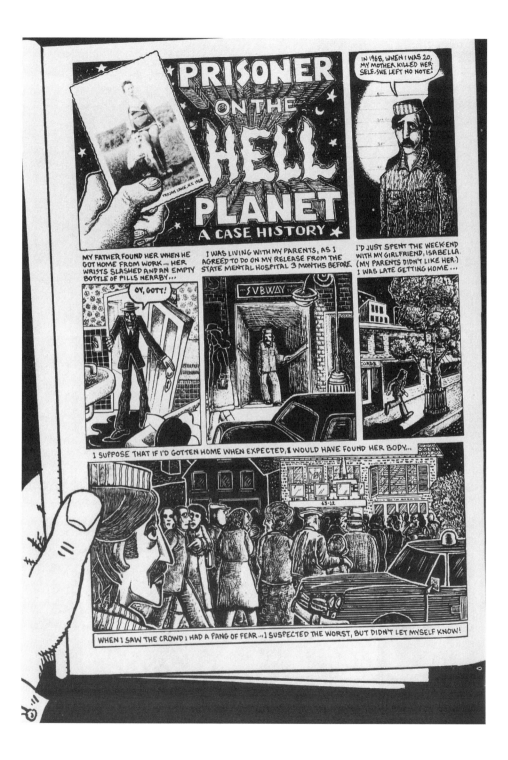

141

144

Chapter 6

On the Yiddish Question

Anita Norich

The contemporary fascination with intellectual autobiographies—especially those written by women, literary critics, and ethnic writers—has made the personal not only political but virtually religious, as if it explained all thought and emotion, rendering it the only necessary contextualization for ideas or behavior. In the academy, the long-acknowledged death of the subject is accompanied by an increased focus on the subjectivity of academic work. At a time when "Question authority" is a cliché reduced to the status of button slogans, the authority of the self seems all that is left. And with the knowledge that all selves are socially constructed, that there is nothing essential about anyone's identity, the attempt to identify the speaking subject has become everyone's pursuit, especially for those empowered to speak. We no longer have apologias for lives lived well but not quite well enough, or lived badly but redeemed at last. Nor do we, for the most part, have exemplary lives or archetypal ones. Many are rightly suspicious of the contemporary academic autobiographical urge: men and women too young to have earned our interest trying to figure out how they acquired their own middle-aged intellects. But, irony aside, there is something utterly appropriate in this turn to the intellectual self at a time when the integrated self is so uncertain a concept.

Often, in Jewish and other ethnic cultures, this turn is expressed through an examination of the connections between various languages and personalities, the word and world of one's developing consciousness. Works as diverse as Irena Klepfisz's English/Yiddish poetry, Alice Kaplan's *French Lessons,* and Eva Hoffman's *Lost in*

Translation illuminate the ways in which acquiring another language is transformative, allowing one to break free of the constraints of a mother tongue or forcing one to become a foreigner, no longer fluently one with the surrounding culture. Acquiring another language for such writers is materially transformative as well, forcing the tongue into different shapes, changing the fluid self into a solid substance, plodding through language rather than flowing in it. I have worried about such changes for most of my thinking life, especially since one of my languages is Yiddish, a language whose ongoing use sometimes requires explanation. Now considered primarily through the language of memory and mourning, defended as a significant part of the Jewish past, Yiddish is analyzed without—in the most literal sense—being understood. It is a language more spoken about than spoken. The personal, individual terms of autobiography trace a more expansive view of Yiddish for me, one that includes the present and future and takes into account that relationships to language, like all relationships, change in response to personal and public life. The very use of concepts such as "relationships" or "expansiveness" suggests a more viable, ongoing set of concerns that resists the dismissal or reification of Yiddish. I have, then, finally succumbed to the autobiographical urge that accompanies the search for meaning in any language.

Half my lifetime ago, I was studying for my Ph.D. in English literature at Columbia University when I embarrassed myself with the following thought: I was about to become, by the standards that were then familiar to me, a highly (over)educated (albeit unemployed) intellectual, and yet I was illiterate in my native tongue. I, who would soon take comprehensive exams concentrating on the history of the English novel, had never read a newspaper—much less a poem—in Yiddish; could name not a single Yiddish novel; and, by dint of much concentrated thought, might have been able to name no more than three Yiddish writers. I decided I should address what I understood as this anomaly, and so, having studied French and—with much resistance—German, I petitioned Columbia to recognize Yiddish as one of my required foreign languages. When they refused, I was offended—offended that "they" would not recognize the language that I, most of my peers, and many of our parents had not acknowledged either. And so I claimed that I needed Yiddish for professional reasons in order to do comparative work in the history of the Yiddish novel. This time, Columbia approved the petition and I was stuck, having at least to pretend to make good on my word. I learned to read Yiddish by sitting with my father, in my parents' Bronx kitchen, as he read volume one of *Ale verk fun Sholem Aleykhem* (The collected works of Sholem Aleichem), a volume I borrowed from a neighbor. I watched his finger move across the letters on the page. He read as I followed, then he followed as I read, and within a few weeks I was reading on my own.

My parents were bemused by this project, at times proud that I seemed to be reclaiming a language we spoke at home but that none of us had particularly valued, at times annoyed that I seemed to be wasting my time. I think I was a bit bemused myself: first, that my father was at long last helping me with my homework (the immigrant experience had reversed those roles long ago), then, at the struggle I had learning to read a language in which I was fluent. The differences between my impeccable kitchen Yiddish and that of the literary world were striking. And, finally, the more I read, the more I became fascinated with the incredible opulence of that literature, the tone of irreverence and love it combined, its social passion, its formal and thematic range. I completed my degree, specializing in the Victorian novel, but continued to read Yiddish as well. My parents continued to be puzzled. In their youth, in Poland, they had read the literature I was now reading, but they had found it stifling, too limited for the expansive promise of European literatures—of Polish, German, Russian, English, and French in the original or translation. Why was their American-educated daughter exhibiting these regressive proclivities?

I exaggerate, a bit, both my parents' bafflement and my own. I have told this story many times, and always with a similar tone of ironic distance, as if it were a story about someone close to me but not actually me, as if it were an intellectual quest on which I had embarked in my impressionable youth, as if it were all about the wonders of Yiddish literature. I try very hard to tell it—to myself as well as to others—as if it had little to do with my parents' experiences in the Lodz ghetto or in Auschwitz, Bergen Belsen, and Dachau; or with my own birth in a Displaced Persons camp in Germany; or with growing up as a child of these survivors. I tell it as if "survivor" needed no translation in my lexicon. But I know better. Yiddish was all the things I was finding in it, but it was also Lodz and my grandparents and a world I could never know. It was the sounds of home and also the sounds of the dead. When my dead spoke to me, they always spoke Yiddish. They never spoke of how they had been murdered but always of Lodz and Zakopane and family and cooking and the fur trade and, sometimes, of the subversive power of books. And they never thought it odd to meet the child born after their deaths. Nor did they ever ask how a happy, well-adjusted American girl had come to speak such a wonderfully rich, unaccented Yiddish. I was passing, I could tell them, passing as an American, as a student, sometimes as an American Jew. But I had not deserted them, leaving them to their fates. I still looked like them, thought like them, spoke like them. It is no wonder that I never told Columbia these reasons for wanting to learn Yiddish. But it is disconcerting that I never admitted them to myself.

My mother worried that Yiddish would literally betray me in ways that my unremarkable name and American English accent never would. One could hide behind Shakespeare or the Victorian novel, but Yiddish offered no safe haven. Though I could imagine myself safely passing as a graduate student and an American, at Columbia and in America no passing was possible for me in Yiddish. On the contrary, it called attention to the hiding places I might have sought. I may not have spoken to the dead of anything but prewar life, but every response I had to my own life was conditioned by their deaths, as if I had been there with them and barely escaped. Whenever I entered a movie theater, I found myself looking for the exit doors. When I entered an apartment, I looked for a corner that could be sealed away. When I met people, I wondered what they would be like in a crisis, if they were the kinds of people whose attics (in New York apartments!) would be safe. When I went to Michigan *(mit di mishigane/meshugane?* [with the mad?] went the inescapable pun that my mother was the first of many to make), things got worse since I was then in unknown terrain, no longer close to family or to the relative familiarity of New York. I don't even remember if my mother ever said these things directly. I knew she thought them, or I thought I knew, because everything in my life had prepared me to have those thoughts myself. I was, in short, a fairly typical child of survivors according to much of the psychological literature and the popular perceptions: highly functioning, successful, loving, with a good sense of humor and social responsibility, frightened much of the time, living in a past I could not bear to name.

I knew the past in the same visceral way I had known as a small child that I should not speak Yiddish on Munich buses, or that my being even fifteen minutes late would make my mother worry beyond endurance, or that calling attention to oneself was dangerous. I had what I imagined to be my parents' reactions to the world. Psychologists no doubt have terms for such things—*secondary post-traumatic stress* or some equally misshapen words—not quite euphemisms, not quite accurate, ugly in sound and sense. The early 1970s, when children of survivors began to speak about the extent to which we shared experiences and reactions, was a great period of liberation for many of us. We, too, were normal, as we had hoped all along. Too soon I came to reject this shared identity, reject the categories that I feared would constrain me, reject the role of victim it seemed increasingly to imply. What right had we—or *I,* the part of speech so hard to claim—to take center stage in the story of the Holocaust? What right to be studied or explained or pitied? It was self-indulgent, and I questioned neither the belief that such self-indulgence was a bad thing, nor that it was self-indulgent, nor what it meant to call it bad.

It was my mother's voice that spoke thus in my ear—again, always, in Yiddish, wittily, ironically, disparagingly. I thought it was my own voice because, while I could not have articulated it at the time, I was accustomed to thinking like my parents, although I had not had (thank God, I still add) their experiences. Years later, I came to call this a dysfunctional reaction formation, proof to me yet again of the ability to hide behind unpleasant language, as if those sober, detached words could reveal what it felt like to respond to experiences I had never had. I wonder, now, what it means to see experiences and feelings on a continuum, as if feelings need to be justified by having an antecedent in personal experience. I understood that my parents' worries, their fears and ambitions, emerged out of their lives before and during the war. (It was always "the war," no gloss or further information ever being required.) Mine, I thought, emerged out of theirs. That left very little room for my own experiences or even for feelings that were not so causally grounded.

In every way imaginable, this myth about responding as if I were someone else—like the myths of self-sufficiency and dependency it partially replaced—was all-encompassing. That, of course, is the power of myth. It was also a different kind of passing (but this time without the illusion of safety), another form of behaving as if I were always masked, the visible hiding the person I could not or would not reveal. This myth gave me a way of explaining to myself why I wanted to be surrounded with a wide circle of friends (because my parents had) although it was so hard for me to trust anyone (as it was for my parents); why I agonized over every decision (as though it meant deciding whether fleeing to Russia or staying put was the better option) but was considered a take-charge kind of person by those who thought they knew me (one always had to be prepared to act); why I needed to know everything (because maybe there was some piece of information that could make sense of the decision to flee or stay) but would reveal little about myself (because it might be used against me); why I distrusted change (it could be for the worse) but was not satisfied with the status quo (it was already bad).

What can it mean to feel as if one must justify emotions, seeking to legitimate them against some cosmic scale on which they rarely even register? On one side of the scale is THE WAR. On the other, my life with its comparatively minor sorrows or depressions or pains. It is difficult to be a strong-willed, self-reflexive individual and yet sustain that level of personal insignificance throughout a lifetime. I have managed to do so for a very long time, but at a cost I have not yet been able to assess adequately. There was a moment in my life when the overwhelming poignancy of it all became clearest. It was a year after my mother's death, a year in which I spoke more Yiddish than usual, because I had spoken it with her, because English could not speak to me of her, because I spent part of the year abroad with Yiddish-speaking relatives and friends. When my father and brother and I were composing the words to place on her headstone, I wanted to follow a custom I had seen in Israel. There, when Holocaust survivors die, a memorial is erected for them and, symbolically, for their immediate family, dead in the war but without graves or markers. Millions are slowly given a place of remembrance, name by name. I wanted to do that for my mother, who had carried the memory of her mother, her sister, and her brother with her throughout her life, and for whom we could do no more (or less) than this final gesture. (Her father had been ill and died—blessedly, as it turns out—young. It was something of a miracle to have had one grandparent who had died in some rather commonplace way.) I knew that the inscription we composed had to be in Yiddish, and it had to name my mother's family. "Tsum eybikn ondenk fun ir mame Khane, shvester Gitl, un bruder Moyshe, umgekumen in letstn khurbn," it finally said—"In eternal memory of her mother Khane, sister Gitl, and brother Moshe, who perished in the last holocaust." They all seemed more alive to me somehow, by being etched in stone with my mother. The English resonates differently from the Yiddish. *Khurbn* is "holocaust" but also "ruin," "devastation"; it invokes the destruction of the temple in Jerusalem as well. *Umkum* is "death," but it is associated with violence. *Letstn* means "last," a gesture to history and all the previous destructions, as well as a hope that this would be the final one, succeeded by no others in Jewish history.

My brother and I, it turns out, responded similarly to the fact that we were able to stand next to our mother's grave, know her *yortsayt* (anniversary of death), compose her memorial: *skhus-oves,* we thought in Yiddish. *Zkhut-avot* in Hebrew. Ancestral merit. Again, a concept that is difficult to translate. It conveys a sense of privilege, unearned except by virtue of one's ancestors. It is because of them that one is blessed. I could choose a language and appropriate words, honor her memory with them, and was privileged to know when and where to utter them. The simple, concrete certainty of place and time became my nostalgia. Instead of photographs, stories, memories, I had a place where names were written. To think of standing near my mother's grave as a *skhus,* a privilege—it was a rare moment of perception about what it meant to me to be a child of survivors. We take our blessings where we can find them, unwilling to let go of the idea of blessings but craving something a little less numinous, too.

Often, then and at other times, I have reached for the tangible as if to reassure myself of the palpability of existence. I have found, instead, that my imagination is peopled by those whom I have never met and lives in places I have never been. I have no desire to return to Munich or to the DP camp of my early years. I have never been to Poland, and it seems wrong to me to go there. To find what? At least once a year for several years now I find myself turning down invitations to teach Yiddish in some part of Eastern Europe. One can now learn Yiddish (again) in Warsaw, Krakow, Vilna, Kiev, Moscow, and the list grows yearly. It is a noble enterprise, this movement of Jews who were compelled for so long to suppress Jewish knowledge now trying to reclaim it, the movement of non-Jews to learn about what no longer survives in their cultures, and the temporary movement of teachers who flourished in the West now going back to the places they have studied. But it is not a movement I can make (yet?). I am more skeptical about all the "marches of the living"—Jews from all over the world returning to this ancestral home. I wonder how many are motivated by *keyver ovus* (the mitzvah of visiting the graves of one's ancestors) and how many by an unacknowledged, magical sense of the metonymic power of this tourism. Seeing these sites comes to signify seeing Jewish history and the inescapability of Jewish identity. To have come out of Warsaw or Auschwitz or Ponar is a sign of victory, the triumph of the Jew over every horror. *Am yisrael chai*—the people of Israel live. "Me too," we can now say on our way out of the gates. But the homology between sight and site, being there and having been there, is deeply disturbing. I cannot imagine myself entering these places willingly, to learn from them, and then to return to real life after a week or two. I think of Poland as one vast cemetery, but there isn't even an actual cemetery where I can find the graves of my dead. It is a kind of palimpsest or *pentimento* for me, a canvas over which new images have been drawn, not quite erasing the old but blurring them beyond recognition.

There is a poem by one of my favorite Yiddish poets, Malka Heifetz-Tussman, called "Keylers un beydemer" (Cellars and attics), in which the speaker and her friend, another poet named Ted, tell one another of their parents' homes. Ted speaks of the objects his children will find in their grandparents' cellar and attic near Boston—the clothes, pots, jewelry, guns—that contain the history and traditions of his family. She tells him of the ritual garments, menorahs, shofars that her children will find in their ancestral home. And when he asks where this house is, she answers "yidishlekh— / A frage af a frage: / Vu iz / dos alte hoyz mayn zeydns?" (Jewishly— / A question with a question: / Where is / That old house of my grandfather's?) Homecoming is not a function of place. Nor, despite what

I have tried to learn from my professional commitments to literary criticism and, particularly, to Jewish culture, do I find a homecoming primarily in texts. I come home *to* language, *in* Yiddish, not only as the language spoken in my childhood home but also as the language spoken in those older homes to which none of us can return.

The first book I wrote had no title until it was completed and a friend, reading my introduction, found the title for me there: *The Homeless Imagination,* he said. It was there all along, a refrain I could not see. Its working title had been a little too precious: "In/Fertile Ground," I thought of calling it, trying to evoke the tensions about the future of Yiddish in Europe and America, the question of whether America could offer fertile soil for Yiddish or whether it was, instead, fated to remain barren, incapable of new generation. Like Israel Joshua Singer, the subject of my book, I sought a location in which Yiddish, the imagination, culture, the future could all coexist. The metaphor of homelessness seemed more apt than that of fertility, perhaps because it was less fraught. I have never, in fact, been homeless. Nor was Singer. Nor was Yiddish. I have a beautiful house, complete with a cellar and attic and antique furniture I have acquired in the last decade or so. (My parents' grandchildren, I thought with each new purchase, will have somewhere to go, to rummage through old things and discover the past.) I am perfectly at home in America, in its landscape and idiom, and I recognize that any alienation or estrangement from which I may suffer is only symbolic. It has never had any serious literal or material consequences. But my imagination continues to live elsewhere. That is something else I share with Yiddish. It can't go home again either, and while it may be welcomed elsewhere, its roots can't quite dig deeply enough.

I resist the impulse to anthropomorphize and psychoanalyze Yiddish, although I know that I am sometimes guilty of doing exactly that. I do not want my students or my readers or myself to see it as another victim of the Holocaust, a precious remnant to be enshrined and guarded. I refuse to make an icon or an idol out of Yiddish, although now and then I cannot help sentimentalizing it a bit. It belongs everywhere and nowhere. It speaks to all Jews whose ancestors ever set foot in Eastern Europe, but few of them can understand it. It occasions a great deal of mawkish nonsense as well as rigorous scholarship. It has a fantastic literature, but few can name its writers. It is

full of pithy, witty, ironic idioms and, in Anglicized form, some of the
worst, most degrading jokes I know. I love these contradictions.
Often, I find them frustrating, but I love the range and energy they
embody. Still, I worry that in casting my lot so firmly—personally and
professionally—with Yiddish I may separate myself from the living,
emerging cultures around me. There is a terrible kind of narcissism
in thinking that one lives as the embodiment of the past, speaking the
language the dead might have used, perhaps even speaking for them.

    I have language nightmares. I walk into a classroom and begin
lecturing, but no one understands me. It is an advanced Yiddish class,
but everyone has signed up for something else and they think I am
mad, speaking in tongues (the *michigane/meshugene* [mad] theme
again). Or I am at a border crossing, nervously handing over my precious American passport but unable to answer simple questions in
English. I am in Germany, but when I speak German, croaking animal
noises are all that emerge. These are overdetermined images, too
easy to tell and to interpret but nonetheless true. Then there are the
daydreams. I am running out of people to talk to, and it scares me to
think of using words that no one around me will understand. I imagine myself, decades hence, a senile, old woman reverting to her first
language, seeming to babble nonsense. I imagine myself after a
stroke, after some horrible accident, stricken with some form of apha-
sia, having forgotten every language but the incomprehensible one. I
imagine hospital staff solicitously worrying about what language most
resembles mine and bringing in some German-speaking doctor to
help. That's as far as my imagination is willing to go.

    Usually (fortunately for me and those around me), my days and
nights are not spent at such a pitch of anxiety. I have learned not to
take myself so seriously, partly because it would make me insufferable,
partly because nothing is as serious as the defining events of my life—
events I did not, in fact, live. I rarely write or speak publicly about
being a child of survivors. I worry that I ran out of new things to say
over twenty years ago, and I am reluctant to offer autobiographical insights that seem inevitably conventional and even self-congratulatory.
("See how I have managed to overcome these obstacles" is what I fear
implying.) The very form of the memoir raises expectations that
make me uncomfortable when I am the writing subject. Again, it is

Malka Heifetz-Tussman who gives me the language to express my hesitation. In a poem titled "Tselokhes" (For spite), she answers those critics who expect that, as a Jew and a Yiddish poet, she must write a poem about *khurbn* (holocaust, destruction). In spite of the destroyers of her people, to spite them, she will live in the world, see her children marry and procreate new generations, and refrain from putting her grief into words. "(A bushe oyftsushraybn / 'troyer' af papir)"— "(A shame to write / 'sorrow' on paper)," she exclaims, containing the vehemence of this outburst within parentheses, as if it were an aside rather than the revelation she must convey to others who write such words too facilely.

(A bushe oyftsushraybn / 'troyer' af papir). Much of what is most important to me is contained within my own parentheses in these remarks: the explanations that seek to make comprehensible what may not be as clear even to me as I would like; those explanations that are utterly clear to me and yet so difficult to convey; translations from Yiddish; even transliterations. *Oyftsushraybn* is a small act of rebellion. Should I write *aftsushraybn,* as standard principles of transliteration dictate, or *oyftsushraybn,* as my Polish-Yiddish accent would encourage? More than a comment about standardization, this question contains within it a range of cultural battles and the recognition that, with the exception of my own child, virtually no one is learning my parents' Yiddish anymore. The accent in which I teach Yiddish language is not the accent in which I speak to my family, so that, even in Yiddish, I seem to be always translating. *Troyer* is sorrow and sadness and grief and mourning. I cannot get all that into one English word. Translators always lament what is lost in the translation, and Yiddish should be considered no more or less difficult to translate than any other language. But in the case of Yiddish, one of the things I fear losing in the translation is me. It is a *troyer*—a source of sorrow and sadness and grief and mourning—to be compelled to translate, and yet I know that if I am to speak to the communities in which I live, I have no choice. My primary materials are almost always in Yiddish, whether they are stories or poems or essays or—as in this case—me. The language in which I form and present these analyses is almost always English. My subject's language is foreign to most of my readers; the language and idiom in which I write are foreign to the cultural

landscape that is my primary subject. Everyone who has experienced bilingual life will recognize some version of this dilemma. But in Yiddish it can assume epic proportions, as speaking populations diminish and we recall their histories in this century.

The stakes in this are extraordinarily high. Sometimes, I feel the act of translation as an act of violence, of betrayal. I want others to know "my" culture as it lived before the war. Translation seems to complete the work of obliteration carried out in Europe. It seems to call into question the viability of the still-living language. But I also think of it as a loving act of resistance, an act of defiance that preserves a culture whose transformations should not be met with silence. Much of my professional and personal life is spent trying to negotiate between these two extremes. My scholarly work has often demanded a dispassionate and objective tone, but there are times in the classroom when all such claims disappear. A Yiddish sentence newly formed by a student from the Detroit suburbs, a Yiddish poem "discovered" by an American who never saw a Yiddish book, a conference in which colleagues my age speak to one another in a richly nuanced Yiddish, Yiddish e-mail (even in transliteration)—these are not the stuff of which revolutions or redemption are made. The delight they give me, though, should require no translation at all. These are among the moments that bring me as close as I will come to Lodz and to the grandparents whose names I bear.

(What is most haunting about the dead is that they always have the last word.)

Or so I thought. There is a coda to these observations, a coda that is actually the center. I have learned that it's not at all the dead who have the last Yiddish word. I have a daughter now, named after my mother and also after another child—a cousin I never met because she died, probably in Treblinka. I thought a long time before giving Sara the middle name of Taibl; I thought about burdening her with my ghosts, about forcing a legacy on her. But I thought, too, about that name, about its sounds, about the little dove *(taibl)* who bore it. And, again in the most literal sense, I wanted the name to continue, to have a happy life. It is such a sweet sound that I thought it should live in the world, even if it would make my daughter stand out a bit.

I never decided to speak Yiddish to my child. I have always chafed at the discussions of Yiddish literature that described the sacrifices poets made by deciding to write in Yiddish rather than becoming part of the larger public literary movements around them. Language, in this sense, is not a choice at all. Multilingual though every Yiddish writer may have been, the imagination tends to speak in one language, and for these modern men and women, who had loved and fought and rebelled in Yiddish, there rarely was such a choice. I understood this anew when I found myself cuddling Sara in the sounds in which I had been cuddled, calling her Surale, adding Yiddish endearments to every sentence. English was suddenly the foreign tongue. I know no language that can describe what it feels like to have her babble in Yiddish intonations or to point to her gorgeous face in response to Yiddish prompts, or to say "Ma-me" aloud—not "mommy" or "mama," but *ma-me* in the kind of accent I thought never to hear again. I am not a romantic Yiddishist in all this. I do not think—the legends of Ben-Yehuda and Hebrew notwithstanding— that she will be the start of a new generation that will be raised as strong, liberal, independent American Jews in Yiddish. I am often at a loss for words in daily conversation with her, refusing to make up Yiddish versions of sippy cup or Raggedy Ann or VCR. I worry, too, that in my lifetime Yiddish really has become the secret language of the Jews, the language that she and I and no one else around us will use, a language that may build a wall around us to cut us off from others. The fear is that she will literally have the last word, that she will be the last non-hasidic or -haredi child to close this particular book. It's not *me* but her upon whom I am imposing this awful responsibility.

At the moment, she hears no distinctions between Yiddish and English; she thinks of them simply as language. They are both, researchers tell us, stored in the same part of her brain now, and she responds with equal energy to both. Like Yiddish writers and like me, she is not choosing one over the other but simply using all the languages at her disposal. For me, the thrill of hearing Yiddish from her mouth is unparalleled even by the daily miracles of her growth. Suddenly, Yiddish is not the language of commemoration or mourning. It is not the Holocaust or prewar cultural life or, to paraphrase I. J. Singer's memoir, "a world that is no more." Sara Taibl is neither my mother Sara nor my cousin Taibl; she is not, cannot be, resurrection or compensation. For now, despite the absence of Yiddish-speaking playmates or caretakers, she is simply a curious, beautiful toddler joyfully growing up in Yiddish. There is nothing really simple in any of that, but it is a much happier ending-by-way-of-another-beginning to this Yiddish story.

Chapter 7

Two Female Characters in Search of a Theory: Mapping Jewish Identity through Personal Narrative

Regina Morantz-Sanchez

The frontispiece of Lydia Kukoff's *Choosing Judaism*, a self-help book written for converts and published in 1981, contains an epigraph that reads, "Whether we are born Jewish or have converted to Judaism, we are all Jews by choice."[1] When I read this passage almost two decades ago, I was moved by the generosity of its message to members new to the fold, but it never occurred to me that it might also have enabled me to better understand my personal history. As a historian, I subscribed to the notion that people become who they are by a conscious struggle with the particularities of family history and sociohistorical experience. But had I been required then to account for my own Jewish identity, I would surely have begun with the fact of birth. I would have gauged my Jewishness against a fixed notion of authenticity, acknowledging that I met some criteria more fully than others. I knew that familial, cultural, economic, and historical circumstances shaped me, though I would have understood these categories to be naturalized, stable, and uncontested. Like most historians at the time, I viewed identity as self-conscious, integral and unified, the product of rational individual struggle.[2] My Jewishness resulted from just such explicit effort, and my life choices—while indeed choices—appeared to me almost teleological in their consistency. Moreover, the version of Judaism that molded me, which celebrated free will and individual choice, would certainly have backed me up.

It is only recently that scholars in my discipline have come to question such premises. My own research in women's history has benefited from several new theoretical approaches to identity formation, and scholarship on the subject has been particularly rich in the last ten years.[3] Some of the best explores the ways in which ideology, culture, bodily experience, and material conditions shape individual subjects. Though we still allow that individuals exercise agency in forming their identities, we understand better the historically specific and culturally ramified conditions in which this process takes place. We have gained a clearer picture of the relationship of the individual to the social world and a fuller understanding of the nature of the cultural dialogue that shapes subjectivity. Stuart Hall's work has been particularly eloquent in articulating these insights. Cultural identity, he has written, is not "eternally fixed in some essentialized past, but is subject to the continuous 'play' of history, culture and power." It "is a matter of 'becoming' as well as of 'being.' It belongs to the future as much as to the past. It is not something that already exists, transcending place, time, history."[4]

This dynamic view of identity formation, one that rejects reductionist and fixed notions of gender, ethnicity, race, and class, has led me somewhat belatedly to reexamine my self-understanding. Because consciousness and identity are never wholly private but are shaped by social phenomena in complex ways, I have come to believe that my own story has significant historical resonance. This chapter revisits key events in my personal history and that of my younger daughter, in order to explore the identity construction of not one but two Jewish women. I suggest that a dominant theme in the narrative of our encounters and contrasting responses to Judaism is the role that feminism has played in both our lives. The ideas, assumptions, and events of women's liberation, though not explicitly articulated, have a foundational role in my reconstruction of the historical context. And because experience is always shaped by the meaning structures that particular individuals inherit and create, I doubt that my daughter would agree with all of what I am about to say.

As a member of a specific generation, I attended to my development as a Jew while responding to a particular set of material and cultural opportunities and constraints. The life-script I wrote for myself helped me comprehend the events I experienced. Understandably, my daughter was profoundly influenced by the choices I made, and my own preferences as a mother clearly shaped her perception of the world. But she came to adulthood under different historical circumstances, and the maternal script, though powerful, needed to be altered. What follows is an experiment stimulated by recent theoretical understandings of identity formation, and it is fair to say that this is primarily my story.[5]

Beginnings

My parents, second-generation Jews who had embraced American values with only a vague and unfocused connection to their Jewish past, were relatively deracinated. Like many children of immigrants, they were disconnected from traditional Jewish lifestyles by a combination of death, assimilation, and family dysfunctionality. Family mythology suggests that it was quite by chance that they rethought their Jewish commitments. Moving from Brooklyn to southern California after World War II, a decision that accelerated the attenuation of their links to a vital Jewish community, they settled in the San Fernando Valley. We lived in a postwar community of typically mixed middle-class ethnicity. We even had a Christmas tree for a few brief years in my early childhood. I'm told that it was a close friendship with the Catholic girl across the street, who taught me to say the rosary and took me to Mass one Sunday, that eventually turned them around. At the age of seven, I returned home full of wonder at the beauty of the church service and announced that I wanted to be Catholic. Though my father was an atheist, a year as a prisoner of war with the Germans had prompted him silently to reclaim his Jewish identity in a quiet and personal way. Having a Catholic in the family was definitely beyond the pale, and much to my astonishment, my parents joined a synagogue the very next day.

Though I'm still amused at this story, I know now that it was this relatively fortuitous event that offered me, a young girl with a passion for belonging, a new set of "conditions of possibility." It allowed me to choose Judaism. I must admit that, like many converts, as I entered into a religious and cultural milieu and connected with a version of history and collective memory that essentialized Jewish identity, I learned to be uncomfortable with this errant family history.

Worse still, there was nary a Bundist or Polish rabbi in my family tree. In fact, I lacked even an appropriately traditional Bubbe or Zaide (grandmother or grandfather). No wonder I felt inauthentic. Adding to my impostor's sensibility was the fact that I had no direct connection to the two toweringly significant historical events that so profoundly shaped Jewish identity in the second half of the twentieth century. I had no family who perished in the Holocaust, and none of my relatives settled in Israel.

Indeed, throughout much of my adolescence I longed for a more orthodox and *haimishe*[6] lineage; I wished for what Stuart Hall has so insightfully called "a transcendental 'law of origin.'" I knew that my fatal flaw, as it were, was that my Jewishness was not as transparent or unproblematic as that of many of my Jewish peers. My great-grandfather attended synagogue because he was a Jew; I went in order to become one. Twenty years later, Stuart Hall's work has laid bare the meaning of that secret shame. I lived in an age that thought of identity as an already accomplished fact. Only now do I understand that my tentative Jewishness was no less "authentic" than my great-grandfather's *shtetl* faith. It was simply the product of a different time and place. Though Hall has helped us to see that cultural identity is "not an essence, but a positioning," such knowledge was beyond my self-understanding in those days.[7]

There is a great deal to say about the shaping of Jewish American cultural self-understanding in the 1950s, when I grew up, and in the 1980s, when my middle child struggled through her adolescence and young adulthood. Depression and world war wrought transformative effects on American politics and society in these decades. Second-generation Eastern European Jews, along with other hyphenated ethnics, transitioned into the middle class, becoming articulate and influential beyond their numbers in politics and society. The Holocaust, the birth of Israel, the Cold War and its aftermath, the campaign for African American civil rights, the social and political revolutions of the 1960s, feminism, Vietnam—all these events profoundly affected the adjustment and acculturation of the Jewish community. It had struggled for almost two centuries with the myriad, complex, and destabilizing effects of emancipation and modernity, first in Europe and then in the United States. These events indirectly shaped me as well as my daughter. They helped produce a version of Judaism that spoke to each of our needs and, perhaps even more important, created a set of needs that a particular version of Judaism was able to satisfy. Obviously, I can only begin here to sort out the place of these events in my self-understanding, but I believe to do so can help decipher the meaning and impact for many individuals of some of the social changes I have just mentioned.

Conservative Judaism Meets Feminism

I must first return briefly to that historical moment when my parents joined a synagogue to prevent me from becoming a Catholic. They were a young couple, newly settled in California and, like many suburban couples, looking for connection and community in the aftermath of a terrible war experience and the typical postwar dislocations and adjustments.[8] The synagogue they chose was a tiny Jewish congregation of fifty families, which today is one of the largest and most successful Conservative *shuls* in southern California. At that time, Conservative Judaism was shaping a version of community practice that could bring young suburban Jews like my parents back into the fold.[9] In the case of my family, the effort was a resounding success. My father, a capable and charismatic young businessman, soon headed up the synagogue's building committee, while my mother, a stay-at-home 1950s housewife with the intelligence, drive, and creativity to become anything she wanted, whipped the Sisterhood into shape in no time flat.

Soon my father was additionally involved with a group of city-wide and nationally connected Jewish lay and religious leaders, who eventually founded a branch of Camp Ramah in California. Since the 1920s, summer camp had gained increased significance as an institution for shaping values among the children of the middle class in the northeastern United States. Jews embraced the institution with zest.[10] Camp Ramah, the brainchild of Conservative Jewish communal leaders at the Jewish Theological Seminary in New York, was initially founded after the war to give faculty children a Jewish experience that could also be American. Before long, camp

advocates understood its value as well in educating the next generation of Jewish leaders, teachers, and intellectuals. With the founding of such camps across the country, advocates learned to combine
the all-American outdoor experience with the dailiness of traditional Judaism in a manner that would aid a new generation to
move comfortably between American society and a modernized but
deeply committed Jewish world.

When Ramah California was established in 1956, my father, the
atheist, sat on its board of directors. That memorable summer, I was
the first girl to become Bat Mitzvah at any of the Ramah camps. And
because it was California, where the Conservative rabbinate had a
reputation for religious radicalism, not only was I allowed to read directly from the Torah, but I even davened the *musaf* service.[11] I am
told that when this news made its way back to the Jewish Theological
Seminary, some of the more traditional members of the faculty suffered mild cases of apoplexy, and in the next few weeks, some very important heads rolled.

But I was in heaven; for the version of Judaism I encountered offered an unconventional and somewhat rebellious young girl in the
1950s a way to opt out of American teenage culture. Profoundly uncomfortable with the feminine stereotypes scripted for me, I was se-
duced not only by the conventional sleep-away camp's stress on sports
and the outdoors (we had some well-placed sabras, native-born Israelis, in our midst, fresh out of the Israeli army and eager to toughen
us up) but also by the commitment to learning and its privileging of
my intellectual abilities. Seminary leaders took seriously the charge of
teaching the next generation of Jewish scholars, teachers, and community leaders. They brought out some of the best minds in Conservative Judaism to serve. Perhaps most important, I found myself in an
environment in which girls, too, could be smart, and the heady intellectual atmosphere of those years has stayed with me. Without a feminist movement to help me work through my discomfort with 1950s
peer culture, Conservative Judaism validated all the personality
traits—including a tendency to be outspoken—that I had to keep
under wraps to be accepted in public school.

In addition, in a decade in which moral values were in flux and
the postwar prosperity produced a youth culture that was often su-
perficially described as apathetic and apolitical, I was drawn to the

deep and passionate questioning the project of creating an Americanized version of Jewish practice invariably generated. We know now that many of the political youth activists of 1960s America were as discontent as I with the cultural vapidity that conformity and materialism evoked in this decade, and that they found outlets other than Judaism in their search for meaning. Thus, in retrospect, my attraction to Judaism in this form is not difficult to comprehend, because it allowed me to enter the political debates of the next decade over civil rights and anti-imperialism with the sense that I spoke in an authoritative, ethical Jewish voice.[12]

But this was the late 1950s, after all, and as time passed, my male peers all went on to study at the seminary, becoming rabbis and teachers and Jewish intellectuals. I went east, too, to Barnard College, and took night courses toward a bachelor's degree in Hebrew literature at the seminary. But I gradually came to see that the equal treatment I had received as an adolescent could not carry over into adulthood. While my male friends were allowed no limits to their ambition and found places for its fulfillment within the Jewish community, I was offered only the possibility of becoming a Hebrew teacher or a *rebetzin*. Although my mentors validated my intellect, no one suggested I make a *career* out of it by channeling my love of history into Jewish directions. So I fell by the wayside. I eventually gave up my Jewish studies and became a professor of American history, specializing in women and the family.

Moreover, by the end of the 1960s, feminism offered me the kind of support for my aspirations that a revitalized Conservative Judaism, still embedded in the gender assumptions of the 1950s, could not. But I always saw my distancing from Jewish practice as temporary. My Jewish identity remained passionate and committed, something to invoke again in an active way when circumstances permitted.

My Jewish path was not an easy one. Alienated from the seminary community because I couldn't find a satisfying place in it, I found camaraderie in the graduate student culture at Columbia. I felt increasingly at home in the tolerant and ecumenical atmosphere of liberal/left academia, especially as we sorted through the meaning of the political upheavals of the 1960s, in which we all took part. I loosened my religious observance. I married a secular Jew profoundly uncomfortable with his Jewish identity who had no sensitivity to my particular Jewish passions. Though I struggled valiantly to produce in our private life the brand of Judaism I was taught, I was forced gradually to acknowledge the uniqueness and singularity of that experience. It simply couldn't be easily explained to a non-initiate or replicated in the real world. One needed a community that oftentimes did not yet exist.

Meanwhile, my husband, fresh from making that long journey from Brooklyn to Columbia, from lower-class ethnic insularity to upper-middle-class cosmopolitanism, that Norman Podhoretz has described so eloquently, was passionately eager to shed the discernible markers of his Jewishness.[13] And, indeed, it was his experience, not mine, that was most typical of the vast majority of Jews of our generation. Still, I was plagued by nostalgia and longing and determined to give my daughters the Jewish enrichment that had meant so much to me. In the late 1970s, we moved from the East Coast to Kansas City. For me it was truly *galut* (exile), and I settled for sending my children to the small, struggling community Jewish day school, much against the wishes of their father.

Fast-forward to the late 1970s. Clearly, I was not the only individual for whom the lasting effect of the Ramah experience was an ongoing compulsion to grapple in one way or another with my Jewish American identity. Few Ramah campers were comfortable returning home, summer after summer, to the suburban Conservative Judaism of our parents' generation. Indeed, existing institutions could not respond adequately to the complexity of our summers' experience. All of us found it difficult to re-create the healthy balance of American culture, Jewish learning, ethical soul-searching, and religious practice that prevailed in camp. Out of this disjunction, many former campers launched intellectual, religious, and organizational innovations within the Conservative movement. Others created new forms of Jewish identity by moving beyond Conservatism in different ways. Ironically for me, the Judaism I had loved and then became estranged from was giving rise to the Havurah movement, the ordaining of women rabbis, the revival of Reconstructionism, critiques of Zionism from a revitalized 1960s Jewish left, and the reframing of Jewish ritual in response to feminism, multiculturalism, and gay liberation.

But I lived in the Midwest, far geographically, institutionally, and ideologically from those extraordinarily creative and history-forming changes. Eventually, I was divorced, and once again it was feminism, not Judaism, that spoke to my personal concerns. Indeed, Judaism's strong commitment to the traditional family served to exacerbate my struggles. In the late 1970s the divorce rate was still relatively low in the ritually active Jewish community of Kansas City. In spite of my Ph.D. and a job at the University of Kansas, my primary status signifier in that community was as the mother of two Hebrew day-school students. Nevertheless, I clung to some version of family life that could integrate feminism and Judaism while satisfying the spiritual and ethical longings that had been very much a part of my concerns in the 1950s. I rekashered my home. My daughters and I began keeping Shabbat. We built sukkahs and dressed up for Purim instead of Halloween. I was active in New Jewish Agenda, an organization of Jewishly committed leftists critical of Israel's burgeoning militarism and occupationist mentality. But Kansas City was a community still arrested, politically, socially, and Jewishly, in the ideology of the 1950s. And here the story twists in ironic ways.

By the early 1980s, America was in the grip of a backlash against the political and cultural upheaval of the 1960s and 1970s. The recoiling was cultural, to be sure, but there was also an emphatic rejection of the politics of the 1960s—civil rights, big government, and, perhaps especially, feminism. Kansas City clung to the ideology and social assumptions of an earlier age. After I was divorced, I used to joke that although, according to statistics, over 50 percent of mothers with school-age children worked for wages outside the home, surely the other 50 percent lived in Kansas City! Because of this atmosphere, both my daughters were hit hard by divorce and single motherhood. For the younger one, it truly seemed that we were the only unconventional family around. Indeed, I don't think she believed we were a family at all. Few looked like us, either in the Jewish community or in the larger neighborhood culture in which we lived.

When this young woman turned fifteen, my delicate balancing act between an ancient tradition and Enlightenment rationality, between modern feminist constructions of self and a love for ritual and family structure still patriarchal in form, between work and family, between a version of public political responsibility learned in the 1960s and a satisfying personal life, appeared increasingly unworkable. The child of divorce and thus deprived of the family both Judaism and

American society in the 1980s privileged in their different ways, she rebelled. She had been obligated against her will to experience the inevitable emotional disruptions and hard times of life with a divorced working mother. These were especially destabilizing against the backdrop of a cultural backlash led by the president of the United States, who attacked two decades of family upheaval and feminist revolution, blaming the victims. In response, she, like her mother before her, turned to Judaism.

But while I chose a Jewish context at least in part to *escape* the reinscription of traditional gender roles during the culturally and politically conservative 1950s, my daughter constructed a Jewish identity that could help her critique and eventually reject the implications of a feminism that had helped me negotiate the personal effects of social change. She became a *baalat tshuvah* (one who embraces a traditional Jewish religious life). Turning her back on the promise of reason, the laws of causality, and, perhaps the most painful of all, the insights of history, she found my personal choices untenable. Recoiling at my attempts to mesh Judaism, feminism, and modernity, she responded with a resounding "No!"

Ironically, she retreated from American teenage culture just as I did. Fearing quite literally the instabilities of gender equality, sex, drugs, and rock and roll, she was very much the product of the Reaganite 1980s. American society sent her in search of a version of Judaism different from the one I offered, one that gave her a "transcendental 'law of origin.'"[14] Rejecting my efforts to live a feminist life in an untransformed and non-feminist world, she retreated into orthodoxy. She would not shunt back and forth between family and work and endure the exhaustion that it breeds; she would not compete in a male professional world that still treated women badly; she would never grapple with the economic and emotional consequences of divorce and single motherhood.

In this discussion, I have been primarily engaged in identifying the pieces of social context that helped shape me and my daughter as subjects. I have concentrated on the differences in our social realities, because we as scholars have theorized the interpretation of public discourses involved in identity construction much more fully than we have the symbolic and the psychic. It is not that I consider the level of the psychic less important to our respective stories; yet how to link the two realms is still problematic. Jacqueline Rose has argued that "the question of identity—how it is constituted and maintained—is . . . the central issue through which psychoanalysis enters the political field."[15] And Stuart Hall insists that "if ideology is effective, it is because it works at both 'the rudimentary levels of psychic identity and the drives' and at the level of the discursive formation and practices that constitute the social field, and that it is in the articulation of these mutually constitutive but not identical fields that the real conceptual problems lie."[16] Clearly, there is much to say about myself and my daughter on this score, and by neglecting that approach here, I do not mean to diminish its importance. But this is not my project now.

Getting (and Losing) My Yichus[17]

Today, my daughter is married to a black-hat Talmud scholar and lives in an Orthodox neighborhood in Jerusalem. She is twenty-four and has just given birth to her third child, her first boy. She is happy, and her husband is a delightful, bright young man. There is much to ponder about the syncretic American Jewish subculture that she chose and how it constructs identity. It has not been lost on me that she made her choices in an age when multiculturalism entered our national discourse. Probably the most cogent critique of multiculturalism from the left is that it aestheticizes and commodifies difference and obscures an insidious and more fundamental material diversity, hegemony, and economic exploitation. Capitalism, many have argued, not only misrepresents and appropriates unity in diversity, it celebrates a superficial pluralism that obscures and often facilitates economic inequality and separates and divides the various groups it exploits.[18] I suggest that my daughter's critique of multiculturalism comes from the right. There is much irony in this, given my own political heritage. But her rejection of Conservative Judaism appears to me to be very much a distancing from American pluralism in its most generous guise; it is a moving away from those democratic and individualistic values that facilitated her own identity formation from the outset.

Equally troubling is that, in a material sense, her ability to live as an Orthodox Jewish woman in Israel is predicated on the success of

American capitalism and the rewards it has garnered for so many American Jews. While my daughter raises children and her husband studies Talmud, their economic needs are met by a father-in-law with few personal obligations other than those he has assumed on behalf of his children. Working as an emergency-room physician in a midwestern American city, his economic contributions remain my daughter's family's primary source of income, now that her college fund has been depleted.

Ironically, the Jewish world she inhabits has not gone untouched by feminism, nor have her expectations of her own future been entirely free of its influence. Jewish American orthodoxy has co-opted some of the language of feminism to praise women and female culture. For example, I am struck repeatedly by the ways in which it can be invoked to validate strict religious observance. My first encounter with this juxtaposition occurred when I heard my daughter and her high school friends defend the importance of modest dress, long sleeves and long skirts, as a way of making clear to men that they are not to be treated as sex objects. More recently, I was struck by a lesson plan left on the table in my daughter's home. A substitute at a female seminary catering to young American Orthodox high school graduates, she was preparing a class organized around the weekly Torah portion. Reviewing the laws against adultery, it dictated that female transgressors be more harshly punished than men. My daughter had prepared a list of questions to stimulate discussion. The first read, "Is it sexist that the woman should be punished more severely than the man?"

Especially among the children of the baby boomers, Orthodox family ideology enjoins young husbands and fathers to participate in child-rearing and household responsibilities. My daughter will argue that fathers participate much more readily in family life in her world than they do in mine. Her husband often does the shopping and cooking. The irony is not lost on either of us that these were important goals on my feminist agenda when she was a child, and that in my life they were never achieved.

Nor does her community simply give lip service to validating women's roles. It offers communal structures and a form of female homosociality that, within certain boundaries, give women a great deal of nurturing and support. My daughter's female teachers at

Yeshiva University Girls High School in Los Angeles were remarkably self-actualized individuals. From the perspective of the outsider, their lives appear dangerously seductive. I do not know whether the appropriation of feminist terms serves to disable feminism's potential for challenging traditional sex roles or whether, as some scholars argue, language will be a first step to altering the accepted meaning structures in which my daughter lives. These are issues I still ponder.

My argument, in the end, is about the self-construction and inventiveness that the shaping of identity requires in the modern world. Only when we take this dynamic and multicausal approach can we see that the ideas and practices that one assumes have long-standing traditional significance are actually being creatively fashioned in contemporary contexts that are novel and unstable. The past provides us only the materials with which to work.

What seems to be apparent is that my daughter's version of Judaism is quite literally dependent on the delegitimating of what I have gradually come to understand as mine. Stuart Hall reminds us that because questions of identity are always also questions about representation, they are "exercises in selective memory and they almost always involve the silencing of something in order to allow something else to speak."[19] My daughter believes that her identity is "eternally fixed in some romanticized and essentialized past."[20] She has no interest in dwelling on how she came to be a Jew; indeed, to do so would deeply threaten her sense of self. Ironically, if I still agreed with her in this, her return to what I used to think was a more "authentic" version of Judaism could give me the comfort and validation—the desire for *yichus*—that I craved as a young Jewish woman growing up in the 1950s. But I am a historian now, and postmodernism has disabused me of simplistic and reductionist versions of social explanation. It falls to me—to us—to follow a different and perhaps more troubled route to self-understanding.

NOTES

1. Lydia Kukoff, *Choosing Judaism* (New York: Union of American Hebrew Congregations, 1981).

2. Stuart Hall, "Who Needs Identity?" in *Questions of Cultural Identity*, ed. Stuart Hall and Paul du Gay (London: Sage Publications, 1996), 1–17, 1.

3. One of the best theoretical discussions of these issues is still Chris Weedon's *Feminist Practice and Poststructuralist Theory* (London: Basil Blackwell, 1987). Also very helpful to me has been the work of Nancy Theriot, especially *Mothers and Daughters in Nineteenth-Century America: The Biosocial Construction of Femininity*, rev. ed. (Lexington: University Press of Kentucky, 1996). The introduction is especially acute.

4. Stuart Hall, "Cultural Identity and Diaspora," in *Identity: Community, Culture, Difference*, ed. Jonathan Rutherford (London: Lawrence and Wishart, 1990), 222–37, 226.

5. See Theriot, *Mothers and Daughters*, 7.

6. Homelike, intimate, comfortable, and traditionally Jewish.

7. Hall, "Cultural Identity," 226.

8. See Deborah Dash Moore, *To the Golden Cities: Pursuing the American Jewish Dream in Miami and L.A.* (Cambridge: Harvard University Press, 1994), for a reconstruction of the various contexts of this migration.

9. For the challenges Conservative Judaism faced, see Marshall Sklare, *Conservative Judaism: An American Religious Movement* (New York: Schocken Books, 1972).

10. See Leslie Paris, "Adirondack Jewish Summer Camps" (paper delivered at the Third Scholars' Conference on American Jewish History, Hebrew Union College, Cincinnati, June 10–12, 1998).

11. The *musaf* service (additional service) is one of the major sections of the service on sabbath and festival mornings that is traditionally regarded as a substitute for the sacrificial service performed in the Temple. It does not easily lend itself to the idea of a woman being the *shaliach tsibur*, the person designated to represent the congregation in public prayer.

12. For the social context of growing up in the 1950s, see Elaine Tyler May, *Homeward Bound: American Families in the Cold War Era* (New York: Basic Books, 1988); Steven Mintz and Susan Kellog, *Domestic Revolutions: A Social History of Family Life* (New York: Free Press, 1988), chap. 9; Stephanie Koontz, *The Way We Never Were: American Families and the Nostalgia Trap* (New York: Basic Books, 1992), chaps. 1–6; Wini Breines, *Young, White, and Miserable: Growing Up Female in the Fifties* (Boston: Beacon, 1992); Susan Douglas, *Where the Girls Are: Growing Up Female with the Mass Media* (New York: Random House, 1994); Brett Harvey, *The Fifties: A Woman's Oral History* (New York: HarperCollins, 1994); and Joanne Meyerowitz, ed., *Not June Cleaver: Women and Gender in Postwar America, 1945–1960* (Philadelphia: Temple University Press, 1994).

13. See Norman Podhoretz, *Making It* (New York: Random House, 1967), 3.

Chapter 1, titled "The Brutal Bargain," begins: "One of the longest journeys in the world is the journey from Brooklyn to Manhattan—or at least from certain neighborhoods in Brooklyn to certain parts of Manhattan."

14. Hall, "Cultural Identity," 226.
15. Jacqueline Rose, quoted in Hall, "Who Needs Identity?" 6–7.
16. Hall, "Who Needs Identity?" 6–7.
17. *Yichus* can be defined as "lineage" and "relatives" but also as "status." I had no status because I had no relatives.
18. Lisa Lowe makes this very important point in *Immigrant Acts: On Asian American Cultural Politics* (Durham, N.C.: Duke University Press, 1996); see esp. chaps. 1 and 4.
19. Stuart Hall, "Negotiating Caribbean Identities," *New Left Review* 209 (January–February 1995): 3–14, 5.
20. Hall, "Cultural Identity," 226.

Chapter 8

The Identity of the Victims and the Victims of Identity: A Critique of Zionist Ideology for a Post-Zionist Age

Adi Ophir

The Position of the Victim

In his revealing discussion of the concept of *differend*, J.-F. Lyotard observed that "it is in the nature of a victim not to be able to prove that one has been done a wrong."[1] In other words, one *becomes* a victim when one undergoes a damage or an injury one is unable to prove. When one is unable to prove a damage, no compensation—no replacement for one's loss—is possible; one's loss is irretrievable. When there is a victim, there is an irretrievable loss; as long as one's loss is irretrievable, one *is* a victim.

Being a victim means being the "owner" of an irretrievable loss. When a damage can be demonstrated and compensation can be claimed and accepted, one's loss is retrievable. When compensation takes place and the loss is retrieved, one ceases being a victim. Through some act of exchange, an object that seemed to be irreplaceable is retrieved or replaced. Such an exchange may be prevented due to certain social, economic, and discursive conditions. It is the victim alone, however, who determines when such conditions take place. It is in the nature of a victim to be unable not only to obtain a replacement for a lost object for which she cares but also to conceive of an obtainable replacement as appropriate. The status of an object or a person as irreplaceable depends on an interested subject that would recognize it, him, or her as such, in its singularity and uniqueness. An object becomes replaceable and one ceases being a victim when one is capable of giving up this sense of singularity and is ready to do so and be content with a certain equivalence of value. A loss becomes absolute and one becomes its "owner" and victim when the lost object is conceived of and experienced as singular and hence irreplaceable.

The subjective economy of loss cannot be reduced to the objective economy of things. The two are obviously inextricably linked, but at the moment of absolute loss, this link seems to be severed. The absolute loss of an object means that the object is now entirely at the mercy of those who remember it. The object is completely subjectivized; it seems entirely flexible; its contours blur; its resistance diminishes; it has been lost and evaporated into the airy stuff of which memory consists. It is at this moment that the subject assumes full mastery over the object; the object is finally fully possessed. But what seems at first a moment of complete subjectivization *of* the object may turn out to be a moment of complete subjectivization *by* the object. The subject who does not forget and refuses to accept substitutes for an absolute loss is preoccupied with the disappearance of the singular object; he or she is possessed by the very cessation of being of the lost object. The victim of absolute loss is subjugated by the presence of an absence, dominated by a void.

To forget and to remember are two seemingly opposite ways of coping with the presence of an irretrievable loss. The forgetting of a lost object can console because—and as long as—the loss is forgotten together with the object. Remembering a lost object (through its representation in tales, paintings, songs, and, recently, in video clips) is capable of consoling because—and as long as—the representing image or text serves as a replacement, and the loss of the irreplaceable is forgotten. In both cases, the singularity of the lost object is negated. When the object is truly singular and irreplaceable and the loss is absolute indeed, even representation must fail, and memory can only betray this failure. It is in the nature of the victim to insist on this failure and never be content with substitutes and consoling representations.

In most cases, the work of memory, both collective and private, conceals the failure of representation through its very use of ordinary language, common tropes and images. Hence it is the duty of the artist or the poet who faces an absolute loss to force into presence, in and through the very activity of representation, the failure of representation.[2] Faced with this failure, readers and spectators, who are not necessarily "owners" and victims of this loss, would be reminded of the immemorial; they would not be allowed to forget a debt[3] that can never be paid. Through this work of representation and mourning, they would acquire a sense of absolute loss and would share the position of the victim of a loss of something that has never been in their possession.

Contemporary Jewish culture, in Israel and elsewhere, is inflated with agents that do just that: urge us not forget the immemorial and remind us of the failure of representation. Several cultural institutions and products come easily to mind here in the context of the commemoration of the Holocaust: Yad va-Shem, the Holocaust Memorial Museum in Washington, the nonmonument for the victims of the Holocaust that is planned for the city of Berlin, the death-camps pilgrimage, Claude Lanzmann's *Shoah*, Steven Spielberg's *Schindler's List*. The learned public often criticizes these institutions and products for their failure to remain within the boundaries of failure, and some of this criticism is justified. The point, however, is not how faithful these cultural agents are to the new standard of representation but that the display of the failure to represent through the work of representation itself has, indeed, become such a standard and is now framing the discourse about memory, remembrance, and loss. At the same time, a sense of an irretrievable loss has become something to be produced, acquired, or purchased; even the experience of absolute loss has become a cultural commodity.

The aura of absolute loss is a cultural construct; cultural agents and institutions of all kinds are involved in its construction. But while much of contemporary Jewish culture is devoted to the production of the aura of absolute loss, other segments of culture are busy, as always, with its effacement—that is, with the systematic effacement of losses as they occur. Both types of cultural practices—both the production and the effacement of the aura of absolute loss—are involved in the making and unmaking of victims, and they do so in opposite directions.

Both types produce victims. In the first case, the position of the victim is acquired through (more or less) willful participation in those practices that produce the aura of singularity by bringing representation to fail. Individuals and groups addressed by an act of failing representation are capable of purchasing a sense of loss with regard to objects that have never been in their possession. They thus learn to share the victim position and are made into subjects of absolute losses. At the same time, in the name of this loss, these individuals are capable of entering social struggles in which some of that loss would be transformed and become retrievable again and thereby would be put back into a circulation in a certain exchange system.

In the second case, when culture effaces absolute losses and negates the aura of singularity of lost objects, the position of the victim may be enforced. The failure of representation is a result of an obstacle imposed by a hegemonic discourse. Such a discourse is inevitably mute to some kinds of phrases; anyone who needs these phrases to articulate a damage would therefore be deprived of the means to prove that damage.[4] This happens because the damage cannot be represented within the constraints of the hegemonic discourse, because one is deprived of access to that discourse, or because there is nobody to take note of one's complaint. The deprived plaintiff becomes a victim.[5]

And yet, as much as *both* types of cultural practices are involved in victimization, *both* may help to unmake victims. When a victim is deprived of the means to prove a damage and the loss she suffers is effaced by a dominant discourse, one should help her re-create an aura of irretrievable loss and let her express her experience in a way that can be shared with others. Against the cultural mechanism and the social system that efface both the loss and the *differend* that accompanies it, one's duty is to identify traces of the loss by recovering a disguised failure of representation. But the reverse may also be true. When consoling practices provide a victim objects and representations to substitute for the lost object, when a consoling discourse distracts attention from the lost object and makes space for forgetfulness and forgiveness, the loss is gradually, even if never completely, effaced. When memory mediates between a subject and the presence of an absence by which he or she has been possessed, the victim may gradually recover.

The Identity of the Victim

People become victims in many, more or less cruel ways. Too often they lose and suffer what they do not deserve, deprived of compensation and relief, in unfair, let alone violent ways. Yet they do not necessarily get stuck in the victim position. They do not identify with this position; they do not conceive of or imagine themselves through the figure of the victim; and they do not commerce and communicate with others through the mediation of this position and that figure. More accurately, they do it quite often, but without consolidating the figure, without insisting on being hooked to that position, and without melting different victim positions they happen to occupy in different social spheres and in different times into one quasi-transcendental position of an eternal victim. They let others occupy the victim position when it so happens and recognize them as such, and they are ready to leave that position vacant whenever it is possible.

Some modern (especially, but not only, Israeli) Jews are not like other people in this respect. They seem fascinated by the victim position, in love with their losses.[6] It is from there that they start constructing their identity. It may seem that it is because they have suffered a great loss—the loss of a coherent Jewish identity—that they are busy reconstructing their Jewish identity to begin with. But in truth, it is the other way around: it is because they have been in need of a discourse of identity, for various, unrelated reasons, that they have reconstructed this Jewish identity as a loss that could never be fully retrieved. Since they already think about this loss from within the victim position—they are always already there—they cannot imagine that loss of identity apart from the many ways in which they or their ancestors have always been victims. In fact, because changes in Jewish life have been so immense and rapid in this century, sharing the victim position with their ancestors has become for many of them the safest and easiest way to relate to their genealogical roots and construct their identity as the victims' heirs. The many, variegated, and quite different cases in which Jews fell victim to non-Jewish aggression throughout history boil down to one long, repetitive story of victimization.

The apogee of this story is the Holocaust, no doubt. Hence the Holocaust is conceived of, thought, learned, and taught through the prism of the question of Jewish identity. The Holocaust is used and abused as a means in the construction of Jewish identity, and identity questions frame and shape the domain of Holocaust discourse. Therefore many Jews tend to think that they have inherited that unimaginable loss as one receives any other inheritance, by virtue of name and genealogy alone. Hence these Jews are mesmerized by an identity constructed around a victim position, which is mesmerized in its turn by an unimaginable loss, into which all other losses lead or are assembled. It is from an understanding of this mechanism of mesmerism by an absolute loss, by a loss invested with an aura of the irretrievable, that a discussion of "the question of Jewish identity" should commence.[7]

Indeed, the destruction of European Jewry is not the only traumatic event around which the identity of the victim is constructed in Zionist discourse. There is a structural similarity between the fascination of the nationalist Zionist discourse with the loss of the Land and the commemoration of the Holocaust in Israeli culture. Both cases involve a similar structure of identification, constructed in an analogous way around two very different losses: Exile (i.e., the loss of the Land and of sovereignty) and the Holocaust. The whole project of colonization initiated by the right-wing Zionist–religious movement Gush Emunim after the 1967 war may be interpreted in this light as an attempt to endow the Land of Israel with an aura of absolute loss.

In 1961 the trial of Adolf Eichmann transformed the way in which Israeli Jews cope with the memories of the Holocaust. It generated a new culture of memory and commemoration in which the extermination of European Jewry became the paradigm of absolute loss around which the new Jewish identity should be constructed. Six years later, during the weeks before the outbreak of the war, the traumatic preoccupation with the Holocaust shaped how Israeli Jews experienced both the threat posed by the Arab enemies before the war and their victory over their enemies after the war. Fear of an imminent Holocaust was replaced by a euphoric celebration of a miraculous triumph, and in both cases the reading of the political, military, and diplomatic reality was utterly distorted. It is from within this distortion that Gush Emunim was born.

Gush Emunim took it upon itself to accomplish a double displacement of the object of absolute loss. The object of the traumatic loss was displaced from the destruction of European Jewry to the destruction of the temple and the dispossession of the Land. The subject of loss was displaced from the position of eternal witness to the unfinished business of extermination, to the position of an eternal agent working in the unfinished business of redemption. What drove the Jewish colonizers was not simply a claim to regain their hold on a lost and now-reconquered piece of Land; something else was manifested in their discourse and activities. It was the insistence on expressing their claims in the most complicated political circumstances, in ways that have always made it impossible to cater fully to their demands. An immanent complaint about an unfinished business was there from the very beginning. In fact, this is a mark of messianism in general—the present is always conceived as an unfinished business of redemption. Gush Emunim did not introduce the messianic moment into Zionist discourse—that moment had been there from the beginning—but the religious nationalists brought it to perfection with a certain twist. In the case of the Jewish colonizers, what is unfinished is not simply the lack in redemption, imagined from the utopian perspective of a world to come, but precisely the opposite: the excess of loss imagined from the nostomanic perspective of a world that passed away long ago.

The work of colonization, that is, the work of return, of regaining the losses, has not been completed not because "the movement" (i.e., the "Gush") was too weak, or the stubborn people of Israel did not respond to the call, or the time was not ripe. The success of the colonizing project has never been complete because an immanent failure has been inscribed in its logic from the very beginning—an incarnation of the remainder of the loss. This has been the colonizers' greatest success so far. A whole nation is now possessed by the loss of an imaginary object that has never been hers—the Land of Israel. A whole nation is now prepared for the losses of a new war soon to come, which it is willing to justify in advance on the basis of the call emanating from the remainders—reminiscences and reminders—of the old loss.

The displacement of absolute loss by the religious nationalists did not, however, mean a replacement of one project (the commemoration of the Holocaust) by the other (the redemption of the Land). In fact, the two projects were quickly interwoven, feeding each other, each thriving on the myths and practices of the other. In both cases, an identification is constructed through the cultural work that makes present an irrecoverable loss. The visit of Benjamin Netanyahu to Auschwitz in the spring of 1998, marching with the Israeli flag in the death fields and preaching his "lesson" covered with a tallith, was a symbol of both the culmination and the merger of these two projects of identification *cum* victimization. It was, as Saul Friedlander would have said, a perfect performance of Kitsch and Death[8] performed by Israel's greatest performance artist, its present prime minster.

Being a Victim of Identity: The "Post-Zionist" Critique

Various cultural practices cope with the presence of absolute loss. The most paradigmatic is probably psychotherapy, but there are many others: bedtime stories; religious myths of redemption; the national oration that renders the stupid, senseless death of war into a beautiful death worth dying.[9] No doubt, it is not only compassion that motivates these discourses. The very presence in society of individuals possessed by a loss is a disruption of social order, a source of annoying embarrassment and a burden on any economy, since that which is beyond substitution immediately becomes a magnet for an unending stream of pacifying substitutes poured in vain into the abyss. The victim position gained by absolute loss creates debts whose interest one may enjoy for a long time; hence, holding a victim position can always be a strategy in social relations. Moreover, an object may always be endowed with the aura of singularity after it has been lost. Indeed, one of the main targets of psychoanalysis is to expose the economy of investments and gains associated with the subject's insistence on hanging onto the position of a victim of absolute loss. When a whole culture clings to such a position, the only therapy possible is critique, cultural and social criticism. This is, I believe (but will not be able to develop here), part of the role of critical theory in Israel today. Here is a case where a hegemonic culture and a hegemonic ideological discourse have not stopped exploiting the position of the victim as a strategy in both internal and external power struggles. And they have made consistent efforts to maintain this position, even in the

many, recurrent situations in which they have represented practices
of cruel victimization of others.

Yet, even when the consoling discourse is not simply pacifying but
critical, exposing the strategic aspect of the victim position, the experience of loss it has to cope with should not be considered a mere
fake. Misrecognition of losses does not reduce pain. The dilemma of
the critic is even more acute when critique exposes a loss as senseless
and its substitutes as bogus, thus forcing the subject to cope with absolute loss. Truth may be as unbearably painful in this case as misrecognition and fantasy were in the former case. What the so-called
post-Zionists, new historians, and critical sociologists have been doing
in Israel in the last decade is precisely to cause this pain. And they
have caused it both ways: by depriving Israeli Jews of their victim position, and by forcing them to confront the fact that they have been
victimizing others.

This new wave of cultural criticism deprives many Israelis of their
ability both to profit from their victim position and to give meaning
to their losses when they truly deserve the victim position. The new
historians thus exemplify a basic truth about *being* a victim. Unlike *becoming* a victim, which may be a result of contingent, ephemeral
forces, *being* a victim means taking, holding to, or being stuck in a victim position, which is always also an effect of a certain structured cultural field. The position of the victim is a cultural construct. It is produced, distributed, acquired, purchased, and sometimes even offered
for free. In the case of the new historians, it is taken away, to a lesser
or greater extent, from those who feel entitled to it by name, right of
inheritance, and personal losses. No wonder those critics have been
met with so much anger, condemnation, and contempt, and with so
few sober counterarguments.

The victim position has been a major asset of the Zionist movement and, later, of the State of Israel. The point is not to ask how Israeli Jews have become victims and heirs to victims whose injuries cannot be healed and whose losses cannot be retrieved. The point is to
understand how the victim position functions in Israeli culture; in the
state's ideology, the apparatuses in which it is embodied; and in the
construction of the constituting narrative of the Jewish state. The critique of Zionism demonstrates that the victim position functions as a

key structural element in the discursive fields in which Jewish and Israeli identities are shaped, negotiated, and fought for.

On the explicit thematic level of the basic Zionist narrative, Israeli Jews are represented as victims and heirs to victims (European Jews) who sought refuge and homeland in their fatherland, where they became victims of Arab violence. Their ongoing struggle against the various forms of violence that permeate every sphere of social life has been carried out in justice with great courage and talent.

In recent years, however, the so-called new historians, using new methodological and ideological perspectives and gathering new historical data, have questioned this narrative. They have taught us that Arab violence was all too often a response to Jewish aggressive colonization. Their writings reveal that Jews had options other than to fight; that their fight was not always courageous and was often unjust and cruel; and that once victorious, Israeli Jews have never shown the generosity necessary to turn an enemy into a friendly neighbor.

On a more implicit level, the new historians question the pragmatics of the Zionist narrative. They expose crucial gaps between this narrative's narrator (the hegemonic subject of Zionist ideology, usually the Ashkenazic Jew), its addressee (every Israeli Jew), and its protaganists (the Chalutz and its contemporary heirs—the settler or the agent of the secret services, etc.) The new historians call into question the all-too-easy collapse of these three narrative figures into the seemingly solid, universal figure of the Israeli Jew. This collapse makes it possible to identify uncritically the narrative's addressee with the figure of the Israeli Jew as a victim-hero.

The problematization of identity enacted by the new historians and critical sociologists, however, does not cease with questioning the identity of victim, whether as a theme of Zionist discourse or as one of its effects. Being a victim is not a ready-made identity but a position with which one identifies, a strategic position to be attained and maintained in various cultural fields. Understanding this enables us to expand and radicalize the critique of the new historians and critical sociologists, for it exposes the ideological work through which the victim position is constructed and maintained. This position is not merely a crucial component of the identity of the Israeli Jew but a key element in the mechanisms that construct it. In other words, what is at stake in the problematization of identity by the critics of Zionism is not merely identity but the forms and practices of identification. It is also the positions that one holds, maintains, loses, or gives up in order to be entitled to an identity and to become authorized to represent it or bestow it on others. The problematization of identification by a critique that radicalizes the work of the new historians subverts the basic structure of Zionist discourse and its ability to continue fabricating the identity of Israeli Jews.

Post-Zionism: Epoch or Cultural Critique?

As in the debates surrounding postmodernism, so, too, in the debates surrounding post-Zionism it is useful to distinguish, if only heuristically, between, on the one hand, (post)moderni*ty* as a set of historical conditions and, on the other hand, (post)moderni*sm* as a style or cultural position or a set of discursive strategies in the realms of art, literature, aesthetics, critical theory, and historiography. Modernism and postmodernism coexist in the contemporary world alongside and against a third major rival—the traditional antimodernist, who longs for a return to a premodern age. One of the main questions at stake in the dispute among these three ideal-types is whether there has been a real epoch-making difference between a modern and a postmodern age. An important difference among the three positions can be articulated through the responses to this question.

Similarly, one may distinguish between two senses of Zionism. On the one hand, Zionism may be conceived as a national movement, a vision, and a discursive regime (all three being interrelated in one project). In this case, anti- or post-Zionism may be conceived as certain critical stances vis-à-vis Zionist ideology. On the other hand, one may think of Zionism in terms of a set of historical conditions created and dominated by the Zionist project. "Anti-Zionist" may express longings for a pre-Zionist age, while "post-Zionist" may herald—or mark—the closure of the Zionist epoch. Once Zionism is understood as an epoch that may come to an end, the Zionist narrative of both ancient and modern Jewish history is called into question. At the same time, a Jewish history told from a non-Zionist perspective emerges as a proper context for a critical examination of the Zionist project, declaring the closure of the Zionist epoch, announcing it as a fait accompli, an imminent event, or a desired goal.

Was there indeed a Zionist epoch in the history of the Jews? What was this epoch? Has it really come to an end? If it has, what are the distinguishing features of this post-Zionist age? The answers to these questions are exactly what is at stake in the debate between Zionists and their anti- and post-Zionist critics. If there are clear-cut distinctions among these three positions, such distinctions must be articulated in relation to the question of the desired, accomplished, or threatening closure of a Zionist epoch in the history of the Jews. At the same time, the question of this Zionist epoch and its closure cannot be approached without taking a stance in the imaginary triangle defined by these three ideal-type positions.

In response to the question "Has the Zionist epoch come to an end?" Zionists, even critical Zionists, answer with a more or less reserved "no." Zionism is an ongoing project; therefore, one should still work hard to accomplish its unachieved goals. The present history of the Jews, it is argued, should still be thought of from the perspective of Zionist discourse, and its future should still be determined by a Zionist agenda. Anti-Zionists are those who, having opposed Zionism from its inception, wish to recover a world that was still devoid of its nationalist ideas and political and cultural practices. Anti-Zionists base their identity on the negation of Zionism. They acknowledge that the Zionist epoch is not over yet, that the Zionist project is still alive and kicking, perhaps more violently than ever. For this reason, Zionism should be opposed whenever possible. Thus, Zionist discourse still determines, by way of negation, the anti-Zionists' cultural and political agenda. Understanding Israeli society through the prism of the Zionist project, they conceive of it as a force that still structures this society and determines many of its ruptures and transformations.

Post-Zionists are presumably those who, while not necessarily accepting old anti-Zionist positions, deny the ongoing viability of Zionism. Thus, for post-Zionists, the Zionist epoch, an epoch in which the Zionist project held center stage, has come to an end. The major political, social, and cultural problems faced by Israeli and Diaspora Jews today should no longer be formulated within the framework of a Zionist discourse; nor can they be solved according to the principles

of a Zionist agenda. Israeli Jews, argue the post-Zionists, should develop a new democratic, civic discourse, or a new non-Zionist political discourse, rooted in the present conditions of Israeli society. Diaspora Jews should develop their own response to the new conditions
of Jewish life; this response is not necessarily related to the Israeli conditions and to the problems facing Israeli Jews.

The Post-Zionist Label

Before elaborating on the question of the (post)Zionist epoch, I
would like to ponder for a moment a simple, somewhat surprising
matter of fact. In Israel today, there are very few real, living and kicking *self-professed* post-Zionists who adhere to the position I have just defined for them. Moreover, very few people identify themselves as post-
Zionists. I personally know only three or four self-proclaimed post-
Zionists. One is Uri Ram, a sociologist from Ben-Gurion University.
For Ram, post-Zionism is a position that critically accepts certain aspects of postmodern culture and uses them to foster a strong Israeli
civil society that would counter recent chauvinistic, nationalist, and
fascist trends. Ram's post-Zionism accepts the existence of a Palestinian state alongside Israel as a fait accompli. Instead of conceiving Israel as a Jewish state, he views it as "a state of all its citizens," Palestinians and Jews alike. In other words, for the post-Zionist, nationality should not determine citizenship but vice versa: citizenship should
determine the boundaries of the Israeli nation. Judaism would then
be regarded as a religion, a community affair, or a matter of a particular ethnicity, one among many.[10]

Important as this ideological position is—and I think it is both important and just—it fails to do justice to the term it tries to define.
Some liberal Zionists, as well as many anti-Zionists, accept the inversion of the relation between nationhood and citizenship. Many Zionists share with Ram the idea of a strong Israeli civil society that would
oppose Jewish nationalism and racism. And, indeed, some of Ram's
closest associates in the debate, scholars and intellectuals like Tom
Segev, Benny Morris, Yoav Peled, Moshe Zuckermann, and Amnon
Raz-Krakotzkin, do not conceive themselves as post-Zionist or at least
have never declared themselves as such. Thus, for example, Moshe

Zuckermann, a social theorist who wrote an important study about the ways the imagery of the Holocaust was used during the Gulf war, is a communist and a straightforward anti-Zionist. Benny Morris, who coined the term *new historians* and whose contribution to the historians' debate is perhaps the most important, is a self-proclaimed Zionist. The historian Amnon Raz-Krakotzkin, whose treatise on Zionist "negation of exile" *(shlilat hagola)* is one of the most influential contributions to the formation of what Zionists understand as a post-Zionist consciousness,[11] refuses the title consistently. Post-Zionism, he argues, is an ideology for Jews only. A Palestinian Israeli cannot identify with it even if he or she accepts it to the letter. Thus, post-Zionism reproduces Zionism's main fault—the radical separation between Israeli Jews and Israeli Arabs.[12] Yet, notwithstanding their disavowal of the label, all these people have been called post-Zionists, and their works have often been presented as paradigms of post-Zionist discourse. For their opponents, at least, they occupy a position that precedes them and determines in advance the way they should be read.

The fact that the post-Zionist position is often associated with postmodernism, as the analogy presented above suggests, only intensifies the impression that the post-Zionist position has been ready and fixed in advance, regardless of the particular features of the works of those who occupy it. Among the growing group of new historians and critical sociologists, only one historian, Ilan Pappe, has tried to develop a postmodern historiography.[13] But even for him, those explicit postmodern historiographical reflections have never become part of his historical studies. Instead, they mainly serve him as a kind of apology for the ideological non-Zionist position he takes as a historian.

Only recently, however, a new generation of scholars, educated in the United States, England, and France, have introduced concepts, sensibilities, theoretical attitudes, and discursive practices that may be associated with postmodern forms of discourse, especially with postcolonial and feminist theories and with gay studies.[14] While they, too, hardly ever claim to be post-Zionist, they have been called post-Zionists by others.

Most of these so-called post-Zionists have been pushed into that position because of their more or less systematic critique of Zionist ideology and the apparatuses of the Israeli state in which this ideology is embodied and which it serves to legitimate. They are often accused of doing what any decent scholar of culture and society is supposed to do—questioning the conceptual grids and discursive practices of those whom they study, Zionists among others. Thus, for example, the so-called post-Zionists do not speak about *olim* but about immigrants; they do not mistake colonization for "redemption of the Land" or occupation for liberation. They examine economic interests behind the "conquest" of the labor market by Jewish hands.[15] Refusing to fully embrace the common image of Israel as "the only democracy in the Middle East," they critically analyze the apartheid aspects of Israeli citizenship.[16] Others explore/reveal the power relations involved in the formation of cultural entities such as Hebrew literature and Israeli art.[17] And they question the binary and teleological structure of the Zionist narrative and its self-evident divisions between "us" and "them," "our enemies." If this is enough to warrant the label "post-Zionist," then they are post-Zionists in the same way that critical students of capitalism are postcapitalists and critical students of liberal democracy are postliberals. The "post" affixed to the Zionist stance of those critics of Zionism designates merely a critical examination of an object of discourse and is not very useful.

The "post" may be more informative if, instead of looking for the meaning of the label, one seeks out its pragmatics. For "post-Zionism" is a label, and labeling is a speech act that serves Zionists as a mechanism of distinction and differentiation, a means of taking and allocating positions in a discursive field. The label functions mainly within Zionist discourse, in academic circles more than elsewhere, and it is certainly used by Zionists much more often than by their critics. Zionist scholars, the old hegemony in the fields of Jewish and Israeli studies (in Jewish history and thought, Israeli sociology, political science, Middle East studies, Hebrew literature), use this label to designate and address certain forms of critique that undermine their claim for legitimacy and authority. By doing this, they achieve two things at once: they determine who is an authorized speaker in the debate and which claims are to be taken seriously.

First, as Raz-Krakotzkin and Silberstein have noted,[18] the label frames the critique of Zionism as an internal Jewish controversy. Israeli Palestinians cannot be post-Zionists; they have been anti-Zionist all along. The critical discourse developed in the radical left in Israel is thus split in two. The all-too-important voices of Azmi Bishara and a few other Palestinian intellectuals, both in Israel and in the territories, are dissociated from those of their Jewish colleagues and relegated to the old niche of irreconcilable anti-Zionism. As for the Jews, they are often divided between an old form of anti-Zionism, mostly presented as outdated and irrelevant, and post-Zionism, which is considered worthy of some attention and presented as a deviation "within the family" caused mainly by the corrupting influences and bad intellectual manners of our time, namely, postmodernist theories and jargon. This association means that one should not take the arguments of the post-Zionists too seriously; it is more important to address the bad, corrupting effects of their discourse. As everyone knows, what postmodernists are best at is the deconstruction of narratives; hence, one should try to retell the narratives they are trying to dismantle.[19]

Indeed, this is the second effect of labeling: it is a convenient way to avoid coming to terms with the opponent's critique. The opponent's position is labeled in a way that undermines his or her authority, sincerity, and objectivity. Post-Zionist critique, we too often hear, is mean, heartless, cynical, full of self-hatred, and ignores the point of view of those it claims to study; it is relativist, ideologically biased, and imposes its interpretation on the facts or ignores them altogether.[20] These denunciations are well recognized and are repeated again and again, like tropes associated with a certain villain type in an old drama. As such, they are part of the preset position of the post-Zionist scholar. Their enunciation is supposed to screen out some of the more disturbing claims and effects of Zionism's contemporary critics. These denunciations protect the Zionist scholar from hearing the claims of its critic and seeing what the latter tries to show. Thus, the label "post-Zionist" functions as an obstacle for a critical dialogue between Zionists and their critics; in other words, it encloses Zionist ideology in a dogmatic position. Or better, it is a symptom of how dogmatic and ossified the latter has already become.

But it is misleading to say that Zionists neither hear what their critics try to tell them nor see what they are trying to show. They hear and see all too well. It is from what they hear and see that the negative reception and vehement rejection of some key post-Zionist works stem. (I think, for example, of the hostile reception accorded Tom Segev's *The Seventh Million,* Idith Zertal's *The Gold of the Jews,* and, of

course, Benny Morris's *The Birth of the Palestinian Refugee Problem.*)[21]
What they hear and see is the slow but irreversible process of untying
that web of beliefs that used to be Zionist ideology.

One of the key factors in the conditions leading to the post-Zionist critique has been a growing sense on the part of Israelis of the post-
1948 generation that they have been lied to and deceived. While
there are many examples of this sense to be found in the writings of
Morris, Gershon Shafir, and Michael Shalev, among others, I offer
here a personal testimony. It was not until the autumn of 1982 that I
learned the truth about the April 1948 massacre in the village of Dir-
Yassin, where two right-wing Jewish militias, the Irgun and the Stern
groups, killed more than two hundred villagers after the village had
surrendered. Before then, I consistently denied the claim of both
Arabs and left-wing Israelis that a massacre had occurred. I refused to
believe these claims because my father, who was a member of the
Irgun and had actually played a minor part in the atrocities, told me
otherwise; and I believed him wholeheartedly. After the massacre in
Sabra and Shatila in September 1982, under the impact of the terrible news, he told me that the massacre reminded him too much of another massacre to which he had been a witness many years ago. These
are the same kind of inhuman people, he said. It was then that I
learned for the first time that he had been lying to me all along. I also
learned that he had distorted the truth in a history book, in which he
documented the Irgun's activities in Jerusalem during the 1948 war.[22]
And I also learned that he did not tell me the whole truth about either the writing of this book or the conflicting versions of the massacre, which the book tries to refute.

I emphasize this experience of disillusionment because it helps
convey a sense of how the rather simple feeling of having been duped
has led many people, including many of the so-called post-Zionists, to
embrace a critical stance toward Zionist ideology. We have all too
often been duped by our parents and teachers, by our army com-
manders, by our public officials, and by so many representatives who
spoke in the name of the state. We have been deceived about the
myth of "a few against the many"—there were more Jewish than Arab
soldiers in 1948;[23] about the flight of the Palestinian refugees—too
many Palestinians were expelled or forced to leave, or shot dead
when they tried to return to their homes and fields;[24] about the rea-

sons for the Sinai war; and about the reasons and planning for the Lebanon war.[25] And even as I write these lines, we are being lied to about the so-called peace process and Israel's responsibilities for the stalemate after Rabin's assassination.

The post-Zionist critique of Zionist ideology, however, goes much further and much deeper than the refutation of some lies or of dubious propaganda. The refutation of these lies and the replacement of euphemisms with proper names clears the space for the acknowledgment that in the Zionist story there are victims other than Jews. Revealing the deception in the dominant Zionist narratives makes possible the representation of the "other" as a victim, not only a victimizer, and consequently allows Israelis the opportunity to accept responsibility for the victimization of others. In other words, the critic of Zionist ideology challenges the dominant image of the Israeli Jew as someone who always already occupies the victim position. This, I think, has been one of the main cultural effects of the research and writing of the so-called new historians and critical sociologists in the last fifteen years.

The Critique of Zionist Ideology

Thus, the new critique of Zionism deprives Israelis of the possibility of continuing to wallow in the identity of eternal, passive, and innocent victims. At the same time, it prevents them from imbuing their losses with a false heroic meaning or significance. "You have not been only victims and heirs to victims," the post-Zionists are telling their fellows, "you have been constantly victimizing others—Palestinians, Arab-Jews, and even the Holocaust survivors themselves."[26] And they argue this as well: "More than a portion of the sacrifices you have made and of the losses you have suffered have not been necessary. These losses cannot be justified by the usual edifying discourse of the 'beautiful death' for the sake of one's homeland—they have simply been superfluous. And they have been caused to a large extent by your insistence on the role of the victim that has made you blind both to your responsibility for the suffering of others and to the real options you have had to prevent at least some of those unnecessary losses."[27]

However, the "lessons" and some of the arguments that the new historians and critical sociologists make are not entirely new. Without going into details, I mention only some earlier critics of Zionism, such as Hannah Arendt, Martin Buber, and other members of Brith Shalom, and later the Ichud movement, the Palestinian Communist Party, the Matzpen movement, Uri Davis, Uri Avneri, and Simcha Flapan.[28] What distinguishes the new historians and critical sociologists from anti-Zionists, however, and makes them "post-Zionists" (as Avi Shlaim and Amnon Raz-Krakotzkin have noted)[29] is the fact that, for the first time, the critique of Zionism is being carried out in the discourse of and with the authorial stamp of the academic world, both within Israel and outside it. And yet, this reflects more than a change in the academic world alone. The critique of Zionism became a legitimate academic enterprise and was undertaken by mainstream intellectuals only because, for many Israelis, some of the major themes of that critique have long been self-evident. What has changed is not so much the content of the critique of Zionism but the place it holds within Zionist discourse and within Israeli culture at large. This very change is one of the clear marks of a post-Zionist epoch.

We may now return to the question posed above: Has the Zionist epoch come to an end? It is through the figure of the victims of the Zionist project, which various kinds of post-Zionist discourse help to delineate, that the closure of the Zionist epoch appears both inevitable and desirable. By this I do not mean a simple judgment of an end according to the means necessary for achieving it or according to the price that has to be paid. What I mean is that the figure of Zionism's victims is a mirror that reflects—for those capable of seeing—the end of Zionism.

The early Zionists conceived of Jews as victims of anti-Semitic persecutions and of their own degenerate way of life in the Diaspora, yet they did not assume the victim position. They engaged not in mourning irretrievable losses but in creating new forms of Jewish life in (what for them was) a new country. Only later, in Palestine, when conditions changed radically and others became the unexpected victims of their enterprise did they gradually assume the position of the victim. Even the Holocaust did not place them in that position before the Eichmann trial, in which David Ben-Gurion, his attorney general, Eichmann's prosecutor, and a group of court journalists made the easy association between the Nazis of yesterday and the Arab enemies of today.[30] Zionists embraced the victim position after June 1967, when their victimization of others grew both in number and in scope. In the summer of 1982 in south Lebanon, many Israeli Jews realized for the first time that they, too, had become victims of the expanding Zionist enterprise and the Israeli state that speaks in its name. And there were tens of thousands of Arab victims as well. Then came the Intifada, in which Palestinian victims claimed their rights in a way that many Israelis could no longer ignore. It was at that moment, perhaps, that the other was perceived not simply as an accidental victim of some "deviations" *(charigim)* in the functioning of an otherwise decent system of governance but as a victim of the Zionist enterprise itself. The figure of the other as victim subverted the self-image of the Zionist occupying the victim position and has come to reflect the end of Zionism.

The reflection of this end may be formulated by a series of inversions of Zionism's initial claims, goals, and tenets. In each of these inversions, the Zionist project is contrasted with its contemporary realization, which always involves victimization of others.

The idea of a national liberation movement and the right of national self-determination, upon which the main political claim of Zionism was based, have been systematically undermined, negated, and denied by the success of the Zionist movement. This success has produced the ongoing oppression of another national movement and repeated attempts to destroy it.

Zionism was a revolt against European anti-Semitism and, later, against racism, and many of those who took part in this struggle were later victims of racism and anti-Semitism. But the struggle has yielded a society that tolerates, and sometimes actively supports, the emergence and consolidation of a Jewish racism that constantly victimizes its others.

The enlightened struggle to guarantee full civil rights to Jews by means of a sovereign Jewish political entity gave birth to an apartheid system of citizenship. The Jewish state administers populations, territories, and lives according to a strict distinction among six classes of subjects: Jewish citizens; Palestinian citizens ("Israeli Arabs"); Palestinians devoid of citizenship under Israeli martial law; Palestinian semi-citizens of the Palestinian authority in the Gaza Strip, under permanent military curfew; Palestinian semi-citizens of the Palestinian authority in the West Bank, under partial military curfew; and, finally, guest workers denied any legal rights, who too often resemble slaves more than guests.

The Jewish state achieved some but by no means all of the objectives of Zionism. Even before it was established, the Zionist vision had been embodied in the ideological apparatuses of the emerging state. Today, the state is not an instrument of the Jewish national movement but vice versa. Jewish nationalism in general and Zionist ideology in particular are the state's instruments, used for political purposes. Old and new forms of Zionist discourse serve to legitimate the apartheid system of the Jewish state, Jewish control of the land, continuous involvement in warfare activities, the ongoing occupation, and the intentional undermining of the processes of negotiation and reconciliation with the Palestinians that were built in Oslo.

Zionism was supposed to transform Jewish economy and turn Jews into productive workers. In the Jewish state, Jews have abandoned most kinds of manual and traditional industrial labor to others. A system of labor relations has formed in which Jews control capital and the means of production while non-Jews work in their fields and factories, sometimes in inhuman conditions, underpaid and exploited.

It is clear that much more than the position of the victim is at stake here. Many of the contemporary conditions of Jewish life in Israel are an inverted realization of the basic tenets of Zionist ideology. The series of inversions presented above may be further extended to include other inversions in which the figure of the other as a victim (or of the victim as other) blurs into the background but does not entirely disappear. At the same time, more Israeli Jews recognize themselves as victims (or potential victims) of the Zionist project and its consequences.

Jews have gained political sovereignty and a mighty army, but Israel, whose population is constantly threatened by conventional, chemical, and nuclear weapons, has become the most dangerous place on the globe for Jews.

Messianic themes have always been present in Zionist discourse, animating its vision. In today's Israeli politics, political themes sometimes animate the messianic form that Zionist discourse has taken. Not that all Zionists have become messianic; but it is in and through discourse dominated by messianic political theology that they articulate their claims.

The melting pot of Jewish ethnic communities has become an overboiling pot of ethnic and religious conflicts. "National Unity" is an empty slogan that witnesses the shattering of unity to pieces. The only thing that keeps all these communities together is the state with its apparatuses, and a war that never ends.

Zionist ideology contained a vision about building a Jewish community in Palestine that would be a spiritual center. To the extent that this Jewish community still maintains spiritual aspirations, they are the most eccentric that Jews have known since the collective suicide on Masada. To the extent that this community maintains a central position in the Jewish world, this position is due first and foremost to the most nonspiritual element in Jewish tradition, the contemporary forms of the sword—conventional, chemical, nuclear. If some spiritual merit is preserved nevertheless, it is either not particularly Jewish or not particularly central.

The Zionist epoch has come to a close precisely because the Zionist vision has been realized. We live in a post-Zionist age as a direct result of the success of the Zionist enterprise; the realization of the basic tenets of Zionist ideology has inverted these tenets. This is not the place to try to explain why it has all happened this way, nor even to demonstrate that the inversion described above really took place. I assume that it did take place, and that to show this, it suffices to juxtapose a series of commonplaces about Zionism with a series of commonplaces about Israel today. The commonsense nature of this juxtaposition is telling. It makes the systematic failure of Zionist discourse to comprehend the present historical conditions of Jewish life, especially in Israel, both understandable and unavoidable. Zionist discourse reflects the reality it seeks to explain, but this reflection is inverted. Zionist discourse denies this inversion and projects that denial on an imaginary enemy, the post-Zionist. Zionism was once a vision, a national movement with a political and cultural agenda. The concrete realization of the vision has turned Zionist discourse into an ideology in the strict and most simplistic Marxist sense of the term, except for one thing: the inversion takes place in the open, outside the *camera obscura* and without its help.

Everything that this ideology touches melts into air, into the void created by the straightforward contradictions between what anyone can see for oneself and what a Zionist can say. The contradictions can be observed by everyone; anyone can be the critic of that ideology. The contradictions I have described above are not something I have exposed with the clear mind and analytic tools of an unbiased observer (which I am not) or of a Marxist dialectician (which I also am not). The interesting point about Zionist ideology, since the mid-1980s at least and certainly in the late 1990s, is that the two contradictory descriptions of social reality coexist, side by side, in the public sphere and in the media. They are pronounced by the agents themselves, by the subjects of ideology. They are sometimes even uttered by the same people in the same context of enunciation. Politicians and generals keep telling us how strong and militarily potent and yet entirely vulnerable Israel is. Those who speak about "national unity" exemplify discord and irreconcilable differences in their very preaching to unity. Those who speak for human rights quite often support the major element of the apartheid system—the so-called separation *(hafrada)* between Israelis and Palestinians. Those who condemn racism in one context are willing to tolerate or even support it in other contexts.

There exists an unbridgeable gap between the Zionist representation of historical-political reality and many of its commonsense representations. Many Israelis, so it seems, are not really bothered by this contradictory situation, perhaps because they hardly care for the Zionist discourse anymore. There is also a frightening minority of dogmatic Zionists who do not care for the real and therefore do not sense any contradiction. But there are many who do sense the contradiction but, being deeply invested in Zionist discourse, are too reluctant to admit it outright and too quick to dismiss or overlook it, hoping that the embarrassment will somehow disappear.

Post-Zionism plays an important role in how ordinary, commonsense Zionists cope with the contradictory situation created by Zionist ideology. Post-Zionism serves as a displacement of the contradiction as well as a screen on which it can be projected and become bearable. The contradiction no longer takes place between Zionist representation of historical-political reality and its ordinary, commonsense representation but rather between Zionism and post-Zionism, conceived as two ideologies with rival truth claims. The figure of the other as a victim also becomes bearable, for it emerges from within a rival ideology that lacks any authority. This displacement may explain why Zionists so often invoke a simplistic association of post-Zionism with vulgar postmodernism and relativism; they need this caricature of postmodernism in order to salvage themselves from their own embarrassing contradiction. The contradiction is related to the existence of a rival ideological position, and the debate is stuck in a methodological muddle, pushing aside issues of substance (see above, page 187). The real, historical conditions that Zionist ideology represents in an inverted way can once again be recognized and ignored, thought and unthought at the same time.

This situation, I believe, is short-lived. In a few years, Zionism will become a relic, an object for museums and history departments only. Post-Zionism will be remembered as the name for the moment in which Israeli Jews became fully aware of the passing of the Zionist epoch in the history of the Jews. This is the moment in which Israeli Jews will allow people other than Jews to assume the position of victim and assume responsibility for all those "other" victims of the Zionist enterprise.

NOTES

1. Jean-François Lyotard, *The Differend: Phrases in Dispute* (Minneapolis: University of Minnesota Press, 1988), 9.
2. Lyotard develops this theme in his reading of Kant's analytic of the sublime and in many of his essays on paintings. See, e.g., Jean-François Lyotard, *Lessons on the Analytic of the Sublime* (Stanford, Calif.: Stanford

University Press, 1994) and "Representation, Presentation, Unpresentable," in *The Inhuman* (Stanford, Calif.: Stanford University Press, 1988).

3. The debt stems from the irreplaceability of the singular. If replacement had been possible, the debt would have been canceled, and the loss would have been lost without a trace.

4. This is Lyotard's definition of "wrong" *(tort)* in *The Differend*, 7.

5. This is Lyotard's paradigmatic case, for which many examples can be easily given: for instance, the Bedouin, the Aborigine, and the American Indian cannot prove their entitlement to a piece of land because their cultures never inscribed the relation between men and their lands in terms of property and ownership.

6. The history of the Jews, in this century at least, may explain this tendency, but it certainly does not justify it. The problem is, however, that this history is already told, for the most part, from within a victim position.

7. I have elaborated on this theme elsewhere. See Adi Ophir, "The Finitude of the Solution and the Infinity of the Loss," in *The Holocaust in Jewish History*, ed. Yehuda Bauer (Jerusalem: Yad Vashem, forthcoming).

8. Saul Friedlander, *Reflections on Nazism: An Essay on Kitsch and Death* (New York: Harper & Row, 1984).

9. Cf. Lyotard, "Beautiful Death," in *The Differend*, 156.

10. Uri Ram, "Post-Nationalist Pasts: The Case of Israel," *Social Science History* 24, 4 (1998): 513–45; idem, "Zionism and Post-Zionism: The Sociological Context of the Historians' Debate," in *Between Vision and Revision: One Hundred Years of Zionist Historiography* [in Hebrew], ed. Y. Weitz (Jerusalem: Merkaz Zalman Shazar, 1997); idem, "Between Neozionism and Post-Zionism: A Sociological Clarification" [in Hebrew], *Gesher* 132 (Winter 1996): 93–97. See also Laurence Silberstein, *The Postzionism Debates: Knowledge and Power in Israeli Culture* (New York: Routledge, 1999), introduction and 89–113.

11. Amnon Raz-Krakotzkin, "Exile within Sovereignty: Toward a Critique of the 'Negation of Exile' in Israeli Culture," *Theoria ve-Bikoret* (1994) 4:23–55 and 5:113–32; Silberstein, *Postzionism Debates*, 175–83.

12. Amnon Raz-Krakotzkin, "Historical Consciousness and Historical Responsibility," in *Between Vision and Revision*, ed. Weitz.

13. Ilan Pappe, "The New History of the 1948 War," *Theoria ve-Bikoret* 3 (1993): 99–114; and "Critique and Agenda: The Post-Zionist Scholars in Israel," *History and Memory* 7, 1 (1995): 66–90.

14. See Silberstein, *Postzionism Debates*, chap. 6.

15. Gershon Shafir, *Land, Labor, and Origins of the Israeli-Palestinian Conflict, 1882–1914* (Cambridge: Cambridge University Press, 1989).

16. See, e.g., Yoav Peled, "Ethnic Democracy and the Legal Construction of Citizenship: Arab Citizens of the Jewish State," *American Political Science Review* 86, 2 (1992): 432–43; idem, "Strangers in Utopia: The Israeli Palestinian Citizens" [in Hebrew], *Theoria ve-Bikoret* 3 (1993): 21–35; Danni Rabinowitz, *Overlooking Nazareth* (Cambridge: Cambridge University Press, 1996).

17. For literature, see, e.g., Hannan Hever, "The Struggle over the Canon," *Theoria ve-Bikoret* 5 (1994): 55–77. For art, see, e.g., Ariella Azoulay, "The Possibility for Critical Art in Israel," *Theoria ve-Bikoret* 2 (1992): 89–117; and Sara Chinski, "The Silence of the Fish," *Theoria ve-Bikoret* 4 (1994): 105–22.

18. Raz-Krakotzkin, "Historical Consciousness and Historical Responsibility"; and Silberstein, *Postzionism Debates,* 113–26.

19. See, e.g., Anita Shapira, "Politics and Collective Memory: The Debate over the 'New Historians' in Israel," *History and Memory* 7, 1 (1995): 9–40; Aharon Megged, "Israeli Suicidal Desire," *Haaretz,* 10 June 1994, 27–28.

20. See, e.g., Megged, "Israeli Suicidal Desire"; Gideon Kersel, "Mentality: Intelligence, Morality, and Jewish-Arab Conflict," *Theoria ve-Bikoret* 8 (1996): 47–72.

21. Tom Segev, *The Seventh Million: The Israelis and the Holocaust* (New York: Hill and Wang, 1993); Idith Zertal, *The Gold of the Jews* (Berkeley: University of California Press, 1998); Benny Morris, *The Birth of the Palestinian Refugee Problem* (Cambridge: Cambridge University Press, 1987).

22. Yehushua Ophir, *Al Hachomot* (On the walls) (Ramat-Gan: Massada, 1960).

23. There were more Jewish than Arab soldiers in 1948, at least until the invasion of the Arab states in May 1948. Cf. Uri Milstein, *History of the War of Independence,* vol. 1 (Lanham, Md.: University Press of America, 1996), 184.

24. Morris, *Birth of the Palestinian Refugee Problem;* and idem, *Israel's Border Wars, 1949–1956: Arab Infiltration, Israeli Retaliation, and the Countdown to the Suez War* (1993; reprint, Oxford: Clarendon, 1997).

25. About the Sinai war, see Motti Golani, *Israel in Search of a War: The Sinai Campaign, 1955–1956* (Brighton: Sussex Academic Press, 1994). About the Lebanon war, see Zeev Schiff and Ehud Yaari, *The War of Deceit* (Jerusalem: Schocken, 1984).

26. See, e.g., Segev, *Seventh Million,* part 3; Ella Shohat, "Sephardim in Israel: Zionism from the Standpoint of Its Jewish Victims," *Social Text* 19–20 (1988): 1–35.

27. Avi Shlaim, *Collusion across the Jordan* (Oxford: Clarendon, 1988); Gershon Shafir, "The Yaring Affair," *Theoria ve-Bikoret* 12–13 (1999): 205–13.

28. Nira Yuval Davis, "Matzpen, the Socialist Organization in Israel" (master's thesis, Hebrew University of Jerusalem, 1977); Simcha Flapan, *The Birth of Israel: Myths and Realities* (New York: Pantheon, 1987); Uri Avneri, *Israel without Zionists: A Plea for Peace in the Middle East* (New York: Macmillan, 1968); Silberstein, *Postzionism Debates,* chaps. 2 and 3.

29. Avi Shlaim, "The Debate about 1948," *Journal of Middle Eastern Studies* 27 (1995): 287–304; Raz-Krakotzkin, "Exile within Sovereignty."

30. See Idith Zertal, "From the People Hall to the Wailing Wall: A Study in Memory, Fear, and War," *Representations* (forthcoming March 2000).

Chapter 9

Mapping Literary Spaces: Territory and Violence in Israeli Literature

Hannan Hever

> As citizens we received identity cards from our state. But as intellectuals, the state will get its identity card from us. And the card which we present to the state will impose on us sublime obligations, missions, and educational roles.[1]

The critic Avraham Kariv, cited here from his 1950 address to the first Writers Association Conference after the founding of the State of Israel, clearly points to the role of Hebrew literature as a cultural mediator, constituting, establishing, and constructing identity. Literature emerges in Kariv's statement as a channel through which to represent—and thus also to model—the national imagined community whose identity would be borne by the collective national "I" of the State of Israel. As an imagined national community in Benedict Anderson's well-known sense,[2] this collective exceeds the boundaries of a community within which subjects maintain a face-to-face acquaintance and presages instead a community based on mediated contacts among its members.

Speaking of Israeli national identity as a mission or task to be fulfilled through literature, Kariv adds his voice to a varied and tortuous series of interventions whereby literary discourse (the texts themselves, but also, and to no less extent, writing and discussion of these texts) is recruited to the task of constituting collective national identity. In the forefront, at the visible plane of the discourse, the literary has served to render a rather coherent narratological process compatible with the hegemonic Zionist narrative since the founding of the State of Israel, and even well before that. In this narration, the metaphor of "Hebrew literature," that is, literature produced in the Diaspora, comes first. Second, the narrative recounts how this literature immigrated to Eretz-Israel, in a process of reterritorialization and transcendence, to become the national literature of a sovereign state. "Hebrew literature," characterized and defined by the use of the Hebrew language, was transformed into "Eretz-Israel" literature, characterized by an attachment to territory. In the last stage, it became "Israeli literature." No longer the literature of a diasporic people, this literature was transformed into that of a sovereign nation in its nation-state.

In the teleological narrative of national identity construction we encounter the confluence of the literary text with space, a space that remains constant and unchangeable. Here, space is understood as the land to be occupied and placed under sovereign rule. In many ways, this particular narrative of identity construction intersects the issue of territory and the quest to achieve sovereign rule over it. This narrative process is variously conceptualized in terms of a future stage yet to be attained, an event that occurred in the past, or one to which the narrated time clings and about which it congeals.

An example of the last instance is the autobiographical piece "Independence '48–'92," published by S. Yizhar in 1992 in the daily *Hadashot* on the eve of Israel's Independence Day.[3] In this text, Yizhar provides a personal account of the expulsion of the people of the southern village of Merar from their territory, an event that took place simultaneously with the announcement of the founding of the State of Israel on May 14, 1948.[4] Thus, in 1992, five years after the start of the Intifada (Palestinian uprising), Yizhar retells the same story of the Palestinian expulsion that he told in his famous text "The Story of Hirbat Hiza'a," published in 1949.[5] The earlier story recounts how a platoon of Israeli soldiers expelled the people of the Palestinian village of Hirbat Hiza'a. However, the two pieces differ in many ways: whereas "Independence" is autobiographical and documentary, "Hirbat Hiza'a" is fictional; the later text occurs on a spring day, whereas the earlier one takes place on a bright wintry day. Most important, however, whereas "Hirbat Hiza'a" is a morality tale that emphasizes the terrible injustice committed against the Palestinians driven from their homes, the emphasis in the 1992 version shifts to a bitter political commentary.

But one thing remains constant in these two narratives, as in all Yizhar's writings—and in all state-era writing. This constant is the space of Eretz-Israel–Palestine as a recurrent turning point in the basic Israeli identity narrative. Time and again in Israeli literature we encounter variations on a basic narrative about a people, the Jewish people, said to possess a shared past rooted in a common origin. In this narrative, a group, the Jewish people, marked by diversity and heterogeneity, is transformed into a single unified body. In the process, the people acquires a new national identity and is integrated with the land, which becomes the literal ground for the existence of the nation-state. Territory is always represented as a space that has already been occupied and violently incorporated—a postcolonial space.

The theme of space, whether as a turning point or a necessary evolutionary stage, recurs in the basic narrative of national constitution, the achievement of national sovereignty. In this identity narrative, the represented space is always the space "after the event"—after the occupation, after the territorial struggle.

The Zionist national narrative thus seeks to resolve the contradiction between Jewishness, perceived as constant over time, and Israeliness, perceived as a break in continuity brought about by the quest to establish a new territory—a dominated, colonial territory, one might add. Significantly, this contradiction is never "just" resolved—it is resolved violently. Violence is the inevitable outcome of the attempt to establish a homogeneous Israeli identity based on sovereign rule over territory.

Alongside this colonial representation of space in Hebrew literary language, we find traces—frequently only partial traces—of the conflict that occurred in that space. For example, the sites of the Jewish National Fund Forest or the Negev Desert, overtly or covertly, encode in themselves traces of the violence that accompanies occupation. The permanent and audible presence of this violence in the representational infrastructures of Israeli space renders problematic the attempt to transform Hebrew literature into Israeli literature. Instead, we are presented with an unusually complex, dynamic, and multilayered picture. A whole range of processes and causal factors disrupts what is presented as a progression. Thus, the continued presence in Israeli literary discourse of a colonized space saturated with violence impedes the final transformation of Hebrew into Israeli literature.

For one thing, the effort to integrate the Jewish people into the physical space repeatedly encounters obstacles: the people(s) living in this territory continually disrupt the smooth progression of this integration. The ongoing need to vanquish this indigenous population cannot be totally erased in the representation of space. "Who could have known," wrote Yizhar in his 1992 piece, "that the question to which [the founders of the State of Israel] did not attend or did not dare ask at the time would become the crucial question . . . What to do with these people? . . . The expulsion did not erase them. The expulsion solved nothing. And there is no other issue for us. [It has been this way] ever since the founding of the state."

The construction of collective "we" that Yizhar represents in his stories and essays, a function of the literary discourse's obsessive preoccupation with the constitution of identity, is never brought to a successful conclusion. There is no point at which "our" confrontation with "them" is completed. Consequently, the movement from Hebrew literature to Israeli literature is neither clear-cut nor fully consummated. It remains, however, an obsessive preoccupation.

Moreover, in the common interchangeable use of the terms *Hebrew literature* and *Israeli literature* to signify the selfsame corpus, the interchangeability of linguistic identity and political-territorial identity is presumed. Also, territorial stability remains elusive. Thus, time and again, the conflict over the territory evokes the conflict of identities, which remains a key to the national story.

Yizhar's "The Story of Hirbat Hiza'a" represents the tension between historical continuity and historical rupture, a tension in which space itself becomes dichotomized. On the one hand, the narrator adopts a static perspective on "the great land [that] stretches in front of you." On the other hand, that space is immediately historicized as "fields which will not be harvested . . . in vain was it all."[6] Not withstanding this dichotomy, the identity narrative of Israeli literature conceals the conflict between rupture and historical continuity. Moreover, in its quest for a stable, coherent subject, the identity narrative also effaces traces of the violence of territorialization.

In response to this precarious situation, the Zionist narrative constricts and reformulates itself into what Stuart Hall calls a "cover story."[7] This cover story seeks to reduce and to condense the conflicted identities arising out of the violent struggle over territory, which the Zionist narrative can neither eschew nor absorb. This failure of the Zionist national narrative also derives from an internal paradox. We have, on the one hand, a story of Jewish continuity, of the Jewish people returning to their land and undergoing a process of territorialization. On the other hand, there is a parallel story of rupture and rebellion: the story of the Hebrews' rejection of the Diaspora Jew. The "New Jew," the newly territorialized Hebrew, seeks to shed his or her Jewish past in order to assume citizenship in the Israeli state.

Highlighting the tension between Jewish ethnic continuity and Zionist discontinuity is a vast, contested territory saturated with violence. On this terrain a number of possible identities emerge, such as native Israeli, Jewish Israeli, Canaanite, and others. These differently articulated identities arise from the constant ambivalence and tension that Homi Bhabha has called the "tension between the synchronic panoptical vision of domination—the demand for static identity—and the counter-pressure of the diachrony of history— change, difference."[8]

Embedded in the teleological narrative of identity formation is a struggle between different approaches to erasing the basic conflict between continuity and discontinuity. The major literary apparatus through which the narrative seeks to construct a coherent collective identity is national allegory, in which the collective story is transformed into a private one. This is evident in "The Story of Hirbat Hiza'a." At the center of the story lies the private sensitivity of the fighter, the gazing "I," who experiences and testifies to the events of the expulsion of the people of Hirbat Hiza'a. Imbuing the quest for a collective national identity with the coherence of a personal story, this allegorical technique seeks to gloss over the conflict within the Israeli collective identity narrative. Over the years, this allegorical technique has functioned as a major reading strategy for literature written in the State of Israel. Through it, the reader is encouraged to read the story of the national collective as a personal drama, which draws on universal models.

Through a coherent personal narrative, the text allegorically blurs or even erases the traces of violence inherent in the process of nation building. Representing the identity of the "I" as an allegory of collective national identity that seeks territorial sovereignty and control has the effect of transforming the violent and often cruel struggle over territory and sovereignty into the more benign discourse of individual identity construction.

Yizhar's story, an example of the literary inscription of the dominant Israeli national narrative, seeks to conceal the violence by distancing the very site of violence from the self. The Other, the object of violence, is displaced in order to render the violence invisible. This "elimination" of the Other is achieved by transforming the Other's concrete, particularized presence into the humanist universal construct of "everyman." This mechanism of universalization transforms "them" into "us" through the erasure of the sharp asymmetry between occupier and occupied. In its most extreme articulation, the Other is made to "become Jewish." Thus, in Yizhar's universalizing trajectory, the expulsion of the Palestinians from Hirbat Hiza'a is represented as exile. In the protagonist's "lightning" flash of epiphany, he sees the expulsion as nothing other than *Jewish* exile: "This is," he says to himself, "what exile looks like."[9] In other words, the protagonist of "The Story of Hirbat Hiza'a" can decipher the fate of the Palestinian Others only through the lens of his Jewish ethnocentricity. This is the case whether he identifies the Palestinians with Jewish refugees or whether he sarcastically dismisses this analogy ("All the stories they told us about refugees. . . . Killing Jews. Europe. Now we are the masters.")[10] Either way, the representation of the Other follows the contours of Jewish identity construction, thereby neutralizing the violent histories of the space populated by the Palestinians and rendering this space pliable to the needs of the history of Israeli integration.

Through the mirror image of the Other, the national allegory tries time and again to constitute Israeli identity by weaving the private story together with the collective one. Through this weaving, it seeks to erase the conflict between Jewishness and Israeliness and to repress the violence resulting from the Israeli appropriation of space. The contradiction between Jewishness and Israeliness is thus linked to a repression of violence. By repressing the Israeli in favor of the anterior Jewish narrative, the contradiction works itself out, but only by deferring the attainment of a distinctive Israeli identity that is free from the effects of exile. This deferral occurs time and again in the attempted transition from Hebrew to Israeli literature. Rather than basing its identity on citizenship in a national state, Israel continues to ground it in ethnocentric considerations.

The universalization of the humanistic national allegory reinforces or reinscribes the myth of *Jewish* origin in the field of representation. The narratology movement from Jewish to Israeli recedes to its Jewish ethnocentric stage. The Jewish element is never lost; it always remains alive and active, metaphorically interchangeable with other identities—territorial, religious, class, gender—which it replaces. And as with all allegories, it always fails to achieve its goal. The private story never fully suits the collective one. The allegory constructing national identity remains always partial. It its representations of the Other, it achieves neither total erasure nor willed blindness, only ambivalence.

Rather than actual erasure, what are usually presented are the failed efforts of erasure. As in Yizhar, the Other is represented as that which will lend itself to erasure in a later phase. At that point, the Other will resume its position of subjection, the better to arouse a fully humanist sensitivity that feeds into the Jewish construction of Israeli identity. Thus, the Other is portrayed not as different and "other" but as a "non-I" who wears my features and speaks in my voice: it is this Other who is today's authentic suffering Jew. In this cycle of avowal and disavowal, the Other is reduced to a trigger for my universal moral sensibilities and, as such, also serves as the object of my desire.

The ambiguous legacy of universalization is still evident in Yizhar's 1992 text, which binds those who expel to those who have been expelled and opts for the universalistic argument that "expulsion solves nothing. Here they are and here are we, the expelling and the expelled." And forty years after "The Story of Hirbat Hiza'a," the same mirror image allows David Grossman, in his book *The Yellow Wind,* to portray Hadijah, the Palestinian refugee living under occupation in the Dehaisha refugee camp, as someone who "reminds me of my grandmother and her stories of Poland, from which she was uprooted. Of the river. Of the fruits there. Time impressed on both their faces the same letter, entirely composed of wisdom and irony, and great skepticism concerning all men, whether relative or stranger."[11]

Moral identification with Palestinian suffering, through which Jewish identity is projected onto the Palestinian, enables the Israeli onlooker to assume an ambivalent stance in which responsibility for this suffering is both avowed and disavowed and is replaced by expressions of weakness and helplessness. Thus, Yizhar relates the cruelty of expulsion from the point of view of the hegemonic collective in whose name he speaks. His allegory is permeated by representational codes of a passive Jewish collective. He describes "the blows" that rain down on the Palestinians as rendering them "in our own likeness"[12] and making them the object of a helpless Jewish gaze. We Israelis, he suggests, are helpless in the face of our own violent identity, and this helplessness enables us to relieve ourselves of responsibility for the violent acts we perform.

One detects a peaking of this ambivalence after the 1967 war and the beginning of the Israeli occupation. At that time, a whole wave of literary works appeared that tried to make sense of the war and its outcome by using national allegories that portrayed the protagonists as powerless and helpless. Such portrayals reflect the inability of such narratives to cope with the new political situation. Instead, the allegories enhance and foreground the inability of allegory to manage and contain the sharp contradiction between the desire for universalizing self-confirmation and the desire to be seen as helpless; the desire for an integrated, unified self-image and the persistence of a schism that became even more visible in the violent aftermath of the war and in the occupation.

In "A Poem about Jerusalem,"[13] published soon after the 1967 war, Meir Wiseltir sarcastically protests against the occupation, noting that there is no point in writing a poem about Jerusalem when its occupation will eventually bring about a political apocalypse and the end of the actual, physical Jerusalem. Yitzhak Orpaz, in his 1968 novella *Ants*,[14] describes the nightmarish life of Jacob and Rachel, a couple whose names allude to the Bible and thus create a national allegory, whose (allegorical) house is steadily being devoured by ants. The new house, which the husband wishes to build, represents the new borders of Greater Israel: it is a house with "one side on a mountain and one side on a sea."[15] This clearly signifies a greatly enlarged Israel, which has, by the end of the novella, shrunk to no more than two words—"new house"—scribbled on a dusty page.[16] The disjunction between the actual condition of the nation and its representation is realized in the disjunction between the absence of the new house and its continuing "existence," so to speak, as representation on the page. The critical parable itself falls apart and exposes the impotence of literary commentary in its confrontation with the crumbling private-national being.

Alongside the construction of the hegemonic allegorical national narrative as the Jewish story of the powerless, we find attempts in Hebrew literature written in the State of Israel to undermine this identity narrative. The 1990s have, in fact, seen a marked tendency to disrupt and disturb the national allegory; Yizhar's 1992 text is one such example. Among other things, he creates a crumbling, partial analogy between the expulsion and David Ben-Gurion's fragmented voice announcing the establishment of the State of Israel, which issues forth from the broken-down radio to which the soldiers listen.

But this subversive tendency is by no means restricted to the last decade of the twentieth century. As early as 1948, Meydad Schif published *Shimon Tzammara*[17]—a text that proposed an alternative to all existing national constructions of ethnicity. Representing his main protagonist as ethnically hybrid, Schif encodes the crossbreeding of identities as an antithesis to monolithic Jewish ethnocentricity. The writings of the Canaanite School, active in the late 1940s and early 1950s, which includes such writers as Yonathan Ratosh, Aaron Amir, Shraga Gafni, Amos Keinan, and Benjamin Tamuz, represent another attempt to undermine the Jewish identity narrative.

The pattern of avowal and disavowal of the Other underwent a dramatic change during the 1960s, which was accompanied by a shift in the role played by the map in literary text. Owing to the centrality of the territory, the map functions as a prominent device for suppressing the conflicts in Israeli identity. This authoritative image represents the institutionalized gaze that orients one in the territory. It also makes territory an object of description, classification, and, accordingly, the desire to control. The map is a literary device that constructs a coherent collective identity through its representation of the violent space. It is particularly the military map that is represented in the fictional text. The literary use of the map is a kind of a glimpse that momentarily arrests the progress of the narrative. It enables the reader's gaze to penetrate the literary apparatus that constructs

Israeli identity. This apparatus recounts the collective story through the literary co-opting of the space, and the map serves as an allegorical code for reading the development of the literature written in the State of Israel.

The military map, which is common in the literature written during the 1948 war, is also found in Yizhar's "Story of Hirbat Hiza'a." There, the map is the most reliable text, providing authoritative knowledge of the expulsion. Hence, the map is the ultimate and most transparent device of appropriation of territory. As recounted in the story, the soldiers are to "'gather the residents starting at point X (see attached map) through point Y (see same map)—to load them on the cars and to move them beyond our lines; to blow up the stone buildings and burn the clay cabins; to gather the young and the suspect, and to clear the area from "hostile forces"' etc., etc."[18]

The map—or the absence thereof—is also a prominent feature in Nathan Shaham's story "Seven of Them," which was later adapted into his play *They Will Arrive Tomorrow*.[19] Because of the absence of the map, the soldiers in the outpost have no idea where another Jewish unit peviously placed seven mines. Thus the external enemy is replaced by an internal one, and the story becomes one of Jewish soldiers against Jewish soldiers. The military collective unravels, for "the death of the one is the redemption of the other." The absent military map could have prevented collapse and preserved the stability of the national war story, with its clear dichotomy between the enemy and us.

Maps play a similar role in Dan Ben-Amos's story "The Camel." This is the story of a soldier who joins a military operation during which a camel wanders onto the battlefield. The narrator protagonist is so disoriented that he is finally made to to prove his loyalty to the military-national cause by killing the innocent camel. In contrast, the maps that accurately signify the actual targets of the battle in Israeli space become the one stable component, not just a "sign" but a constant validation of control.

The map functions as an important part of the national allegory, the major literary device through which the text constructs a coherent collective identity. As discussed above, Yizhar's prominent allegory "The Story of Hirbat Hiza'a," which tells the story of the War of Independence—a crucial and dramatic stage in the national narrative, also employs the personal perspective of the fighter to function in the manner of the map in Shaham's and Ben-Amos's stories, that is, as a means of covering the conflict within the collective identity narrative. But unlike the Jewish "conversion" of the Other that we see in Yizhar's 1949 text, the literature of the 1960s employs a universalistic oedipal model of intergenerational struggle. This oedipal model, applied to the Arab-Jewish conflict, frames the conflict in terms of "universal" intergenerational or paternal relationships, rather than in moral or political terms.

In "Facing the Forests," by A. B. Yehoshua,[20] one of the most prominent stories of the 1960s, both the map and the oedipal model come into play. The map is portrayed by the forest ranger, who writes a study on the Crusades in the refuge of the forest of the Jewish National Fund. The new forest symbolizes the new Zionist settlement, which is built on an Arab village that was destroyed in the 1948 war. The forest ranger ultimately joins a Palestinian, a former resident of the destroyed Arabic village, who is planning to burn the forest down.

What on the surface looks like a moral and political act is transformed in the story to an act of oedipal rebellion by the forest ranger against the old generation. Thus, Yehoshua privileges psychology over politics, and the moral act of burning down the forest is transformed into a private struggle of an agonized soul in its battle against the older generation.[21]

In the end, what remains from the fire is a map:

> The words are confusing to him. For the time being, for the past few weeks, that is, he has been zealously devoted to one single sheet of paper. A picture? No, a map. A map of the area. He will display it on this wall for the benefit of his ancestors, that they may remember him. Look, he has already signed his name, signed it to begin with, lest he forget.[22]

The man who constructed a map of the area as a message to his heirs, in the hope of recovering his problematic place in the patriarchal line, is the man who helped the Palestinian burn down the forest. In the end, only the map, his private map, remains.[23] The cartographic representation signifies the narcissism of those who seek to evade their responsibility as the majority in a sovereign state by adopting the position of an apparent minority. Rather than serving as an instrument for orientation and control of the unknown, as represented in 1948 literature, the map in 1960s literature is a substitute for reality.

Shimon Ballas, a writer of Yehoshua's literary generation, was one of the few who wrote from a Mizrahi non-Zionist perspective, which he defines as that of an "Arabic Jew." Rejecting the Zionist Ashkenazi hegemony, Ballas tries to displace the binary opposition between Jews and Arabs onto Baghdad, a site in which Zionist nationality will not fulfill a meaningful function.[24]

Like other Israeli writers, Ballas, too, uses the map as a way of privileging the imagination over reality. But, unlike the prevalent 1960s oedipal story of struggle with authorities, where, in the end, the protagonist finds his identity, Ballas undermines the oedipal hegemonic story by foregrounding the space and its typical representations in paintings, photographs, and maps. Privileging the constitution of identity in space over its constitution in time or through the oedipal story, Ballas subverts any clear center of national identity.

This is evident in Ballas's story "Imaginary Childhood," in which he tells about his conversation with a friend who has been exiled from Baghdad. Although they share experiences from their place of birth, Ballas prefers his imagination to the tourist map of Baghdad his friend brings to him. Refusing to use the map, Ballas suggests an imagined map.

> "I have a different map"—I said to him—"a map of alleys twisted and intertwining like an intricate cobweb. I can draw it on paper because I remember every single curve, every single niche, every single arch, every single window and every single side of a house that protrudes in a sharp angle near which men stood and pissed."

> "Many quarters have been pulled down," my friend replied promptly, "yours too, perhaps."

> Whether it has been pulled down or not, what is the difference? As far as I'm concerned, It will stand forever. The world of childhood is beyond Time, located in the imagination rather than reality. It is a complete experience that cannot be apprehended by mere words. We are used to telling stories in an allegorical way. The language we use is arranged according to fixed rules and it obeys Time. Every re-

sult has a cause, and causality is the guideline of the sentences we utter. Otherwise, no one will understand. How should we relate an experience that is beyond Time? Childhood experiences can only be retold at the expenses of locking them up in Time, of binding them in a tight chain of cause and effect. Such are the childhood stories that we read. They are stories, a faded shadow, or a polished reflection of an imaginary experience. I do not put great trust in childhood stories, just as I do not put great trust in dream stories. I particularly do not believe writers' childhood stories.[25]

Ballas posits the map as an antithesis to the semi-autobiographical story that, in the oedipal pattern, contributes to the formation of the new Israeli nation. Instead of the oedipal struggle with the father over the love of the mother, Ballas's narrative represents the bonding of son and mother in an effort to overcome his childhood fear of snakes: "I would lie beside my mother on a mat spread on the floor when I saw the snakes crawling in a long row underneath a wooden stool close to the wall."[26] The hegemonic critical establishment, however, has responded to Ballas by reading him within the rubric of an ethnic category created by the Zionist hegemony. Calling Ballas's production "local or tribal literature,"[27] they reaffirm *Jewish* ethnicity as the stable and totalizing feature of this literature.

In addition to the Israeli Jewish writers previously cited, we can also cite Israeli Palestinian writing in Hebrew. In recent decades, we find a large body of translations from Arabic and Palestinian literature into Hebrew. These interventions propose an alternative understanding of the category of the "national" by exposing its ethnically Jewish foundation. The very act of Palestinians writing in Hebrew undermines the Jewish ethnic identity principle of Hebrew literature. The writers expose the linguistic identity of Hebrew literature (its being exclusively *Hebrew* literature) as no more than a cover for its ethnic identity as *Jewish* literature. This type of exposure reached its pinnacle in Anton Shammas's novel *Arabesques*,[28] which undermined the narrative of national allegory through the iconography of the arabesque, disrupting the narrative's linearity and thus also disturbing the construction of narratological agency as that which generates a clear and representative identity available for use in the name of national identification.

"Nationalism," writes Prasenjit Duara, "is often considered to override other forms of identification within a society, such as religious, racial, linguistic, class, gender, or even historical ones—to encompass these differences in a larger identity."[29] In Israeli literature, the ethnocentric Jewish narrative strives to dominate. This is evident in the way in which Palestinian writing in Hebrew is consistently appropriated into the Jewish national narrative by labeling Palestinians as "non-Jews." Previously, the radical challenge posed to the hegemonizing ethnic Jewish identity by Canaanite writing was also reappropriated into the ethnically Jewish parameters of the literature through being labeled a radical version of the Zionist negation of the Diaspora.

In what can be read as a response to Shammas's novel, A. B. Yehoshua, in his novel *Mr. Mani* (published in 1990),[30] exposes the roots of Israeli identity's construction, without granting it the authority of being "natural." He sends an ancestor of the Manis to the Palestinians during the British Mandate to invite them to share the Balfour Declaration and split the territory between the two nations. The map he draws for the Palestinians demonstrates the arbitrariness of the political act and their missed historical opportunity.

This is, in a way, a reaction to Shammas's subversion of the notion of "origin" in the Israeli-Palestinian conflict. Yehoshua answers that there were other origins as well, and that all could have been different. While he does not abandon the notion of origin, the map becomes an independent signifier, a tool for political-conflict solution that could have materialized not because of geopolitical circumstances but by virtue of the map's autonomous authority.

None of the subversive models I have just described has confronted the hegemonic identity narrative head-on. Their subversion of the myth of allegorical continuity linking Hebrew literature to Israeli literature proceeded by exposing the basic contradiction within the stitching or suturing that allegory is always called on to perform in national narrative.

To read the traces of the violence against the persuasive hegemonic national narrative, to resist the allegorical movement that erases and smoothes over those traces of violence, it is necessary to displace the gaze and perform an alternative reading. This alternative reading must discard the teleology inherent in the notion of a uniform Israeli identity, grounded in the shared roots of the Jewish people; a teleology that has the effect of erasing traces of violence toward the Other. To reveal these traces of violence, one has to perform a reading in the space of the "post"—a reading that rejects the naturalness of violence and reveals its erasure. One has, in short, to perform a postcolonial reading of allegory "that exist[s] as an aftermath, as after—after being worked over by colonialism,"[31] a reading that opens space for exploration and that also lays bare the efforts to efface violence in the attempted construction of a coherent, homogeneous, noncontradictory identity.

A recent effort to create a postcolonial text that lends itself to such a reading can be found in the writings of Orly Castel-Bloom, which radically subvert the dominant Zionist narrative. To Castel-Bloom, Zionism is a meta-category that subordinates "woman" to the "nation"—a claim that exposes the limits of the national as Zionist and male. The hegemonic criticism, however, seeks to appropriate Castel-Bloom by classifying her writing as a form of "female writing" that can be "appropriately" placed within a Jewish ethnic framework.

In "A Story of Someone Else," Castel-Bloom tells of a group of children who refuse to heed a sign at the border ordering them to stop. This refusal, a denying of the authority of the Israeli borders, undermines the use of territory as a basis for national identity. This subversion of fixed territorial boundaries represents a discontinuity with the dominant Hebrew literary narrative.

Castel-Bloom also appropriates the map differently than the dominant Israeli literature. In her novel *Dolly City* (1992),[32] she tells the story of Dolly, who lives in Dolly City. A mother and physician, Dolly cares for her son (a baby she found) by piercing his body and makes him a target of her medical experimentation by drawing a map of Israel on his back. This allegorical act transforms the map from an imagined representation to a bodily act. Unlike the map in the literature of the 1960s, which represented a narcissistic escape from the Zionist Israeli nationality, Castel-Bloom's map represents political protest.

Castel-Bloom resolves the central question in Israeli politics—the conflict over occupied territories and the borders between Israel and the Arabs—through the body of the child. After some time, she realizes that, according to the map inscribed on his body, the withdrawal to the 1967 border has been completed. Thus, in an act of protest, she reads the public situation in the private body. Castel-Bloom encounters the lack of a political solution, the dead-end situation, presented by the accepted narratives that portray the process of national territorialization. The political act of mapping the body, rather than the territory, is an act of exposure—an exposure of the deceit imposed by national texts on the reader. Castel-Bloom goes back to the integration of the map and the collective. As in the literature of 1948, her map guides the collective. But whereas in 1948 the literature subordinated the individual to an external, objective orientation, in Castel-Bloom's work of the 1990s, the external reality is determined by the private body. Dolly, the mother, finds her lost son and is astonished by the changes in his body:

> "Turn around," I said.
>
> He obeyed and I saw the map of Eretz-Israel, which I inscribed on his back some years ago. The map was accurate and updated. Someone redrew it and enlarged it according to the growth of the kid. I looked carefully at the map and noticed that he returned to the '67 borders. It was unbelievable!
>
> Ah, the gap between generations. My Mom spat at Arabs, I gaze at them with my eyes, and my son is going to lick their ass.[33]

Castel-Bloom dismisses the 1960s oedipal narrative of generational power struggle, but even more radically, for her the body becomes the signifier. The materiality of language, which is inscribed in the body, becomes the main cultural arena. Just as *Dolly City* is named after Dolly, so Dolly finds a locksmith in Locksmith Street, a known street in Tel Aviv. In her novel, Castel-Bloom rejects the standard pattern of an adventure story and unravels the national male mapping that orients the individual in the national territory. In an act of reversal, Castel-Bloom orients the collective according to the borders framed in the body of the individual.

In her refusal to suppress the violence embedded in the occupation of the national space, Castel-Bloom deviates from the dominant Israeli literary narrative. In contrast to most Israeli writers, she exposes the violence. For Castel-Bloom, who rejects the territorial basis of Israeli literature, the private body rather than the collective territory fixes and portrays the national space. Concentrating on the body as a point of departure for geopolitical changes, she transforms it into a political agent that exceeds the boundaries of the nation. The body itself, read as a text of violent acts, thus transgresses the national narratives and their concealment of collective violence.

Notwithstanding her radical moves, Castel-Bloom, like the other writers discussed above, has refused to confront the hegemonic Israeli identity narrative head-on. Instead, she seeks to subvert the allegorical myth of continuity that links Hebrew literature to Israeli literature by exposing the basic contradiction within the stitching or suturing of the national narrative. In this regard, she succeeds in highlighting the disruptions in the hegemonic national narrative. By opening space for the emergence of that which was repressed (ethnicity, gender), she subverts the effort to create the illusion of one coherent, monolithic national identity. This act of subversion foregrounds exactly that which allegory endeavors to conceal so as to overcome its inner contradiction. By preventing the dominant literary narrative from successfully representing an unbroken continuity, this literature contributes to undermining the seemingly seamless movement from Hebrew to Israeli literature.

NOTES

1. Avraham Kariv, "Ha-Sifrut Ve-Hamedina" (The literature and the state), in *Atara Le-Yoshna* (To restore to pristine) (Tel Aviv: Dvir, 1956), 244.
2. Benedict Anderson, *Imagined Communities: Reflections on the Origin and Spread of Nationalism* (London: Verso, 1991).
3. S. Yizhar, "Azmaut, '48–'92" (Independence, '48–'92), *Hadashot*, 6 May 1992.
4. The exact date of the expulsion from Merar is May 18, 1948. See Benny Morris, *Leidata Shell Beayat Ha-Plitim Ha-Falastinim, 1947–1949* (The birth of the Palestinian refugee problem, 1947–1949) (Tel Aviv: Am Oved, 1991), 591.
5. S. Yizhar, "Hirbat Hiza'a" (The story of Hirbat Hiza'a), in *7 Sippurim* (7 stories) (1949; reprint, Tel Aviv: HaKibutz HaMeuhad, 1971), 37–88.
6. Yizhar, "Hirbat Hiza'a," 72.
7. Stuart Hall, "Ethnicity: Identity and Difference," in *Becoming National: A*

Reader, ed. G. Eley and R. G. Suny (New York: Oxford University Press, 1996), 344.

8. Homi K. Bhabha, "Of Mimicry and Man: The Ambivalence of Colonial Discourse," in *The Location of Culture* (London and New York: Routledge, 1994), 86.

9. Yizhar, "Hirbat Hiza'a," 84.

10. Ibid., 87–88.

11. David Grossman, *Hazman Ha-Tzahov* (The yellow wind) (Tel Aviv: Siman Kria HaKibutz HaMeuhad, 1987), 7–8.

12. Yizhar, "Hirbat Hiza'a," 84.

13. Meir Wiseltir, "Shir al Yerushalaim" (A poem about Jerusalem), in *Kah* (Take) (Tel Aviv: Siman Kria, 1971), 87.

14. Yitzhak Orpaz, *Nemalim* (Ants) (Tel Aviv: Am Oved, 1968).

15. Ibid., 88.

16. Ibid, 103.

17. Meydad Schif, *Shimon Tzammara* (Tel Aviv: Twerski, 1952).

18. Yizhar, "Hirbat Hiza'a," 38.

19. Nathan Shaham, *They Will Arrive Tomorrow* [in Hebrew] (Merhavia: Sifriat Poalim, 1949).

20. A. B. Yehoshua, "Mul Ha-Yearot" (Facing the forests), in *Ad Horef 1974* (Until winter 1974) (Tel Aviv: HaKibutz HaMeuhad, 1975).

21. Mordechai Shalev, "Ha-Aravim Ke-Pitaron Sifruti" (The Arabs as a literary solution), *Haaretz*, 30 September 1970.

22. Yehoshua, "Mul Ha-Yearot," 111.

23. When the man in charge of the forests finds out that the ranger is not familiar with Israeli forests, he offers the ranger a map—a map courtesy of the fathers' generation. Ibid., 95.

24. Shimon Ballas, *Mul HaHoma* (In front of the wall) (Ramat-Gan: Massada, 1969).

25. Shimon Ballas, "Imaginary Childhood," trans. Hanna Amit-Kochavi, *Jerusalem Quarterly* 21 (Fall 1981): 60.

26. Ibid., 56.

27. Gershon Shaked, *Ha-Siporet Ha-Ivrit 1880–1980* (The Hebrew fiction, 1880–1980), vol. 4 (Tel Aviv and Jerusalem: Keter and HaKibutz HaMeuhad, 1993), 67–68.

28. Anton Shammas, *Arabeskot* (Arabesques) (Tel Aviv: Am Oved, 1986).

29. Prasenjit Duara, "Historicizing National Identity, or Who Imagines What and When," in *Becoming National*, ed. Eley and Suny, 161.

30. A. B. Yehoshua, *Mar Mani* (Mr. Mani) (Tel Aviv: HaKibutz HaMeuhad, 1990).

31. Gyan Prakash, "Postcolonial Criticism and Indian Historiography," in *So-*

cial Postmodernism: Beyond Identity Politics, ed. L. Nicholson and S. Seidman (Cambridge: Cambridge University Press, 1995), 87.

32. Orly Castel-Bloom, *Dolly City* [in Hebrew] (Tel Aviv: Zemora- Bitan, 1992).
33. Ibid., 88–89.

Chapter 10

Reterritorializing the Dream: Orly Castel-Bloom's Remapping of Israeli Identity

Deborah A. Starr

I have a dream that Jews, not only writers, not only Israelis, not only women Israeli writers, will find a way, or the ways, to get rid of that *noblesse oblige*, the obligation complex of Judaism that produces nothing but paralyzing guilt feelings and shame on us. . . . This way of thought that there is only one country, one people, one religion, one way, is ugly, suffocating and could kill the whole idea of Israel as a free place.
—Orly Castel-Bloom, Jewish Writers Conference, 1998

Orly Castel-Bloom, a young, highly acclaimed Hebrew novelist, has taken a position within contemporary Israeli cultural debates by publicly airing her socially critical views. Calling for a secular, democratic, and pluralistic Israeli society, Castel-Bloom's discourse leaves little room for doubt about her distaste for those who claim to represent Israeli identity univocally:

Others attack my books by saying that I am anti-Zionist—that my books aspire, as it were, to destroy what is already achieved—that I describe chaos, or even Hell. Unfortunately these people think they have Jewish consciousness by its horns. They think that they have a monopoly on Hebrew, that their generation had long since resolved the problem of the new Israeli identity, and that there are several questions that should not be reopened. They are wrong. They are so wrong that there is no dialogue. (1993b, 30)

Through her fiction writing as well, Castel-Bloom attempts to subvert the cultural hegemony of male, Ashkenazi (descended from Jews in northern France and Germany in the medieval period) voices in Israeli culture and recover the repressed voices of women and Mizrahim ("Oriental" Jews and their descendants).[1]

Castel-Bloom's critical reappraisal of Israeli society emerges in an atmosphere of widespread self-critique and reexamination of social values in Israel, concurrent with major social, political, and economic changes. For almost thirty years, the Labor Party of the Socialist-Zionist movement governed Israel, putting into place its own interpretation of Jewish history and maintaining its hegemonic vision through various state apparatuses. In 1977 the Likud Party mobilized the previously underrepresented Mizrahi population, or "Second Israel," to win the parliamentary election.[2] Thus, ironically, Israel's conservative party took up the banner of promoting Israeli multiculturalism to attract and maintain support from its diverse constituency. The subsequent dissolution of a single, hegemonic interpretation of Zionism, coupled with the installation of a government characterized by its mandate from a plurality of voices, symbolized the social changes already underway and hastened their impact on Israeli society. As a result of the same forces, in recent years the Israeli economy has undergone a deliberate shift away from state-owned enterprise toward privatization, international trade, and private foreign investment (Aharoni 1998). Particularly noticeable is the growing Americanization of Israeli society.

Castel-Bloom's cultural criticism and the social phenomenon of which it is emblematic have been popularly labeled "post-Zionist."[3] Broadly defined, post-Zionism can be described as disruptions of the cultural hegemony of the Zionist master narrative, or more specifically, the various social and academic trends that undermine, fragment, or reinvestigate some or all of the tenets of Zionist ideology on which the state and its society were founded. In a recent study, Laurence Silberstein (1999) has isolated and analyzed independent trends that have all been labeled "post-Zionism." According to Silberstein, many works that are so labeled never entirely escape the preexisting paradigms of thought. The one major exception is the regular contributors to the journal *Theory and Criticism,* cultural critics who self-consciously reinvestigate the modernist categories of Zionist discourse and frame their study of Israeli culture through concepts and forms of analysis that Silberstein describes as postmodern.

Others have demonstrated the conceptual shortcomings of various post-Zionist writings. For example, Ilan Pappe illustrates how post-Zionist discourses in the political realm, even as they diverge significantly from the Socialist-Zionist ideology that characterized the pre- and early state period, remain largely focused on issues of Israel's Jewish national character (1997). In a Gramscian move, Yerach Gover argues that much presumably counterhegemonic literature labeled as post-Zionist "stems from the same hegemony it claims to oppose" (1998, 31). I would add that the Israeli literary critical establishment, by lauding the "arrival" of postmodernism in Israel and by unceasingly comparing Israel's literary output to great European writers and works, tends to reinscribe the normalization goals of Zionism.

The labeling of her writings as post-Zionist notwithstanding, Castel-Bloom's literary works, as critic Anne Golomb Hoffman argues, "interrogate without dislodging" Zionist master narratives (1997, 63). In her fiction, Castel-Bloom pits herself against the Socialist-Zionist, Ashkenazi hegemony, the primacy of a culture of violence, and the persistence of patriarchy. Her writing in effect gives her repressed subjects voice by creating a language in which they can speak and by testing the limits of the territorial boundaries so as to offer them a place from which to tell their stories. Through this multipronged approach, Castel-Bloom interrogates a unitary construction of Israeli national identity.

In this chapter, I examine and evaluate the loci of Castel-Bloom's critiques of Israeli society and her attempts to create space for alternative subject-positions. At the same time, I seek to clarify the ways in which her work fails to transcend the categories she sets out to critique. First, I investigate how her experimentations with language attempt to disrupt the normalizing function Hebrew has played in Israeli society. Next, I explore her efforts to delegitimate Israel's patriarchal military culture. Finally, I examine the ways in which she seeks to reterritorialize Israeli national identity.[4]

Mapping the Territory of Language

Many influential Israeli literary critics have singled out Castel-Bloom as the exciting voice of a new idiom in Hebrew fiction.[5] Castel-Bloom, whose first collection of stories *Not Far from the Center of Town* appeared in 1987, claims that she "jazzes" her writing by spontaneously improvising on the central themes of a piece to create a kaleidoscopic, fragmented fantasy world (1998). The jarring, disorienting effect she achieves has been lauded as unprecedented in Hebrew literature.

Although Castel-Bloom's work has received much praise, a close examination of the critical discourse reveals an unease with her use of language that may derive from the critics' unstated awareness of its potentially explosive content. In an otherwise gushing review of Castel-Bloom's first novel, *Where Am I* (1990), critic David Gurevitz reveals an underlying anxiety in his insistent rhetorical question, "In what language will we speak tomorrow?" (1990). Without acknowledging the negative connotations of the terms, critics have praised her unique style by labeling it "schizophrenic" and "autistic" (Gurevitz 1990), "flat" and "thin" (Naiger 1993), "anorexic" (Miller 1990), and "dead" (Miron 1989). Other supportive critics have described her prose as a "poetics of ugliness" (Hertzig 1989) and have likened it to George Orwell's (demagogic) newspeak (Nissim 1992).

A review by critic Meir Schnitzer reveals the source of his unease: "We are speaking about a familiar Hebrew: the language of the street and of the corner market, a secular, spoken, non-elevated language. . . . Yet . . . Castel-Bloom avoids using slang and the metaphors of the Carmel Market" (Schnitzer 1987). For this critic, vernacular, spoken Hebrew is acceptable, even applauded, as long as it does not degenerate into the juicy, low-class metaphors or Mizrahi-coded tough talk of the open-air marketplace. And though the other critics steer clear of such elitist commentary, their thinly veiled anxiety derives from the subtle and not-so-subtle leakage of such "undesirable" elements into Castel-Bloom's prose.

Indeed, in a 1995 interview, Castel-Bloom expressed her commitment to portraying Israel's underrepresented Jewish minorities in her writing:

> We are descendants of *adot ha-mizrah*. Therefore, I make sure that
> most of my main characters are *Mizrahim*, or *Samekh-Tetim (sefaradim
> tehorim)* ["pure" Sephardi—descendants of the Jews who inhabited
> Spain and Portugal before the expulsion in the late fifteenth cen-
> tury] like my father. It is very important to me to construct people
> from *adot ha-mizrah* in a non-folkloristic or stereotypical way. (Negev
> 1995)[6]

Pairing a multilingual narrative texture with a range of characters
drawn from all walks of Israeli society, Castel-Bloom attempts to
broaden the base of Hebrew expression in order to acknowledge the
presence of Israel's repressed languages and identities. In Israel, the
teaching of modern Hebrew has, in fact, served as an important tool
in the assimilation and acculturation of Jewish immigrants to Israel.
Indeed, within one generation Hebrew significantly displaced Jewish
diaspora languages in Israel.[7] In her writing, Castel-Bloom, herself
the daughter of Francophone Jewish immigrants from Egypt, seeks to
reverse this normalizing trend that threatens Israel's multilingual
heritage.

For example, in a chapter from her novel *Where Am I* titled "She
Speaks Only Hebrew," the protagonist takes a break from her work as
a typist on the night shift at a newspaper to get some fresh air. She encounters a mercenary assassin in a carpenter shop who claims to be
stalking the newspaper's shift supervisor. "She speaks six languages,"
he explains. "I want them" (Castel-Bloom 1990, 17). When she returns to work, the protagonist warns her supervisor, who responds
testily, "I speak six languages? Who concocted such nonsense? I speak
Hebrew. That's it. Do you understand? . . . Hebrew, and that's it" (18).

This curious image of language poaching presumes a sort of market in which languages are assigned a commercial value. For the assassin, the identifying feature of his target is her multilingualism, a
presumably commodifiable marker of difference. To kill the carrier is
to erase the difference. In Israel, as in any culture, languages are assigned relative values. Yet the social pressures and internal drive for
Jewish immigrants to assimilate into mainstream Israeli culture have
tended to render languages other than Hebrew less rather than more
valuable—as represented in the story by the supervisor's petulant denial of her multilingualism.

In another playful move, Castel-Bloom strategically drops foreign words, phrases, and vulgarities (sometimes in Latin script, other times in transliteration) into the text of her narrative. In a later scene from *Where Am I,* the then-unemployed protagonist is called on to entertain her highly educated French cousins during their stay in Israel. One morning, she informs them that they will visit Jerusalem together. One cousin exclaims in French, "Jérusalem . . . Le mur de la Montation" (32). Here the cousin offers up a pun structured around the French name for the Wailing Wall *(le mur des Lamentations)* and the French translation *(monter)* of the Hebrew term *(l'alot)* that represents travel to Jerusalem as an ascent. This interlingual play on words intersects these idiomatic expressions in two languages.[8]

One also senses this ludic tendency in Castel-Bloom's use of empty English phrases in her novel *Mina Lisa* (1995). Mina, the title character, sprinkles her narration with such gems as "Dear me" (70); "To make a long story short" (75); "That's for sure"(99); and "It's now or never" (114). Castel-Bloom taps into the cosmopolitan cachet English carries in Israel, citing recognizable but distinctly unassimilated terms. Yet her inclusion of banalities mocks both Mina, an upper-class housewife, and the faddishness English has come to denote in Israeli popular culture.[9]

Critical theorist Mikhail Bakhtin places a great deal of value on the significance of comic or parodic effects of such polylingualism or interanimation between languages. His conception of *polyglossia* serves to reveal the potentially subversive impact of Castel-Bloom's critique of language usage on the national myth of a unitary Israeli Jewish identity. Historically, Bakhtin argues, monoglossia played a significant role in shaping the unitary myths on which traditional Greek literary forms—epic, lyric, and drama—developed. The multilingual world of the Hellenistic empire later gave birth to a polyglot genre, a precursor to the novel. Yet the rise of polyglossia also meant the death of the "unitary and totalizing national myth" (Bakhtin 1981, 65), an outcome Castel-Bloom seeks through her work (Castel-Bloom 1993b).

Castel-Bloom's effort to legitimate counterhegemonic subject-positions through language is perhaps most apparent in a story titled "Ummi Fi Shughl," Arabic for "My Mother's at Work," which appeared in the collection *Involuntary Stories* (1993a). The protagonist sets out for a solitary walk on a winter day. Resting on a park bench, she feels something sting her leg. She looks down to discover an old woman in dirty, tattered clothes lying beneath her. The old woman joins her on the bench and tries to convince the protagonist that she is her mother. When, in the course of conversation, the protagonist says that her family came to Israel from Egypt, the old woman repeats her insistent assertions of their familial relations in Arabic:

> "*Ana ummik.* [I'm your mother.]"
> "*Ummi? Ummi mush hina, ummi fi shughl.* [My mother? My mother isn't here. My mother's at work.]"
> "*Ana ukhtik.* [I'm your sister.]"
> "*Inti mush ukhti, ukhti fi shughl.* [You're not my sister. My sister's at work.]"
> "*Ana ummik.* [I'm your mother.]"
> "*Inti mush ummi, ummi fi shughl.* [You're not my mother. My mother's at work.]"
> And she went through the same routine about twenty times. (1993a, 10–11)[10]

Although Arabic long functioned as an important language of the Jewish diaspora, a recent study argues that the Israeli educational and cultural establishment overwhelmingly perpetuates the perception of Arabic as solely a language of Arabs (Ben-Rafael 1994, 211).[11] For the non-Mizrahi Jewish reader of "Ummi Fi Shughl," the repetition of assertion and denial of Jewish lineage and familial relations *in Arabic* disrupts this dominant perception.

The infusion of various mother tongues of Israel's minorities, in this case Arabic, into Castel-Bloom's Hebrew constitutes an attempt at remapping the boundaries of identity formation. In this story, both language and the image of the mother evoke memories of a repressed identity. The bench *(safsal)* that functions as the material border dividing the protagonist from the "mother" also represents the limen *(saf-hacara),* or shadowy threshold of consciousness. Rising from under the "bench" into the protagonist's consciousness, the "mother" attempts to identify herself through a performative evocation of the "I" ("*Ana ummik*"), but she is rebuffed by the protagonist and thus reverts to imperceptibility below. The confrontation with the repressed imago of the mother nevertheless shakes the foundations of the protagonist's self, rendering her immobile—she expresses discomfort in staying on the bench, for fear that the "mother" will prick again into her consciousness, yet she also feels it would be impolite to get up and leave. In this example, the language of the Other (both the Other without, the Arab, and the Other within, the Arab Jew) permeates the borders of the (Israeli Hebrew) self.

The significance of recurrent structures, like the repetitive dialogue in the story, in the creation of subversive identities has been effectively argued by critic Judith Butler in her book *Gender Trouble*:

> In a sense, all signification takes place within the orbit of the compulsion to repeat; "agency," then, is to be located within the possibility of a variation on that repetition. . . . Then it is only *within* the practice of repetitive signifying that subversion of identity becomes possible. (Butler 1990, 145)

Although Butler's analysis is concerned specifically with alternative gender identities, the rhythmic repetition in the story of the Arab voice within—a repressed mother tongue—may be seen as a performative articulation of a subject-position that subverts the Zionist Ashkenazi construction of Israeli national identity.

In the terms laid out by Jacques Derrida in his essay "Des Tours de Babel," Castel-Bloom's attempt to create a Hebrew capable of representing and supporting the multiplicity of its speakers may be regarded as dialectical. For Derrida, the impulse to universalize language simultaneously creates "peaceful transparency of the human community" alongside "colonial violence and linguistic imperialism" (1985, 174). This dialectic, evident in "Ummi Fi Shughl," is additionally manifested in Castel-Bloom's speech at a 1998 Jewish writers' conference. There, the writer further radicalizes her calls for the creation of a pluralistic Israeli culture and a multiethnic Hebrew literature:

> With great anticipation I am looking at the foreign workers who enter Israel legally and illegally. . . . "Do stay for a long time," I plead with them with all my heart, "Do mingle in our society, you and your descendants. . . ." This pluralism should be part of our daily life and culture. Israel should be heaven and a haven to all refugees. Accept and welcome the foreigner, it is an investment. One day he will surely write good Hebrew literature. (Castel-Bloom 1998)

Not surprisingly, Castel-Bloom's comments provoked a great deal of discussion. Noted Hebrew critic Chana Kronfeld pointed out a problematic power relationship in Castel-Bloom's conception: "I hope that . . . what you are talking about is not inviting the *gastarbeiter* to lose their own identity by enriching ours—and similarly, [inviting] the literal refugee to enrich our identity by allowing us to feel metaphorically like refugees" (Castel-Bloom 1998). Yet, as Hillel Halkin, a noted translator and critic, responded, there is the danger that the debate over assimilating or refusing to assimilate foreigners into Israeli society could be reduced to finger-pointing, each side calling the other culturally imperialist (Castel-Bloom 1998).

This brings us to an apparently irresolvable paradox in Castel-Bloom's writing. On the one hand, her polyglossia, to use Bakhtin's term, threatens the Israeli myths of seamless integration of Jews into an Israeli Hebrew culture. On the other hand, her desire to universalize Hebrew suggests another kind of radical assimilation, the assimilation of non-Jewish guest laborers. Despite the inherent shortcomings in the conceptual framework, when considered within the Israeli hegemonic social structure, Castel-Bloom's multilingualism nevertheless disrupts the continuity of the Hebrew-Jewish nexus.

Mapping Historical Memory

In Castel-Bloom's attempt to broaden Israeli identity construction to accommodate a broader range of experiences, she turns to the image of the Holocaust. Castel-Bloom's Mizrahi characters bear internalized guilt feelings for having been spared personal exposure to the Holocaust, which she represents as almost a familial rite of passage into the society. In the story "Ummi Fi Shughl," when the "mother" asks the protagonist her ethnicity, she replies, "I'm not a Holocaust survivor. But lately I have been dreaming that I am. As a matter of fact, my parents are from Cairo" (Castel-Bloom 1994, 10). Dolly, the protagonist of Castel-Bloom's second novel, *Dolly City* (1992), also expresses guilt feelings that all the relatives of her parents' generation are alive. Dolly sets up a street-side curiosity show including an arm with a tattooed number, which she identifies to an onlooker as "my teacher's arm, from grade school. . . . I hated her. . . . She made me ashamed I wasn't the daughter of Holocaust survivors. Because of her, I was ashamed that my uncles weren't murdered by the Nazis but are still alive and kicking in Kiryat Ata" (1992, 77; 1997, 114).

In a review of *Dolly City*, critic Ariel Hirschfeld (1992) authorizes the notion of the Holocaust as a key to gaining access to Israeli culture. According to Hirschfield, the culturally steeped use of the Hebrew language, particularly through the inclusion of Holocaust references, firmly locates the novel within Israeli culture and, indeed, exemplifies it. The novel, he points out, starts with the evocation of the ritual sacrifice of a fish (likened to the animal sacrifices at the Holy Temple) and ends with the six million. Such an argument might be taken to confirm the suspicions of Dolly and the woman on the bench that for Sephardim and Mizrahim, representation of the Holocaust in Hebrew is a primary avenue for locating oneself within mainstream Israeli culture.

However, such was not always the case. As Tom Segev (1993) relates in his groundbreaking study of the ways in which Yishuv (Jewish settlement in prestate Palestine) and later Israeli leadership have manipulated the representations of the Holocaust in shaping national identity, European Jewry's passive acceptance of their fate during the Holocaust was viewed as endemic to the diaspora mentality. Indeed, various branches of Zionism had long advocated for "dissolving the diaspora" to do away with the passive mentality that had no place in their vision of the new, empowered Jew who would build the state. In this context, the Holocaust served as the irreversible violent rupture legitimating the nationalist aspirations of the Jewish people—a notion inscribed in the wording of the Declaration of Independence of the State of Israel (Mendes-Flohr and Reinharz 1980, 478). The prevailing atmosphere in the Yishuv immediately after the war and in the early years of the state was to avoid discussing the topic, and thus individual experiences of Holocaust survivors were largely repressed (Segev 1993, 185).[12]

However, to Castel-Bloom's Mizrahi characters, the Holocaust is another means of social exclusion. And thus, in its dual repression—the repression of the lived experience and the repression of the excluded—the Holocaust returns as repressed memories, bubbling through the Israeli psyche just as in the cyclical recurrence of the protagonist's nightmare in "Ummi Fi Shughl." While the inclusion of this imagery does not in any way subvert the significance of the Holocaust in the creation of Israeli national identity, it nevertheless indicates the way in which it has functioned to further alienate and delegitimate certain subject-positions.

Territorializing Violence

Castel-Bloom's work also entails a critique of Israel's culture of violence that, in a self-perpetuating manner, privileges (masculine) militarism as the protector of territory and the (Jewish) bodies that occupy it. As critic Anne Golomb Hoffman writes of *Dolly City*: "[Castel-Bloom's] imagination seizes upon and intermingles deeply held conceptions of the mother-child relationship and the notion of 'territory' as both body and homeland" (Hoffman 1997, 63). Castel-Bloom's work maps these territories onto each other, delimiting the heavily defended, narrow corridor in which her characters exist. While her female protagonists do not succeed in escaping their confines, they are granted two limited responses: embracing a romanticized notion of their role as victim, and appropriating violence as a tool to control territory and the body, thereby perpetuating rather than subverting the system.

Castel-Bloom's short story "Heathcliff" from the collection *Not Far from the Center of Town* (1987) describes a teenage girl, Smadar, embarking on a cinematically inspired fantasy adventure with the wild, romantic hero of the movie version of Emily Brontë's *Wuthering Heights*. The story opens with a description of a lingering war. Over the din of the public debates about the war's merits, the narrator introduces the protagonist's adventures by saying, "There were also people for whom the war held no interest whatsoever, to the point they didn't know with certainty who was losing and who was winning. Their hearts tended toward other directions entirely" (53). Smadar, like other members of society, could participate in the pervasive war talk. However, she outright rejects or ignores the discourse of militarism.

Indeed, as a teenage girl whose future army service is unlikely to bring her anywhere near the front, Smadar enters the discourse of violence through (imagined) victimization.[13] As she wanders from the theater toward her home, envisioning Heathcliff galloping by, a bus of Arab laborers pulls up alongside her. The image of Heathcliff disappears from view, and she turns to fantasizing herself the victim of a terrorist attack at the hands of one of the workers.[14] As described by Freud's notion of the pleasure principle, by controlling her fantasy she preemptively enacts her victimization to establish control over her anxiety (Freud 1955).

When Smadar attempts to escape her physical confines, however, she makes herself (her body) vulnerable to real violence. After the imagined threat, she continues wandering, refusing to return home: "A little more than one hundred meters separated Smadar from her parents' house, but she preferred to continue until she got to the green hills on the other bank of the stream that delimited the city on the north side" (Castel-Bloom 1987, 59). By doing so, she has crossed over to the "other side," where she completely gives herself over to movie-inspired fantasies. Indeed, this action represents Smadar's singular attempt to escape from the confines of the territory (as land); rejecting "home," she signifies her total submission to the illusion by renaming the park "Yorkshire" (60). However, by denying the safety of home, however restrictive, she puts her body at risk. She is subsequently raped in the park, all the while imagining her assailant to be Heathcliff. The brutal appropriation of Smadar's body in the Israeli park by a Hebrew-speaking attacker violently reterritorializes the wayward girl.[15]

Unlike Smadar, Dolly *(Dolly City)* adopts the culture of violence to effect change, providing an option other than that of passive victim. In the most often cited image of the novel, Dolly, a crazed, overprotective, abusive mother, plays doctor, making incisions on the back of her adopted son in the shape of a map of the biblical land of Israel. Her cartography graphically evokes the violence of the conquests of the territory (both ancient and modern) as she describes the wadis filling up with blood (1992, 29; 1997, 44). This act of mutilation is an attempt to control both her authority over her son and the mythic territory he represents.

Dolly City, however, is as much about uncovering the myths and mysteries of the memory of the father as it is about imposing them on the (fatherless) son. Throughout the novel, Dolly gleans shards of evidence of her father's former employer, the national airline, meddling in her life and in the life of her son. Only on her mother's death can Dolly gain access to the world of the father and symbolically settle accounts with the corporation of the nation. Yet, despite Dolly's best efforts to "cure" the society of social ills (manifested as cancerous growths), the patriarchal system ultimately perpetuates itself; her attempts to remap the patriarchal legacy onto and through her son ultimately fail.

The boy, as he becomes a man, assumes his active role in the society, and Dolly is ultimately subdued, losing her voice and her independence. Initially, it had been Dolly who silenced her son by never properly teaching him to speak. As he approaches adulthood, however, on his thirteenth birthday, or Bar Mitzvah, he begins to assert his authority over her. Rather than following silently behind her as he once had, the boy leads Dolly along on his errands and verbally engages with others as his mother looks on silently. At the same time, Dolly discovers that the map she has carved has "reverted" to the pre-1967 boundaries of the state of Israel—some unseen hand has reclaimed the territory of the boy's body (1992, 88; 1997, 132). Later, in the presence of her adult son, Dolly completely loses her power of speech (1992, 96; 1997, 144). Finally, at the end of the novel, the reversal is complete. The son enacts his retribution on his mother by first preventing her act of self-destruction (saving her from drowning), then committing her, silenced and completely disempowered, to an institution (1992, 122; 1997, 181). In the end, her best efforts fail—her attempts to break the reproduction of patriarchy through her violent perversion of the role of mother in order to stake a territorial claim are subdued.[16]

While neither Dolly nor Smadar succeeds in overcoming the sources of her victimization and oppression, Castel-Bloom's writing serves critically to represent the limited options Israeli women experience. Neither character ever manages to transcend her double bind as female subject in a society in which violence both within (rape, terrorism) and without (war, military threats) so restrictively inscribes her body in territory. Perhaps it is only through a subversion of the notion of home, as manifested in other texts by Castel-Bloom, that the possibility of transcending the dual mapping of territory exists.

Mapping Borders

Zionism, in its radical remapping of the focus of Jewish identity, privileges the role of territory, particularly as a legitimation of statehood. Although Castel-Bloom, too, privileges territory in her construction of identity, she resists confining her notion of home to a rigid, hegemonically contrived map. Castel-Bloom's mapping of territory represents a departure from the Socialist-Zionist mapping (both physical and cultural) of a patriarchal and monocultural society in Israel. Rather, she calls into question the integrity of Zionist borders, thereby permitting a reinterpretation of their cultural content.

In a speech delivered at a writers' conference in Turin, Italy, Castel-Bloom argues that, despite the lack of representational characterization of Israel in her writing, her characters cannot be divorced from their home:

> *Dolly City,* [is] about a city that exists only in the mind and spirit of the protagonist. Despite the seemingly uncertain connection between those same characters and the daily ground on which one treads, I think that if someone were to take one of those characters and transported her to, let's say, Saigon, or Turin or North Carolina—she would disappear immediately because that is not her home. (Castel-Bloom 1993b)

In this passage, Castel-Bloom insists that Dolly exists only within a location-specific context. In a sense, such a construction of identity represents a playful yet literal interpretation of the concept "subject-positionality." Although Castel-Bloom appears to essentialize place, her fiction nevertheless disrupts hegemonic and also essentialistically contrived spatial constructs.

The titles of Castel-Bloom's first collections of stories, *Not Far from the Center of Town* (1987) and *Hostile Surroundings* (1989b), confirm her particular concern for the relationship between self and place. The issue of place is also explored at length in the previously mentioned novel *Where Am I*, which plots the search for the "I" of the nameless female protagonist (Gurevitz 1990). The character incessantly bounces from experience to experience, from brief stints at drama school and university to short-lived careers as typist and prostitute, but none of her ventures ever succeeds. As the novel progresses, her encounters become progressively more bizarre and fantastic. The fragmentary but largely chronological picaresque "plot," however, takes her from her home in Ne'ot Afeqa and, later, Ramat Aviv—both affluent suburbs of Tel Aviv—to Jerusalem, Beersheba (desert city), Eilat (southernmost port city), and Qiryat Shemona (northernmost city), in effect tracing Israel's outer limits. Thus, since throughout the novel her physical location is always identifiable, it seems to operate as the only fixed variable in the ever-shifting matrix of identity formation. In other words, the "where" of the title serves to point to the fixity of place in the novel while indicating the character's ongoing existential search within that space. Further, when the characters disappear off the map, as it were, to spend several months trekking in Tibet, the narrative ceases, picking up again at the airport on their return (Castel-Bloom 1990, 52). In other words, as Castel-Bloom claims about Dolly in her speech at Turin, the characters in *Where Am I* effectively vanish outside their identifying territory.

Yet, as we shall see, Castel-Bloom does not take the map for granted; her explorations serve to highlight the historical fluidity of Israel's borders. For much of its existence, Israel had no land borders, only armistice lines. The ambiguous status of the territories occupied in 1967—Gaza, the West Bank, and the Golan Heights—has only contributed to the uncertainty of Israel's territorial boundaries. Even after the 1979 peace treaty established an internationally recognized border between Israel and Egypt, territorial disputes, most notably the claim over the resort settlement of Taba, were settled only by arbitration more than six years after Israel's withdrawal from Sinai in 1982. Israel's continued occupation of a "security zone" in southern Lebanon, along with its repeated military forays into Lebanese territory, has undermined the integrity of Israel's northern boundary. Israeli political geographer Oren Yiftachel casts further doubt on Israel's territorial integrity on different grounds:

> Israel as a definable, democratic political entity does not exist. The legal and political power of extraterritorial Jewish bodies and the rupturing of state borders [in the form of settlements] empty the notion of "Israel" of the broadly accepted meaning of a state as territorial-legal institution. (1998, 11)

The boundaries of Castel-Bloom's writing explore the nature of Israel's borders and their permeability. For example, in the story "Peach Monster" from *Hostile Surroundings* (1989b), the characters' territory of identification is not directly concomitant with Israel's borders, pushing the limits of the defining space of identity. This question of porousness becomes immediately apparent as the story opens with suspicious gunfire, presumed to be an infiltration of an Israeli army outpost along the border with Egypt shortly after the return of the Sinai peninsula to Egyptian control.

On one level, this story represents national anxieties provoked by Israeli withdrawal from Sinai.[17] The title of the story, "Peach Monster," refers to the recurrent nightmare of the main character, Od, an uneducated dwarf who serves as sergeant major in charge of discipline. Od's childhood memories of the twitching bodies of headless chickens in his father's butcher shop cast the Israeli withdrawal from Sinai as a violent severing of territory from a living body (Castel-Bloom 1989b, 145). After witnessing his father's symbolic emasculation through his father's loss of his ability to provide for the family, Od began to dream of a threatening peach, intent on biting him with its giant, toothy mouth (139). There is no mistaking the significance of the menacing pinkish, fleshy fruit as a vagina dentata representing Od's own castration anxiety. Drawing out the analogy to the national psyche, Od's fear of loss and impotence mirrors, to a certain extent, societal apprehension about Israel's security without Sinai and concerns over the viability of the peace treaty with Egypt.

In the story, however, the feared attack against Israel never takes place, as the shot fired in the opening sequence turns out to be the suicide of a blonde female Israeli soldier from a highly secretive outpost next to the main base, not a terrorist infiltration. In other words, the focus of the narrative turns inward with the investigation of an act of self-destruction initially assumed to be a penetration of the border by enemy forces. Indeed, Od suspects all along that the sinister yellow building housing the outpost, not the border with Egypt, represents the true threat. Od's paranoia proves to have some merit as, at the end of the story, anonymous Israeli agents summoned from the outpost open fire on the commander's car to prevent his pursuit. The same shots that puncture the tires—the only aggressive military action in the story—deflate the portent of external threat, further underscoring the utter futility of the base's mission.

Israel's first land border would seem the perfect locus for the sort of existential inquiry evoked by the story "Peach Monster." One would expect the border to function as a clear definition of the limits of one entity as defined against an Other. Indeed, we have come to think of that Other as indispensable in the definition of the self. As Derrida argues:

> The rapport of self-identity is itself always a rapport of violence with the other; so that the notions of property appropriation and self-presence, so central to logocentric metaphysics, are essentially dependent on an oppositional relation with otherness. In this sense, identity presupposes alterity. (Derrida 1984, 117)

In "Peach Monster," however, all violence is self-inflicted, and there is no representation or acknowledgment of an Other. In addition, the experience of one Israeli soldier, Itamar, demonstrates that the border is to be treated as an arbitrary, unnatural, and permeable boundary. Itamar disappears from the base after reportedly raving "about . . . desires of his to cross the border to Egypt to see how we seem from there, [and] . . . about some Hanokh Benvenisti who committed suicide by hanging" (Castel-Bloom 1989b, 135). Itamar, it seems, like the female soldier and his friend Hanokh, contemplates taking his own life but rejects his suicidal urges, turning toward the border for answers—answers about the society ("we") to which he belongs.

Yet crossing, in essence, reinscribes rather than obliterates the existence of the borders. Indeed, Itamar relies on the border, however porous, to define inside and outside. Nevertheless, to cross over is to abandon one's allegiance to the collective, even if the goal, as for Itamar, is to understand one's place in it. Thus, ultimately, both options—crossing and suicide—can be cast as subversive acts leading to the dissolution of the self. The permeability of boundaries implied by the crossing represents a desire to return to an undifferentiated state, to regain the fluid continuity of primary narcissism, while death is, of course, the ultimate destruction of the subject. In returning to our original reading of the story, this dissolution must be viewed within the context of national reckoning.

"Someone Else's Story," from the collection *Involuntary Stories* (Castel-Bloom 1993a), further investigates the permeability of borders and their role in the dissolution of the self. During a beach trip, a group of ten anonymous Israeli children embark on a journey along the coast to reach Israel's northern border to see the sign reading, "Stop Border Ahead." The story opens by clearly establishing that they departed not from Nazareth, an Arab city in the Galilee, but from Haifa, an ethnically mixed port city. As in *Where Am I*, each landmark along the way is clearly identified: Acre (an Arab fishing port), Nahariyya (a Jewish beach resort), Rosh Haniqra (the chalk cliffs on the Israel-Lebanon border).

The group is undifferentiated, all children of petty clerks. Their leader derives his authority from his age and his father's independent employment status, yet he, too, remains nameless. This son of the "independent one" or the "son of the accountant" *(ro'eh heshbon)*, or prophet *(ro'eh)* of reckoning *(heshbon)*, leads them in their journey to identify and locate themselves through space. Their goal, the sign behind the black-and-white striped bar that literally reads "Stop Border Before You," marks a material boundary against which to delimit themselves.

Yet at the moment of their arrival, the search is deferred; their "prophet" postpones the reckoning:

> The son of the accountant told us that this was nothing compared to a minefield. There, written on a crooked sign it says, "Caution: Minefield!" Everything seems normal. On our parents' next trip to the Golan Heights, we will run away again and hike in a minefield, there you don't know what you're stepping on, until after the step is taken. (86)

The reckoning to which he leads them is self-destruction; in other words, the search for identity turns out to lead to its dissolution. Yet, ultimately, their search and the threatened blowup of identity are deferred—the longed-for destruction of the self never actually occurs.

Castel-Bloom thus rejects the fixity of boundaries, stressing permeability and highlighting the fluidity that calls into question a national identity defined against the heavily defended borders. For Castel-Bloom, borders are arbitrary markers, and to abide by them means to be restricted to hegemonic constructions of (national) identity (both Zionist and Ashkenazi). Such a vision is in keeping with her self-described "chemistry" with and "poetic" connection to the Middle East, stretching beyond the arbitrary political boundaries (Castel-Bloom 1993b). In the context of a writers' conference on the cultures of the Mediterranean Basin, after poetically describing her family's crossings of the Mediterranean over the course of five hundred years (from Andalusia to the Levant in the fifteenth century and again from Egypt to France in the twentieth), Castel-Bloom nevertheless rejects the basic premise of the conference linking the cultures connected primarily by a body of water. She rather sees herself as an organic outgrowth of the contiguous territory of the Middle East. In keeping with this vision, borders (albeit somewhat prone to shifting) are cast as a ruthless and unnecessary carving up of the flesh of the Middle East (as signified in *Dolly City*).

Mapping the Levant

Unlike her contemporary Ronit Matalon, an Israeli-born writer of the same generation also descended from Egyptian Jews, Castel-Bloom does not directly evoke the work of Egyptian-born Anglophone writer Jacqueline Kahanoff, whose essays appeared regularly in Hebrew translation in the journal *Keshet*.[18] One cannot, however, discuss Castel-Bloom's construction of Middle Eastern-ness or its porousness without first understanding Kahanoff's "Levantinism," its intellectual precursor.[19] Through nostalgic reminiscences about her life in Cairo, Kahanoff comes to represent the multicultural interactions and admixture of Eastern and Western cultures within the upper class her family occupied as the ideal incarnation of a pluralistic society. By labeling this social model the Levant, she identifies its historically fluid locus, but, more important for her Israeli readership, she appropriates a term *(levantiniyut)* that had taken on negative connotations as a description of the poverty and "backwardness" of the Jewish immigrants from Arab countries (Kahanoff, "Israel: Ambivalent Levantine," 3).

However, Kahanoff's Levant is neither European nor Arab. She criticizes social Darwinism and European brutality but is likewise critical of Arab Islamic culture for its rejection of everything European.

The Levantines, the minorities—Jews, Greeks, Armenians, and Copts—are cast as arbiters, successfully negotiating the best of both cultures. The blind spots of her notion are, however, instructive for our purposes.

Kahanoff's construction of the Levant was inherently unstable. She attributes these characteristics to a specific generation of upper-class youths growing up in interwar Egypt at a crossroads of cultures and during a specific period of great political upheavals:

> The Arabs and the other colonized peoples were the crossbreeds of many cultures by accident, while we Levantines were inescapably so, by vocation and destiny. . . . We belonged to the Levantine generation whose task and privilege it was to translate European thought and action and apply it to our own world. We needed to find the words that would shake the universe out of its torpor and give voice to our confused protests. We were the first generation of Levantines in the contemporary world who sought a truth that was neither in the old religions nor in complete surrender to the West. (Kahanoff 1985, 40)

In other words, by describing the Levantine as the unique experience of her generation, she casts the notion as momentary and fleeting. Indeed, in one of a series of articles titled "The Generation of Levantines," Kahanoff describes the Levantine Egypt she knew as "the frail little world, seemingly so perfect, but in reality so rotten that it had to fall apart" ("Europe from Afar," 14).

Despite the inherent instability in this cultural construct, Kahanoff returns to positive characterizations of the Levantine and adopts it prescriptively as an antidote to Israel's problems, particularly its social divide between Sephardim/Mizrahim and Ashkenazim, and as a step toward regional peace:

> Israel is in the unique position of having this process of mutual influence and transformation take place within the same country: Levantine due to its geographic location between east and west, and through the very mixture of its people. It can thus reconcile its two main component groups into one dynamic, creative unity which, because it must fit together and fuse conflicting elements, can strive towards universality, as did the great Levantine (Byzantine and Islamic) civilizations of the past. They, too, represented a composite

of peoples and cultures, indeed, the same as did Western Europe in
its formative period. ("Israel," 10–11)

In this passage, she attributes to the Levantine a sort of universality
not supported by the model from which it was drawn. But also significant, we come to see that she is projecting a social cohesion of
Jews, through a model derived from "Levantine civilizations" but
devoid of the majority culture of the same Levant. Going back to
her characterizations of her childhood, we see that while Arab culture served as a host, it is described as somewhat superfluous to the
(explicitly non–Arab Islamic) Levantine "bridge" culture that flourished within it.

Likewise, while Castel-Bloom's claim to Levantinism is ultimately based on her sense of belonging within the larger regional
"culture(s)," her depiction of the Levant, even beyond Israel's borders, is almost entirely devoid of Arabs.[20] There are not even any
Egyptian or Lebanese soldiers visibly stationed along the borders in
either "Peach Monster" or "Someone Else's Story." The process of
self-realization in confronting the outer limits takes place, as discussed above, without a notion of alterity. If Castel-Bloom and her
characters are organically related to the region, then Jews and
Arabs, Israelis (particularly Sephardim and Mizrahim), Lebanese,
and Egyptians are all transitively part of the same culture. Notwithstanding the subversive impact of Castel-Bloom's writings and her
representations of the Levant on the Ashkenazi hegemony over Israeli society, her perspective nevertheless forcibly deprives the Arab
of a unique identity.

In the discussion provoked by Castel-Bloom's call for Israel's
guest laborers to enrich Hebrew language and literature, let us recall that, throughout the debate, none of the participants voiced
concern over how the discussion about the potential role of foreign
laborers in Israeli society deflects attention from Israel's preexisting sources of diversity, as well from the struggle of Palestinians in
Israel to integrate into or make an impact on the same society. Such
a perspective is unfortunately also circumscribed in Castel-Bloom's
notion of Levantinism.

In this sense, Castel-Bloom's work, like many other critiques designated as post-Zionist, fails to transcend the dominant processes of

Israeli identity construction. Indeed, by refusing to establish an Other against which to define the self, Castel-Bloom's writing is vulnerable to Yerach Gover's critique of other post-Zionist literary texts: "What cannot occur is the recognition of a moral other in whose gaze the Jew would find him or herself suddenly objectified as Jew, made an essence, in the face of the then existentially vital, subjective and self-reflective Arab" (1998, 35). Yet Castel-Bloom's project clearly differs from those of the texts Gover dismisses. Since she is striving to obliterate the notion of the "Jew" from Israeli identity, it follows that she would want to see the equally hegemonic category "Arab" eliminated as well. Yet such a presumption of power only invites further accusations of cultural imperialism such as that implied in Chana Kronfeld's question, cited above.

Thus, like other post-Zionist discourses that reproduce the Zionist paradigm against and through which they define themselves, Castel-Bloom's conception falls short of constructing a viable new locus for a regionally based identity. Nevertheless, her writing serves to problematize the prevailing Zionist representations of Israeli society and culture, with their valorizations of violence and the erasure of difference among Jews. Her experimentations with language function to disrupt the hegemonic role of Hebrew in assimilating Jews of vastly different cultures. Her stories also map the limited territory of women's identity within a militaristic culture. Although she adopts Zionism's fetishization of land, she subversively transforms the fetish object from a Jewish territorial homeland to a multicultural Middle East. Finally, she effects critiques of these weighty social issues through strategic employment of her characteristic biting wit. Despite the limitations of Castel-Bloom's conceptual models, her work succeeds in breaching and revealing the weak points of some of the most heavily defended outposts of hegemonic Israeli identity construction.

NOTES

1. As a literary endeavor, the categories Castel-Bloom investigates do not necessarily bear similar valences; likewise, the subject-positions she validates, women and Mizrahim, are necessarily overlapping categories.

2. For a good analysis of the demographic forces behind the election, see Swirski 1984.
3. There is a great deal of slippage between the notions "post-Zionism" and "anti-Zionism" (as Castel-Bloom describes the criticism of her detractors). Poet, novelist, and critic Yitzhak La'or, for example, claims that there is no such thing as post-Zionism: "It is just a bluff that permits them to live with the critique they have of Zionism without letting slip from their mouths the word anti-Zionist" (cited in Sheleg 1995, 59).
4. I do not mean to suggest that Castel-Bloom's work is either the first or the only attempt to effect such reterritorialization. However, in the interest of conducting an in-depth analysis of Castel-Bloom's work, I have elided some significant precursors, influences, and contemporaries. Take, for example, Yonah Wallach's radical remapping of gender identity in her poetry of the 1960s and 1970s.
5. A 1989 article titled "Encouraging Surroundings" (Golan) describes a colloquium at Hebrew University on Castel-Bloom's recently published collection of stories, *Hostile Surroundings* (1989b), in which Dan Miron, Hayim Pesach, and Yigal Schwartz offered positive critical appraisals of her work. A second article titled "A Celebration for Orly Castel-Bloom" describes a publication party for Castel-Bloom's first novel, *Where Am I* (1990), hosted by Dan Miron in his home—a rare occurrence, according to the journalist—attended by many notable Israeli literati, academics, and editors. In her review of Castel-Bloom's novel *Mina Lisa* (1995), Ariana Melamed (1996) claims that she has never seen such attention paid to a living, active writer.
6. Although most Israelis say *edot* for the plural of the noun *edah*, grammatically the proper plural form is *adot*, as used in my transliteration above. For an insightful analysis of the concept of *adatiyut*, see Domínguez 1989, 3–20 and 158–88.
7. The impact was particularly significant during the large waves of immigration to Israel in the early 1950s (Doron 1998). The 1972 Population and Housing Census found that 57 percent of Jewish Israelis then above the age of fourteen (i.e., those who would currently be over forty) were bilingual in Hebrew and another language. However, the data also showed that, at that time, 88 percent of the bilingual Israeli Jews already used Hebrew as their principal language of communication every day (cited in Rosenbaum et al. 1977, 193). Another study found that bilingualism was on the decline in Israel and predicted that "Jewish Israelis may cease to be multilingual in the various European and Middle Eastern languages known by the immigrant genera-

tions" (Nadel and Fishman 1977, 165). While demographic studies list twenty-four languages other than Hebrew currently spoken natively by Jews in Israel, the data bear out the conclusions drawn by these sociolinguistic studies in the late 1970s, as many of these languages are reportedly maintained only by the aging immigrant generation (*Ethnologue* 1996). See Katz (1982) for a study of the ideological component to pedagogy in *ulpanim*, Hebrew language courses. However, according to the research of Schmelz and Bachi, such courses had only a limited reach, since only an estimated one hundred thousand of the eight hundred thousand adults (over the age of twenty) who immigrated to Israel between 1949 and 1969 attended *ulpanim* (1974, 768–69).

8. To her cousin's pun the protagonist replies, "Qui"—or "Who"—evoking a different comic genre, the sort of slapstick routine generated from a verbal miscue.

9. In terms of the assimilation of languages in Israel, English has come to represent a somewhat special case. In a survey conducted in 1967, English-speaking immigrants to Israel were shown to be linguistically assimilating at the same rate as other immigrant groups (Isaacs 1967, cited in Seckbach and Cooper 1977, 168). A 1975 study, however, demonstrated increasing retention of the native language among English-speaking immigrants because of the relative increase in social value of English in Israeli society (169). Yet, as evidenced in Castel-Bloom's writing, in recent years English has made great inroads into Hebrew, with words cropping up at all levels of discourse, from colloquialisms to academic writing, and among native and non-native speakers of English alike (Ben-Rafael 1994).

10. I have modified the translation of Dalya Bilu that appears in *Ribcage* (see Castel-Bloom 1994) to match more closely the rhythm and structure of Castel-Bloom's transliteration, the translation of which appeared as footnotes at the end of the story. I have also changed Bilu's transliteration to reflect more accurately the pronunciation of the dialogue in Egyptian colloquial Arabic (following a simplified version of the transliteration system used in el-Said Badawi and Martin Hinds, *A Dictionary of Egyptian Arabic*). I thank Anton Shammas for pointing out the use of a nonstandard transliteration in the original Hebrew. In academic transliterations from Arabic to Hebrew, the Arabic letter *gh* in *shughl* should appear as an *'ayin* with a stroke. Shammas suggests that it is only through Ashkenazi, nonguttural pronunciation that the *gh* is mistaken for the "standard" Israeli *r* as employed by Castel-Bloom. If

such is the case, to a certain extent she undermines the subversiveness of the inclusion of Arabic by transliterating in an Ashkenazi-inflected voice.

11. Ammiel Alcalay (1993, 276–77), in his discussion of *The Yellow Wind*, identifies an inability on the part of noted Israeli writer and peace activist David Grossman to imagine the possible source for the assimilation of Arabic words into Hebrew as the large number of Jewish immigrants from Arabic countries. Grossman instead considers Israel's 1967 occupation of the West Bank and Gaza and the ensuing contact between Hebrew and Arabic speakers as the sole source. Alcalay cites this as an example of endemic social repression of the contributions of Mizrahim to Israeli culture.

12. See also Morahg (1997) for a discussion of shifts in Israeli literary representations of the Holocaust.

13. If Smadar's voice has no forum for expression in Israel's militaristic society, neither does she have a voice in her imagined romance because, as she expresses in one of her encounters with Heathcliff, she fears that she would break the magic by speaking in imperfect and accented English. There is no talking back to the film or the culture that produced it; yet to accept its terms is to become a passive consumer of the violence of the erasure of difference it perpetuates.

14. She appears to be unable to assimilate the violent fantasy, born out of a uniquely local environment, with the foreign romantic hero.

15. Castel-Bloom's representation of the movie adventure as a form of dangerous escapism becomes even more apparent in contrast to Robert Coover's story "Intermission" (1987). Coover's story describes a teenage girl being whisked out of the movie theater by a handsome movie hero and carried along from one action scene to another. In contrast to Smadar, however, her naïveté remains intact. As she gets dropped back into the theater in the midst of a scene from a horror movie, she reassures herself, "Isn't there always a happy ending? Has to be. It comes with the price of the ticket" (134).

16. One thinks here of Chodorow's *Reproduction of Mothering* (1978).

17. For an interesting report of public reaction to the peace treaty between Israel and Egypt, see Elon 1980.

18. In her novel *The One Facing Us* (1995), Matalon portrays Kahanoff as a friend of the narrator's family and reproduces Kahanoff's essay "An Egyptian Childhood" in the narrative. See Beckwith 1997, 226–68, for a discussion of the influence of Kahanoff's writing on Matalon's work. The Hebrew journal *Keshet* appeared from 1958 to 1975. Kahanoff's essays were published in a collected volume titled *From East the Sun* in 1978, a

year before she died. *Keys to the Garden: New Israeli Writing* (Alcalay 1996) includes some of Kahanoff's work.

19. Yonatan Ratosh's ideology, most commonly referred to as Canaanism, also calls for regional assimilation. I understand Castel-Bloom's position, however, to represent a second-generation adoption of Kahanoff's model, which was drawn from the memory of the lived experience of a vibrant, multiethnic Levant, rather than as being based on Ratosh's poetic but unprecedented regionwide rejection of religious culture. Although the primary translator of Kahanoff's work and the editor of the journal in which her essays were featured, Aharon Amir, identified with Canaanite ideology, Kahanoff's writings nevertheless express her independent philosophy. For a discussion of Ratosh's ideology, see Diamond 1986.

20. Only four of Castel-Bloom's stories portray Arab characters, three of them, not surprisingly, appearing in the collection titled *Hostile Surroundings* (1989b). In "Death in the Olive Grove" (Castel-Bloom 1989b), there is an Arab drug dealer. While in "Heathcliff" (Castel-Bloom 1987) the stereotype of the Arab as terrorist is presented in the context of a sort of Jewish persecution complex, there is an almost subliminal impact of the fleeting moment when Smadar presumes the Arab laborer to be a terrorist.

Castel-Bloom's only two historical narratives, however, both take place in the Arab world, providing a certain variety of Arab subject-positions. "Joe, a Man from Cairo" (Castel-Bloom 1989b) describes the effects of the 1948 war on an Egyptian Jewish family. There is a certain care in her portrayal of the Muslim neighbor's concern for the Jewish family's well-being in contrast to the accusations of the anti-Jewish, nationalist rioters. "The Man from Sudan" (1989b) describes a Sudanese bicycle repairman who had come to Lebanon for work. In an attempt to flee the village from Israeli air raids, he agrees to accompany a villager to deliver a fully loaded truck to a spot near a foreign embassy in Beirut. Before they can leave, however, the village is bombed and they are both killed. Both stories depict victims of aggression (the Egyptian Jews and the Lebanese villagers), yet there is a certain extent to which the victims are also perceived as aggressors. Joe is considered a suspect in the bombing of a café in Port Said, while his mother is accused of leaving her Sabbath candles lit as a beacon to the Israeli air force during a raid. The Lebanese villager suspects that the Sudanese repairman may be an Israeli spy, and there are clear implications that the villager himself intends to carry out a bombing on the foreign embassy. One wonders if the Arab for Castel-Bloom is purely a historical construct.

REFERENCES

Aharoni, Yair. 1998. "The Changing Political Economy of Israel." *Annals of the American Academy of Political and Social Science* 555 (January): 127–46.

Alcalay, Ammiel. 1993. *After Jews and Arabs: Remaking Levantine Culture*. Minneapolis: University of Minnesota Press.

———, ed. 1996. *Keys to the Garden: New Israeli Writing*. San Francisco: City Lights.

Bakhtin, Mikhail. 1981. *The Dialogic Imagination*. Edited by Michael Holquist. Austin: University of Texas Press.

Beckwith, Stacy. 1997. "The Conceptual State of Israel: Textual Bases for Dominant and Alternative Impressions of the Nation." Ph.D. diss., University of Minnesota.

Ben-Rafael, Eliezer. 1994. *Language, Identity, and Social Division*. Oxford: Clarendon Press.

Butler, Judith. 1990. *Gender Trouble: Feminism and the Subversion of Identity*. New York and London: Routledge.

Castel-Bloom, Orly. 1987. *Not Far from the Center of Town* [in Hebrew]. Tel Aviv: Am Oved.

———. 1989a. "The End of a Decade: Orly Castel-Bloom" [in Hebrew]. *Yediot Aharonot*, 29 December.

———. 1989b. *Hostile Surroundings* [in Hebrew]. Tel Aviv: Zemora-Bitan.

———. 1990. *Where Am I* [in Hebrew]. Tel Aviv: Zemora-Bitan.

———. 1992. *Dolly City* [in Hebrew]. Tel Aviv: Zemora-Bitan.

———. 1993a. *Involuntary Stories* [in Hebrew]. Tel Aviv: Zemora-Bitan.

———. 1993b. "The Lost Article" [in Hebrew]. Speech at International Writers Conference "The Mediterranean Basin: An Ancient Future" in Turin, Italy, 21 May. Reprinted in *Yediot Aharonot*, 11 June 1993: 30.

———. 1994. "Ummi Fi Shurl" [*sic*]. Translated by Dalya Bilu. In *Ribcage: Israeli Women's Fiction*, A Hadassah Anthology, edited by Carol Diament and Lily Rattok, 259–62. Hadassah, n.p.

———. 1995. *Mina Lisa* [in Hebrew]. Jerusalem: Keter.

———. 1996. "Someone Else's Story." Translated by Sheila Jellen. In *Israel: A Traveler's Literary Companion*, edited by Michael Gluzman and Naomi Seidman, 206–10. San Francisco: Whereabouts.

———. 1997. *Dolly City*. Translated by Dalya Bilu. UNESCO Collection of Representative Works. London: Loki Books.

———. 1998. Speech (untitled) at colloquium "Reflections on Literature and Identity," National Foundation for Jewish Culture Writers' Conference, "Writing Jewish Futures: A Global Conversation," San Francisco, 1

February. [Session audiotapes 103.1–103.2 include oral responses to Castel-Bloom by Chana Kronfeld and Hillel Halkin.]

Chodorow, Nancy. 1978. *The Reproduction of Mothering: Psychoanalysis and the Sociology of Gender.* Berkeley: University of California Press.

Coover, Robert. 1987. "Intermission." In *A Night at the Movies, or, You Must Remember This.* New York: Simon and Schuster.

Derrida, Jacques. 1984. "Deconstruction and the Other." In *Dialogues with Contemporary Continental Thinkers: The Phenomenological Heritage*, edited by Richard Kearney, 107–25. Manchester: Manchester University Press.

———. 1985. "Des Tours de Babel." In *Difference in Translation*, edited and translated by Joseph F. Graham, 165–207. Ithaca, N.Y.: Cornell University Press.

Diamond, James. 1986. *Homeland or Holy Land: The "Canaanite" Critique of Israel.* Bloomington: Indiana University Press.

Domínguez, Virginia. 1989. *People as Subject, People as Object: Selfhood and Peoplehood in Contemporary Israel.* Madison: University of Wisconsin Press.

Doron, Gideon. 1998. "The Politics of Mass Communication in Israel." *Annals of the American Academy of Political and Social Science* 555: 163–79.

Elon, Amos. 1980. *Flight into Egypt.* Garden City, N.Y.: Doubleday.

Ethnologue: Languages of the World. 1996. Edited by Barbara Grimes. http://www.sil.org/ethnologue/countries/Isra.html (13). Summer Institute of Linguistics, Inc.

Freud, Sigmund. 1955. "Beyond the Pleasure Principle." In *Standard Edition of the Complete Psychological Works of Sigmund Freud*, vol. 18, 3–64. London: Hogarth Press and the Institute of Psycho-Analysis.

Golan, Yaron. 1989. "Encouraging Surroundings" [in Hebrew]. *Kol Ha'ir*, 31 March, n.p.

Gover, Yerach. 1998. "Post-Zionism and Zionist Utopia." *News from Within* 14 (January): 31–35.

Gurevitz, David. 1990. "In What Language Will We Speak Tomorrow?" [in Hebrew]. Review of *Where Am I*, by Orly Castel-Bloom. *Yediot Aharonot*, 20 February.

Hertzig, Hannah. 1989. "The Poetics of Ugliness" [in Hebrew]. Review of *Hostile Surroundings*, by Orly Castel-Bloom. *Ha'aretz*, 24 March, B8–9.

Hirschfeld, Ariel. 1992. "Chasms behind the Medlar Tree." *Ha'aretz*, 29 May.

Hoffman, Anne Golomb. 1997. "Bodies and Borders: The Politics of Gender in Contemporary Israeli Fiction." In *The Boom in Contemporary Israeli Fiction*, edited by Alan Mintz, 35–70. Hanover, N.H.: Brandeis University Press.

Isaacs, Harold. 1967. *American Jews in Israel.* New York: J. Day.

Kahanoff, Jacqueline. 1978. *From East the Sun* [in Hebrew]. Tel Aviv: Hadar.

Kahanoff, Jacqueline. 1985. "Childhood in Egypt." *Jerusalem Quarterly* 36: 30–41. Originally published in Hebrew in *Keshet* 1, 2 (Winter 1959): 72–79; and reprinted in *From East the Sun*, 11–19.

——. n.d. "Europe from Afar." Unpublished English manuscript. Originally published in Hebrew in *Keshet* 1, 3 (Spring 1959): 52–62; and reprinted in *From East the Sun*, 24–34.

——. n.d. "Israel: Ambivalent Levantine." Unpublished English manuscript. Published in Hebrew as "Black on White" in *Keshet* 1, 4 (Fall 1959): 121–32; and reprinted in *From East the Sun*, 47–59.

Katz, Pearl. 1982. "Ethnicity Transformed: Acculturation in Language Classes in Israel." *Anthropological Quarterly* 55: 99–111.

Matalon, Ronit. 1995. *The One Facing Us* [in Hebrew]. Tel Aviv: Am Oved.

——. 1998. *The One Facing Us*. Translated by Marsha Weinstein. New York: Metropolitan.

Melamed, Ariana. 1996. "Views from the Depths of Repression" [in Hebrew]. Review of *Mina Lisa*, by Orly Castel-Bloom. *Ha'ir*, 9 June.

Mendes-Flohr, Paul, and Jehuda Reinharz. 1980. *The Jew in the Modern World: A Documentary History*. New York and Oxford: Oxford University Press.

Miller, Tal Niv. 1990. "Emotional Novel. Anorexic Language" [in Hebrew]. *'Iton 77*, 126 (July): 8.

Miron, Dan. 1989. "Something on Orly Castel-Bloom" [in Hebrew]. *Al-Hamishmar* 16 (3 June): 19.

Morahg, Gilead. 1997. "Breaking Silence: Israel's Fantastic Fiction of the Holocaust." In *The Boom in Contemporary Israeli Fiction*, edited by Alan Mintz, 143–84. Hanover, N.H.: Brandeis University Press.

Nadel, Elizabeth, and Joshua A. Fishman. 1977. "English in Israel: A Sociolinguistic Study." In *The Spread of English: The Sociology of English as an Additional Language*, edited by Joshua A. Fishman, Robert Cooper, and Andrew Conrad, 137–67. Rowley, Mass.: Newbury House.

Naiger, Motti. 1993. "The Mother, the Son and the P. M. Spirit" [in Hebrew]. Review of *Dolly City*, by Orly Castel-Bloom. *Efes Shtayim* 2: 128–32.

Negev, Eilat. 1995. "To Take a Married Woman" [in Hebrew]. Report on interview with Orly Castel-Bloom. *Yediot Aharonot*, 2 June.

Nissim, Kobi. 1992. "With Arrogance" [in Hebrew]. Review of *Dolly City*, by Orly Castel-Bloom. *Al-Hamishmar*, 5 June.

Pappe, Ilan. 1997. "Post-Zionist Critique on Israel and the Palestinians, Part III: Popular Culture." *Journal of Palestine Studies* 26, 4: 60–69.

Rosenbaum, Yehudit, Elizabeth Nadel, Robert Cooper, and Joshua Fishman. 1977. "English on Keren Kayemet Street." In *The Spread of English: The Sociology of English as an Additional Language*, edited by Joshua A. Fishman,

Robert Cooper, and Andrew Conrad, 179–96. Rowley, Mass.: Newbury House.

Schmelz, U. O., and R. Bachi. 1974. "Hebrew as Everyday Language of the Jews in Israel—Statistical Appraisal." In *Salo Wittmayer Baron Jubilee Volume 2*, 745–85. Jerusalem: American Academy for Jewish Research.

Schnitzer, Meir. 1987. "Wild Head, Steady Hand" [in Hebrew]. *Koteret Rashit*, 12 August.

Seckbach, Fern, and Robert Cooper. 1977. "The Maintenance of English in Ramat Eskhol." In *The Spread of English: The Sociology of English as an Additional Language*, edited by Joshua Fishman, Robert Cooper, and Andrew Conrad, 168–78. Rowley, Mass.: Newbury House.

Segev, Tom. 1993. *The Seventh Million: The Israelis and the Holocaust.* New York: Hill and Wang.

Sheleg, Ya'ir. 1995. "Zionism: The Battle on Writing" [in Hebrew]. *Kol Ha'ir*, 6 October, 57–70.

Silberstein, Laurence. 1999. *The Postzionism Debates: Knowledge and Power in Israeli Culture.* New York and London: Routledge.

Swirski, Shlomo. 1984. "The Oriental Jews in Israel: Why Many Tilted toward Begin." *Dissent* 30: 77–91.

Yiftachel, Oren. 1998. "Democracy or Ethnocracy: Territory and Settler Politics in Israel/Palestine." *Middle East Report* 207: 8–13.

Chapter 11

Weighing the Losses, Like Stones in Your Hand

Ammiel Alcalay

Prologue

Since I have come to scholarship through poetry and poetry through philology, my work has always questioned and disrupted categories that would separate intelligence and music, public discourse and personal narrative, politics and form. Just prior to being asked to participate in the conference "Mapping Jewish Identities," held by the Berman Center for Jewish Studies in May 1998, I was graciously invited to a conference in Beirut commemorating the fiftieth year of *al-Nakba*, the disaster of Palestine, organized by the Lebanese novelist Elias Khoury. More than any gesture of my public intellectual life, this invitation lent a profound and moving legitimacy to the kind of concerns I had been voicing for close to twenty years.

The conference in Beirut was to feature a section specifically discussing the question of Arab Jews, titled "Roots and Exile," with prominent figures such as the Moroccan novelist Edmond el-Maleh, the writer and psychoanalyst Jacques Hassoun, and the former Moroccan political prisoner Abraham Serfaty. I had corresponded with Serfaty a number of years ago, while he was still in Kuneitra Prison, and found—to my amazement and delight—that he had read a number of my articles on Israel and Palestine and the cultural politics of Middle Eastern Jews. When political pressures were brought to bear on abbreviating the Beirut conference and canceling the participation of Arab Jewish intellectuals and others discussing the issue, Elias Khoury and others presented a united front. Although many of the participants could not be present, our work was read and discussed, turning a possible form of censorship into both a real and a symbolic test of the limits of public discourse in a context where the consequences of these limitations are quite concrete. While the principle of openness and historical recuperation was upheld, Elias Khoury was also quoted as saying: "I am sad and feel ashamed that I was unable to defend Abraham Serfaty, the man who taught me the love of the Palestinian cause."

It is precisely this kind of breach and recognition that I find fuels my work and is what I most clearly recognize in the work of others as having the possibility of evoking and effecting the kinds of change that make a difference. The events surrounding my own possible participation in the Beirut conference—coupled with my wish to represent this to a group engaged in "mapping Jewish identities"—also made me think about key moments in my own Palestine, in my own ways of interpreting and mapping the world. In terms of a specific "Jewish" identity, I found these isolated moments from my own specific experience—poetic, personal, textual, and historical—provided very different ways of reading and mapping the kinds of elements that go into making up what we usually consider such an identity to consist of. Thus, for example, a text like Virgil's *Aeneid*, central to me at a certain point in my life, is reread through the filters and experiences of Phoenicia, Lebanon, and Palestine. This, I would emphasize, is not merely an exercise in free association but rather a particular form to engage and recognize markers that have been made invisible on the charts we have been given. It is only by engaging and reconfiguring the contours of these markers that we can summon the kinds of complexity that can lead us to begin learning what personal, national, and other collective identities have been and might again become.

Weighing the losses, like stones in your hand

Often I Am Permitted to Return to a Meadow

> as if it were a scene made-up by the mind,
> that is not mine, but is a made place,
>
> that is mine, it is so near to the heart.
> —Robert Duncan, *The Opening of the Field*

1.

In seersucker overalls, I'm trying to balance myself on the huge old Hudson, the sunlight glaring off the hood. 1960. I'm four years old, still blond from my grandmother, the darker genes haven't kicked in yet. The family's only been in the New World nine years. In the next set of pictures, it's 1963. My hair is dark and, in every picture in the series, I'm holding Jip, my stuffed terrier. What happened?

2.

It takes a long time to learn, not just with the head but with the head and the heart, just how false the models of sophistication and complexity we have been given are. Of beauty. And understanding. The enormous amount of work ("one method is the restoration of memory's remembering on its own terms, organizing along the lines of experience's trace, a reconstruction released from the pressures of uniform exposition—'the only true moments' the ones we have lost, which, in returning to them, come to life in a way that now reveals what they had previously concealed—the social forces that gave shape to them")[1] needed to reach what seem, once finally arrived at, the most obvious conclusions: "One does not write in order to say something, but to define a place where no one will be able to declare what hasn't taken place."[2] Back "home" for just a little over a year (PUBLIC OPINION: "I think he's a slimebag: kill him"),[3] I am trying to reconstruct some sense of our time elsewhere. Because here (in that ritualized disengagement from the world that is the fetish of consumption: lonely at dusk "the monologue of objects, as if they are to ricochet, requiring an anesthesia which skirts this morbidity, at least for now, in this America which one would occupy,"[4] guessing at models and license plates, waiting) and there ("As I left the house behind, I left my childhood behind too. I realized that our life ceased to be pleasant, and it was no longer easy for us to live in peace. Things had reached the point where the only solution was a bullet in the head of each one of us"),[5] inside and out, are two absolutely different places. There is always somewhere else, but here is where this takes place.

3.

My father took a Greyhound cross-country. Newly arrived, and hungry to catalog another set of images, he went from the steel mills (sound bite: "The danger, of course, has to do with the hostile environment . . . the Middle East is nothing like the Middle West . . . with Damascus, Syria, near Youngstown, Ohio, Baghdad, Iraq, would be close to New York City") to the Grand Canyon and the West Coast. I got a postcard from the Enchanted Castle at Disneyland and one from Lombard Street in San Francisco. My brother got some reddish chunks of Petrified Forest. It seemed a happy time, before the summer of high fever, dreams of the pit with prehistoric birds hovering over it, fainting in the bathroom, the stillness of playing alone in the abandoned tractor, the terror of seeing someone dragged away in a straitjacket at a night game.

4.

The fable of our father Abraham just means unfinished business, long after the garden and the flood and the tower. Abraham's brother Haran died before his father, in his native land of Ur-kasdim. But their father, Terah, died in Haran. Abraham was already seventy-five when he set out for Canaan, going through the Negev and on down to Egypt, even before he changed his name.

5.

To want to retrieve or recuperate memory (kids with schoolbags running after a trolley in Cairo, late afternoon; cutting curves on the way to eat at Abu George's in Bethlehem, past midnight; Easter in Athens) would be to concede defeat: "There is no hope in returning to a traditional faith after it has once been abandoned, since the essential condition for holders of a traditional faith is not to know they are traditionalists."[6] An old story: if those who can only grasp things (the masses, the crowd, the people of the land) through the imaginative faculties (not the "intellect" and "reason"), are given an argument that leads to a loss of faith, it's nevertheless obvious that they've understood the argument. Such thinking (or not-thinking) assumes "progress," so the philosophers (and other custodians of order) exert "caution," usually by creating hierarchical systems, with-holding information and mystifying terms of relation and descrip-tion: "You had imagined that people would be more worn out . . . You would have expected to see the signs of rebellion and of anger marked on the face of each one of life's disinherited. In fact, you no-tice nothing like that. You find the same good nature, the same smile ready to flower, the same lively emotions expressed on each face. Fa-talism? Cultural temperament? There's a little of that. But you feel convinced that this is not the essential element. . . . So you tell your-self that it's so much the better that they show this enigmatic en-durance, so much the better that they do not allow their oppressors to see the image of their defeat or weakness, and so much the better that they hide beneath their skin the yeast of future awakenings."[7]

6.

Not sympathy, never pity, but gesture, movement "raising the thresh-old of the urgent."[8] Public discourse admits a breach grinding off to a halting start. ("Given this sense of a 'hidden' community of workers such as myself, I replaced 'the story of the Revolution' with 'the story of turning to words.' This is not quite the same as saying that my writ-ing became a substitute for political action, or that it is something I'll do in between periods of political activism. Rather, I think that I for-mat my writing to go in and out of narrative to coincide with the way I respond to any worlded activity").[9] In the dusty thicket intrepid lib-erty traps light. The discourse AD HOC, active and unfossilized, con-nected to the actual situation of people put away, assumes and ad-umbrates a poetics of the real, a politics intensely felt. Tomorrow it will be someone even closer. Submerged in a return that had begun when. And the intention of that desire carried by a language that grows out of itself and is the magic of fully living within the mother tongue: anyone from someplace can feel it, the brutal anonymity. The ripe the ready the soft the naked flesh. Memory of another time. This crowd, these vistas. Not enough noise. Excessively punctual. We are going (CLIPPETY) to the good (CLOP) people of Zamalek: "Saddika puts down her doll and goes to paddle in the canal. Suddenly a cart dragged by an infuriated mule emerges onto the road. The wheels turn rapidly, madly, with a creaking sound. Before Saddika can climb up the slope again, the cart sweeps round, bowls along, passes her, has passed by. . . . There is nothing left on the ground but a few rags, a little straw and some tiny splinters.

"'I will make you another one,' says Nabila, her elder sister.

"'Never, never . . . This is the doll I want.'

"'I'll make you another one just like it, with these same rags, this same straw, these same sticks.'

"'No, no . . . I want mine.'

"With nothing but this little heap of mud and stuff in her hands, Saddika sobs. She will never be comforted.

"However, by the middle of the night she has already come to the end of her tears. Astonished and disappointed that her tears should so soon be used up, she returns to the canal and ceremoniously lays the remains of her doll on the water. It floats away, rolled up in a damp winding-sheet."[10]

7.

They were cut off from everything else, my "studies": the view across St. Nicholas Park, the old massive Gothic structures, the Vietnam vets I hung out with in the cafeteria who studied ancient Greek. (*The cafeteria almost like grade school, like the school lunches I never ate, preferring bread-and-butter sandwiches with a carton of milk at first and cold cuts later on.*) That far uptown didn't have much to do with downtown and the life I was leading. The Latin class had become a tutorial, since there were only two of us, me and a girl whose name I don't remember but who turned out to be Croatian and spoke a language as familiar and broken as my Serbian the few times we haltingly exchanged a few words as she rushed off to meet her boyfriend before asking me which lines of Virgil were due: we both bore a burden, and it seemed we were on the verge of becoming other people.

8.

And so the story of the vanquished is turned into that of another victory:

> *I'm on a train. I'd considered not mentioning it, but we are passing ship-building yards—and great steel hulls, & cranes rising from the water: ugly & beautiful, dull & fascinating—and houseboats—stark and dreary but for the small parts made of rich warm highly varnished wood—and now the train yards—smallish red cars—hundreds of them. We've left Calais behind. On my way to Paris, I've finally gotten used to London. Now it's easy to be there. In Paris, perhaps you know, there's a neighborhood called Le Marais—it is where you see this ✿ on every shop, the children are dark-skinned with curly black hair, you read "N'oubliez pas!" on the facade of a grammar school, and you can get borscht at Joe Goldenburg's Delicatessen. It's getting to be spring in NY and when I left it was getting to be winter. I think of your life there, envy it in fact—balanced, full, well-conceived—like you. At first I hated everything new and strange—now I grow tense at the thought of the throbbing arrogant familiarity of every building and pile of dog shit in NY. I'm coming for a week or so around the end of May—for the unveiling. It's one year—time is all different because nothing has happened this year, just watching it pass. And I fear nothing will change. I'd like you to come to the ceremony. Horrible as it will be, would you be there anyway?*

9.

It was as if the unyielding logic of the grammar, united with the absurdity of the sentences, provided me with the only mental exercises I'd ever encountered analogous to the kind of menial work I'd done so much of, like bundling papers, shingling, wrapping fruit, sanding fiberglass, or unloading trucks:

The man said that he himself would praise the girl.

Marcus said that he (Claudius) had not praised the woman.

The girl said that the woman had been praised by the man.

The woman thought that the leader should not be praised by the men.

The girl will deny that she (herself) has praised the man.

The man said that the women were praising their own sons.

The boys believed they were being praised by the leader.

The man praising the woman praised by the girls about to praise the boys about to be praised will come to the city.

You came back to the city, but just as you did I was about to leave and I'd be gone for years. Maybe you did envy me when you thought of me from that distance—You wrote about your choices, and I was happy for you, I would only want you to have the best—but what choices could I speak of?

10.

Not much of a transcript, really. A "C" average in high school, and even that was luck and a certain sympathy some of the teachers had for "a great deal of ability that his record does not really show." Then college: a "C" in Shakespeare my first semester, troubles with the registrar, financial aid, disbarred at some point for an unsettled debt. A lot like my students now who, as Kimiko described them, seem extremely pissed off and must have been considered screwups at some point. True survivors. "My life in New York," "your envy." The way up the hill from Broadway, after switching from the express to the local at Ninety-sixth Street. I don't even remember what I carried my books in, it was before knapsacks. A shoulder bag, I guess. Or maybe even my old canvas delivery-boy bag with the wide fluorescent orange strap that I used for brushes and spackle knives and the hawk I was so proud of having bought after learning the finer points of plastering from Jokeem.

11.

STORM	CALM	
Sails	———————	<u>a mission</u> i.e., to do something seeking something

shipwrecks}

                outside

    drowns}

      -DREAM-

---

appears to Halcyone naked &
      dripping—(she sees him as he is)

---

    goes to shore

(his last prayer)

      {body washes ashore at

      {her feet

she leaps into sea

    reverse?   her death = life (sea)
                jumping to <u>him</u>
                as he is
            unable to <u>be sated</u>?

EGGS IN NESTS ON THE SEA

hatched seven days before &
seven after winter solstice

(Ceyx, king of Trachis, disregarding the entreaties of his wife Halcyone [who, as a daughter of Aeolus, knew the power of the sea
winds], sailed to Ionia to consult the oracle of Apollo, and was ship-
wrecked and drowned. All naked and dripping, he appeared to her
in a dream and told her of his death. She hastened to the seashore
and his body [in accordance with his last prayer] was washed
ashore at her feet. She leaped into the sea to kill herself, but the
gods, taking pity, changed her and Ceyx into kingfishers, and Zeus
forbade the winds to blow for seven days prior to and seven days
after the winter solstice when they are hatching their eggs in nests
on the sea.)

12.

The rich purple woven into robes by Dido, from the same sea: "[Will] no color content your eye, but such as is stained by the fish *Murex?*"[11] Such common English usage dates back to 1589, four hundred years after the Third Crusade: *Sarranus murex,* known throughout the Roman Empire. Purple from Tyre. Dido, the refugee in Carthage: "upon her shoulders / she wears a robe of Sidon with embroidered / borders. Her quiver is of gold, her hair / has knots and ties of gold, a golden clasp / holds fast her purple cloak."[12] My old, beat-up copy of Virgil, the spine already broken off when I got it, only some grayish cardboard showed between the nondescript, muddy-colored boards. I kept my notes in it with a mechanical pencil, to get between the lines of the tiny print as I struggled with the text. Dido: a Phoenician woman given in marriage by her father as a virgin to a man who was then murdered by her brother. Dido: a Lebanese refugee, a suicide. The fingernails of her sister Anna scratching her face and wounding her flesh in lamentation as Aeneas sails off with his son toward Italy, leaving behind the glowing flames of Tunis: "Because the Marquis of Sidon, who was waiting for a dispensation from the pope to put his sister under a Muslim, or if not his sister then his niece, was not suitable as a genuine ally against the English, who were holding Acre under siege . . . Because the aim of partitioning the land into coast and mountain between Arab and Frank was not, under prevailing conditions, to guarantee for the Arabs whatever forts and terrain had remained in their hands but to grant the enemy a respite that enabled him to establish a pattern that sanctioned his transition from exception to rule . . . And they read the history of forts and citadels conquerors used as signatures to keep their names alive in lands not theirs and to forge the identity of rocks and oranges . . . Forts and citadels that are no more than attempts to protect a name that does not trust time to preserve it from oblivion . . . It has had a long history, this double operation of searching for a place or a time on which to put a signature and untie the knot of the name facing the long caravan of oblivion."[13]

13.

How can I even begin to describe Jaffa, as a repository of memories that could never have been mine but which still remain familiar, or as material proof of a forbidden and concealed history that is still being lived despite the extent of the defeat? What was I looking for, in Rome, Jerusalem, Egypt, Palestine? The cities, towns, and villages my family once hid out or lived in? The physical presence and texture of places that had once been a part of what I would become? The gaze of Ascanius I had read about in a book, looking back at the kind and beautiful Queen who had hoped to kidnap the heart of the father by embracing the son? Could this possibly be what the "distinguished" professor meant when he said that students have to read the "Western" classics since that is part of "our" "heritage"?

14.

There aren't any known historical depictions of Dido, also known as Princess Elissa. Punic coins made of electrum, a mixture of silver and gold, depict a woman's face in profile that has variously been claimed as Dido, Demeter, Persephone, and the Phoenician deity Tanit, believed to be of Libyan origin. Her nose is long and angular; her eyes are also long, set deeply into her high cheeks. Her lips are resolute but bend ever so slightly to the sloping curve of her chin. Her hair is extremely curly, set in a diadem that also seems to have a thick braid pulled through it. She is wearing a long earring, with three hanging pendants. Her neck is thin and elongated; at the bottom of the coin, a simple embroidered lace adorns her clothing. As the granddaughter of King Mattan of Tyre, she would have been the great-niece of King Ahab's wife Jezebel, the daughter of Ethbaal, king of Sidon and a former high priest of the goddess Astarte. It was Jezebel's daughter, Athalia, who was instrumental in bringing forbidden Phoenician practices back to the southern kingdom of Judah.

15.

Phoenician and Hebrew are regional dialects of the Canaanite language. In my son's encyclopedia, it says: "A tiny group of cities perched along the coast of the Mediterranean produced the most famous sailors and traders of the ancient world. These seafaring people were called the Phoenicians. The cities of Phoenicia were linked by the sea, and they traded in many goods, including purple dyes, glass, and ivory. From 1200 to 350 B.C. the Phoenicians controlled trade throughout the Mediterranean." In another entry, under alphabet, it says: "The Phoenicians, who lived about 3,000 years ago in the Middle Eastern country now called Syria, developed the first modern alphabet. The ancient Greeks adapted the Phoenician alphabet, and later the Romans improved it. The Roman alphabet is now widely used throughout the world."[14] Phoenician inscriptions have been found in Cyprus, Greece, Egypt, Africa, Italy, France, Spain, and the islands of Melitus, Gaulos, Sicily, Cossura, Sardinia, and Corsica. The following text is from Carthage:

> Tariff of payments set up by [the
> men in charge of the payments . . .].

[For an ox, as whole offerings or *substitute offerings*], the priests [shall have] the skins, and the person offering the sacrifice the *fat parts* [. . .].

For a stag [as whole offerings or *substitute offerings*], the priests [shall have] the skins, and the person offering the sacrifice the *fat parts* [. . .].

For a ram or a goat, as whole offerings or as *substitute offerings*, the priests shall have the skins of the goats, and the person offering the sacrifice shall have the *ribs* [. . .].

For a lamb or for a kid or for a *young* stag, as whole offerings or *substitute offerings*, the priests shall have the skins [. . .].

For any sacrifice which shall be offered by persons poor in cattle, the priest shall have nothing whatever.

For an *'gnn* bird or for a *ss* (bird), 2 *zr* of silver for each.

[For any *substitute offering* wh]ich he shall have to carry to the God, the priest shall have *necks* and *shoulder joints* [. . .].

[Upon any] holy [*oblation*] and upon a hunt offering and upon an oil offering [. . .].

Upon a *cake (fodder)* and upon milk (fat) and upon a sacrifice as a meal-offering and upon [. . .].

Any payment which is not specified in this tablet shall be made [according to the written document . . .].

Any priest who shall take [. . .].

Any person offering a sacrifice who [. . .].

Any person who shall trade [. . . , and who] shall shatter this tablet [. . .].[15]

16.

A talent of gold a talent of silver, the sound of crushed shells under our feet. Shells at the bottom, shells from the top, shrapnel and shards. Any person who shall trade, any person who shall shatter. This name, this likeness. That I carry myself. And of you within me. And your curly hair as we untangle the spreading roots that take us farther and farther away only that we "may learn what is the winged oak and the decorated cloth upon it."[16] The fabric a veil we never placed between us to consecrate our union. Now the shells, in a bottle on the shelf of a room you're not in. "Shelf." "Ledge." "Room." "Chamber." "Window." "Portico." "Fabric": "cloak," "shirt," "tunic," "gown," "dress." Clay, brick, lime, slate, mortar, ash, sand, gravel, wood, glass, copper, brass, lead, plaster, burnt umber: the materials of the building you sift through my hands as we survey the wreckage. Walking up the hill from the beach past the lighthouse, the lack of fish and tainted water, the breakers choppy. This sea. This body we drift and skirt, the water rushing past your toes as I run after you in the wind of a winter sun in Jaffa. The chiming bells dangle past garages and welding shops and junkyards, the pavement soaked in oil and the flash of acetylene lost in the din of spinning rims, grinders, generators, jacks, pumps, and compressors. Most of the world is like this road—a place in between other places—the hood open, someone busy peering down into a carburetor as a bus careens around a hairpin turn, picking up speed for the next hill. Today the sun burst through the clouds over the elevated at Fourth Avenue and in the distance the girders looked just like the awning of a ruined Roman amphitheater, where the cornice has been chipped away, the inner and outer shells blending with vaults and columns, arches and windows, brackets and arcades.

17.

As I look at pictures of us in different places I wonder what made Virgil tell the version of Dido's story that he told. More than seventy years before the poet was born, right on Byrsa Hill (where the Queen Dido Hotel now overlooks the excavations of Punic houses), as the Romans set fire to building after building, the wife of Hasdrubal—the last commander of Punic Carthage, who begged at the knees of Scipio—cursed her husband and, dressed in her finest robes, jumped into the flames of a funeral pyre she had prepared for herself. Legend has it that the widow Dido or Elissa, having escaped the blood feud of her brother Pygmalion and made her way to Carthage (after getting a group of maidens about to offer their virginity at a temple of Astarte in Cyprus to join her expedition), also leaped into the flames of a funeral pyre rather than submit to a local Libyan king. Even Virgil cannot deny her pride, as he put these words in Dido's mouth: "We Tyrians / do not have minds so dull and we are not / beyond the circuit of the sun's yoked horses."[17]

18.

To see the very shadows cast by precisely that sun; to feel the heat of the rocks before evening and their coolness before daybreak, to rub pepper leaves and rosemary between my fingers, to dream of ancestral homes we never knew, gardens fallen into ruin, memorials never erected or left unvisited. I keep looking through the pictures, putting some aside and concentrating on others. An older one, in black and white: you are leaning against a stone pillar in the ruins of the old olive press in Sheikh Badr, just across the road from where we lived; you wear a long black coat—it's winter. Then a more recent one: our son running with a friend along the plaza of smooth paving stones leading up to the stairs below the archway that frames the magnificent golden dome of the Haram as-Sharif in full sunlight. Their shadows are distinct and slant at perfect forty-five-degree angles below the slender cedars where you once nursed him before we left. Another one: this time Mahmoud swings our boy through the air as he grips his baseball hat, screaming with glee—they're right in front of the fountain that never works marking the twenty-fifth anniversary of Sultan Abdul Hamid's rule, near the Muristan and the Aftimos Market. Which chapters of *his* life will these images attach themselves to, like so many barnacles seeking an anchor in the sea of this world?

19.

I am here now (*"here—in the whirlpool of the city, in the incessant noise of masses of refugees and exiles from different lands and of different races, among sad displaced peasants in broad blue gowns who had left a homeland not their own to oppressors and bloodsucking landlords to escape emptyhanded to the distant and enchanting city of promise and to try their fortune there as porters and street-cleaners, doormen and pickpockets"*).[18] Here, now: these are the innocents. Over and over, they claim they have no one to talk to. I can touch the clouds, the trees, my window. Light all over, fast, under: love's body rocks the child to sleep. The staff of youth. A wooden figurehead: skeletal hands holding a small globe. Columbus. Cement tower of Pisa behind on a hill, streetlight to the right: David, Machiavelli, Atahuallpa, a Pope, Pizarro. Naked women holding a fish. Going from the Grand Canal to Lido and seeing St. Mark's Square for the first time, the line "I hear Arabia calling" kept repeating itself over and over again to me, like some long-lost amulet whose coolness I could finally feel against my chest: "The final page of my notes is about deception, a tree falls. There is the blank face of indifference in the afternoon of staring happily and thoughtlessly into your child, the ultimate learning, there is the face of hardheartedness, the adorned face of the confusion of having been taken by storm before thought could leap up, take you higher, and there is the face of wickedness, again the face of my education upon which I walk backwards like a devil on a moral precipice to cast off."[19]

NOTES

1. Charles Bernstein, "The Dollar Value of Poetry," in *The L=A=N=G=U=A=G=E Book*, ed. Bruce Andrews and Charles Bernstein (Carbondale: Southern Illinois University Press, 1984), 139.
2. Bernard Noel, "The Outrage against Words," in *The L=A=N=G=U=A=G=E Book*, ed. Andrews and Bernstein, 190.
3. 1989 television news opinion poll on Noriega and the invasion of Panama.
4. Jerry Estrin, *in motion speaking* (San Francisco: Chance Editions, 1986), 49.
5. From Ghassan Kanafani's "The Land of the Sad Oranges," in *Men in the Sun and Other Palestinian Stories* (London: Heinemann, 1982), 61.
6. Phrase commonly attributed to Abu al-Ghazali, the eleventh-century Islamic theologian and mystic.
7. Abdellatif Laabi, *Rue du Retour* (London: Readers' International, 1989), 99–100.
8. Quoted from Erica Hunt in a talk given on the panel "Poetry for the Next Society: Design for Continuing Investigation" at the St. Mark's Poetry Project, New York, N.Y., May 7, 1989.
9. Tina Darragh, "Error Message," *Poetics Journal* 5 (May 1985): 120.
10. Andree Chedid, *The Sixth Day* (London: Serpent's Tail, 1987), 141–42.
11. *The Compact Edition of the Oxford English Dictionary* (Oxford: Oxford University Press, 1971), 772.
12. *The Aeneid of Virgil*, book 4, 182–86, trans. Allen Mandelbaum (New York: Bantam Books, 1972), 85–86.
13. Mahmoud Darwish, *Memory for Forgetfulness: August, Beirut, 1982*, trans. Ibrahim Muhawi (Berkeley: University of California Press, 1995). This is a collage of quotes from 47–48 and 14–15.
14. *The Random House Children's Encyclopedia* (New York: Random House, 1991), 412 and 25.
15. This text, known as "The Carthage Tariff," is one of a number of fragments found in Carthage over a number of years, beginning in 1858 (*The Ancient Near East: An Anthology of Texts and Pictures*, ed. James B. Pritchard [Princeton: Princeton University Press, 1958], 223–24).
16. A fragment from Isidorus the Gnostic, first to second century A.D., in G. S. Kirk and J. E. Raven, *The Presocratic Philosophers* (Cambridge: Cambridge University Press, 1957), 62.
17. *Aeneid of Virgil*, book 1, 798–800, trans. Mandelbaum, 20.
18. This description of Cairo appears in Yitzhak Shami's *The Vengeance of the Fathers*, in *Eight Great Hebrew Short Novels*, ed. Alan Lelchuk and Gershon Shaked (New York: New American Library, 1983), 126.
19. Bernadette Mayer, *Eruditio ex Memoria* (Lenox, Mass.: Angel Hair, 1977), n.p.

Chapter 12

The Close Call; or, Could a Pharisee Be a Christian?

Daniel Boyarin

For Bluma, Chana, David, Erich, Naomi, Dina, and Galit—
colleagues, conversationalists, friends

The So-Called Parting of the Ways

Even scholars who have recognized that Christianity can hardly be
derived as a "daughter" religion from Judaism have still tended to
assume a distinct "parting of the ways" sometime in the first or second century, after which there was hardly any contact between the
two religions. Philip Alexander has written, "Since there are clearly
radical aspects to early Christianity the tendency has been to see
the parting of the ways as having taken place early, usually in the
first or early second century C.E. Some analyses so stress the radicalism of early Christianity as to suggest that the parting of the ways
occurred almost *ab ovo.*"[1] Many would place this final break as early
as 70 A.C., after the destruction of the Jerusalem Temple. Others
put it somewhat later. One of the leading Israeli historians has put
it thus: "With the Bar Kokhba rising the final rift between Judaism
and Christianity was complete."[2] Such a statement is possible only
on a reading according to which "Jewish Christians," that is, for instance, almost the entire Syrian church, are neither Jews nor Chris-

This article appears in *Dying for God: Martyrdom and the Making of Christianity and Judaism,* by Daniel Boyarin (Stanford: Stanford University Press, 1999), and is used with
the permission of the publishers. No part of the text may be reproduced without the
written permission of Stanford University Press. The notes have been abridged considerably for this publication, and various other abridgements have also been made.

tians, rather than both. This is, I claim, a dogmatic judgment, not a historical one.[3] Indeed, there has been a kind of general collusion between Jewish and Christian scholars (as earlier between Rabbis and doctors of the church) to insist on this total lack of impact and contact, each for their own reasons.[4] This mutual stake has been described, once more by Alexander: "The attempt to [lay down a norm for Judaism in the first century] barely conceals apologetic motives—in the case of Christianity a desire to prove that Christianity transcended or transformed Judaism, in the case of Jews a desire to suggest that Christianity was an alien form of Judaism which deviated from the true path."[5] Indeed, the very distinctness of Judaism has been articulated by Jews as precisely its distance from a "syncretistic" Christianity whose defining feature is that it is somehow a composite of Judaism and Hellenism.[6]

Alexander has provided a fairly simple, graphic metaphor for an alternative approach: "If we picture Judaism and Christianity as circles we can graphically represent how we reached the present state of affairs as follows. Today the circles stand side by side essentially in self-contained isolation. If we move the horizon of time backwards this monadic relationship remains more or less constant until we come roughly to the fourth century of the current era. Then an important development takes place: we observe the circles approaching and beginning to overlap."[7] It is to Alexander's credit that he complicates the picture of a simple "parting of the ways" that took place once and for all, but it seems that his Venn diagrams provide too simple a model for the reconfiguring that needs to be done.

Changing Paradigms: Religions and Family Resemblance

The breaking down of the cultural boundaries between groups in close spatial contact is a point at issue not only in the writing of histories of late antiquity but in our understanding of cultures and their interactions in general. The newly developing perspective on Judaism and Christianity as intertwining cultures is thus dependent on a developing climate of opinion or even *Zeitgeist.* As Homi Bhabha has written:

The theoretical recognition of the split-space of enunciation may open the way to conceptualizing an *international* culture, based not on the exoticism of multiculturalism or the *diversity* of cultures, but on the inscription and articulation of culture's *hybridity*. To that end we should remember that it is the "inter"—the cutting edge of translation and negotiation, the *in-between* space—that carries the burden of the meaning of culture.[8]

Bhabha, in other words, suggests that cultures are never bounded and singular entities.[9] In accord with much current cultural theory, then, with its focus on hybridity (and with models of identity construction that are favored today), I offer here a revised model for understanding the historical relationship of the two "new" religions of late antiquity, Judaism and Christianity.

First of all, I suggest that the kinship metaphors need to be abandoned, for they imply, ipso facto, the kinds of organic entities and absolute separations that it is precisely the work of this text to displace, or at any rate to call into question. Instead, I think we might usefully substitute something like Wittgenstein's notion of family resemblance as a semantic, logical category. All Judaisms and all Christianities share features that make them a single semantic family in the Wittgensteinian sense. This essentially logical category has its historical analogue as well. Rather than parallel but essentially separate histories, I propose a model of shared and criss-crossing lines of history and religious development. To make sense of how such developments could take place, we need to imagine the modes by which new religious ideas, practices, and discourses could be shared. I tend to think of Judaism and Christianity as points on a continuum from the Marcionites (the followers of the second-century Marcion, who believed that the Hebrew Bible had been written by an inferior god and had no standing for Christians) on one end, who completely deny the "Jewishness" of Christianity, to many Jews on the other end for whom Jesus meant nothing. In the middle, however, were many gradations that provided social and cultural progression from one end to the other of this spectrum. In other words, to use a linguistic metaphor, I am suggesting a wave theory of Christian-Jewish history, one in which convergence is as possible as divergence, as opposed to the traditional *Stammbaum* model, within which virtually only divergence is possible after 70 A.C., or in some versions, 135 A.C.[10]

Let me develop this point. In one form of linguistic historiography, groups of languages are taken as descended from a common ancestry, a "proto-language," from which they have diverged as their populations separated from each other. Similarities between the resulting languages are ascribed to their common ancestry. This is called the *Stammbaum*, or family-tree model, which we so often see in handbooks. According to this model, for example, all of the Romance languages are daughter languages of the vernacular, spoken Latin of European late antiquity. Notice the kinship metaphor employed, similar to the kinship metaphors used until now for describing the relationship between Judaism and Christianity. According to another model, however, the languages in a given group might very well have similarities that are the product of convergence, of new developments in one that have passed to the others, because the languages are still in contact with each other. This is called wave theory, on the assumption that an innovation takes place at a certain location and then spreads like a wave from that site to others, almost in the fashion of a stone thrown into a pond. Separate languages are, on this theory, artifacts of the canonization of a particular dialect as the official language of a given group. An example may be helpful: If one were to travel from Paris to Florence speaking only the local dialect in each town or village, one would not know when one had passed from France to Italy. There is no linguistic border "on the ground." The reason we speak of French and Italian as separate languages is precisely that the dialect of Paris and the dialect of Florence have been canonized as the national languages. Similarly, I suggest, social contact and the gradations of religious life were such that, barring the official pronouncements of the leaders of what were to become the "orthodox" versions of both religions, one could travel, metaphorically, from rabbinic Jew to Christian along a continuum where one hardly would know where one stopped and the other began.

This model allows us to see Judeo-Christianity (not in its modern sense of a homogenized common culture) as a single circulatory system, within which discursive elements could move from non-Christian Jews and back again, developing as they move back and forth and around the system. My perspective here is very close to that of Galit Hasan-Rokem, who writes:

> I base my discussion on a cultural model which a) prefers to look at interaction between cultures in terms of dialogue rather than "influence" (often defined, . . . according to a unidirectional conceptualization) . . . ; b) deals with exchange rather than polemics (Lieberman's model) . . . ; c) instead of opposing canonical vs. noncanonical texts, looks at the constant dynamics between them as represented in the interaction between oral/literal, religious/ secular. . . .
>
> The discursive model which has been the implicit or explicit basis for most discussions on intergroup relations in Rabbinic literature, namely the one which conceptualizes intergroup relations as polemic, stems from a very elitist view of the formation of the texts, and does not reflect the full complexity, multivocality and dynamic points of view introduced in the folk narrative texts themselves.[11]

Following this model, there could and would have been social contact, sometimes various forms of common worship, all up and down the continuum of "Jews" and "Christians." This social continuity provided for the possibility of cultural interaction and shared religious development. Thus, for instance, H. J. Drijvers has argued that "Christianity" in Edessa had virtually nothing to do with "Judaism" until the *end of the third century*, when connection with and influence of the Jewish "conversation" expanded dramatically.[12] A further corollary to this revised model of Jewish and Christian history is that there might very well be a gap between the explicit claims of certain texts that groups are different and separate and the actual situation "on the ground," in which there was much less definition, much more fuzziness at the borders, and thus much more possibility of converging religious and cultural histories than would otherwise seem the case. Such gaps between people's perceptions or articulations of social relations and what can be observed are a commonplace of cognitive anthropology and would be more even expected in the highly charged situation of formative religious groups. Indeed, as both Virginia Burrus and Dina Stein have emphasized to me, denials of sameness are precisely what we would expect in situations of difficult difference. I am not suggesting, for instance, that there is no distinction at all between "Judaism" and "Christianity" by the second century, only that the border between the two was so fuzzy that one could hardly say precisely at what point one stops and the other begins. "It is monstrous to talk of Jesus Christ and to practice Judaism," thunders Ignatius, thus making both points at once: the drive of the nascent orthodoxy to separation and the lack thereof "on the ground" (*Magnesians* 10.3).[13] The monster, it seems, was very lively indeed. It is important, moreover, to emphasize that in order to assume convergence as well as divergence, we hardly have to assume noncompetitive or irenic relations between subgroups.[14] As Israel Jacov Yuval has recently written of the intersecting developments of Passover and Easter liturgies: "Parallel development of two different narratives about the same Festival among two rival groups living in close proximity necessarily produces great similarity together with mutual tensions."[15]

All these considerations raise serious terminological problems, because at the same time that I wish to deny the early existence of separate Judaism and Christianity, I am also speaking of the relationship between two entities that are, in some senses, recognizably different.[16] I will accordingly try to be careful to speak not of "Judaism" and "Christianity" in what follows but of *rabbinic* Judaism and *Catholic* Christianity, or sometimes, as contextually appropriate, of Christian Jews and non-Christian Jews (a reversal of the usual Jewish Christians and non-Jewish Christians), as the two main (in the sense of finally "successful") formative entities within this system. Finally, in accord with the usage of the third-century Syriac text the *Didascalia*, I shall (at least erratically) refer to Judaism and Christianity, not as religions but as "conversations," thus capturing, somewhat anachronistically to be sure, the sense of nondifferentiation that I wish to emphasize.

I think that we need to take seriously the extent to which non-Christian Jews and Christians were themselves "in conversation" with each other at many sites throughout the Roman Empire, including notably Palestine, Antioch, and Rome but not only in those places. More scholars are beginning to adopt the perspective articulated so well by Wayne Meeks and Robert Wilken: "For the understanding of early Christianity, it is necessary to study Judaism, not only as it existed in the so-called 'intertestamental period,' i.e., as 'background' to Christianity, but as a vital social and religious force during the early centuries of the Common Era. Its presence as an independent religion alongside Christianity during this period helped to shape the context in which Christianity developed."[17] The same is true, of course, in the reverse direction. But I would go even a bit further. These religio-cultural histories were inextricably intertwined to the point where the very distinction between syncretism and "authentic" Judaism, Christianity, and "paganism" will finally seem irrelevant.

Let me cite some colorful examples of various types and various weights in support of this hypothesis. W. H. C. Frend has noted that, according to a document preserved in Eusebius's church history, the famous martyrs of Lyons of 177 had been eating kosher meat, which they must have been purchasing at "a kosher market established for the Jews, and this in turn indicates fairly close personal relations between the Jews and Christians in the city."[18] Although in this case we can hardly speak of shared observance, since the Lyonnais Christians were merely following apostolic rules preserved in Acts, nevertheless, if Frend is correct in his assumption that they purchased the meat from a "kosher" butcher, this observance brought them into intimate contact with Jews. An example of quite a different type is the general observation of both Saturday and Sunday as holy days among fourth-century Eastern monastics.[19] Now, according to Eusebius, this double observance is precisely the marker of the so-called Ebionite heresy: "They observed the sabbath and the other Jewish customs, . . . yet, on the other hand, each Lord's day they celebrated rites similar to ours, in memory of the Saviour's resurrection" (2.27.5).[20] In other words, in the very heartland of developing Eastern Orthodox Christian life, the monasteries and hermitages of Egypt and Palestine, something that Eusebius would regard as a "judaizing heresy" and as only belonging to the past was central to the religious actuality.[21] It becomes much easier now to understand why there would be Christians who would attend synagogue services on the Sabbath and church on the Lord's Day. This puts a somewhat different cast on the "problems" that both Origen and John Chrysostom faced of those who followed such "syncretistic" practices.[22] Jerome complains as well that the Christians imitate the liturgy of the Jews.[23]

Some of the most striking examples come from actually shared worship (admittedly rarely attested but not the less significant for that).[24] In fifth-century Minorca, "Theodore and his relatives stood at the head of a community where Jews and Christians had learned to coexist, sharing, for instance, in the same haunting beauty of their chanted psalms."[25] At Mamre, the site of the Abrahamic epiphany, Jews, Christians, and pagans were carrying on a common religious festival, apparently also as late as the fifth century (according to the Palestinian church historian Sozomen), in which

> the inhabitants of the country and of the regions round Palestine, the Phoenicians and the Arabs, assemble annually during the summer season to keep a brilliant feast; and many others, both buyers and sellers, resort there on account of the fair. Indeed this feast is diligently frequented by all nations: by the Jews, because they boast of their descent from the patriarch Abraham; by the pagans, because angels there appeared to men; and by Christians because He who has lately revealed himself through the virgin for the salvation of mankind once appeared there to the pious man. . . . Some pray to the God of all; some call upon the angels, pour out wine, or burn incense, or offer an ox, or he-goat, a sheep or a cock . . .

and "all abstain from coming near their wives."[26] This description presents a remarkable picture. Not only do the three religious groups that Sozomen describes gather together for a common fair, but they celebrate together what is essentially the same feast, a festival in honor of Abraham's angelic epiphany, each with a slightly different explanation for the feast, and each with slightly different practices, including practices of one conversation that theoretically would be anathema to the others. We have no reason to suppose that such "regional cults" were common, but this description is certainly indicative, as late as Sozomen in the fifth century, of social conditions within which religious interaction was possible between the so-called separated religions in Palestine.

In short, without the power of the Orthodox Church and the Rabbis to declare people heretics and outside the system—"neither Jews nor Christians," in Jerome's words[27]—it remains impossible to declare phenomenologically who is a Jew and who is a Christian. At least as interesting and significant, it seems more and more clear that it is frequently impossible to tell a Jewish text from a Christian text.[28] The borders are fuzzy, and this has consequences.[29] Religious ideas and innovations can cross the borders in both directions.

These border crossings can take place sometimes where we expect them least. In her recent Hebrew work *The Web of Life*, Galit Hasan-Rokem has analyzed a fourth-century Palestinian midrash text that tells of the birth of the Messiah in Bethlehem.[30] Hasan-Rokem demonstrates that this story comes from a level that might be called (for want of a less anachronistic term) folk literature of the Jews of Palestine and has been adopted into and canonized, as it were, in a high rabbinic text. The choice of Bethlehem as the birthplace of the Messiah is based on the same midrash on the same verse (Micah 5:1) as the midrashim on which Matthew and Luke base their birth narratives, and indeed, the stories are alike in many narratively significant details: the Messiah is revealed by a traveler; there are three wise men; there are gifts for the mother and the child; and the mother is destitute. In a brief recent English version of this discussion, Hasan-Rokem emphasizes:

> The preservation of this legend both in the Talmud and the Midrash attests to the fact that the consolidation of the gospel tradition did not result in an elimination of the legend from the Jewish folk literary corpus, as could have been expected. As far as I can see, the rabbinical inclusion of the tale does not direct itself to the polemical potential of the text. It may rather be interpreted as a folk literary dialogue, an oral intertextuality between two interpretative paradigms of the same plot.[31]

Thus, she elaborates, this collection

> indicates that there is not necessarily a polemic or imitation here, but similarity of details which is typical of folk narration. It seems to me that this is a parade example of folk traditions that are common to Jews who belong to the majority of the people and to the minority who believe in the Messiahship of Jesus and join the early Christian church, whose main social base is Jewish.[32]

In her recent publication, however, Hasan-Rokem goes even further:

> If, however, we prefer to explain the appearance of the legend in the Jewish corpus as ancillary to the gospel tradition rather than parallel to it, then the absence of polemical overtones leads us to a view . . . [that] some of the narrative and idiomatic alternatives developed by ecclesiastical Christianity into dogmas echo folk narra-

tive elements extant in Jewish, both Rabbinical and early Christian, communities in Palestine and its vicinity in the first centuries of the Christian era. The Midrash texts include them in their exploration of potential sources of consolation in a troubled era."[33]

Hasan-Rokem's analysis suggests strongly that Jews and Christians were not only confronting each other, determined to shore up their identities as well as triumph over each other; they were also listening to each other and learning.[34]

When Rabbi Eliezer Was Arrested by Christianity

A third-century Palestinian text tells the shocking story of a Pharisee who was arrested during the Trajanic persecutions of Christianity:

> It happened to Rabbi Eliezer that he was arrested for sectarianism (Christianity),[35] and they took him up to the βημα to be judged.
> The ruler said to him: A sage such as you having truck with these matters!?
> He said to him: I have trust in the judge.
> The ruler thought that he was speaking of him, but he meant his Father in Heaven. He said to him: Since you trust me, I also have said: Is it possible that these gray hairs would err in such matters? *Dimus [= Dimissus]*! Behold, you are dismissed.

To avoid being martyred as a Christian, Rabbi Eliezer exploits an ambiguity of language. He answers the charge of Christianity, implicitly a charge of disloyalty to the Empire, by indicating his fealty to the Roman *hēgemōn* (leader). The Rabbi is nevertheless quite distressed. He understands that he would not have been arrested at all were it not for some sin that he had committed, and he cannot rest until he discovers that sin, for indeed, he does have trust in the Judge of the World that does not do injustice:

> When he had left the βημα, he was troubled that he had been arrested for sectarianism. His disciples came in to comfort him, but he was inconsolable. Rabbi Akiva came in and said to him: Rabbi, I will say before you a word; perhaps you will not be troubled.
> He said to him: Say!

He said to him: Perhaps one of the sectarians said something to you of sectarianism, and it caused you pleasure.

He said to him: By heaven, you have reminded me. Once I was walking in the marketplace of Tsippori, and I found there Yaakov, the man of Kefar Sikhnin,[36] and he recounted a saying of sectarianism in the name of Yeshu the son of Pantiri, and it caused me pleasure, and I was arrested by/for the words of sectarianism, for I violated that which is written in the Torah, "Keep her ways far away from you, and don't come near the opening of her house, for she has brought many victims down!" [Proverbs 5:8]. (Tosefta *Hullin*, 2:24)[37]

Our story illustrates beautifully the hypothesis of simultaneous rabbinic attraction to and repulsion from Christianity. On the one hand, we find here a narrative which, like the letter of Jerome to Augustine, is very anxious to exclude anything Christian from the realm of proper rabbinic Jewish proximity. Jerome's important notice that the sect of Nazarenes are to be found "in all of the synagogues of the East among the Jews" and that they consider themselves both Christians and Jews but are really "neither Christians nor Jews" is highly revealing. Christianity and Judaism can be kept apart, it seems, and thus produced as separate religions only by fiat, whether from Rabbis or Doctors of the Church: "Keep her ways far away from you." On the other hand, in the same Tosefta narrative, the attractiveness of Christianity to even a centrally located rabbinical hero, Rabbi Eliezer, is brought to the fore, and perhaps even more than this, as we shall presently see.[38]

There is an important interpretative question with respect to this text that needs to be addressed, namely: Why did Rabbi Eliezer not simply deny his Christianity? Why the evasiveness? An accused Christian had to perform two acts in order to prove his or her "innocence." The first was to sacrifice to the emperor, and the second was to curse Jesus. We have an excellent contemporary description of this practice from Pliny the Younger's famous letter to Trajan:

Those who denied that they were, or had ever been, Christians, who repeated after me an invocation to the Gods, and offered adoration, with wine and frankincense, to your image, which I had ordered to be brought for that purpose, together with those of the Gods, and who finally cursed Christ—none of which acts, it is said, those who are really Christians can be forced into performing—these I thought it proper to discharge.[39]

Although, to be sure, we cannot assume uniformity and systematization of the judicial process, this text is certainly evocative of the possibilities that were available for proof of non-Christianity.[40] The *Martyrdom of Polycarp* provides further evidence that this was not, at any rate, a mere fluke, as the proconsul offers the aged bishop the option: "Take the oath and I will let you go; revile Christ [λοιδορησον τον Χριστον]."[41] Although a Jew could not prove his non-Christian leanings by sacrificing to the emperor, he could curse Jesus.[42] Why, then, did not Rabbi Eliezer simply say: *Christianus non sum. Iudaeus sum?* My teacher, Professor Saul Lieberman, of blessed memory, raised this problem and offered what I, with due modesty, take as an intentionally tricky answer, namely, that Rabbi Eliezer feared further questioning on the "intimate internal affairs of the rabbinic academies."[43] I suggest in all diffidence and respect that the very implausibility of the explanation offered by Lieberman is intended precisely to lead us to a warranted, if highly unsettling, answer.[44] I hypothesize, accordingly, that the text is hinting that Rabbi Eliezer did not *want* to curse Jesus. Rabbi Eliezer, the text implies, had more than some sympathy to Jesus and his followers and their Torah, an implication that is supported as well by the Rabbi's irenic Torah conversation with this Yakov/James. I have pointed to the proximity of Rabbi Eliezer to Christianity in cultural/ideological matters before, particularly with respect to his attitudes toward sexuality.[45]

There is a double meaning, a bit of trickster language or indirection, in this text that is not directed at the *hēgemōn* but perhaps at the very readers of the text. The phrase that I have translated as "arrested for sectarianism" could just as easily be translated from the Hebrew as "arrested by sectarianism," that is, captured intellectually or spiritually by Christianity.[46] It is important to recall that the tradition itself remembers that Rabbi Eliezer was declared heretic by the Rabbis for a period of his life (see below). If, indeed, there is a sort of repressed motive here of this central rabbinic figure's attraction to Christianity, then the point that I am making against drawing strict lines between the histories of what only *much* later became defined as separate religions is considerably strengthened. In inscribing Rabbi Eliezer—one of the most canonical and central of rabbinic culture heroes—in a fictive plot situation that would lead him to extreme marginality and then, in the end, recuperating him, the biographical narrative is inscribing, I suggest, the under-construction, being-invented nature of the divide between Christians and Rabbis in the third century.[47]

In an important discussion of the Pseudo-Clementines, Albert Baumgarten has shown from the Christian side evidence of attachments of at least some Galilean Jewish Christians (in the strict sense, i.e., Christians who were apparently ethnically Jews) to the Pharisees, and their disdain for the Sadducees, because only the Pharisees properly observe the Law. As he writes: "The Pseudo-Clementines therefore do not only think well of the Pharisees in this case, but they reflect a Pharisaic point of view on a particularly sensitive issue." "The Pseudo-Clementines describe the Sadducees as the real heretics deserving denunciation," because they did not acknowledge the resurrection of the dead. The denunciation is identical in terms, Baumgarten notes, with similar rabbinic denunciations of the Sadducees. The text acknowledges the Gospel condemnations of Pharisees as hypocrites, but only to argue that is true of only some Pharisees, no more or less than the Talmud itself would do. Altogether, the picture of a Christian group with strong Pharisaic allegiances is ineluctable. Baumgarten establishes that when the Pseudo-Clementines argue that, were it not for the *kanon,* the Jews would not know how properly to interpret the self-contradictory Bible, the word *kanon* refers to the rabbinical hermeneutical rules. He then concludes that the third-century

> Pseudo-Clementine texts exhibit detailed and specific knowledge of rabbinic Judaism. Their awareness is not of commonplaces or of vague generalities which might be based on a shared biblical heritage, but of information uniquely characteristic of the rabbinic world. There can be no doubt that we are dealing with two groups in close proximity that maintained intellectual contact with each other. The authors of the Pseudo-Clementines quite obviously admired rabbinic Jews and their leaders.[48]

So, in the third century there were such contacts and such groups.[49] Could our Rabbi Eliezer be a figure for such a group—a group that threatened the neat binary opposition of the world into Jewish and

Christians? Could there have been Christian Rabbis, or Pharisaic Christians among the rabbinic party? How might the text provide answers to such questions?[50]

I am obviously not making any claim whatever that this text teaches us anything about the "real" Rabbi Eliezer and any truck with sectarianism, magic, or heresy that he may or may not have had, but rather that we ought to read this text as the historian would read fiction. Keith Hopkins has written, "Serious historians of the ancient world have often undervalued fiction, if only . . . because by convention history is concerned principally with the recovery of truth about the past. But for social history—for the history of culture, for the history of people's understanding of their own society—fiction occupies a privileged position."[51] The method of analysis employed here is close-reading of fictional or legendary narrative texts, that is, essentially classical talmudic methodology. In an earlier version of talmudic studies, one that we might, for want of a better term, call traditional Yeshiva study, such close-reading was normative, without it being made to do any historical work at all. Rashi (tenth century), his grandson Rabbenu Tam, and myriad others until perhaps the middle of the nineteenth century, when the Jewish early modern period begins, simply wanted to understand the logic of the talmudic text to the best of their ability, whether it was a legal (halakhic) or a narrative (aggadic) text. *Wie es eigentlich gewesen ist* was simply not a question. Talmudic history, at any rate, had simply not been invented yet.

These early scholars' methods of questioning and answering questions about the text were substantially the same as those exhibited here. Or, better formulated: Their questions about the text were similar to mine; their answers might and frequently would have been very different, in part precisely because they were not motivated by any questions "outside the text." In a sense, they might be comparable to the "new critics"—also religious conservatives—of American literary culture. At a later stage in talmudic study—let us call it the beginnings of *Wissenschaft des Judentums*—texts such as the ones that I am "reading" in this chapter were simply ignored. Since they were obviously "legendary" or even "folkloristic," they had "no value" for the reconstruction of events that was the goal of such history writing as that of scholars from Graetz to Urbach. At best, occasionally, such narratives were understood to contain somewhere a "kernel of truth," which could be extracted by very carefully breaking the shell and dis-carding most of the meat as well. In any case, one did not ask the sort of logical-consistency questions that a Rashi would have asked, or the Talmud itself, or that I ask below, such as "Why didn't Rabbi Eliezer say this and not that?" Since it was understood, at best and at least, that the likelihood that the "real" Rabbi Eliezer had said anything of the sort at all was virtually nonexistent, there just didn't seem to be any point. Now we have new methodologies. Rabbi Eliezer is no longer a historical character of the first century but a "fictional" char-acter of the third century. I return to the methods of questioning of the text of the traditional learning; ask questions about coherence, internal and external; and draw historical conclusions, not about events but about ideologies, social movements, cultural construc-tions, and particularly repressions, the work of the text. Rabbi Eliezer's close call can be uncovered—if, indeed, it is uncovered and not invented—only by close-reading.

Much of the source material in this chapter consists of the analy-sis of what are technically called "legends of the Sages" in the literary-critical and folkloristic work on rabbinic literature. These represent scattered, frequently disjointed, and often contradictory episodic narratives with one of the Rabbis (or sometimes other figures in their world) depicted in a single incident. We have no extended biogra-phies or hagiographies in any of the classical rabbinic texts (virtually the only Jewish texts we have between the second and the sixth cen-turies A.C.).[52] A naive positivism once regarded these scattered narra-tives as the elements for a quest for the historical Rabbis. Thus, for in-stance, in one of the best of that genre, Louis Finkelstein produced a book-length biography of Rabbi Akiva.[53] Such positivism by and large is no longer credited in the scholarly literature. The work of scholars from Jacob Neusner to Jonah Frankel has discredited it.[54] Never-theless, I believe one can derive meaning by studying together the sto-ries about a particular Rabbi (or other figure), because these named characters are themselves a kind of sign or emblem, almost embodied complexes of particular ideas or possibilities for thought (sometimes even impossibilities for thought) within the religious world of the Rabbis and the communities in which they are embedded.

I am suggesting that through the medium of the legend, the Rab-bis are, as they do so often, teaching us something of the complexities of their world and their worldview. They are, we might say, recognizing and denying at one and the same time that Christians are us, marking out the virtual identity between themselves and the Christians in their world at the same time they are very actively seeking to establish difference.[55] Rabbi Eliezer is thus the character who, in his person, thematizes the tension between the most "orthodox" space of rabbinism and the most "sectarian" space of Christianity.[56] He is the very figure of liminality. This story is a representation of the complexities of the relationship between rabbinic Judaism and Christianity in the era leading up to the fourth century.

As Professor Lieberman already pointed out in his unpublished lectures, one can conjecture a strong connection between this story and the well-known talmudic story of the excommunication of Rabbi Eliezer.[57] According to the version of the story that is preserved in the Babylonian Talmud, Rabbi Eliezer refused to accept the will of the majority of the sages in a halakhic matter and was cursed and sentenced to complete isolation and removal from the rabbinic and even the Jewish community for this relatively minor—if not insignificant—malfeasance. I suggest that rather than the point of halakhic disagreement, in the view of that Talmud at least, it was precisely the manner of Rabbi Eliezer's support for his position, by quasi-prophetic or magical means, that so enraged the Rabbis:

> On that day, Rabbi Eliezer used every imaginable argument, but they did not accept it from him. He said: If the law is as I say, this carob will prove it. The carob was uprooted from its place one hundred feet. Some report four hundred feet. . . . A voice came from heaven and announced: The law is in accordance with the view of Rabbi Eliezer. Rabbi Yehoshua stood on his feet and said "it [the Torah] is not in heaven." (*Baba Metsia* 59a)

On a given halakhic question (the question of the purity or impurity of a certain kind of ceramic stove), Rabbi Eliezer initially tried to support his position using the "normal" rabbinic modes of rational argument, the very modes of argument [תשובות] that might be said to define rabbinic rationality. When that failed, however, he didn't accept defeat but rather turned to another source of authority entirely, miracles and heavenly oracles. According to the Talmud's version of this story (the one that I am quoting here), Rabbi Eliezer was then punished by an extremely harsh version of excommunication, a highly unusual practice in cases of halakhic disagreement: "On that day, all the objects that Rabbi Eliezer had declared clean were brought and burned in fire. Then they took a vote and excommunicated him." Lieberman already suggested that the singular severity with which Rabbi Eliezer was treated was a product of the Rabbis' suspicion that he was intimate with the Christian sectarians, as intimated clearly, almost openly, in the Toseftan story treated here.[58] Alexander Guttmann has argued that it was Rabbi Eliezer's use of magic and prophetic means to argue his halakhic case that so provoked the Rabbis.[59] Through his usage of appeals to forms of authority and authorization that were not rabbinic, Rabbi Eliezer was demonstrating, according to the tellers of our story, that he was "infected" with sectarianism, the most salient case of which was, for them, Christianity.

As Guttmann writes:

> The employment of miracles, among them the *Bat Kol* [voice from heaven], becomes more weighty if we realize that this was done by a personality who appeared to be friendly toward Christianity and its leaders, as was R. Eliezer. . . . Suspicion of Christian leanings combined with the employment of a device which, at this time, was fundamental and successful for Christianity, might have worked almost automatically against R. Eliezer as circumstantial evidence of his pro-Christian sympathies. In this connection likewise, the fact has to be remembered that R. Joshua, leader of the victorious opposition against R. Eliezer, was an outstanding polemicist against Christian influence.[60]

My only corrective to Guttmann's formulation would be to translate it from a set of positivist statements about the historical Rabbis Eliezer and Yehoshua into a set of considerations of the place of Christians and Christianity in the rabbinic world as represented through these figures as characters.[61] Guttmann's point is particularly cogent when we remember from the above rabbinic story of its founding that, in the eyes of the Rabbis of the Talmud, one of the main stereotypes of Christianity was that it was a species of magical practice.[62] The representation of Rabbi Eliezer's appeal to magic and prophecy might well have been precisely the way in which the text thinks about the complicated nexus between the rabbinic and Christian forms of Judaism.

That this was the interpretation method in which rabbinic texts "read" this story can be further supported by means of another story about Rabbis and their relations with Christians—indeed, apparently with the same Christian who encountered Rabbi Eliezer. In the Tosefta *Hullin,* immediately preceding the story of Rabbi Eliezer's arrest, we find the following account:

> It happened to Rabbi Elazar Ben Dama that a snake bit him. And Yaakov the man of Kefar Sama came to cure him in the name of Jesus the son of Panthera, and Rabbi Ishmael refused to allow him. They said to him: You are not permitted Ben Dama.
> He said to him: I will bring a verse from the Torah that proves that this is permitted, but he did not suffice to cite his proof, until he died.
> Rabbi Ishmael said: Blessed art thou, Ben Dama, for you left in peace, and you did not violate the fence of your colleagues, for anyone who breaks down the fence of the Sages, terrible things happen to him, as it says, "One who breaks down a fence, let a snake bite him." (Ecclesiastes 10:8)[63]

In this story, we have another instance of a tale about very close contact indeed between the early Rabbis and the same (fictional) apostle of Jesus whom we have already met in the Tosefta above. There, he offered to Rabbi Eliezer some pleasant and profitable words of Torah. Here, he offers healing in the name of Jesus, his teacher. The patient dies, however, before the sectarian cure can be effected, and the uncle of the deceased exalts him, saying that he is blessed in that he died before he would have been able to break down the fence, that is, transgress the boundary of rabbinic authority. Receiving the cure of a Christian in the name of Jesus is, accordingly, a similar offense to that of Rabbi Eliezer, receiving Jesus' Torah. In neither case there a question that the Torah is itself false or wrong or, *mutatis mutandis,* that the cure is ineffective; but since both come from the mouths of sectarians, they must be avoided like a snakebite. An inconsistency in the story, however, noticed by earlier commentators but not resolved by them, suggests another moment of interpretation here, for according to the cited verse, the snakebite is a punishment for the transgression that Ben Dama had not made yet but was only considering making because of the very snakebite he had suffered. The snake had bitten Ben Dama even before he contemplated making use of the Jesus doctor; indeed, had he not been bitten, he would not have thought of doing so. So the punishment has, as it were, come before the crime. As a late gloss in the Palestinian Talmud wonders: "But wasn't he already bitten by a snake?! Rather it means that he won't be bitten by a snake in the next world" (*Avoda Zara* 2:2, 51a; compare *Shabbat* 14:4, 14d). The clumsiness of the answer discloses the validity of the conundrum. Once more, I think, by indirection, hint, and insinuation, the story is indicating that this Ben Dama, otherwise a kosher rabbinical Jew, just like Rabbi Eliezer, had been an intimate of the Christians—which would explain, by the way, why this Yakov/James showed up so quickly to cure him. This also explains why Ben Dama is already primed and ready with a halakhic justification for the appropriateness of cures in the name of Jesus. In contrast, the story is also indicating the work of strict separation that was taking place at the explicit ideological level of the rabbinic text. Rabbi Ishmael, after all, would rather see Ben Dama die than be saved by "Christian" magic.

The story thus provides a remarkable parallel to the story of Rabbi Eliezer—indicating the same tensions between manifest and "suppressed" elements within the narrative—and in fact, in both early Palestinian sources for this narrative tradition, the Tosefta and the midrash *Qohelet Rabba*, we find the two stories of Rabbi Eliezer's near martyrdom and Ben Dama's near cure together as doublets of each other.

Even though the two stories are not placed together syntagmatically in the Babylonian Talmud, we find a startling verbal similarity, a sort of rhyming, that suggests that they are doublets there as well. First, we need to see the version of the Ben Dama story that appears in the Talmud:

> It happened to Ben Dama, the son of the sister of Rabbi Ishmael that a snake bit him. And Yaakov the man of Kefar Sekhania [= Sikhnin] came to cure him, and Rabbi Ishmael refused to allow him.
> He said to him: Rabbi Ishmael my brother, let me be cured by him, and I will bring a verse from the Torah that proves that this is permitted, but he did not suffice to finish the matter until his soul left him and he died.

Rabbi Ishmael cried out over him: *Blessed art thou, Ben Dama, for your body is pure and your soul left you in purity,* and you did not violate the words of your colleagues, who would say, "One who breaks down a fence, let a snake bite him" (Ecclesiastes 10:8). (*Avoda Zara* 27b)

Now let us look at the end of Rabbi Eliezer's life story as the Babylonian Talmud relates it:

> It is taught: When Rabbi Eliezer was sick, Rabbi Akiva and his colleagues went in to visit him. He was sitting in his canopied bed, and they were sitting in his anteroom. That day was the eve of the Sabbath, and his son Horkanos went in to take off his [father's] phylacteries. He rebuked him and [the son] went out with a scolding. He said to the colleagues: I believe that Father is out of his mind.

According to rabbinic law, the phylacteries are not worn on the Sabbath. The son wishes to remove the father's phylacteries in order that he should not be in violation, but the father rebukes him. The son concludes that either his father is in a highly irrational state of mind or, perhaps, that he is following some sectarian practice. "Out of one's mind" is used as a technical term for sectarianism or for *superstitio*, which does not mean a foolish belief to be laughed at but "everything which opposed the true Roman *religio* such as the activities of astrologers and fortune-tellers."[64]

> [Rabbi Eliezer] said to them: He and his mother are out of their minds. How shall I leave that which is liable for stoning and take care of that which is only a minor commandment?!

Eliezer is apparently exercised that the boy and the mother are not attending properly to their own preparations for the Sabbath, while worrying about his apparent "sectarian" practice. Although the aggression toward his wife, the famous Imma Shalom, seems totally gratuitous here, the Rabbi offers a rational, that is, rabbinic, explanation for his behavior.[65] He was engaged in preparing for the more stringent aspects of Sabbath observance—and they ought to have been too—and didn't want to be bothered with the relatively minor stricture to remove his phylacteries. Although by leaving his phylacteries in place he is violating a rabbinic injunction and therefore seemingly still transgresses the boundary, he explains that this

is not his intention at all. He is simply angry that his wife and son
are concerned with his transgression of a mere rabbinic commandment, while they are putting themselves in danger, thereby, of light-
ing candles or cooking on the Sabbath, which are much more serious violations. He is neither insane nor insensible of the nuances
and details of rabbinic halakha:

> When the sages saw that his mind was clear, they went and sat down
> four cubits from him.
> He said to them: Why have you come?
> They said to him: To learn Torah we have come.
> He said to them: And until now, why have you not come?
> They said: We didn't have time.
> He said to them: I will be amazed if they will die a natural death.
> Rabbi Akiva then said to him: What about me?
> He said: Yours is more severe than all of them.
> He took his two arms and placed them on his heart and said: Aiih to
> these two arms that are like two Scrolls of the Torah rolled up. I have
> learned much Torah, and I have taught much Torah. I have learned
> much Torah and I didn't lose from the teaching of my masters even
> as much as a dog licks from the sea. I have taught much Torah, and
> my disciples have not lost from my teaching so much as the brush in
> its case.[66]
> And not only that but I teach three hundred laws in the matter of
> leprosy, and no one ever asked me a question about them, and in
> the planting of cucumbers, and no one ever asked me about them,
> except for Akiva ben Yosef. Once he and I were walking on the way.
> He said to me: Teach me their planting. I said a word and the field
> was all full of cucumbers. He said to me: Rabbi, you have taught me
> their planting; now teach me their uprooting. I said another word,
> and they were all gathered into one place.
> The [sages then] said to him: A ball, a slipper, and a cameo that are
> [made of leather and filled with wool]. He said to them: They are
> pure.
> *And his soul left him in purity.*
> Rabbi Yehoshua stood on his feet and said: The vow is released. The
> vow is released!
> On the going out of the Sabbath, he met Rabbi Akiva on the way [in
> the funeral procession] from Caesarea to Lydda. He was flagellating
> his flesh until the blood flowed to the ground.

He opened his eulogy and said: My father, my father, the chariot of Israel and its horsemen (2 Kings 2:12).[67] I have many coins and no banker to change them. (Babylonian Talmud *Sanhedrin* 68a)

Among its other meanings, this story certainly thematizes the conflicted and conflictual aspect of the representation of Rabbi Eliezer. On the one hand, he is a kind of holy man, almost a magic-worker, of a type that rabbinic religiosity has a constant suspicion of. On the other hand, he is the very type of an "orthodox" Pharisee and a halakhic authority par excellence. Indeed, Rabbi Eliezer's response to his original excommunication only confirmed his sectarianism, since he, like Jesus with the fig tree, reacted by blasting a third of the olive crop, a third of the wheat crop, and a third of the barley crop, "for everything at which Rabbi Eliezer cast his eyes was burned up." On one reading at least, for this text Rabbi Eliezer's magical activity of planting and harvesting cucumbers with a word continues to mark his liminality, indeed, his closeness with "sectarianism." That he refers to both the "orthodox" issue of purity laws—that is, leprosy—and the suspect planting and harvesting of cucumbers by magic as "halakhot" laws, creates an almost comical effect and emphasizes his heterodoxy. This is closely analogous to his attempt to prove a point by way of the magical uprooting of a carob tree that, according to my reading, precipitated Rabbi Eliezer's excommunication in the first place.[68] As we have seen, early rabbinic texts repeatedly refer to Jesus as a magician.[69]

It could be fairly argued that this is not a particularly telling point, since, as Peter Brown has remarked, "the image of the sorcerer lay to hand in all circles to cut the exceptional and the threatening human being firmly down to size."[70] Indeed, as Brown, among others, has emphasized, the very distinction between magic and miracles was a function of the evaluation and location of the practitioner and not a phenomenology of the practice.[71] I am suggesting nevertheless that the rhetoric and "plot" of our narratives suggest that Rabbi Eliezer was accused of being exceptional and threatening when he used language in a certain way to affect "reality," and that he was deemed to have been cut down to size when he used language in a way that indicated he, too, believed that "it [the Torah] is not in heaven." Even Brown seems to allow some measure of "essentialism" in the definition of the sorcerer: "The superstitious man was like the sorcerer. He replicated in his relation to the supernatural patterns of dominance and dependence that were best left unexpressed."[72] This sounds like a fair enough representation of the character of Rabbi Eliezer in our stories. Note, of course, the tight association of *superstitio* and sorcery, both threats to a kind of civic order. The precise issue between Rabbi Eliezer and his colleagues is "the difference between legitimate and illegitimate forms of supernatural power."[73] Hence, perhaps, his insinuated association with Christians, who did boast, à la Eusebius, of "foreknowledge of the future, visions, and prophetic utterances; laying on of hands"; healing of the sick; and even raising of the dead.[74] In contrast to the commonplace characterization of Rabbi Eliezer as a figure for extreme conservatism, he begins to look like a harbinger within Jewish society of the same cultural changes that were "the making of late antiquity" according to Brown.[75] Indeed, some of the same conflicts within Christian groups that led to such movements as Montanism, the "new prophecy," and its opponents might well have been motivating the tensions within rabbinism between prophetic and rabbinic modes of authority and authorization for halakhic practice. As Christine Trevett has remarked: "The matters at issue between the earliest New Prophets and the developing Catholic tradition . . . concerned not heresy but *authority*."[76] One might easily conclude the same as to the issue between Rabbi Eliezer and his former fellows.

The Rabbi's seeming refusal to obey the laws of the Sabbath in his apparent desire to retain his phylacteries seems also to mark him as being "out of his mind," that is, suspect, in a mystical and perhaps sectarian state. His answer, belligerent as it is, thus marks him as "within," because it is a rational answer based on a good halakhic principle. He is saying: Do not risk a major violation of the Sabbath, a violation that results in the punishment of stoning, in order to see about the removal of my phylacteries, since the wearing of phylacteries on the Sabbath is only a minor violation. Since his answer is according to the laws of ordinary rabbinic rationalities, the Rabbis conclude that he has "returned" from his mystical, sectarian, perhaps *ex hypothesi*, Christian deviance.[77] He is sane again, that is, a proper Pharisee in his worldview. It is not, then, a question about cucumbers that the Rabbis ask him but a perfectly ordinary question in the everyday laws of purities, and it is his appropriate answer to this question that repatriates him into the rabbinic community, that releases the vow of ex-communication. It does not even finally matter whether or not his answer is correct, only that it obeys the structure and strictures of rabbinic authority. From a literary point of view, the fact that the last word out of his mouth is *pure* serves iconically to signify his repurification. Now, in addition to the fact that both of our Palestinian sources, the stories of Rabbi Eliezer's arrest and of Ben Dama's near fall into heretical behavior, appear as doublets, the formal similarity between the two death stories in the Babylonian Talmud—namely, the use of the phrase (attested in only one other place) "his soul left him in purity"—suggests that the two were once a pair in an earlier corpus, apparently a variation of the two forms in which the stories appear together in the early Palestinian texts. In any case, the formal echoes suggest that it is legitimate to read them together.

What do we learn from reading these stories together? Ben Dama was genuinely tempted to engage in some kind of medical sorcery offered by a disciple of Jesus in order to be cured from his snakebite, just as Rabbi Eliezer had been genuinely tempted to enjoy and render definitive the Torah that he heard in the name of Jesus. I have already pointed, however, to a telling inconsistency in the first story as it is told: on the one hand, the implication is that Ben Dama was saved from heresy entirely through his timely death; on the other hand, there is more than an implication in the cited verse that the cause of death, the snakebite that brought him low, was itself a punishment for *prior* engagement with Christianity. The death by snakebite is precipitated, according to the story's interpretation of the verse, by the very breaking down of fences from which he was ostensibly saved by that death. His death in purity was therefore a kind of atonement or reparation for his earlier sin, a recuperation, and the idea of death as atonement for one's own sins is a familiar rabbinic concept. Since the death was by snakebite, we have prima facie evidence that the narrative implicates Ben Dama in antecedent involvement with the Jesus sect. Similarly, then, we can understand the death of Rabbi Eliezer and, accordingly, the lengthy and total isolation and excommunication into which he had been placed. Rabbi Eliezer was also suspected by his fellows of untoward closeness to the Christians; and if my argument about his refusal to curse Jesus is cogent, it is not entirely surprising that he was so suspected. He was indeed, the narrative seems to suggest, an adjunct or perhaps a fellow traveler of Jesus, and his death "in purity" represents the same kind of recuperation or salvation from heresy that Ben Dama's does. The text thus records both the intimacy of the Rabbis with Christianity and the explicit cultural work of separation that was being undertaken.

The story of the so-called parting of the ways is a much more ambiguous and complicated narrative than is usually imagined. Jews and Christians, as much as they tried to convince themselves and others differently, traveled along similar paths for a long, long time, if not always. Indeed, paradoxically, with respect to certain discourses and practices, far from a "parting of the ways" we will observe a startling convergence of roads taken.[78]

NOTES

1. Philip S. Alexander, "'The Parting of the Ways' from the Perspective of Rabbinic Judaism," in *Jews and Christians: The Parting of the Ways A.D. 70 to 135*, ed. James D. G. Dunn, The Second Durham-Tübingen Research Symposium on Earliest Christianity and Judaism (Durham, England, September 1989) (Tübingen: J. C. B. Mohr [Paul Siebeck], 1991), 2.

2. Yitzhaq Baer, "Israel, the Christian Church, and the Roman Empire from the Time of Septimius Severus to the Edict of Toleration of A.D. 313," in *Studies in History*, ed. Alexander Fuks and Israel Halpern, Scripta hierosolymitana VII (Jerusalem: Magnes Press, 1961), 82.

3. Charlotte Fonrobert, "The Concept of Jewish Christianity as Retrospective Fallacy: The Case of the Didascalia," *Journal of Early Christian Studies*, forthcoming.

4. For this collusion, see Alexander, "Parting of the Ways." See also discussion in Gedalyahu Stroumsa, "The Hidden Closeness: On the Fathers of the Church and Judaism" [in Hebrew], *Jerusalem Studies in Jewish Thought* 1, 2 (Fall 1982): 170–75.

5. Alexander, "Parting of the Ways," 3.

6. I acknowledge here the productive influence of Karen King's work, on the use of "syncretism" vis-à-vis Gnosticism in the construction of "authentic Christianity," on the development of my own thinking about the use of Christianity in the production of "authentic Judaism."

7. Alexander, "Parting of the Ways," 2.

8. Homi K. Bhabha, *The Location of Culture* (London: Routledge, 1994), 38.

9. Dina Stein has suggested to me that already Mary Douglas, *Purity and Danger: An Analysis of Concepts of Pollution and Taboo* (1969; reprint, London: Routledge and Kegan Paul, 1978), is articulating this understanding, at least implicitly.

10. I prefer B.C. (before Christ) and A.C. (after Christ, as in the French usage) as a more honest designation than the politically correct assertions of a "common era" or the theologically loaded A.D.

11. Galit Hasan-Rokem, "Narratives in Dialogue: A Folk Literary Perspective on Interreligious Contacts in the Holy Land in Rabbinic Literature of Late Antiquity," in *Sharing the Sacred: Religious Contacts and Conflicts in the Holy Land First–Fifteenth C.E.,* ed. Guy Stroumsa and Arieh Kofsky (Jerusalem: Yad Ben Zvi, 1998), 127. For a fascinating example of such dialogical interchange, see Elchanan Reiner, "From Joshua to Jesus: The Transformation of a Biblical Story to a Local Myth: A Chapter in the Religious Life of the Galilean Jew," in *Sharing the Sacred,* 248–69, who shows that many local Galilean Jewish traditions about various Joshuas are very similar to Gospel accounts about Jesus, also, of course, Joshua. He writes specifically: "The polemical interpretation is not the only possible explanation for the existence of sources that exhibit mutual literary ties" (Reiner, "Joshua to Jesus," 268). This is not, of course, to deny the possibility of "folk narratives" being polemic in their own right. The *Toledot Yeshu* literature, as folk parodies of the Gospels, is a perfect example. See, inter alia, Daniel Boyarin, "A Corrected Reading of the New 'History of Jesus' Fragment" [in Hebrew], *Tarbiz* (1978): 249–52.

12. H. J. W. Drijvers, "Jews and Christians at Edessa," *Journal of Jewish Studies* 36, 1 (1985): 88–102.

13. See Judith Lieu, *Image and Reality: The Jews in the World of the Christians in the Second Century* (Edinburgh: T. & T. Clark, 1996), 28ff., for an exploration of the anxieties that this fuzzy border gave rise to. Ignatius already seems very actively engaged in policing the border, again suggesting that it was clearly extant but also very permeable and unstable. See especially his *Letter to the Philadelphians*, in William R. Schoedel, *Ignatius of Antioch*, Hermeneia—A Critical and Historical Commentary on the Bible (Philadelphia: Fortress, 1985), 195–215. This position is partially pace Keith Hopkins, "Christian Number and Its Implications," *Journal of Early Christian Studies* 6, 2 (1998): 187, who seems to regard such fuzziness (or "porosity," in his language) as particularly characteristic of Christianity. Hopkins's paper is very important and will have to be reckoned with seriously in any future accounts of Judeo-Christian origins and genealogies. See also Shaye J. D. Cohen, "'Those Who Say They Are Jews and Are Not': How Do You Know a Jew in Antiquity When You See One?" in

Diasporas in Antiquity, ed. Shaye J. D. Cohen and Ernest S. Frerichs, Brown Judaic Studies 288 (Atlanta: Scholars Press, 1993), 1–45.

14. Indeed, relations do not have to even sort themselves out into either polemic or irenic but can occupy complex spaces between these two extremes (Dina Stein, *Folklore Elements in Late Midrash: A Folkloristic Perspective on Pirkei de Rabbi Eliezer* [in Hebrew with English abstract] [Ph.D. diss., Hebrew University, 1998], 169).

15. Israel Jacov Yuval, "The Haggadah of Passover and Easter" [in Hebrew], *Tarbiz* 65, 1 (October–December 1995): 5; see also Israel Jacob Yuval, "Easter and Passover as Early Jewish-Christian Dialogue," in *Passover and Easter: Origin and History to Modern Times*, ed. Paul F. Bradshaw and Lawrence A. Hoffman, Two Liturgical Traditions, vol. 5 (Notre Dame: University of Notre Dame Press, 1999).

16. These terminological problems dog all our attempts to write about these relations. Thus, in the course of two sentences, we find Frend writing that "it is in the pages of Revelation with their terrible comparison between the 'true' and the 'false' Jews and the denunciation of the 'Synagogue of Satan' whose members were enemies and persecutors of the Saints that the intensity of ill-feeling between the two groups can be seen." Which are the two groups? Obviously from this quotation, they are both Jews, even from the perspective of the author of Revelation himself; but for Frend, in the very next sentence, "the struggle between Jew and Christian was bitter and incessant"—two groups of warring Jews have now become the "Jew" *tout court* and the Christian, by now necessarily not a Jew (W. H. C. Frend, *The Early Church* [Minneapolis: Fortress, 1965], 37). This consistent distortion (on the part of most writers, certainly not only Frend) renders it nearly impossible to see the more complex sets of relations that obtained.

17. Wayne A. Meeks and Robert L. Wilken, *Jews and Christians in Antioch in the First Four Centuries of the Common Era*, Society for Biblical Literature Sources for Biblical Study 13 (Missoula, Mt.: Scholars Press, 1978), vii. See also Baer, "Israel," 79. See now Lieu, *Image and Reality*, passim, esp. 11–12. Note that Miriam S. Taylor, in *Anti-Judaism and Early Christian Identity: A Critique of the Scholarly Consensus*, Studia Post-biblica 46 (Leiden: E. J. Brill, 1995), demonstrates that a "vital social and religious force" and an "independent religion alongside Christianity" do not imply, at all, a Jewish mission to the Gentiles, Jewish competition for converts, or Jewish aggressiveness toward Christianity.

18. W. H. C. Frend, *Martyrdom and Persecution in the Early Church: A Study of a Conflict from the Maccabees to Donatus* (Garden City, N.Y.: Doubleday, 1967), 18.

19. This double observance was the case in the Palestinian *lauras* of the fourth century, and in the Pachomian and Nitrian foundations as well; Derwas J. Chitty, *The Desert a City: An Introduction to the Study of Egyptian and Palestinian Monasticism under the Christian Empire* (1966; reprint, Crestwood, N.Y.: St. Vladimir's Seminary Press, 1995), 15, 23, 31. See R. L. Odom, *Sabbath and Sunday in Early Christianity* (Washington, D.C., 1977). According to both the Didache and Ignatius, observance of the Lord's Day rather than the Sabbath was the mark of the Christian as opposed to the Jew (Joan E. Taylor, "The Phenomenon of Early Jewish-Christianity Reality or Scholarly Invention," *Vigiliae Christianae* 44 [1990]: 317, 319).

20. Hugh Jackson Lawlor and John Ernest Leonard Oulton, trans. and eds., *Eusebius, Bishop of Caesarea: The Ecclesiastical History and the Martyrs of Palestine* (London: Society for Promoting Christian Knowledge, 1927), 89.

21. This point is all the more striking since, already in the third century, observing the Lord's Day rather than the Jewish Sabbath was seen in some texts as a touchstone of orthodoxy (Arthur Voobus, *The Didascalia Apostolorum in Syriac I and II* [with English translation], CSCO 401–402 [Louvain: Peeters, 1979], 233). I am grateful to Charlotte Fonrobert for calling this text to my attention in this context.

22. Nicholas de Lange, *Origen and the Jews: Studies in Jewish Christian Relations in Third-Century Palestine* (Cambridge: Cambridge University Press, 1976), 188.

23. Samuel Krauss, "The Jews in the Works of the Church Fathers," *Jewish Quarterly Review* 5–6 (1892–93): 238 n. 2.

24. However, much of the extant scholarship on religious interaction between Judaism and Christianity in late antiquity has, indeed, to do with shared liturgical innovation. See Jefim Schirmann, "Hebrew Liturgical Poetry and Christian Hymnology," *Jewish Quarterly Review* 44 (1953–54): 123-61; Phillip Sigal, "Early Christian and Rabbinic Liturgical Affinities: Exploring Liturgical Acculturation," *New Testament Studies* 30 (1984): 63–90.

25. Peter Brown, *The Cult of the Saints: Its Rise and Function in Latin Christianity*, The Haskell Lectures on History of Religions (Chicago and London: University of Chicago Press, 1981), 103. Sadly, what transpires on p. 104 is the violent destruction of this concord. On this whole incident, see now Severus of Minorca, *Letter on the Conversion of the Jews*, trans. and ed. Scott Bradbury, Oxford Early Christian Texts (Oxford: Oxford University Press, 1996).

26. Sozomen, *Ecclesiastical History* 2, 4 in the translation of Aryeh Kofsky,

"Mamre: A Case of a Regional Cult?" in *Sharing the Sacred*, ed. Stroumsa and Kofsky, 24–25; and see discussion there as well.

27. Jerome, *Correspondence*, ed. Isidorus Hilberg, Corpus scriptorum ecclesiasticorum Latinorum (Vienna: Verlag der Oster reichischen Akademie der Wissenschaften, 1996), vol. 55, 381–82.

28. David Satran, *Biblical Prophets in Byzantine Palestine: Reassessing the Lives of the Prophets*, Studia in veteris testamenti Pseudepigrapha 11 (Leiden: E. J. Brill, 1995), 4–6, and literature cited there. Also Brent D. Shaw, "Body/Power/Identity: Passions of the Martyrs," *Journal of Early Christian Studies* 4, 3 (1996): 281, on the *Testament of Job*.

29. See Lieu, *Image and Reality*, 161–62.

30. I am not implying, of course, that it is impossible that this text has an earlier origin than its context.

31. Hasan-Rokem, "Narratives in Dialogue," 121.

32. Galit Hasan-Rokem, *The Web of Life—Folklore in Rabbinic Literature: The Palestinian Aggadic Midrash Eikha Rabba* [in Hebrew] (Tel Aviv: Am Oved, 1996), 165.

33. Hasan-Rokem, "Narratives in Dialogue," 122.

34. Reuven Kimelman has cited impressive patristic evidence for Jewish aid to Christians in time of trial and for Jewish attempts to persuade Christians to follow the law without necessarily "converting" to Judaism ("Birkat Ha-Minim and the Lack of Evidence for an Anti-Christian Jewish Prayer in Late Antiquity," in *Aspects of Judaism in the Greco-Roman Period*, ed. E. P. Sanders, A. I. Baumgarten, and Alan Mendelson, Jewish and Christian Self-Definition, vol. 2 [Philadelphia: Fortress, 1981], 239–40).

35. Jerome knows that the term *mîn*, "sectarian," is a name for Jewish Christians, as we see from his famous letter to Augustine (*Correspondence*, ed. Hilberg, vol. 55, 381–82). This letter was written about 404 (Ray A. Pritz, *Nazarene Jewish Christianity: From the End of the New Testament Period until Its Disappearance in the Fourth-Century* [Jerusalem: Magnes, 1992], 53). See also M. Friedlander, *Patristische und Talmudische Studien* (1868; reprint, Farnborough, England: Gregg International Publishers, 1972), 62.

36. This place, referred to in other texts in an Aramaicized form as Kefar Sekhania, cannot, it seems, be identified with certainty (Pritz, *Nazarene Jewish Christianity*, 120).

37. M. S. Zuckermandel, ed., *Tosephta: Based on the Erfurt and Vienna Codices, with Saul Lieberman "Supplement" to the Tosephta* [in Hebrew] (Jerusalem: Bamberger and Wahrmann, 1937), 503.

38. See also Gedaliah Alon, *The Jews in Their Land in the Talmudic Age (70–640 C.E.)*, ed. and trans. Gershon Levi (Jerusalem: Magnes, 1984), 1:292–93.

39. Pliny, *Pliny the Younger: Letters and Panegyricus,* trans. Betty Radice, Loeb Classical Library (Cambridge: Harvard University Press, 1969), 2:402–3.

40. Indeed, as one anonymous reader pointed out, the "whole point of Pliny's letter is to ask advice *because he doesn't know what exactly the procedure is,* not because he is outlining an established practice."

41. William R. Schoedel, translation and commentary, *Polycarp, Martyrdom of Polycarp, Fragments of Papias,* vol. 5 of *The Apostolic Fathers: A New Translation and Commentary,* ed. Robert Grant (New York: Thomas Nelson and Sons, 1967), 65.

42. Saul Lieberman, "Roman Legal Institutions in Early Rabbinics and in the Acta Martyrum," in *Texts and Studies* (1944; reprint, New York: Ktav, 1974), 79 and esp. n. 150. Kimelman has interestingly interpreted the notice in Justin Martyr that the Jews "scoff at the King of Israel" after their prayers as owing to the Jewish need to demonstrate to the Romans, *at the time of Justin,* precisely that they are not Christians, for purpose of escaping martyrdom and persecution as such ("Birkat Ha-Minim," 235).

43. Lieberman, "Roman Legal Institutions," 78.

44. There is indeed evidence that my conjecture is correct, i.e., that the published answer offered by Lieberman was evasive and intended to lead the reader to the suggestion offered here within. In unpublished lectures delivered to his students, Lieberman openly proposed a partial version of the hypothesis that I tender and argue for here. According to Marc G. Hirshman (*Midrash Qohelet Rabbah* [Ph.D. diss., Jewish Theological Seminary, 1982], part 1, 52), Lieberman "connected the suspicions of Rabbi Eliezer of sectarianism (being Christian) with his excommunication on the part of the Sages in the matter of the Akhnai Stove."

45. See Daniel Boyarin, *Carnal Israel: Reading Sex in Talmudic Culture,* The New Historicism: Studies in Cultural Poetics, vol. 25 (Berkeley and Los Angeles: University of California Press, 1993), 47. See also Stein, *Folklore,* 173–81.

46. Rashi, in what I take to be yet another bit of "hidden transcript" making, improbably interprets the phrase to mean "arrested [in order to make him into] a sectarian," i.e., that the Romans were trying to force him to become a heretic. This interpretation is so linguistically strained and so inadequate to the narrative context that it is hard to believe that Rashi intended it as other than a cover-up. Cover-ups upon cover-ups, but ones that leave the marks of the covering all over the place.

47. The division is always, obviously, a constructed one. My argument, then, is that in this period, much more active work is being done to construct it than would be necessary at later times (although in the early modern period it becomes necessary again; but that is another story). This active

work is both diachronic, in that the division is being made through history, and synchronic, in that certain discursive forces are actively trying to make it appear as a given. We are observing the effects of those forces in our texts.

48. Albert I. Baumgarten, "Literary Evidence for Jewish Christianity in the Galilee," in *The Galilee in Late Antiquity*, ed. Lee I. Levine (New York: Jewish Theological Seminary of America, 1992), 46–47.

49. For the dating of the Pseudo-Clementines, see F. Stanley Jones, *An Ancient Jewish Christian Source on the History of Christianity: Pseudo-Clementine Recognitions 1.27–71*, Texts and Translations: Christian Apocrypha Series (Atlanta: Scholars Press, 1995), 1.

50. For another possible (if somewhat improbable) connection of this type, see Arthur Marmorstein ("Judaism and Christianity in the Middle of the Third Century," *Hebrew Union College Annual* 10 [1937]: esp. 233), who also discusses the relation between the *Didascalia* and the Pseudo-Clementine literature. See also Georg Strecker, "On the Problem of Jewish Christianity (= Appendix 1)," in Walter Bauer, *Orthodoxy and Heresy in Earliest Christianity* (Philadelphia: Fortress, 1971), 251; and especially Charlotte Fonrobert, *Constructing Women's Bodies in Late Antique Jewish Cultures,* Contraversions: Jews and Other Differences (Stanford: Stanford University Press, 1999), chap. 6, n. 33; Fonrobert, "Concept of Jewish Christianity."

51. Keith Hopkins, "Novel Evidence for Roman Slavery," *Past and Present* 138 (1993): 6.

52. See Jacob Neusner, *Why No Gospels in Talmudic Judaism?* Brown Judaic Studies, no. 135 (Atlanta: Scholars Press, 1988).

53. Louis Finkelstein, *Akiba: Scholar, Saint and Martyr* (1936; reprint, New York: Macmillan/Atheneum, 1964).

54. Jacob Neusner, *Eliezer Ben Hyrcanus: The Tradition and the Man* (Leiden: E. J. Brill, 1973); and Yonah Frankel, *Readings in the Spiritual World of the Stories of the Aggada* [in Hebrew] (Tel Aviv: United Kibbutz Press, 1981), to take just two examples of their prodigious writings, particularly related to the present subject.

55. Jonathan Z. Smith, "Differential Equations: On Constructing the 'Other'" (lecture and pamphlet, Tempe, Arizona, 1992), 13–14; and see King, "Gnosticism as Heresy." This process goes both ways, of course. A beautiful example is the famous passage in the Didache in which the author exhorts the faithful: "But do not let your fasts fall on the same day as 'the hypocrites' [i.e., the Jews; see Matt. 6:16ff.], who fast on Monday and Thursday. Rather you should fast on Wednesday and Friday"

(Robert A. Kraft, translation and commentary, *Barnabas and the Didache,* vol. 3 of *Apostolic Fathers,* ed. Grant (1965), 165.

56. See also Alon, *Jews in Their Land,* 1:183.
57. See also Alexander Guttmann, "The Significance of Miracles for Talmudic Judaism," *Hebrew Union College Annual* 20 (1947): 386. I would like to thank Dr. Dina Stein for reminding me of this reference.
58. In unpublished lectures, cited in Hirshman, *Midrash Qohelet Rabbah,* part 1, 56.
59. Guttman, "Significance of Miracles," 383.
60. Ibid., 386.
61. See also Stein, *Folklore,* 175 n. 124.
62. In addition to the passage cited above, see *Sanhedrin* 43a and 106a–b, in which Jesus is implicitly compared to Balaam. Celsus also emphasizes particularly Jewish charges against Jesus that he was an Egyptian magician (*Contra Celsum* 1.28), and we find identical indictments in the parodic Jewish anti-Gospel known as *Toledot Yeshu* (Boyarin, "History of Jesus"); and see, indeed, Mark 3:22 and Matthew 12:24.
63. Zuckermandel, ed., *Tosephta,* 227.
64. Jan den Boeft and Jan Bremmer, "Notiunculae martyrologicae," *Vigiliae Christianae* 35 (1981): 44–45.
65. On the halakhic issue, see Yitzhak D. Gilat, *R. Eliezer Ben Hyrcanus: A Scholar Outcast,* Bar-Ilan Studies in Near Eastern Languages and Culture (Ramat Gan: Bar-Ilan University Press, 1984), 161.
66. On this passage, see discussion in Neusner, *Why No Gospels?* 52; Stein, *Folklore,* 166–67.
67. This is, of course, the verse that Elisha cried out upon the death of Elijah. For Elijah as a model for Christian ascetics, see Sebastian P. Brock and Susan Ashbrook Harvey, trans. and eds., *Holy Women of the Syrian Orient,* 2d ed., updated with a new preface, Transformations of the Classical Heritage 13 (1987; 2d ed., Berkeley and Los Angeles: University of California Press, 1998), 8; and Stein, *Folklore,* 178.
68. Cf. Guttmann, "Significance of Miracles," 380–82.
69. According to a passage in the manuscripts of the Babylonian Talmud *Sanhedrin* 43a,b, Jesus was crucified by the Sanhedrin on the eve of Passover for sorcery and for misleading Israel into idol worship.
70. Peter Brown, *The Making of Late Antiquity,* The Carl Newell Jackson Lectures, 1976 (Cambridge: Harvard University Press, 1978), 24.
71. Ibid., 21.
72. Ibid., 39.
73. Ibid., 60.

74. Lawlor and Oulton, *Eusebius*, 152.
75. Brown, *Making of Late Antiquity*, 17.
76. Christine Trevett, "Gender, Authority and Church History: A Case Study of Montanism," *Feminist Theology* 17 (January 1998): 14.
77. Guttmann further argues that it was precisely the fact that Rabbi Eliezer was responsive in the matter of purities, an aspect of Jewish law that "Christian leaders" allegedly opposed, that indicated to the Rabbis he was no longer suspect of Christian leanings ("Significance of Miracles," 388–89).
78. For fascinating evidence of continued cultural interaction between rabbinic Jews and Christians in an area entirely different from the one considered in this essay, see Shaye J. D. Cohen, "Menstruants and the Sacred in Judaism and Christianity," in *Ancient History, Women's History*, ed. Sarah Pomeroy (Chapel Hill: University of North Carolina Press, 1991), 273–99. More recently, on the same topic, see Charlotte Fonrobert, "Women's Bodies, Women's Blood: Politics of Gender in Rabbinic Literature" (Ph.D. diss., Graduate Theological Union, 1995), microfilm; and her forthcoming *Menstrual Purity: Rabbinic and Christian Reconstructions of Biblical Gender* (Stanford: Stanford University Press, 2000).

Chapter 13

On Thinking Identity Otherwise

Susan E. Shapiro

In this chapter,[1] I offer a reading of Emmanuel Levinas's critique of and intervention into the logic of identity in the West. In this logic, the instance is subsumed under the concept, and the particular utterly disappears into the universal. This disappearing of the particular is associated by Levinas with Western thought from Parmenides onward. The consequence of this logic, according to Levinas, is the desire to exterminate the other without remainder.[2] Because this logic thus leads to both totalizing thinking and totalitarianism, the stakes of such a critique are very high.

In brief, for Levinas totalizing logic entails a movement from part to whole that simultaneously understands, explains, and utterly subsumes the part, both containing and completing it. There thus is no beyond or other than the whole or "totality." In terms of the logic of identity and difference, this move from part to whole negates difference. All that remains is identity, the Same. Levinas links this logic of identity with ontology and, especially, with the subsumption of the many by the One. Finally, this logic of identity that underlies ontology and totality in the West produces violence toward the other person(s). This violence, for Levinas, is not limited to but is represented by totalitarianism.

It is this totalizing that Levinas critiques through a logic of infinity that refers—as suggested by the title of his second major work—"otherwise than being or beyond essence." This critique entails treating ethics, and not ontology, as first philosophy. In this ethical logic, the irreducible alterity of the other person(s) is maintained. Ontology's logic of identity thus is made ethically significant only after and in relation to this prior and unsurpassable logic of difference.[3]

I do not here further rehearse Levinas's basic philosophical argument in which he treats ethics as first philosophy, although it is central to his critique of the logic of identity and identification. Rather, I look at the two main avenues through which Levinas enacts his critique: one through a thinking otherwise of what he terms "sexual difference" and the other through thinking otherwise of Jewishness/Judaism in the West, or the relation between Hebrew and Greek. In this chapter I principally focus on the first path, although I return to the importance of the second approach in concluding.

Introduction: Thinking Sexual Difference Otherwise

Oppositional gender difference and the subordination of the feminine to the masculine are ancient philosophical topoi. Indeed, Levinas traces this subordination back to Parmenides and the "Eleatic" notion of Being.[4] In his work *Time and the Other* (1947),[5] Levinas suggests that the very otherness of the other person cannot be recognized when difference is mapped spatially and when matter is utterly subordinated to form. For Levinas, without an irreducible and impassible difference between self and other, ethics is impossible. To locate such an alterity, Levinas calls for a thinking otherwise of "sexual difference."[6] Critiquing the subordination in spatial terms of the feminine as matter to the masculine as form, Levinas instead turns to time as the locus of thinking sexual difference. Levinas thereby seeks a way to locate difference that will not always already return it to the economy of the Same. Thinking sexual difference otherwise, for Levinas, becomes a condition of the very possibility of ethics itself:

> Human alterity is not thought starting with the purely formal alterity by which some terms are distinguished from others in every multiplicity (where each one is already other as the bearer of different attributes or, in a multiplicity of equal terms, where each one is other than the other through its individuation). The notion of a transcendent alterity—one that opens time—is at first sought starting with an *alterity-content*—that is, starting with femininity. Femininity—and one would have to see in what sense this can be said of

masculinity or of virility; that is, of the differences between the sexes in general—appeared to me as a difference contrasting strongly with other differences, not merely as a quality different from all others, but as the very quality of difference.[7]

The "feminine" is a trope running throughout Levinas's work. In order to ask whether, and, if so, to what extent, Levinas succeeds in thinking sexual difference otherwise, I here attend only to selected aspects of his writing on this subject. In particular, I consider two of his Talmudic readings. I address first his "And God Created Woman"[8] and then aspects of his "Desacralization and Disenchantment."[9] I employ the terms *feminine* and *Woman* in accord with their usage in these texts, a use that is patently heteronormative.

Levinas's characterization of both rhetoric and idolatry bears directly on his understanding of sexual difference. I show how they function in his work to reinscribe the very gender hierarchy and subordination of female to male and Woman to Man that Levinas would apparently undo.

First, I more fully lay out Levinas's portrayal of the "Eleatic notion of being."[10] The founding question of this metaphysical tradition was whether the nature of the world is irreducibly multiple and changing or ultimately One and static. In reducing the many to the One, this style of philosophizing feminizes matter as intrinsically plural, passive, and changing and, then, utterly subsumes and subordinates it— without a trace—to the unity of form. Levinas claims that this mode of philosophizing leaves no room in which to think difference or alterity. Nor, he claims, does what he terms "neutered" or nongendered philosophical thinking (such as Martin Heidegger's) offer a way in which to locate irreducible otherness. Thinking sexual difference otherwise is thus a necessary precondition of making space—or rather, for Levinas, making time—for the Other. Ethics in Levinas's thought thus becomes intrinsically related to the task of thinking sexual difference in terms of temporality.

This task persists throughout Levinas's writings. In his "Philosophy, Justice, and Love" (1982), Levinas remarks as follows:

> I used to think that otherness began in the feminine. That is, in fact, a very strange otherness: woman is neither the contradictory nor the opposite of man, nor like other differences. It is not like the

opposition between light and darkness. It is a distinction that is not contingent, and whose place must be sought in relation to love. . . . Before Eros there was the Face; Eros itself is possible only between Faces. The problem of Eros is philosophical and concerns otherness. Thirty years ago I wrote a book called *Le temps et l'autre* [Time and the other]—in which I thought that the feminine was otherness itself, and I do not retract that.[11]

Sexual Difference in "And God Created Woman"

If thinking sexual difference otherwise is not only part of what distinguishes Levinas's work but also that which significantly makes possible his Other-oriented ethics, how can we account for the persistent subordination of the feminine and, especially, of the category "Woman" in his thought?

With this question in mind, I turn now to Levinas's essay "And God Created Woman," his commentary on *Berakhot* 61a. In this text we find both the promise and the problems of Levinas's attempts to think sexual difference otherwise. In this essay, Levinas explicitly turns away from Greek accounts—such as that of Aristophanes in Plato's *Symposium*—of the origin and relation of male and female. In their place, he turns to rabbinic arguments about how to interpret God's creation and thus the relation of man and woman as told in Genesis. One may wonder, however, at Levinas's choice in particular of *Berakhot* 61 as a text through which to raise these issues, for it is one of the most misogynist rabbinic readings of the creation stories. Indeed, as I will show, the argument in *Berakhot* 61a constrains Levinas's interpretation of the creation, character, and relation of Man and Woman in ways that seem opposed to his attempts to think sexual difference otherwise. For example, in "And God Created Woman," Levinas treats Woman as the "accessory" to Man, made out of his "tail," not his "Face." Also, as I will demonstrate, the fact that Eve is, in this biblical account, created second is important for Levinas in that she does not then interfere with the primordial intimacy of the relationship between God and Man. She comes "after the event," that is, after the creation of Adam. Indeed, Levinas finds in this mode of temporality—this coming after—Woman's very feminine difference from Man. Does Levinas consider his essay a thinking otherwise about sexual difference? I repeatedly raise this question in different ways throughout my exposition of this text.

For Levinas, it is important that Eve is like Man because she is created out of him. Woman thus is primarily understood as a part of the human inasmuch as she is like Man. But "Woman as Woman," that is, in her sexuality, is regarded by Levinas as the eroticized Other. As such, she is less than human. It is Man who has the greater proximity to both the Universal and the Divine. Woman may someday catch up with Man and join him on this universal plane, made possible, according to Levinas, by the priority of the masculine. Not only, then, is the feminine "after the event," but Woman lags behind and always follows Man. Indeed, Levinas thinks that Woman may be just "two centuries" behind Man.

In this way, Levinas can have it both ways. He can set up a prior masculine universality in which Woman can take her place, to the extent to which she becomes capable of putting aside her feminine sexuality. Woman thus bears within herself erotic otherness, in all its ambiguity. Woman's exclusive bearing of eros thereby leaves undisrupted Man's primordial masculine relation to God and the Holy, because sexuality enters the scene only with the feminine, that is, with the second creation of Woman from Man. The feminine is made secondary and subordinated to the masculine so as to preserve the primordial relation of Man to the Divine and to the Universal through the masculine alone.[12]

Furthermore, if God had, in the beginning, created Man and Woman as two separate and equal beings instead of as an original, unitary being, according to Levinas, these two "principles" would have issued in an unending state of war. To avoid war in the *polis* and "family scenes" at home, then, Levinas argues that God created Woman so that she is subordinated to Man, knowing that this arrangement produces—indeed, relies on—injustice. It is an injustice that is, for Levinas, "justified" inasmuch as the "part" (that is, Woman) suffers injustice for the sake of peace for the whole (that is, Man and Woman joined in marriage and society).[13]

Levinas draws on *Berakhot* 61a in these terms as follows:

Our text [*Berakhot* 61a] asks itself, however, in what way the idea of two equal beings—man and woman—in the first man is "the most beautiful idea." Does the image of God mean from the outset the simultaneity of the male and the female? Here is the answer of Rav Abbahu: God wanted to create two beings, male and female, but he created in God's image a single being. He created less well than his original idea. He would then—if I may venture to say so—have willed beyond his own image! He wanted two beings. In fact, he wanted that from the beginning there should be equality in the creature, no woman issuing from man, no woman who came after man. From the beginning he wanted two separate and equal beings. But that was impossible; this initial independence of two equal beings would no doubt have meant war. It had to be done not strictly according to justice, which would demand two separate beings. To create a world, he had to subordinate them one to the other. There had to be a difference which did not affect equity: a sexual difference and, hence, a certain preeminence of man, a woman coming later, and as woman, an appendage of the human. We now understand the lesson in this Humanity is not thinkable on the basis of two entirely different principles. There had to have been a *sameness* that these *others* had in common. Woman was set apart from man but she came after him: *the very femininity of woman is in this initial "after the event."* Society was not founded on purely divine principles: the world would not have lasted. Real humanity does not allow for an abstract equality, without some subordination of terms. What family scenes there would have been between the members of that first perfectly equal couple! Subordination was needed, and a wound was needed; suffering was and is needed to unite equals and unequals.[14]

In what sense is this a thinking of sexual difference otherwise than in the Eleatic notion of Being? Is Woman's temporal difference from Man her "coming after the event," that is, her having been created second? Is this "coming after," lagging behind Man, the "very femininity" of Woman? Is this what Levinas means by thinking sexual difference otherwise? It would appear so.

Levinas's turn to biblical and rabbinic rather than to Greek sources does not seem to have affected the subordination of Woman to Man, especially with regard to her "sexual difference" from Man.

While Woman is not here equated with matter or to the receptacle of Being, as for Plato, the injustice marking Woman's temporality as "coming after the event" and as requiring her subordination to ensure peace may merely be a somewhat softer version of this gendered Eleatic metaphysics. Further, Levinas's siding in his essay "And God Created Woman" with the interpretation that Woman derives from the "tail" of Man is in tension not only with his critique of the Eleatic notion of Being but with another—although much more brief and fragmentary—reading of *Berakhot* 61a found in his essay "Judaism and the Feminine."[15] There Levinas (provisionally) differentiates between the Rabbis and Plato on sexual difference, whereas here Levinas collapses this distinction.[16] How, then, may we account for this apparent failure to think sexual difference otherwise?

Keeping Up Appearances

To address this question, I now turn to a consideration of the inscription of the feminine, deception, and idolatry in Levinas's writing as tied especially to the deformations of appearance. While he seeks to undo the negative association of the feminine with matter, plurality, and change, as well as her subordination to masculine form, Levinas necessitates subordinating Woman to the masculine, a principle he regards as prior to the feminine. Levinas, I suggest, institutes a gender hierarchy within his ethics in part as a consequence of his continued attachment to certain residues of the Eleatic notion of Being. For example, in repeating Plato's negative feminizing of rhetoric as deception, Levinas reintroduces the very metaphysics he would wish to think otherwise. Further, in appropriating biblical and rabbinic feminizings of idolatry and sorcery in terms of appearance, he treats them—like rhetoric—as constitutionally deceptive. Rhetoric, idolatry, and Woman, as I will show, are all tied to appearance understood as opposed to the Real.

For example, Levinas treats Woman as having been created by God, at least in part, through the arts of appearance and illusion. His views on this matter become clear in his discussion of the following midrash in *Berakhot* 61a:

For the text "He fashioned the rib into woman," it has to be understood that the Holy One, Blessed be He, plaited Eve's hair into braids and took her to Adam, for in other countries plaiting is called *binyatha* (building) [*Berakhot* 61a].[17]

Levinas interprets this passage, focusing on the connections between the feminine, artifice, appearance, and deception, as follows:

In the feminine, there is face and appearance, and God was the first hairdresser. He created the first illusions, the first make-up. To build a feminine being is from the outset to make room for appearance. "Her hair has to be done." There is in the feminine face and in the relation between the sexes this beckoning to the lie, or to an arrangement beyond the savage straight-forwardness of a face-to-face encounter, bypassing a relationship between human beings and approaching each other in the responsibility of one for the other.[18]

In this midrashic reading, Levinas invites an association between rhetoric and deceptive femininity. God functions for Levinas not only as the "first hairdresser" but as the first makeup artist. The always already made-up face of the feminine thus is associated with artifice, deception, and the lie. These feminized tropes for appearance reinscribe in the heart of his thought the very pernicious gender ideology that Levinas would otherwise undo.

Levinas casts his suspicion of appearance in gendered terms that resemble Plato's view of rhetoric, in particular in his *Gorgias*.[19] Levinas repeatedly draws on Plato's views of rhetoric in his work, treating it as a seduction of the other's freedom. Like Plato, he considers rhetoric a deceptive and shadowy knack with speech that imitates, haunts, and would supplant being or truth. In its attempt through ruse to seduce the neighbor into a "bad proximity," rhetoric is synonymous with injustice. As Levinas writes in his *Totality and Infinity*:

Rhetoric, absent from no discourse, and which philosophical discourse seeks to overcome, resists discourse. . . . It approaches the other not to face him, but obliquely. . . . Truth is bound up with the social relation, which is justice. . . . Justice is . . . access to the Other outside of rhetoric, which is ruse, emprise, and exploitation. And in this sense justice coincides with the overcoming of rhetoric.[20]

Levinas seems even less optimistic than Plato about the ability within discourse finally to separate and distinguish between rhetoric and philosophy when he suggests:

> This threatening ideology hides in the core of the Logos itself. Plato is confident that he can escape it by means of good rhetoric, but he soon hears within discourse the simian imitation of discourse.[21]

In Levinas's writings, the difficulty and importance of distinguishing between rhetoric and philosophy—and, as we will see, of demarcating between the proximities of idolatry or sorcery and metaphysical or ethical desire—is inscribed in gendered oppositions and terms. The stakes of "telling the difference" between bad and ethical proximity to the Other, like distinguishing between idolatrous and proper love of God, could not be greater. Further, distinguishing between these two forms of proximity is as difficult—according to Levinas, even more so—as was distinguishing between rhetoric and philosophy for Plato.

This near incapacity to distinguish between two forms of proximity, the unjust and the ethical, is a problem that haunts Levinas throughout his writings.[22] When this entanglement between closely related but opposed discourses is taken up in Levinas's thought in explicitly religious terms, the role of gender in disciplining this difference emerges most strongly.

Sorcery, Sister of the Sacred

In Levinas's Talmudic essay "Desacralization and Disenchantment," a commentary on *Sanhedrin* 67a–68a, the ability to distinguish between appearance and reality is registered and put into question—now, however, in the context of discerning the differences between the Sacred and sorcery as well as between the Sacred and the Holy. Levinas writes of the difficulty of distinguishing sorcery from the Sacred in a manner strikingly reminiscent of the problem of deceptive appearance in Plato's and Levinas's views of rhetoric (as well as, of course, in those of many philosophers temporally between them). Levinas writes:

> Sorcery, first cousin, perhaps even sister, of the sacred, is the mistress of appearance. She is a relative slightly fallen in status, but within the family, who profits from the connections of her brother [the Sacred], who is received in the best circles.[23]

As the "mistress of appearance," sorcery is feminized. Furthermore, she trades on her connections to "her brother," the Sacred, to gain credibility. Sorcery appears to be what she is not. She appears like and confuses herself with the Sacred, her brother. To undo this sorcery, appearance must be separated from the true.

The problem of distinguishing appearance from the true is addressed by Plato in his *Gorgias* when he describes rhetoric as masquerading as that which she is not:

> Now these four [gymnastics, medicine, legislation, and justice], which always have the greatest good of the soul or the body in view, the art of flattery takes note—I won't say with full knowledge, but by shrewd guessing—and divides herself into four, entering secretly into each of the branches, and pretends that she has become what she has entered, caring nothing for the greatest good, but seeking to entrap ignorance with the bait of pleasure of the moment. And she accomplishes her deceitful design to the extent that she has come to be considered of the highest value.[24]

The similarity between these descriptions is not accidental. Rhetoric, sorcery, idolatry, and the feminine are all figured through each other as deceptive uses of appearance. And appearance is understood as other than—even as opposed to—the true and the Real.

The feminization of appearance in Levinas's thought draws on several genealogies—those pertaining to the creation of Woman (as in *Berakhot* 61a), the history of the feminine figuration of rhetoric in relation to logic and philosophy, and the association of women with sorcery and idolatry in the Jewish tradition. Indeed, Levinas reserves his most negative treatment of the feminine for Woman's association with idolatry and sorcery.

In "Desacralization and Disenchantment," Levinas examines the following text from the Gemara in *Sanhedrin* 67a:

> The sorcerer, if he performs an act, etc. There is a *baraita*: The text says "sorceress" whether it be man or woman; but one says "sorceress" because the vast majority of women engage in sorcery.[25]

After assuring his audience that "this text cannot be taken literally" and that "Sarah did not engage in sorcery, nor did Rebecca, Rachel, Leah, Ruth, or Bathsheba," Levinas tells us that we should "rest assured of the dignity of the biblical woman" and "of the dignity of the feminine in itself."[26] He will, however, further suggest:

> It is on the basis of a certain degradation of the feminine—but each essence is responsible for its own modes of degradation—that the charm of sorcery would function: appearance in the *very heart* of the real, dissolution of reality through the ungraspable resources of appearance, the nonreal received in its unreality, as a trace of the surreal; equivocations perceived as enigmas; and, in the "fling" experienced as an ecstasy of the sacred, the law suspended.[27]

As I have already indicated, this characterization of sorcery fits not only Plato's treatment but Levinas's view of rhetoric as well. The problem of rhetoric is that it appears to be true and takes the place of philosophical discourse. Disentangling the two, however—whether appearance and reality or rhetoric and philosophy—is (near) impossible. This is what makes both rhetoric and sorcery so dangerously potent. Indeed, the philosophical problem Levinas addresses in "Desacralization and Disenchantment" has to do with the problem of distinguishing appearance and reality, sorcery and the Sacred:

> But hence there is a philosophical problem: How is degradation possible? How can holiness be confused with the sacred and turn into sorcery? How can the sacred transform itself into enchantment, into power over human beings?[28]

These are questions for which there are no direct or easy answers. Indeed, as I have already suggested, gender plays an important role in giving the appearance of answering these questions (and others like them). Thus, gender is used, in the first instance, to cover up the insufficiencies within these discourses definitively to separate such closely related but opposed terms and ways of life. Relatedly, gender also provides images, terms, and practices ready to hand for the further disciplining and keeping in place of these opposed—but dangerously, indistinguishable—discourses and experiences. As I will demonstrate, Levinas even splits the "Face" into two in such gendered terms.

Two Faces

As I have noted, in his essay "And God Created Woman," Levinas interprets the creation stories of Genesis as supporting the view that Woman was made out of the tail, not the Face, of Man. Further, he considers that there are two Faces, one feminine and the other masculine. The feminine is always already made-up, whereas the masculine is direct and unadorned, even to the point of a certain savagery. In this context Levinas asks:

> Which of the two faces, the masculine or the feminine, leads? Here equality would end in immobility or in the bursting apart of the human being. The Gemara opts for the priority of the masculine. A man must not walk behind a woman, for his ideas may become clouded. The first reason stems perhaps from masculine psychology. It assumes that a woman bears the erotic within herself as a matter of course.[29]

Given that the Face is, perhaps, the ethical term *par excellence* in Levinas's thought—referring to the infinite alterity of the other person for whom "I" am responsible—this is a troubling split. Although there is a trace of awareness in his thought that the feminine is a projection of what Levinas here terms "masculine psychology," it does not undo this split between Faces, in which the masculine is prior. In the conclusion of "And God Created Woman," Levinas explains that the Gemara prefers a man choose to walk behind a lion rather than behind a woman: "The text of the Gemara prefers the danger of the lions to this intimacy."[30] After Woman comes idolatry, showing—according to Levinas—that the Gemara "still prefers the sentimental road [of following Woman] to that of idolatry."[31] Then comes a passage in this essay that brings one to again question what Levinas might mean when he refers to thinking sexual difference otherwise:

> You see: the feminine is in a fairly good position in this hierarchy of values, which reveals itself when choices become alternatives. It is in second place. It is not woman who is thus slighted. It is the relation based on sexual differences which is subordinated to the interhuman relation—irreducible to the drives and complexes of the libido—to which woman rises as well as man. Maybe man precedes—by a few centuries—the woman in this elevation. From which a cer-

tain—provisional?—priority of man. Maybe the masculine is more directly linked to the universal, and maybe masculine civilization has prepared, above the sexual, a human order in which a woman enters, completely human.[32]

It is as if Levinas, in locating the creation of Eve from a subordinate part of Adam, makes Woman subordinate to Man in the present, in space, in our imperfect world, but also as capable of "coming after" Man and eventually returning fully to the human from which she came. In so doing, Levinas imagines Woman as eventually—that is, in time—transcending and leaving behind her feminine sexuality, joining Man on a higher plane to which he has both preceded her and paved the way in terms of a masculine universality.[33] Levinas regards this version of sexual difference as an improvement on the Eleatic notion of Being. In thus thinking sexual difference, however, Levinas seems to associate the feminine and the "bad proximity" of rhetoric, idolatry, or sorcery in terms of space and the deformations of appearance. In thinking sexual difference in terms of time, he also allows for an ethical proximity to the Other in which Woman can eventually be included inasmuch as she leaves behind and transcends her feminine sexuality into a sort of universal masculinity. This eschatological solution to thinking sexual difference otherwise, however, is continually haunted by the ontological way in which Levinas reads the Genesis stories of creation and by the residues of the Eleatic notion of Being he would elude.[34] While succumbing to the temptation of reading Genesis ontologically is understandable, it is lamentable that Levinas did not, instead, begin with an ethical interpretation of that text.

That Levinas succumbs to the use of gender stereotypes in order to institute, enforce, and govern the differences between ethical and bad proximity is most disappointing in one who has set out to think sexual difference otherwise as a basis for ethics. Further, temporalizing sexual difference still locates it not only within a heteronormative and essentialized understanding of Man and Woman, male and female, but exclusively within the feminine and Woman. Levinas thus fails adequately to think identity through sexual difference otherwise. Again, I ask: How are we to account for these systematic failures, so as not simply to dismiss Levinas's thought, especially his turn to ethics as first philosophy? Can we think "sexual difference" otherwise? Can we think the logics of identity and identification in the West otherwise?

Reconfiguring Rhetoric

I have argued that the gendered configuration of the relationship between rhetoric and philosophy (and in Jewish philosophy the related feminizing of idolatry) is a crucial locus for both the constituting and the regulation not only of these disciplines and forms of life but of sexual difference. As Levinas argues, the history of the Eleatic philosophy of Being has demonstrated a systematic subordination of matter as passive and feminine to form as constitutive and masculine. To think sexual difference otherwise so as to institute the possibility of ethics, including that of gender justice, I argue, a reconfiguration of the gendered character of the relationship between rhetoric and philosophy must be undertaken. A critique and reconfiguration of representations of gender is important as well for those genealogies of the Sacred and idolatry that, as in Jewish philosophy, have developed out of and along the same lines as those of rhetoric. This is necessary because these feminized views of rhetoric and idolatry are remains of an Eleatic metaphysic that negatively configures and subordinates woman and the feminine to man and the masculine. The reinscription of gender stereotypes through the appropriation of rhetoric in these terms repeats the problematic subordination of difference to the Same and the Other to the self. Contrary to Levinas's insistent identification of justice with the "overcoming of rhetoric," therefore, I believe that at stake in the revaluing of the relationship between rhetoric and philosophy is precisely the question of justice.

Without such a critique of this negative figuration of both rhetoric and idolatry, Jewish (and not only Jewish) philosophy and theology will inexorably repeat the marginalization of women, the feminine, and the body. When not treated as simply the other of philosophy—that is, as the bearer of error, delusion, and prejudice—rhetoric offers resources for and methods of critical reading that enable us both to uncover and to reconfigure otherwise the pernicious gender ideology within philosophy itself.[35] Only then may we undo the problematic rendering of the feminine, the Other, body, and Woman in the Eleatic notion of Being that Levinas both calls for and, alas, fails to perform. Levinas thus may have left unfulfilled the promise to think sexual difference otherwise, a challenge that I choose to pick up. We must ask, however, whether notions of sexual difference will provide a way toward gender justice or whether, as in Levinas's case, they will lead to yet another ethical cul-de-sac.

Thinking Identity Otherwise

In responding to this challenge and concern, I suggest that sexual difference is not the only, and perhaps not the most promising, mode of thinking identity and identification otherwise in Levinas's thought. While, as late as 1982, Levinas again affirms his 1947 view that "the feminine was otherness itself," need we also stake Levinas's ethics of alterity on this notion of sexual difference? I suggest not. Indeed, we may pick up an unexpected clue from that work which so early offered a critique of Levinas's notion of "sexual difference" as the othering of Woman as the "second sex."

In her work of that title, Simone de Beauvoir reads Levinas as enacting the concomitant othering and subordination of Woman to Man. De Beauvoir's critique concerns sentences such as the following from Levinas's *Time and the Other:*

> Does a situation exist where the alterity of the other appears in its purity? Does a situation exist where the other would not have alterity only as the reverse side of its identity, would not comply only with the Platonic law of participation where every term contains a sameness and through this sameness contains the Other? Is there not a situation where alterity would be borne by a being in a positive sense, as essence? What is the alterity that does not purely and simply enter into the opposition of two species of the same genus? I think the absolutely contrary contrary [*le contraire absolutement contraire*], whose contrariety is in no way affected by the relationship that can be established between it and its correlative, the contrariety that permits its terms to remain absolutely other, is the *feminine.*[36]

Levinas puts in question the Platonic law of participation and instead seeks alterity "in a positive sense . . . that does not purely and

simply enter into the opposition of two species of the same genus." As
I have noted, however, in grafting the "absolutely other" onto the
feminine associated with the deformations of appearance, Levinas
reinscribes just this metaphysic onto sexual difference. Thus, while de
Beauvoir's reading of Levinas may be both reductive and, in part, incorrect, it is not entirely so. As de Beauvoir describes the situation:

> She [Woman] is defined and differentiated with reference to man
> and not he with reference to her; she is the incidental, the inessen-
> tial as opposed to the essential. He is the Subject, he is the Ab-
> solute—she is the Other.[37]

De Beauvoir then goes on to suggest:

> I suppose that Levinas does not forget that woman, too, is aware of
> her own consciousness, or ego. But it is striking that he deliberately
> takes a man's point of view, disregarding the reciprocity of subject
> and object. When he writes that woman is a mystery, he implies that
> she is mystery for man. Thus his description, which is intended to be
> objective, is in fact an assertion of masculine privilege.[38]

Levinas's important and distinctive understanding of the asymmetri-
cal obligation (not power) of the self to and for (not over) the other
person is not registered in de Beauvoir's insistence on "reciprocity"
and mutual recognition as a basis for ethics. Still, she is not incorrect
in noting a persistent androcentrism in his writing that threatens to
undo the very efficacy of Levinas's notion of sexual difference as a critique of participation metaphysics.

If de Beauvoir does not offer a way out of the cul-de-sac of sexual
difference in Levinas's thought, the way in which she attempts to
frame her inquiry into gender and sexuality in *The Second Sex* does
offer another way of thinking about difference and identity in the
West. Rather than seeking essentialized differences, following Sartre,
de Beauvoir suggests that identity is dependent on a "situation."[39] In
locating her problematic, de Beauvoir first attempts to draw analogies
between the situations of women, blacks, and Jews.[40] She also, however, finds important differences between them. Some of the ways in
which she pursues this track are rather awkward. For example, she
seems to overstretch her point when she supports her claim that
women are dispersed among men, thus lacking the power derived

from mutual identification and solidarity, in the following extreme terms:

> The proletariat can propose to massacre the ruling class, and a suf-
> ficiently fanatical Jew or Negro might dream of getting sole posses-
> sion of the atomic bomb and making humanity wholly Jewish or
> black; but woman cannot even dream of exterminating the males.
> The bond that unites her to her oppressors is not comparable to any
> other.[41]

Although, despite this claim, she maintains analogies between blacks and women,[42] de Beauvoir ends up drawing an impassable distinction between the situation of women and that of Jews:

> "The eternal feminine" corresponds to "the black soul" and to "the
> Jewish character." True, the Jewish problem is on the whole very dif-
> ferent from the other two—to the anti-Semite the Jew is not so
> much an inferior as he is an enemy for whom there is to be granted
> no place on earth, for whom annihilation is the fate desired. But
> there are deep similarities between the situation of woman and that
> of the Negro.[43]

While de Beauvoir finds more helpful for her purposes analogies between the situations of women and blacks, she steps back from thinking through the relations of misogyny and antisemitism.[44] In 1949, what is foremost in de Beauvoir's understanding of anti-semitism is the realization of its telos in annihilation. For her, this breaks analogies and halts further thought in this direction. She makes one last comparison of the situations of women, blacks, and Jews, however, in which she importantly puts the dominant subject in question as follows:

> If we cast a general glance over this history, we see several conclu-
> sions that stand out from it. And this one first of all: the whole of
> feminine history has been man-made. Just as in America there is no
> Negro problem, but rather a white problem; just as "anti-semitism is
> not a Jewish problem: it is our problem" [Jean-Paul Sartre, *Réflexions
> sur la question juive,* translated as *Anti-Semite and Jew*]; so the woman
> problem has always been a man's problem.[45]

By renaming the source and subject of the "problem," de Beauvoir has significantly shifted the terms of the discourse.

Conclusion

While de Beauvoir is at times successful in thinking race, ethnicity, sexuality, gender, and religion together, often she is not. This is not surprising given the difficulty of such a task. Nor, as I have shown, is Levinas successful in thinking sexual difference otherwise and thereby undoing the binding logics of identity in the West. The importance, however, of his ethical critique of these logics and of his attempts to undo or unsay them in other terms persists. In seeking a critique of identity, then, it is perhaps not in the announced location of Levinas's attempt to undo the knots of Western metaphysics that we should look. Rather than entering the cul-de-sac of sexual difference one more time, we might turn to Levinas's rethinking of the relation of Hebrew and Greek and of Jewishness/Judaism for a more consistently effective critique and transformation of the logic of identity. Further, although Levinas traces this logic back to Parmenides and the Eleatic notion of Being, the place where Jewish difference is most pressingly at stake in these terms is in the dialectic of the Enlightenment/Emancipation.

To think identity otherwise, I suggest that we turn not to Levinas's notion of sexual difference, but to how Levinas differently appeals to Judaism and gender in thinking the relationship of particular to universal. For it is here that Levinas has been more successful in thinking identity otherwise than being, through such notions as "election" and "translation" and in (my) excessive and immemorial "responsibility" for the Other. While these are not untroubled notions, they hold within them a promise that should be further explored. Furthermore, since (male) Jews and Judaism have, in post-Emancipation Europe, often been figured as and through the feminine, an interrogation of Levinas's work on the question of thinking identity otherwise should also include a study of the *intersections* of gender and Jewishness in his work. One might, for example, ask what happens in Levinas's writings when terms for race, ethnicity, and religion are sexed or gendered, and when "sexual difference" is interpreted through the categories of religion, race, and ethnicity. By tracing the mutual implications of and between these various terms and categories, one might better articulate the dialectics of feminizing the Other and othering Woman and the feminine in Levinas's writings.

Finally, by contextualizing Levinas's thought in terms of the dialectics of Jewish emancipation in the aftermath of the Enlightenment (and, finally, the Shoah), the import of his critique of its very terms and limits will become evident. While Levinas has inaugurated just such a sustained critique through his interpretation of Judaism, his inscriptions of sexual difference all too often reinstate the very terms of the emancipation he would otherwise critique. In thinking through their intersection and thereby refusing the opposition between the problematics of identity in Judaism and those of sexual difference, we may finally move beyond a persistent impasse in Levinas's thought, toward a thinking of identity otherwise.

NOTES

1. I thank Laurence Silberstein for generously inviting me to contribute to this book, even though I was unable to attend the conference at Lehigh University on which it was based. I also thank the Harvard University Program in the Study of Women and Religion for granting me a fellowship during the 1997–98 academic year, enabling me to work on my project "Figures of Marginalization: Rhetoric, Gender, Judaism," of which this chapter forms a part. Finally, aspects of this chapter were presented at the Harvard University Divinity School in April 1998 and at the annual meeting of the Association for Jewish Studies in December 1998. I thank those in attendance at these lectures for their insightful and engaged responses, and especially Laura Levitt for her superb (and timely) editorial advice.

2. In an explication (resembling that of Levinas) of the social consequences of this logic in genocide, Theodor Adorno writes: "Genocide is the absolute integration. It is on its way wherever men are leveled off— 'polished off,' as the German military called it—until one exterminates them literally, as deviations from the concept of their total nullity. Auschwitz confirmed the philosopheme of pure identity as death" (Theodor W. Adorno, *Negative Dialectics* [New York: Continuum Publishing, 1983], 362; originally published as *Negative Dialektik* [Frankfurt am Main: Suhrkamp Verlag, 1966]).

3. I do not here engage Jacques Derrida's important critique of Levinas's logic as, precisely, failing to elude the grammar and logic of identity and totality after Hegel. See, especially, Jacques Derrida, "Violence and Metaphysics: An Essay on the Thought of Emmanuel Levinas," in

Writing and Difference (Chicago: University of Chicago Press, 1978), 78–153; originally published in French as *L'Écriture et la différence* (Paris: Editions du Seuil, 1967). For a reconsideration of some of his earlier views of Levinas, see Jacques Derrida, "At This Very Moment in This Work Here I Am," in *Re-reading Levinas* (Bloomington: University of Indiana Press, 1991), 11–48, translated by Ruben Berezdivin from the French: "En ce moment même dans cet ouvrage me voice," in *Texts pour Emmanuel Levinas*, ed. F. Laruelle (Paris: Jean-Michel Place, 1980).

4. One must also consider, however, the sources of this subordination, as evidenced in Levinas's thought, in the stories of the creation of Man and Woman in Genesis.

5. Emmanuel Levinas, *Time and the Other*, trans. Richard A. Cohen (Pittsburgh: Duquesne University Press, 1987). Original texts appeared as follows: "Time and the Other" as "Le Temps et l'autre," in J. Wahl, ed., *Le Choix, le monde, l'existence* (Grenoble-Paris: Arthaud, 1947), republished as *Le Temps et l'autre* (St. Clement, France: Fata Morgana, 1979) with a new preface by Levinas; "Diachrony and Representation" as "Diachronie et représentation," *University of Ottawa Quarterly* 55, 4 (1985); "The Old and the New" in *L'Ancien et le nouveau* (Paris: Editions du Cerf, 1982).

6. As Levinas writes: "Sex is not some specific difference. It is situated beside the logical division into genera and species. This division certainly never manages to reunite an empirical content. But it is not in this sense that it does not permit one to account for the difference between the sexes. The difference between the sexes is a formal structure, but one that carves up reality in another sense and conditions the very possibility of reality as multiple, against the unity of being proclaimed by Parmenides" (*Time and the Other*, 85).

7. Ibid., "Preface," 36.

8. Emmanuel Levinas, "And God Created Woman," in *Nine Talmudic Readings*, trans. Annette Aronowicz (Bloomington: University of Indiana Press, 1990), 161–77. This essay was published in French in Emmanuel Levinas, *Du sacré au saint: Cinq nouvelles lectures talmudiques* (Paris: Les Editions de Minuit, 1977).

9. Emmanuel Levinas, "Desacralization and Disenchantment," in *Nine Talmudic Readings*, trans. Aronowicz, 136–60. This essay appeared in French in Levinas, *Du sacré au saint.*

10. "The Eleatic notion of being dominates Plato's philosophy, where multiplicity was subordinated to the one, and where the role of the feminine was thought within the categories of passivity and activity, and was reduced to matter. Plato did not grasp the feminine in its specifically erotic notion. In his philosophy of love he left to the feminine no other role

than that of furnishing an example of the Idea, which alone can be the object of love. . . . Beginning with Plato, the social ideal will be sought for in an ideal of fusion. It will be thought . . . in its relationship with the other, by being swallowed up in a collective representation, a common ideal. . . . Set against the cosmos that is Plato's world, is the world of the spirit *[l'esprit]* where the implications of eros are not reduced to the logic of genus, and where the ego takes the place of the same and the Other takes the place of the other" (Levinas, *Time and the Other*, 92–94).

11. Emmanuel Levinas, "Philosophy, Justice and Love," in *Entre Nous: Thinking-of-the-Other*, trans. Michael B. Smith and Barbara Harshav (New York: Columbia University Press, 1998), 113.

12. Levinas is aware of the dangers of the very temptation to which he ultimately succumbs:

> The various relations that can exist in man and being are always judged according to their proximity or distance from unity. What is relation? What is time? A fall from unity, a fall from eternity. There are many theologians in all religions who say that the good life is a coincidence with God; coincidence, that is, the return to unity. Whereas in the insistence on the relation to the other in responsibility for him or her the excellence of sociality itself is affirmed; in theological terms, proximity to God, society with God. (Levinas, "Philosophy, Justice, and Love," 112)

13. This part-whole relation functions here despite Levinas's views as represented in n. 16, below.

14. Levinas, "And God Created Woman," 173.

15. Emmanuel Levinas, "Judaism and the Feminine," in *Difficult Freedom: Essays on Judaism*, trans. Sean Hand (Baltimore: Johns Hopkins University Press, 1990), 30–38; originally published as *Difficile liberté: Essais sur le judaïsme* (1963; reprint, France: Editions Albin Michel, 1970).

16. "If woman completes man, she does not complete him as a part completes another into a whole but, as it were, as two totalities complete one another—which is, after all, the miracle of social relations. The discussion between the schools of Rav and Shmuel on the creation of Eve can be viewed from this perspective. Did she come from Adam's rib? Was this rib not a *side* of Adam, created as a single being with two faces that God separated while Adam, still androgynous, was sleeping? This theme perhaps evolved from Plato's *Symposium*, but it is one which in the Doctors takes on a new meaning. The two faces of the primitive Adam from the beginning look towards the side to which they will always remain turned. They are faces from the very outset, whereas Plato's god turns them round after separation. Their new existence, separated existence, will

not come to punish the daring of too perfect a nature, as in Plato. For the Jews, separated existence will be worth more than the initial union" (Levinas, "Judaism and the Feminine," 35). However, in the same essay, Levinas counters this view, emphasizing the priority of the masculine in the following terms: "These ideas are older than the principles in whose name modern woman struggles for her emancipation, but the *truth* of all these principles lies on a plane that also contains the thesis opposed to the image of initial androgyny and attached to the popular idea of the rib. It upholds a certain priority of the masculine. The latter remains the prototype of the human and determines eschatology. . . . The differences between masculine and feminine are blurred in this messianic age" (Levinas, "Judaism and the Feminine," 35).
17. Levinas, "And God Created Woman," 174.
18. Ibid.
19. For more on the importance of Plato's *Gorgias* in forming the predominant negative view of rhetoric in (Jewish) philosophy, see my "Rhetoric as Ideology Critique: The Gadamer-Habermas Debate Reinvented," *Journal of the American Academy of Religion* 62, 1 (Spring 1994): 123–50; and "A Matter of Discipline: Reading for Gender in Jewish Philosophy," in *Judaism since Gender,* ed. Miriam Peskowitz and Laura Levitt (New York: Routledge, 1997), 158–73. For a more extensive treatment of the shifting views of rhetoric in Levinas's philosophy, see my "Rhetoric, Ideology, and Idolatry in the Writings of Emmanuel Levinas," in *New Essays in Rhetoric and Religion,* ed. Walter Jost and Wendy Raudenbush Olmsted (New Haven, Conn.: Yale University Press, forthcoming Spring 2000).
20. Emmanuel Levinas, *Totality and Infinity,* trans. Alphonso Lingis (Pittsburgh: Duquesne University Press, 1969), 70–72; originally published as *Totalité et infini: Essai sur l'extériorité* (The Hague: Martinus Nijhoff, 1961).
21. Emmanuel Levinas, "Ideology and Idealism," in *The Levinas Reader,* ed. Sean Hand (Oxford: Basil Blackwell, 1989), 241.
22. Emmanuel Levinas, *Otherwise Than Being or Beyond Essence,* trans. Alphonso Lingis (The Hague: Martinus Nijhoff, 1981), from *Autrement qu'être; ou, Au-delà de l'essence,* Phaenomenologica 54 (The Hague: Martinus Nijhoff, 1974).
23. Levinas, "Desacralization and Disenchantment," 141.
24. Plato, *Gorgias,* trans. C. Helmbold (New York: Bobbs-Merrill, Library of Liberal Arts Press, 1952), line 465.
25. Levinas, "Desacralization and Disenchantment," 142.
26. Ibid., 142.
27. Ibid., 143.
28. Ibid., 146–47.

29. Levinas, "And God Created Woman," 174–75.
30. Ibid., 175.
31. Ibid., 176.
32. Ibid., 177.
33. The priority and constitutive character of the masculine in the human with regard to both creation and eschatology, the end of days, is evident elsewhere in Levinas's writing as well. In "Judaism and the Feminine," Levinas describes the subordination of the maternal to the masculine in the messianic as follows:

> It upholds a certain priority of the masculine. The latter remains the prototype of the human and determines eschatology, in relation to which maternity itself is described as the salvation of humanity. The justice which will rule the relations between men amounts to the presence of God among them. The differences between masculine and feminine are blurred in this messianic age. . . . In the rabbinic interpretation of love, maternity is subordinate to a human destiny which exceeds the limits of "family joys." . . . The forms of romance that one finds in the Bible are at once interpreted by the *midrash* in such a way as to bring out the eschatological side of the romance. . . . Poetic images of amorous life are discreet in the Bible, outside the Song of Songs, which is soon interpreted in a mystical sense. . . . The feminine will never take on the aspect of the Divine [in Judaism]. . . . The dimension of intimacy, not the dimension of loftiness, is opened up by woman. Doubtless the mysterious interiority of feminine existence will be used to experience, like a betrothed, the Sabbath, the Torah itself; and sometimes the divine Presence in the nearness of men, the *sheckhinah*. The images do not in any way become feminine figures. They are not taken seriously. Amorous relations in Scripture are interpreted symbolically and denote mystical relations. . . . True life, joy, pardon and peace no longer belong to woman [at the end of days]. Now there rises up, foreign to all compassion for itself, spirit in its essence, virile, superhuman, solitary. It recognizes itself in Elijah, the prophet without pardon, the prophet of anger and punishment, a suckling of crows, inhabiting deserts, without kindness, without happiness, without peace. . . . But the biblical figure which haunts Israel on the paths of exile, the figure that it invokes at the end of the Sabbath, in the dusk where it will soon remain behind without help, the figure in whom is stored up for the Jews all the tenderness of the earth, the hand which caresses and rocks his children, is no longer feminine. Neither wife nor sister nor mother guides it. It is Elijah, who did not experience death, the most severe of the prophets, precursor of the Messiah. (Levinas, "Judaism and the Feminine," 35–38)

This treatment of the relation between the masculine and the feminine recalls Elliot Wolfson's important interpretation of the role of gender in

Jewish mystical traditions. See, especially, his *Through a Speculum That Shines* (Princeton: Princeton University Press, 1994) and *Circle in the Square* (Albany: SUNY Press, 1995). While many critics read Kabbalah and philosophy as utterly opposed and incompatible discourses, the displacement and subsumption of the feminine by the masculine is also constitutive of a central stand of Jewish philosophy from (Philo or) Maimonides to Levinas. See, e.g., my essay "A Matter of Discipline," in Peskowitz and Levitt's edited book *Judaism since Gender*, on this and related topics. Here, I emphasize how Levinas's understanding of eschatology in "Judaism and the Feminine" (as well as in other of his texts) undoes his articulations elsewhere of the importance of distinguishing between ontology and ethics. This masculinist eschatology is, alas, both symptomatic of and compatible with Levinas's failure to think sexual difference otherwise than the Eleatic notion of Being, in which the end is a return to the beginning and difference is absorbed in the Same.

34. This despite Levinas's clear statements elsewhere disavowing the desire of a return to a primordial unity:

> One last thing that is very close to my heart. In this whole priority of the relationship to the other, there is a break with a great traditional idea of the excellence of unity. The relation would already be a deprivation of this unity. That is the Plotinian tradition. My idea consists in conceiving sociality as independent of the "lost" unity. ("Philosophy, Justice, and Love," 112)

35. For more on the importance of rereading philosophy rhetorically, see my "Rhetoric as Ideology Critique: The Gadamer-Habermas Debate Reinvented" and "A Matter of Discipline: Reading for Gender in Jewish Philosophy."

36. Levinas, *Time and the Other*, 85. Translator Richard A. Cohen in his editorial notes cites this passage in particular as drawing de Beauvoir's negative comment. In fact, she casts a somewhat wider net, one that nevertheless captures this passage as well. (See below in my text, as well as n. 37.) I thank Elisabeth Schüssler Fiorenza for repeatedly drawing my attention to the importance of considering de Beauvoir's reading of Levinas.

37. Simone de Beauvoir, *The Second Sex*, trans. H. M. Parshley (New York: Vintage Books, 1989), xxii; published in France in two volumes as *Le Deuxieme Sexe: I. Les Faits et les mythes; II. L'Expérience vécue* (Paris: Librarie Gallimard, 1949). Original English translation published by Alfred A. Knopf (1952).

38. Ibid.

39. "The biological and social sciences no longer admit the existence of un-

changeably fixed entities that determine given characteristics, such as those ascribed to woman, the Jew, or the Negro. . . . To decline to accept such notions as the eternal feminine, the black soul, the Jewish character, is not to deny that Jews, Negroes, women exist today—this denial does not represent a liberation for those concerned, but rather a flight from reality" (ibid., xx).

40. "There are, to be sure, other cases [beside that of Woman] in which a certain category has been able to dominate another completely for a time. Very often this privilege depends upon inequality of numbers—the majority imposes its rule upon the minority or persecutes it. But women are not a minority, like the American Negroes or the Jews; there are as many women as men on earth. Again, the two groups concerned have often been originally independent; they may have been formerly unaware of each other's existence, or perhaps they recognized each other's autonomy. But a historical event has resulted in the subjugation of the weaker by the stronger. The scattering of the Jews, the introduction of slavery into America, the conquests of imperialism are examples in point. In these cases the oppressed retained at least the memory of former days; they possessed in common a past, a tradition, sometimes a religion or a culture" (ibid., xxiv).

41. Ibid., xxv.

42. "The similarity just noted is in no way due to chance, for whether it is a race, a caste, a class, or a sex that is reduced to a position of inferiority, the methods of justification are the same" (ibid., xxvi).

43. Ibid.

44. De Beauvoir's interest in comparing the situations of blacks (especially in the United States) and women is to be accounted for by Nelson Algren's suggestion that she follow out this analogy and, in part, by her friendship with Richard and Ellen Wright (Deidre Bair, "Introduction to the Vintage Edition," in de Beauvoir, *Second Sex*, xii). As were so many of her views, de Beauvoir's perspectives on Jews and antisemitism are clearly shaped by Jean-Paul Sartre, especially his *Réflexions sur la question juive* (Paris: Paul Morihien, 1946).

45. De Beauvoir, *Second Sex*, 128.

Chapter 14

Individuation without Identity: A Deleuzian Aesthetics of Existence

Gordon C. F. Bearn

It's a strange business, speaking for yourself, in your own name, because it doesn't at all come with seeing yourself as an ego or a person or a subject. Individuals find a real name for themselves, rather, only through the harshest exercise in depersonalization, by opening themselves up to the multiplicities everywhere within them, to the intensities running through them. (Deleuze [1973] 1995, 6)

To become is never to imitate, nor to "do like," nor to conform to a model, whether it's of justice or of truth. There is no terminus from which you set out, none which you arrive at or which you ought to arrive at. Nor are there two terms which are exchanged. The question "What are you becoming?" is particularly stupid. (Deleuze and Parnet [1977] 1987, 2)

In one of its guises, the problem of identity strikes as deep as the Platonic problem of participation, the problem that started the stammering endemic to philosophical questions: what makes chairs chairs, the wicked wicked, the beautiful beautiful, scrapple scrapple, or the French French. From the beginning, this problem was defined as a problem of authenticity. In the *Republic*, for instance, it is the problem of what makes an action an authentic instance of justice and not simply the will of the stronger. Even Plato found that these problems of identity turned in on themselves, for, especially in the wake of Socrates' execution, it was important to distinguish authentic philosophy, however poorly conducted, from the inauthentic, which was not even bad philosophy but only its inauthentic simulacrum, only sophistry. Challenges to traditional approaches to identity can thus be expected to swell into novel characterizations of philosophy itself.

Identity and Authenticity

In a late essay on Herman Melville's "Bartleby," Deleuze offers a characterization of the traditional approach to identification:

> Most often, an identification seems to bring into play three elements, which are able to interchange or permutate: [1] a form, image, or representation, a portrait, a model; [2] a subject (or at least a virtual subject); and [3] the subject's effort to assume a form, to appropriate the image, to adapt itself to the image and the image to itself. (Deleuze [1993] 1997, 76)

There is almost nothing original in this characterization: on the one side is the subject manifesting motley properties; on the other side is the perfect model, the ideal normative instance; and in between we find the subject, huffing and puffing in an effort to imitate the ideal model. In contemporary philosophical discussions, one is less likely to speak of normative instances than of defining criteria, necessary and sufficient conditions for being just or beautiful. And here discussion is likely to go in one of two ways: either in the direction of squabbling over which criteria are the real criteria for being just or in the direction of a concern with a subject's difficulty ever, perfectly or completely, to adapt itself to those criteria. In the rest of these remarks, I allow myself to be drawn in the second, pessimistic direction: not to settle into the black space of postmodernism charted by Jean-François Lyotard but to escape it, to ride a line of thought beyond authenticity and inauthenticity.

It was the existentialists who, in our century, did the most with the language of authenticity, and I will dwell for a moment on the failure of their account of authenticity in order to emphasize the existential origins of what is called poststructuralist thought, origins often lost in a rush to read Saussure. Heidegger and Sartre both thought that, most of the time, we allow others to lead our lives for us, becoming not authentic individuals but, in Heidegger's terms, merely one of them, a they-self. The existentialist criticism of inauthentic they-selves seems to demand an account of a truly authentic self, and it would be natural to picture this authentic self as a kind of jewel hidden by what "they" think and do, an authentic emerald caked with the muck of inauthenticity. It comes as a surprise, therefore, to discover that the existentialists did not believe there was such a thing as an authentic self at all. On their account, at bottom there is no bottom. The fundamental mood of anxiety reveals that, fundamentally, human beings are nothing. I return to attempt a diagnosis of this existential nothingness later, but for now I simply remark that if there is no authentic self, then the famous existentialist discussions of authenticity are metaphysically bootless.

Instead of an authentic self, these existentialists offer the leap, a resolute commitment to a single possible way of being, for example, being a surgeon or a dancer. By chaining ourselves to one such possible mode of existence, our existence, so we are told, can be made authentic. These modes of existence are ways of living our lives, and each of our lives points inevitably to death; so, fully to affirm any such possibility is to live it in the face of the inevitability of death. But on this Heideggerian account, the task of becoming a surgeon is never finished. Since being a surgeon is a way of living into the future, it cannot be finished in the present moment of choice, and so to become authentic, one must *repeat*[1] in the face of death's inevitability the resolute commitment to a life of surgery.

This story of existentialist authenticity is bleak enough as it stands. There is no self. The task of making oneself an authentic surgeon can never be completed. And then you die. But in fact, the story is bleaker still. For it is not as if at each moment, just for a moment, one is an authentic surgeon, in all one's being, down to one's toes. In that case, a long series of moments of authenticity summed up over a life would amount to an entirely authentic life. Each cupful of our lives, although only a cupful, would still be an authentic instance of a type. But since, on this existentialist account, there is no authentic self, it is not as if one becomes, for a moment, authentic. What one is trying, in one moment, to be—a surgeon—is something that inevitably reaches into the future and so cannot possibly be present in a moment. Each resolute attempt to make oneself an authentic surgeon is therefore a failure, and the sum of these failures—complete failure—is the best we can make of our lives. We were not using cups to fill our lives after all; they were sieves.

In contemporary discussions of identity, this is the place where some think they can save the notion of identity by turning from being to becoming. In one respect this is no help at all; for if we simply replace a representative picture of a person's being a surgeon with a teleological model of a person's becoming a surgeon, we will be no closer to identity. The turn to becoming can help, but only if we do not force it into a teleological framework, only if we stop asking, "What are you becoming?" (Deleuze and Parnet [1977] 1987, 2). Consider that form of the turn to becoming in which we are tempted to say that it is not the destination that matters but the journey. This familiar formula is reaching for the truth, but it will not get us there. A journey has a direction, a point, and it makes sense as an effort to arrive at its destination. So a journey that never arrives is, in its own terms, a failure. If the best we can say about our quest for authentic identity is that it is the journey that counts, not the destination, then we will have said nothing to help us understand how our lives could be worth more than nothing.

The turn to becoming will help only if it is cut off from the teleological interpretation of becoming. Thus it already seems that unless we can reverse our evaluation of pointlessness, unless we can find the good side of pointlessness, pessimism or nihilism will be our only option.[2]

These criticisms of existentialist authenticity recapitulate Derrida's discussion of signatures (Derrida [1971] 1988). Signatures authenticate identity. When I sign a check, my signature proves that and who signed the check: it validates the identity of the signer. These acts of signing are the fiduciary equivalent of existentialism's resolute choice, and like that choice, they must fail. To function as a signature, a signature must be able to reappear at the bottom of other checks. It must be recognizably the signature of the same person, the identical person. But this reproducibility—Derrida will call this the signature's "iterability"—not only makes possible the use of my signature to cash checks, it also makes possible the use of my signature to forge checks;

for it is precisely the fact that my signature is a recognizable and re-peatable form that makes forgery possible. But this ruins all hope that a signature might, on its own and without appeal to power, work. This is why, in an adjacent context, Jacques Derrida writes: "Ultimately there is always a police and a tribunal ready to intervene each time that a rule . . . is invoked in a case involving signatures, events or con-texts" (Derrida [1977] 1988, 105).

If a signature were really to guarantee that I, and I alone, had been present, at that date, authenticating with one flourish both my presence and my deposit, then my signature could be used only that once. But were it able to be used only once, it could not function as a signature. So, paradoxically, if a signature were really to work, it couldn't work at all. Whenever anyone signs anything, they are not, as it were, *signing;* they are merely portraying their signature—portray-ing in the sense of portraying a character on stage, simulating an identity. Every act of signing a check is a theatrical act and, like every theatrical act, merely simulates an identity, especially if what is the-atricalized is sincerity or authenticity.

This Derridean version of the necessary failure of authenticity can be generalized. If we are looking at identification in the tradi-tional way, a subject trying to exemplify the defining characteristics of a normative instance, then being a surgeon or a dancer or Jewish will be as possible and as impossible as signing your name. For the defining characteristics of being a member of a class are like signa-tures, repeatable, iterable, and so these defining features make pos-sible—at one and the same time—identification and masquerade. And just as the result of our brief consideration of signatures was that every act of signing is a theatrical act, so every attempt to make oneself an authentic surgeon or authentic Jew will be theatrical, a masquerade of authenticity. Identity, authenticity, is trapped in the theater of representation.[3] Subjects struggle to represent them-selves *as* a surgeon or dancer or Jew and so can do no more than *portray* the marks of authenticity. And as with signatures, it is always the police that arrest every question of identity. There can be no es-cape from this theater of representation, which is not also an es-cape from representation itself. But how can we understand an es-cape from representation itself? Surely not by representing it. Then how? I am getting ahead of myself.

Representation Dry

Consider identification, representation at its most dry: desiccated and secular. A particular, x, is identified as a thing of a certain kind: a dancer, a surgeon, a Jew, a scalpel. Imagine a particular object, for example, the wastepaper basket now near my desk. Now, suppose we wanted to represent that particular wastepaper basket. We might try to represent it simply as a "wastepaper basket." But, of course, there are many wastepaper baskets, so this concept will not permit us to talk about just that one. Our first thought will be to add more concepts to eliminate the unintended other particulars that we are not intent on representing. So we might try "brown wastepaper basket" or "light-brown plastic wastepaper basket"; but the problem of representing more than a single particular is still with us. Sophisticates might try to represent just that particular particular, by invoking the concept of a "shaped light-brown plastic trajectory through space-time"; but although that might seem to do the trick, it is still not a particular, only a rather devious *universal*. So, even if a concept picked out only one particular in the actual world, it would still represent many different particulars in other possible worlds, that is, in this world had things happened differently. Success would nevertheless be ours if we could restrict our sophisticated space-time trajectory to the actual world; but the actual world is another particular, and if we could represent particulars we wouldn't be having this problem in the first place. So any appeal to the actual world only begs the question. The problem can be put like this: a particular is a particular and a long sum of universals is still a universal. In principle, universals refer to more than one particular thing, even if there is, in actual fact, only one thing in the world to which they refer.

Perhaps that is just a human limitation; perhaps, although our finite minds cannot represent a particular, god's can. Grant that since god is god, god can think about particulars; the question I want to ask is: Can god think a particular by doing what we call *representing* it?

How big is the space of actual particulars? Huge. How big is the space of possible particulars? It has no end. Now, suppose that god can grasp an infinite conjunction of concepts; would that allow god to narrow down the extension of that infinite concept to one particular wastepaper basket? No! Imagine this infinite conceptual conjunction growing. Each new concept would eliminate more of the infinite space of possible particulars, but the size of the remaining space would be the same: it would have no end. And no matter how many concepts we added to this monster conjunction, the space of particulars that might satisfy it would remain the same size: endless. Hence, although god might be able to think particulars somehow or other, even god cannot *represent* a particular wastepaper basket.

It is important for me that however god thinks particulars, it not be by means of conceptual representation, because I want particulars to be unrepresentable in principle. It is obvious, any fool can see, that the wastepaper basket is there, but we have just found that, in its particularity, it is unrepresentable. I don't want to turn this into skepticism. I want to ask: What does the unrepresentability of particulars tell us about the being or identity of the particular? What do we learn about particulars when we learn that they cannot be captured by concepts?

> If a particular were *one,* self-identical thing, then it
>   would be conceptualizable, representable.
> But it is not.
> —So a particular is not one, self-identical thing.

Alternatively:

> If a particular were *many,* self-identical things, then it
>   would also be conceptualizable, representable.
> But it is not.
> —So a particular is not many, self-identical things.

Neither one nor many, particulars evade identification; they evade the millennial problem of the one and the many. They are neither. What are they?

We are approaching what Gilles Deleuze calls his transcendental empiricism (Deleuze [1968] 1994, 56). According to Deleuze, the limitations of representational thinking tell us about the real nature of those particulars that exceed representation. And what we are told is that a particular is not a thing, it is not an it; a particular is a multiplicity: "a swarm of differences, a pluralism of free, wild, or untamed differences" (50). Deleuze even dares to say, "Difference is not the phenomenon but the noumenon closest to the phenomenon" (222). Between the one (n = 1) and the many (n + 1), Deleuze and Félix Guattari find multiplicities (n − 1) (Deleuze and Guattari [1980] 1987, 6). They write:

> This is our hypothesis: a multiplicity is defined not by the elements that compose it in extension, not by the characteristics that compose it in comprehension, but by the lines and dimensions that it encompasses in "intension." (245)

These are difficult moments in Deleuze and Guattari's thought, but they are central; it is here that they insist on pack phenomena. A pack of wolves is defined not by the wolves (the elements) that it includes, nor is it defined by the concept of wolf that each wolf exemplifies; a wolf pack is defined by the changing relations among the wolves that compose it, by the differences of intensity or ordering among the wolves (Deleuze and Guattari [1980] 1987, 31).[4] Pack systems have some similarities with rhizomes, crabgrasses, for which every root can become a stem and every stem a root; so Deleuze and Guattari announce, characteristically without hesitation, "multiplicities are rhizomatic" (Deleuze and Guattari [1980] 1987, 8). Pack systems also have some similarities with certain computer networks; already in 1980, Deleuze and Guattari could write of

> acentered systems, finite networks of automata in which communication runs from any neighbor to any other, the stems of channels do not preexist, and all individuals are interchangeable, defined only by their *state* at a given moment—such that the local operations are coordinated and the final, global result synchronized without a central agency. (17)

But before I turn to the notion of individuation without identity, I will assess the consequences of this discussion of representing the wastepaper basket for the general notion of identity.[5]

Beyond Representation: Swarms of Intensities

If identification is construed in the traditional fashion, as a subject trying to identify with a group or a way of being, then although people may be identified as Jewish and may identify themselves as Jewish, this identification will be metaphysically suspect. Deleuze writes:

> The primacy of identity, however conceived, defines the world of representation. But modern thought is born of the failure of representation, of the loss of identities, and of the discovery of all the forces that act under the representation of the identical. The modern world is one of simulacra. Man did not survive God, nor did the identity of the subject survive that of substance. *All identities are only simulated, produced as an optical "effect" by the more profound game of difference and repetition.* (Deleuze [1968] 1994 xix; my emphasis)

"All identities . . . only simulated"? How can this be true? Are there then no chairs, no surgeons, no dancers? Of course there are. But these categories—chairs, surgeons, dancers—are unable to pick out just one particular, and so the particular escapes.[6] At this point, one move is to make identity partial or relative. For instance, we could say that this chair and that one are both identical high chairs. But they are different individuals, so being a high chair will not represent either one completely, only partially, relatively—as when a dog and a cat have the same weight. Notice, however, that we should not conceive partial identification as if we were trying to represent a checkerboard and were able to represent the particular black squares but not the particular white ones. If particulars escape representation, as I have suggested, then the black squares will escape the concept "black" just as the white ones escape the concept "white." So there is something very misleading about speaking here of partial identification, and it will not save our interest in identification. It is not that a multiplicity has a partial identity; Deleuze and Guattari write that "a multiplicity has neither subject nor object, only determinations, magnitudes, and dimensions that cannot increase in number without the multiplicity changing its nature" (Deleuze and Guattari [1980] 1987, 8).[7]

If multiplicities have no subject, no center, no self-identical core, what happens when one identifies oneself as a dancer or as Jewish? Is it *impossible* to identify oneself as a dancer? It can be done, of course, but inadequately. And the reason is familiar from my first discussion of existential authenticity: the identification can only be theatrical. It is a masquerade of identification. And as with the existentialists, the masquerade is metaphysical. But the metaphysics has changed: where the existentialist thought that humans were, at bottom, nothing, Deleuze will say that we are, at bottom, swarms or packs or rhizomes or becomings or lines. One of his showstoppers is: "There are only lines" (Deleuze and Guattari [1980] 1987, 8).[8]

The only way to recognize the fundamentally swarmlike characteristics of individuals is to escape the "iron collars of representation" (Deleuze [1968] 1994, 262). If we remain within the striated land of representation, then the other side of representation will simply be nothing. Deleuze seems to be offering this as a criticism of existentialists such as Heidegger and Sartre when he writes:

> Representation, especially when it becomes infinite, is imbued with a presentiment of groundlessness. Because it has become infinite in order to include difference within itself, however, it represents groundlessness as a completely undifferentiated abyss, a universal lack of difference, an indifferent black nothingness. (Deleuze [1968] 1994, 276)

This is a Deleuzean diagnosis of the existentialist characterization of the self as fundamentally nothing. The existentialists correctly discerned the inadequacy of representational thinking but did not take the turn to transcendental empiricism, and so did not discover multiplicity between the one and the many. Thus, although Deleuze can agree that identification, the quest for authenticity, is a metaphysical masquerade, he will not agree that we are fated to the inauthentic, because he holds out the possibility of releasing the swarms of difference, differences of intensity; he holds out the possibility of a life "beyond authenticity and inauthenticity" (Derrida 1991, 45).[9] These differences of intensity are presupposed by the diversity and change revealed in what Deleuze smears as the orthodoxy of common sense and good sense (Deleuze [1968] 1994, 223–28). Deleuze urges us to release the "animality peculiar to thought, the genitality of thought; not this or that animal form but stupidity *[bêtise]*. . . . Stupidity (not error) constitutes the greatest weakness of thought, but also the source of its highest power" (275).

An Honorable Postmodernism: Lyotard

Lyotard goes part of the way. He recognizes the failures of representation and makes it the task of what he calls an "honorable postmodernism" (Lyotard [1983] 1988, xiii) to bear witness to the inevitable inadequacy of representation, an inadequacy to which he gives the name "differend." Lyotard operates with a metaphysic of phrases, bits of significance including much more than words, for example, the twitching tail of a cat (Lyotard [1983] 1988, para. 198). The representational significance of a phrase is partly determined by how a phrase is "linked" to a given phrase. And since silence is a way of linking onto a given phrase, there is no choice about whether to link or not. This is a necessity (para. 102). But how to link is not necessary, and it is in the space of that "how" that the differend happens (para. 40). It is "signaled by what one ordinarily calls a feeling: [for example, that] 'One cannot find the words'" (para. 22). The sign that Lyotard sees no way out of the land of representation is that he (like the existentialists) describes the space between phrases as nothing: "the abyss of Not-Being which opens between phrases" (para. 100, para. 188). According to Lyotard, "what is at stake in literature, in philosophy, in politics perhaps, is to bear witness to differends by finding idioms for them" (para. 22). This would be the task of an "honorable postmodernism."

Picture the field of representation as a field on which are scattered many conceptual cups, containers of various shapes and sizes.[10] As the particulars rain down, they will be caught by the conceptual containers; but many will escape. On Lyotard's account, what is at stake in philosophy and the arts is to find idioms for what escapes the cups. And this can take at least two forms: one good and one melancholic. The first and more familiar is the effort to extend respect and dignity to those currently denied it; to add new cups to help extend respect to those who are immigrants, refugees, minorities. Lyotard does not deny that these activities are admirable: "These commandments of liberal democracies are good. They allow, and even request, Amnesty International to exist" (Lyotard [1993] 1997, 119 and 203). But the second task is more melancholic and more distinctively Lyotardian: the task of bearing witness to the fact that the field of representation will never be able to contain all (or even any) of the particulars raining down on it. The differend is without end. Here is Lyotard, at some length commenting on the effort to invent idioms for what escapes the conceptual containers of representation:

> This life is not without "melancholy," however. It is true that we owe others respect for their rights and that they owe us respect for ours. And that everyone owes it to him or herself to be absolutely respected. But there is in this self [deserving of respect] another, whomever or whatever the self meets or seeks to meet during the hours of secrecy. This other exerts an absolute right over the self that was never contracted and is unaware of reciprocity. It is utterly other than "the others."[11] It requires our time and our space in secret, without giving us anything in exchange, not even the cognizance of what it is, or what we are. We have no rights over it, no recourse against it, and no security. (Lyotard [1993] 1997, 121)

This self beyond representation is unrepresentable, and yet, according to Lyotard, it is the deep and melancholic task of philosophy and the arts to attempt the impossible to represent the unrepresentable. According to Lyotard, music, for instance, "struggles, it *labors* in the strong sense of the word . . . to leave a trace or make a sign, within the audible, of a sonorous gesture that goes beyond the audible" (218).

Individuation without Identity

However unclear you find the idea of releasing swarms of intensities, I hope that, even now, it is clear *that* (if not *how*) Deleuze will want to escape Lyotard's melancholy in the direction of those very swarms. The question of identity and identification is closely related to the question of "the other," and this is also true in Deleuze's thought. To be represented as a self-identical individual is to be represented as a thing of *this* kind—not that, not that other. And so the space within which we succumb to the metaphysical masquerade of identity is a space characterized by the other of our identity. But Deleuze takes pains to separate himself from the (existentialist) interpretation of the other as an other person. The other, he insists, is not an other I (Deleuze [1968] 1994, 61).

> The error of philosophical theories is to reduce the Other some-
> times to a particular object, and sometimes to another subject. . . .
> But the Other is neither an object in the field of my perception nor
> a subject who perceives me: the Other is initially a structure of the
> perceptual field, without which the entire field could not function
> as it does. (Deleuze [1969] 1990, 307)[12]

The other-structure works to divide our group from other groups. It
organizes the perceptual field into us and them. Deleuze again:
"Everything happens as though *the Other integrated the individuating
factors and pre-individual singularities within the limits of objects and subjects,* which are then offered to representation as perceivers or perceived" (Deleuze [1968] 1994, 281–82).

In later work, authored jointly with Guattari, the other-structure
seems to have become "faciality," the white wall/black hole system
(Deleuze and Guattari [1980] 1987; see Deleuze and Parnet [1977]
1987, 42 and 45). The idea of faciality can come into focus as a joining of Derridean and Foucauldian elements. The white wall is Derrida's endless disseminating play of representational signifiers, too
fluid by themselves even to be able to authenticate a check. Or again,
the white wall is the space within which Lewis Carroll's Tortoise ruins
the logic of Achilles (Carroll 1895). In contrast, the black holes are
foci of Foucauldian normalization. So the face itself is a combination
of significance and subjectification (Deleuze and Guattari [1980]
1987, 167). It is the power of the face that permits logic to work, and
it is the face that functions to individuate the swarms of intensities
into majoritarian groups and those who should be majoritarian but
"whose crime it is not to be" (178).

The difference between Lyotard and Deleuze may be put this
way: only Deleuze imagines that it is possible to escape the other-
structure, the face, the white wall/black hole system. If we can't escape the face, then seeking identity within a group will logically risk
inciting hatred directed against those whose crime it is to be unlike
us, to be at some distance from the normalizing, black holes on the
face that make us subjects. And if we are anxious to escape that hatred, we might join Lyotard in either of the tasks of his honorable
postmodernism, either the good task of inventing idioms to extend
respect to the disrespected, to recover lost literatures, ignored cul-

tures, or the melancholy task of mourning the endlessness of this good work.

But is there any way to escape the other-structure altogether? What would a *world without others* be?[13] Deleuze's answer to this question was first presented in a reading of Michel Tournier's novel *Friday*, a retelling of the story of Robinson Crusoe (Tournier [1967] 1997). As Tournier tells it, when Crusoe lands on the island, he is all alone but still living on the Christian face that he brought with him from his British island home: he keeps very busy and replicates, as much as he can, his life in England, even punishing himself when he does not obey the rules he has invented for his new island. Friday changes all that. Friday is an example of what Deleuze and Guattari refer to as an "exceptional individual" or simply as the "anomalous" (Deleuze and Guattari [1980] 1987, 243 and 244). They claim that wherever you find a multiplicity, wherever you have escaped the iron collars of representation, there you will find an exceptional individual, a Friday (243). The anomalous "has neither familiar or *subjectified* feelings, nor specific or *significant* characteristics" (244, my emphasis). The anomalous cannot find a home on the face, either in the white wall of the endless play of signifiers or in the black holes of subjectification. It is neither I nor other; it is a diagonal line that can throw off the whole system. It is the white whale that turns an ordinary whaling captain at home on the bottom line into Ahab racing along a line of destruction, a line of death. But it can also be Friday releasing Crusoe from his Yorkshire roots to the delirious intensities of the sun and Speranza, his new island.

Deleuze and Guattari do not go into much detail about how an anomalous individual helps release swarms of intensities, but the outlines of an account can be sketched. Our lives and our languages are, first of all, regimented, not free; striated, not smooth; organized, not disorganized. And each organizational technique will box off some thoughts or pleasures or races or religions or sexes as "other." Those that are so boxed off are not anomalous, for anything that fits in the other box will fit the organizational scheme. The anomalous (the werewolf, the vampire)[14] must disrupt the verticality of the majority and the horizontality of what appears as other. The anomalous releases the incommensurable diagonal: the square root of two.

The anomalous can also help make sense of Deleuze and Guattari's strange notion of becoming-minoritarian, which we may transpose as a becoming-anomalous, becoming-diagonal.[15] Deleuze and Guattari insist that they do not mean minority in a numerical sense. Their concern is to point to an incommensurable anomalous, not a numerically rare:

> The opposition between minority and majority is not simply quantitative. Majority implies a constant, of expression or content, serving as a standard measure by which to evaluate it. Let us suppose that the constant or standard is the average adult-white-heterosexual-European-male-speaking a standard language. . . . It is obvious that "man" [so hyphenated] holds the majority, even if he is less numerous than mosquitos, children, women, blacks, peasants, homosexuals, etc. . . . That is why we must distinguish between: the majoritarian as a constant and homogeneous system; minorities as subsystems; and the minoritarian as a potential, creative and created, becoming. (Deleuze and Guattari [1980] 1987, 105–6)

Becoming-minoritarian is not a matter of becoming or simulating a certain minority; that would simply reproduce the organized framework of representation. This is why we are encouraged to initiate becomings but warned that it would be "particularly stupid" to ask, "What are you becoming?" (Deleuze and Parnet [1977] 1987, 2). Rather, what we should be doing is initiating a becoming-minoritarian of the majority. "We should distinguish between minor languages, the major language, and the becoming-minor of the major" (Deleuze and Guattari [1980] 1987, 106).

It is in a discussion of becoming-minoritarian that Deleuze and Guattari come as close as they ever come to explicitly discussing the question of Jewish identity and becoming-Jewish as a becoming-intense of life and language. In the following extended passage, they broach the question of Jewish identity, but not in terms of a static model that authentic Jews ought to represent, and not in terms of a temporal model in which one can never reach the ideal or in which a pattern of change is itself identified with being Jewish. Rather, they address the question of becoming-Jewish as a becoming-minoritarian of all people. All people. Universal fraternity, not self-identity, is the goal, but this universal fraternity is a molecular universality, not a mere sum of identities as if there were a togetherness of all identities: a sack of all the kinds of person that there are.[16] "For everybody/ everything is the molar aggregate. But *becoming everybody/everything* is another affair, one that brings into play the cosmos with its molecular components" (Deleuze and Guattari [1980] 1987, 279–80). Here, then, is the extended quotation that addresses becoming-Jewish:

> Jews, Gypsies, etc., may constitute minorities under certain conditions, but that in itself does not make them becomings. One reterritorializes, or allows oneself to be reterritorialized, on a minority as a state; but in a becoming, one is deterritorialized. Even blacks, as the Black Panthers said, must become-black. Even women must become-woman. Even Jews must become Jewish (it certainly takes more than a state). But if this is the case, then becoming-Jewish necessarily affects the non-Jew as much as the Jew. . . . Conversely, if Jews themselves must become-Jewish, if women must become-woman, if children must become-child, if blacks must become-black, it is because only a minority is capable of serving as the active medium of becoming, but under such conditions that it ceases to be a definable aggregate in relation to the majority. Becoming-Jewish, becoming-woman, etc., therefore imply two simultaneous movements, one by which a term (the subject) is withdrawn from the majority, and another by which a term (the medium or agent) rises up from the minority. . . .[17]
>
> A woman has to become-woman, but in a becoming-woman of all man. A Jew becomes Jewish, but in a becoming-Jewish of the non-Jew. A becoming-minoritarian exists only by virtue of a deterritorialized medium and subject that are like its elements. (Deleuze and Guattari [1980] 1987, 291–92)

What is going on here? Are we in the face of some dubious romanticization of minorities? If so, this passage would simply update the romantic fascination with an idealized pastoral. But I don't think this is what is going on. There is no question that a sort of privilege is granted to becoming-minoritarian, but it is not the privilege of a segmented minority cultural life, still in the grip of the facial organization of the other structure, still in the grip of the white wall/black hole system. Rather, the privilege is that in breaking through the face, a becoming-minoritarian of the majority is a first step.[18] The claim seems to be that to break through the white wall of representation, we will have to initiate a becoming-minoritarian of the majority—even the majoritarian category of the minority.

Insofar as becoming-Jewish has any privilege in the passage through representation, releasing swarms of intensities, it is a function of the stature of Christianity in the face. As Deleuze and Guattari describe the face, the face is not only male, it is Christian. Indeed, they tell us: "The face is Christ" (Deleuze and Guattari [1980] 1987, 176).[19] In this way, Deleuze and Guattari revise Nietzsche's premature obituary of the Christian God. Becoming-Jewish, read as something that Jews and non-Jews must both undertake, is a way of assembling a plane of spiritual life that breaks away from molar identifications of all sorts, including Christian and Jewish; a plane of pure immanence: A LIFE (Deleuze [1995] 1997).

The face, however, is more fundamentally male than it is Christian, so becoming-woman is the form of becoming-minoritarian that comes first. At one point, Deleuze and Guattari enumerate the various steps on the way to breaking through the wall of representation: "If becoming-woman is the first quantum, or molecular segment, with the becomings-animal that link up with it coming next, what are they all rushing toward? Without a doubt, toward becoming imperceptible" (Deleuze and Guattari [1980] 1987, 279).

Again, this does not mean representing women; that would remain within the system of faciality, in the same way as pretending to be Jewish would preserve the other structure that makes identity possible. Becoming-women will begin to break away from identifications in general, so both the identity of men and that of women begin the process of releasing swarms of intensities, rushing toward becoming-imperceptible along lines of becoming-Jewish, becoming-woman, becoming-animal, becoming-music.

Deleuze's regular example of the imperceptible is Soren Kierkegaard's knight of faith, who, in *Fear and Trembling*, looks like nothing so much as a mundane civil servant (Deleuze and Guattari [1980] 1987, 279). Like a camouflaged fish, becoming-imperceptible requires drawing disorganizing lines that draw the fish into its world, constructing a new world without fish and without rock, just lines: becoming-imperceptible (280). By drawing lines connecting our selves to everything surrounding us, our self is obliterated. "Where the psychoanalyst says 'Stop, find your self again,' we should say instead,

'Let's go further still . . . we haven't sufficiently dismantled our self'" (151). Dismantled, self-identity disappears, leaving an imperceptible individual without identity: a rhizome.

> To be present at the dawn of the world. Such is the link between imperceptibility, indiscernibility, and impersonality—the three virtues. To reduce oneself to an abstract line, a trait, in order to find one's zone of indiscernibility with other traits, and in this way to enter the haecceity and impersonality of the creator. One is then like grass: one has made the world, everybody/everything into a becoming, because one has made a necessarily communicating world, because one has suppressed in oneself everything that prevents us from slipping between things and growing in the midst of things. . . . Saturate, eliminate, put everything in. (Deleuze and Guattari [1980] 1987, 280)

Drawing lines from here to everywhere will make of what used to be an identifiable self a new creature: an individual without identity. Drawing lines from here to everywhere is one way of characterizing a powerful work of art: not merely propaganda for this or that cause, not merely cute, not merely formally intriguing, not merely erotically exciting, but all of these and more. A powerful work of art can overwhelm us by disorganizing our identity along the lines it feeds us; not a sublime art that confronts us with the unrepresentable but a beautiful art that incites pointless play along the multiple lines—neither one nor many—that constitute us. An existential imperative to become-imperceptible is thus, paradoxically, an existential imperative to make of one's life a work of art. A Deleuzean aesthetics of existence: draw a beautiful life in a world without others.

A new mode of individuality appears, individuality without identity. Haecceities. But what are these?

> There is a mode of individuation very different from that of a person, subject, thing, or substance. We reserve the name *haecceity* for it. A season, a winter, a summer, an hour, a date have a perfect individuality lacking nothing, even though this individuality is different from that of a thing or a subject. They are haecceities in the sense that they consist entirely of relations of movement and rest between molecules or particles, capacities to affect and be affected. (Deleuze and Guattari [1980] 1987, 261)

Approach haecceities from the side of the person. Suppose the mode of individuation of a person is given by the standard model of identification with which I started this chapter (Deleuze [1993] 1997, 76). A person struggles to maintain his or her identity by conforming to a form or an ideal that the person conceives of as his or her identity. It is a repressive project: our actions hemmed in by the goal of simulating the ideal person we would be.

Haecceities, however, are meant to be individuated without identity, or at least without identity of that sort. Consider the example of an hour, but don't be misled by the fact that an hour can be clocked. Think rather of times and hours defined otherwise: recess, graduation, spring, five o'clock in the afternoon.

> "What a terrible 5:00 in the afternoon!" It is not the moment, and it is not the brevity, which distinguishes this type of individuation. A haecceity can last as long as, and even longer than, the time required for the development of a form and the evolution of a subject. (Deleuze and Parnet [1977] 1987, 92)

It is possible to experience five o'clock in the afternoon for two or three hours. Even when it is still winter (by the rotation of the Earth), it can be spring—warm air, the melting ground filling the air with the spring smell of dirt. These are haecceities that can join with features of our lives normally kept separate: releasing them to meet in "unnatural nuptials" (Deleuze and Guattari [1980] 1987, 241). Spring, construed as a haecceity, does not represent a model of spring. It is not a date on the calendar; it has no center or origin. Neither is it pointed in one direction; it has no culmination or climax. "A haecceity has neither beginning nor end, origin nor destination; it is always in the middle. It is not made of points, only lines. It is a rhizome" (Deleuze and Guattari [1980] 1987, 263). Haecceities are multiplicities, swarms of subrepresentational particles that join with others forming further multiplicities. Haecceities are sometimes recalled by brief Japanese poems that, according to Deleuze and Guattari, "include indicators as so many floating lines constituting a complex individual" (261). Perhaps the following poem is an example of what they have in mind:

In the utter silence
Of a temple,
A cicada's voice alone
Penetrates the rocks. (Basho [ca. 1690] 1977, 123)

Nor should this be surprising; because I have already provided the means for defending the claim that a work of art—where powerful—can be construed as a haecceity.

How can a life be made into a haecceity? Instead of seeking to organize our lives around a central identity, instead of seeking identity and organization at all, we should seek disorganization, the cusp of conceptualizability, which Kant called the beautiful: purposiveness but without a purpose. Not black pointlessness craving for a point, not the theater of representation craving perfect authenticity, but pointlessness unburdened of the craving for a point; a theater of repetition, not a theater of representation. The points become lines.

We are drawing our lives, but not with our eye on any model, so not burdened by either the existentialist dream of authenticity or the Lyotardian discovery of inevitable differends. How do you draw out your life, how do you ride a line of flight, how do you break through the white wall of representation and identification, how do you become imperceptible in a world without others? It will not seem like much to be told that *pointlessness* is the way. But it can be enough, and we already know how to do it. Nevertheless, in this case, the slippers will neither return us to Kansas nor leave us in Oz. Neither taking us home nor leaving us in exile, these diagonal slippers will launch us on a delirious, nomadic line of flight.

If you think about your ordinary life and about the experiences that are the best, I think you will find that they are *not* often the experiences that aim at a goal, a point. —A drive to the store can be enjoyable, but just going on a drive to nowhere in particular, this is better.[20] —A walk to a lookout in the forest is a good thing. But it ends. You look out and that's it. A nice view. But stopping along the trail, sitting by the side of tree, the world of the dirt, the ants, the dead twigs, the decaying leaves, the beetles running, the grubs hiding: this is much more than a view. —Thought, too: the best thinking alone or with others is hardly a treatise, never question and answer; rather, it is a fragment here, a fragment there, scribbling in your notebook, trading incomplete thoughts with a friend, shouts, jumping up in excitement from your desk. —Even, or especially, sex: intimacy governed by the quest for genital climax, enjoyable surely, but honestly, a little too close to work . . . however . . . caresses . . . pointlessly wandering your lover's body . . . this is much more. Caressing is not possible unless the hand forgoes goals, ignores the biological glory of our opposable thumb, and simply moves. Desire does not seek pleasure, a lack filled: desire desires desire, not satisfaction. How do you draw a pointless life? With caresses.

It will be theatrical, yes, but it will not be aiming at a model or goal, and so it will be neither authentic nor inauthentic. Remember when we played with blocks? We could aim at a model, give our actions a point: this, we told our friends proudly, is the *Titanic.* Or we could just play, allowing our desires to grow, one block here, another there, let's put a row over here, and the pointless play continues without aiming at a model. The first is play with a point, like a dice game you might lose, Deleuze refers to the second kind of play as a divine game where "every time the whole of chance is affirmed in a necessarily winning throw" (Deleuze [1962] 1983, 25–27; [1968] 1994, 283). And he suggests that the closest human game to this divine game is the work of art ([1968] 1994, 283). Theatrical, yes, but a theater not of representation but of repetition, repetition repeated without a goal, without a point, unconstrained by any conceptual or representational model. Unconstrained by the longing for identity; beyond authenticity and inauthenticity.

The theater of repetition is a theater of intensities. It will require an anomalous individual, not necessarily a human, to get us moving—it might be alcohol or drugs, but this would risk initiating a line of destruction, risking not just the death of the self but of the body as well.[21] These things must be done carefully. Deleuze and Guattari suggest we learn from one of their favorite bits of Henry Miller: "To succeed in getting drunk, but on pure water" (Deleuze and Guattari [1980] 1987, 286). To be drunk on water, to have passed up goals for goallessness, to turn from the existentialist leap to the Nietzschean dance (Deleuze [1962] 1983, 37): this would be to make our lives works of art, not purified lives, but intensified. And I can imagine these pointless, intensified lives moving in two directions: in the direction either of goallessness achieved through meditation and isolation, the intensities of Apollo, or of goallessness achieved through connection, the intensities of Dionysus. We thought the postmodernists were Nietzscheans, but we were wrong. Their mentor was, rather, Schopenhauer, and we have yet to discover what a real life of affirmation might be. Beyond identity, beyond authenticity and inauthenticity, life as a work of art, an aesthetics of intensified existence.[22]

NOTES

1.   This notion of repetition is one of two that Gilles Deleuze distinguishes in *Difference and Repetition* (1968; reprint, London: Athlone, 1994), 23–25. One kind of repetition is repetition of conceptually identical individuals, two counter stools; but the "primary sense of repetition" is "the essence of that in which every repetition consists: difference without a concept, non-mediated difference" (25).

      In the Heideggerian context of authenticity, repetition in this "primary sense" seems not to be the sense of repetition *(Wiederholung)* invoked (Heidegger [1927, German p. 308] 1996, 284).

      In Jacques Derrida's discussion of iterability, he says that what iterability names is "the logic that ties repetition to alterity" ([1971] 1988, 7). This claim appears very close to Deleuze's that the primary sense of repetition is one that ties repetition to difference. Most of the time, however, Derrida looks at the work of alterity on repetition from, so to speak, *this* side of representation: *italicizing* the play thereby introduced to representation. On rare occasions, Derrida can hazard a discussion of the other side of representation (the metaphysics of presence), "the as yet unnameable" beyond metaphysics (Derrida [1967] 1978, 293). But on these occasions, the beyond of representation is misconstrued according to the early Nietzsche of *The Birth of Tragedy* as a primordial unity, not as swarms of differences of intensity, a position Deleuze attributes to the mature Nietzsche (Deleuze [1968] 1994, 276–77).

2.   Nietzsche's interest in reversing the evaluation of pointlessness is visible in this passage: "When one moves toward a goal it seems impossible that 'goallessness as such' is the principle of our faith" (Nietzsche [1901] 1967, para. 25).

3.   In due course, I will distinguish two kinds of theater that will pair off with the two kinds of repetition distinguished in n. 1: a theater of representation and a theater of repetition.

4. Deleuze speaks of what lies beneath phenomena of diversity and change as differences of intensity (Deleuze [1968] 1994, 222). These differences of intensity are what bind together packs and swarms. It is not unlike the vision of reality current in parts of physical theory today: if the world is fundamentally arrangements of waves, then what an individual really is, is an arrangement of waves, and (1) it doesn't matter what waves (wolves) make up the arrangement and (2) the concept of a wave (wolf) is not what will define the arrangement; rather, the arrangement is an emergent pack phenomenon. (Thanks to Mark Bickhard for connections to physics.)

5. Deleuze's argument against the possibility of representing one and only one particular is cousin to Derrida's argument against the possibility of invoking one and only one serious significance of our words. I owe to Mark Bickhard the suggestion that perhaps Derrida's argument is directed to singularity in time and Deleuze's to singularity in space.

6. What keeps the particulars from escaping is what Derrida calls force (Derrida [1989] 1992) and what Deleuze and Guattari call "faciality" ([1980] 1987, 167–91). I do not mean that these are the same, only that in both cases the stability, such as it is, of the play of signifiers is derived from a place beyond semantics, beyond truth and falsity.

7. Deleuze and Guattari turn away from partial identities when, in spite of respect, they turn from Melanie Klein's "partial objects," which they saw as too tied to the language of completion, wholeness, identity (Deleuze [1969] 1990, 197).

8. Perhaps the most accessible example of the primacy Deleuze gives to lines is in "Many Politics" in Deleuze and Parnet ([1977] 1987, 124–47).

9. I am stealing these four words from Derrida's remarks not because I want to arrive at the mournful Derridean experience of the impossible; quite the reverse. I steal them, rather, because four years ago, they pointed my thinking not toward a new goal but in a new direction—a direction I had not even thought possible but that I now find deliriating.

10. Interpreting concepts as containers is not the only way to interpret concepts. It is a "negative" interpretation, not unrelated to the negative interpretation of desire as lack. Deleuze and Guattari are dead set against the morbid conception of desire as lack, and when they announce that "concepts are lines," they reveal that they are also opposed to the negative conception of concepts as containers (Deleuze and Guattari [1980] 1987, 22).

11. Like Lyotard, Deleuze also wants to get beyond the "others," but not to find a *thing* (Lyotard [1993] 1997, 140, 189ff.). This preserves the other-

structure but purges the other of all representable content. Deleuze will want to slip away from the other-structure altogether.

12. This brings the other-structure fairly close to Heidegger's "they" *(das Mann)*.

13. There is a lobster diagram here:

LIFE

A with other-structure and identity		B without other-structure and without identity	
1 hating others	2 honorable postmodernism	1 empty body without organs	2 full body without organs
	a. politics of rights	death	pointless delirium
	b. mourning		

14. "From 1730–1735, all we hear about are vampires" (Deleuze and Guattari [1980] 1987, 237); "In order to produce werewolves in your family . . . " (246).

15. "Free the line, free the diagonal: every musician or painter has this intention" (Deleuze and Guattari [1980] 1987, 295).

16. Although I am arguing for individuation without identity, this can also be understood as inventing a novel conception of identity, one that Deleuze distinguishes as *psychotic*, in opposition to the *neurotic* standard conception of identity that I invoked in the first section of this paper (see Deleuze [1993] 1997, 78). We can table the distinction between a neurotic and a psychotic conception of identity this way:

	NEUROTIC Identification	PSYCHOTIC Identification
1.	model/form	formless trait
2.	subject	zone of indistinction
3.	effort of the subject to model the subject	universal fraternity/unnatural nuptials

17. These two simultaneous movements ("one by which a term [the subject] is withdrawn from the majority, and another by which a term [the medium or agent] rises up from the minority") can be understood in two complementary ways: (1) To become-woman you need to find a molecular medium within which to draw a line of flight, and this molecular medium is probably girls (Deleuze and Guattari [1980] 1987, 277). But

you also need to be the becoming of a deterritorialized subject, and here
the majoritarian versions of men and women need to be deterritorialized, becoming-minoritarian. (2) The two simultaneous movements
could also be understood as the two simultaneous movements in the
production of a BwO (body without organs): first a disorganization of
the organs, and then setting intensity and gaiety to flow through them
(Deleuze and Guattari [1980] 1987, 152–53). Melville's Bartleby can be
construed as having emptied himself but not having filled himself with
intensities; motionless he faces the wall but does not move through it beyond representation.

18. "If the face is a politics, dismantling the face is also a politics involving
real becomings, an entire becoming clandestine. Dismantling the face is
the same as breaking through the wall of the signifier and getting out of
the black hole of subjectivity" (Deleuze and Guattari [1980] 1987, 188).

19. If the face is Christ's, then Deleuze and Guattari seem to be open to the
same criticism that is sometimes launched against Lyotard's *Heidegger
and 'the jews'* ([1988] 1990), namely, that of encouraging the historical
figuration of the Jew as the other. Whatever the merits of this criticism
directed against Lyotard, in Deleuze's case both the Christian and the
Jew are a function of the face of Christ, so that breaking through the face
would be to move beyond the categories of the Christian and the Jew
and, indeed, beyond representation altogether.

20. It was a discussion of pointless driving with Alison Freeman in the early
fall of 1997 that first convinced me pointlessness, in a positive sense,
might be the answer to the riddle of existence.

21. The line of death here risked is B.1 of the lobster in n. 13.

22. Michael Mendelson helped enormously in the writing of this chapter.
The central argument against particulars was worked out with him during an intense (what else?) forty-five minutes just before I rushed off to
teach a bit of *Difference and Repetition* on 15 April 1998; and a month later
he helped me find the lobster in note 13. But I would never have pulled
these ideas together without Larry Silberstein's characteristically generous invitation to participate in the Berman Center conference "Mapping
Jewish Identities."

REFERENCES

Basho. [ca. 1690] 1977. *The Narrow Road to the Deep North.* Middlesex, England: Penguin Books.
Carroll, L. 1895. "What the Tortoise Said to Achilles." *Mind* 4: 278–80.

Deleuze, G. [1962] 1983. *Nietzsche and Philosophy*. New York: Columbia University Press.

———. [1968] 1994. *Difference and Repetition*. London: Athlone.

———. [1969] 1990. *Logic of Sense*. New York: Columbia University Press.

———. [1973] 1995. "Letter to a Harsh Critic." Also called "I Have Nothing to Admit." In *Negotiations*, 3–12. New York: Columbia University Press.

———. [1993] 1997. *Essays Critical and Clinical*. Minneapolis: University of Minnesota Press.

———. [1995] 1997. "Immanence: A Life . . ." *Theory, Culture, and Society* 14, 2 (May): 3–7.

Deleuze, G., and F. Guattari. [1980] 1987. *A Thousand Plateaus: Capitalism and Schizophrenia*. Minneapolis: University of Minnesota Press.

Deleuze, G., and C. Parnet. [1977] 1987. *Dialogues*. New York: Columbia University Press, 1987.

Derrida, J. [1967] 1978. *Writing and Difference*. Chicago: University of Chicago Press.

———. [1971] 1988. "Signature Event Context." In *Limited Inc.*, 1–23. Evanston: Northwestern University Press.

———. [1977] 1988. "Limited Inc a b c . . ." In *Limited Inc.*, 29–110. Evanston: Northwestern University Press.

———. [1989] 1992. "Force of Law: The 'Mystical Foundation of Authority.'" In *Deconstruction and the Possibility of Justice*, edited by Drucilla Cornell, Michel Rosenfeld, and David Gray Carlson, 3–67. New York: Routledge.

———. 1991. "Summary of Impromptu Remarks." In *Anyone*, edited by Cynthia Davidson, 39–45. New York: Rizzoli International.

Heidegger, M. [1927] 1996. *Being and Time*. Translated by J. Stambaugh. Albany: SUNY Press.

Lyotard, J.-F. [1983] 1988. *The Differend: Phrases in Dispute*. Minneapolis: University of Minnesota Press.

———. [1988] 1990. *Heidegger and 'the jews.'* Minneapolis: University of Minnesota Press, 1990.

———. [1993] 1997. *Postmodern Fables*. Minneapolis: University of Minnesota Press.

Nietzsche, F. [1901] 1967. *The Will to Power*. New York: Vintage Books.

Tournier, M. [1967] 1997. *Friday*. Baltimore: Johns Hopkins University Press.

About the Editor

Laurence J. Silberstein is Philip and Muriel Berman Professor of Jewish Studies in the Department of Religion Studies, Lehigh University, and director of the Philip and Muriel Berman Center for Jewish Studies. He is author of *Martin Buber's Social and Religious Thought: Alienation and the Quest for Meaning* (1989) and *The Postzionism Debates: Knowledge and Power in Israeli Culture* (1999). He is the editor of *New Perspectives on Israeli History* and *Jewish Fundamentalism in Comparative Perspective*, as well as co-editor with Robert Cohn of *The Other in Jewish Thought and History*.

About the Contributors

Ammiel Alcalay is chair of Classical, Middle Eastern, and Asian Languages and Cultures at Queens College and a member of the faculty of Comparative Literature and the Medieval Studies Program at the CUNY Graduate Center. He is author of *After Jews and Arabs: Remaking Levantine Culture; Keys to the Garden: New Israeli Writing; the cairo notebooks;* and *Memories of Our Future: Collected Essays 1982–1997.*

Gordon C. F. Bearn is the Selfridge Associate Professor of Philosophy at Lehigh University. He has published *Waking to Wonder: Wittgenstein's Existential Investigations* and a number of articles on relativism, aesthetics, and deconstruction. He is currently working on a book, *Life Drawing: An Aesthetics of Existence,* which details some of the ideas sketched in his chapter in this book.

Daniel Boyarin is the Taubman Professor of Talmudic Culture at the University of California. Author of numerous volumes, journal articles, and scholarly papers, he recently published *A Radical Jew: Paul and the Politics of Identity* and *Unheroic Conduct: The Rise of Heterosexuality and the Invention of the Jewish Man.* His current work engages the question of Jewish-Christian religious relations and interactions between the second and fifth centuries after Christ.

Michelle A. Friedman, a Ph.D. candidate in English at Bryn Mawr College, is writing her thesis on "Transforming Acts of Witness: Reading Contemporary American Holocaust Literature." She was the recipient of the 1994 National Women's Studies Association Grant in Jewish Women's Studies and has taught at Bryn Mawr College, Haverford College, and Lehigh University.

Tresa L. Grauer is lecturer in the Department of Foreign Literatures and Linguistics at Ben Gurion University of the Negev. She has published essays on Philip Roth, Jerome Badanes, Cynthia Ozick, and Vivian Gornick and is completing a study of narrative explorations of Jewish American identity in contemporary Jewish American literature.

Hannan Hever is associate professor of poetics and comparative literature at Tel Aviv University and has served as a visiting professor at Columbia, Northwestern, and the University of Michigan. He authored two books on modern Hebrew poetry and fiction and its relationship to the Hebrew national character: *Captives of Utopia: An Essay on Messianism and Politics in Hebrew Poetry in Eretz-Israel between the Two World Wars* and *Poets and Zealots: The Rise of Hebrew Political Poetry in Eretz-Israel.*

Laura S. Levitt is associate professor of religion and chair of Jewish Studies at Temple University. Her recent publications are *Jews and Feminism: The Ambivalent Search for Home, Judaism since Gender,* which she co-edited with Miriam Peskowitz; and "Blurring the Familial: An Afterword," in *The Familial Gaze.*

Regina Morantz-Sanchez is professor of history at the University of Michigan. She has published widely in women's history and the history of sexuality and is the author of three books, including *Sympathy and Science: Women Physicians in American Medicine* and *Conduct Unbecoming a Woman: Medicine on Trial in Turn-of-the-Century Brooklyn.*

Anita Norich, associate professor of English and Judaic studies at the University of Michigan, is author of *The Homeless Imagination in the Fiction of Israel Joshua Singer* and co-editor of *Gender and Text in Modern Hebrew and Yiddish Literatures.*

Adi Ophir is senior lecturer in the Institute for the History and Philosophy of Science at Tel Aviv University. He is editor of *Theory and Criticism,* an interdisciplinary Hebrew journal for Israeli cultural studies and critical theory. His publications include *Kinds of Evil: An Outline for an Ontology of Morals* (forthcoming) and essays in Hebrew, English, and French journals and books.

Marilyn Reizbaum is professor of English at Bowdoin College and is currently also on the faculty of Tel Aviv University. She is the author of *James Joyce's Judaic Other* and is co-editor with Kimberly Devlin of *"Ulysses"—En-gendered Perspectives: Eighteen New Essays on the Episodes.* She also works in the areas of contemporary Scottish and Irish literatures and postcolonial theory.

Susan E. Shapiro teaches Jewish philosophy and the philosophy of religion at Columbia University. Her essay in this book is part of a larger project titled "Figures of Marginalization: Rhetoric, Gender, Judaism." Other articles related to this project include "A Matter of Discipline: Reading for Gender in Jewish Philosophy," in *Judaism since Gender*, and "Rhetoric as Ideology Critique: The Gadamer-Habermas Debate Reinvented," in the *Journal of the American Academy of Religion.*

Deborah A. Starr is a doctoral candidate in comparative literature at the University of Michigan. Her dissertation examines issues of identity formation in contemporary literature by and about Egyptian Jews. She is also the author of "Egyptian Representation of Israeli Culture: Normalizing Propaganda or Propagandizing Normalization?" in *Review Essays in Israel Studies.*

Index

Abraham, 253, 273

Adam, 302, 306, 311, 319n. 16

Adorno, Theodor, 21, 122, 124, 317n. 2

Adultery, 170

Aeneid (Virgil), 251, 259, 263

African Americans: de Beauvoir comparing women and, 314–15; racism as inspiration for Spiegelman's *Maus,* 128–29; in Spiegelman's *New Yorker* cover, 21, 125–29

Agency, 10, 27, 30n. 11, 160

Akiva, Rabbi, 275, 280, 285, 286

Alcalay, Ammiel, 24–25, 244n. 11

Alexander, Philip, 266, 267

Algren, Nelson, 323n. 44

Allegory, national, 205–7, 209, 210, 214

Alter, Robert, 41, 58n. 4

American Jews: desire to be really American, 74–75, 82; Holocaust in shaping identity of, 98; Holocaust mythologized by, 98, 101–4, 115, 117n. 2; and Israeli Jews remembering the Holocaust differently, 23, 32n. 29; in Jewish American literature, 37–64; names of, 85; photographing, 65–96; picture books about, 65, 70; self-representation contrasted with that of Israeli Jews, 135–36; sustaining narrative desired by, 76; women seeking Jewish identity, 159–73; Yiddish speaking by, 145–58

Amir, Aaron, 209, 245n. 19

Anderson, Benedict, 201

"And God Created Woman" (Levinas), 302–5, 310

Anomalous, the, 337–38

Anti-Semitism, 85, 193, 315

Anti-Zionism, 184, 185, 188–89, 242n. 3

Ants (Orpaz), 208

Appearance: distinguishing the Sacred from sorcery, 307–9; the feminine associated with, 305–7

Arabesques (Shammas), 17–18, 213–14

Arabic language, 226, 244n. 11

Arabs. *See* Palestinians

Arborescent systems, 6–8

Arendt, Hannah, 192

Art, 16, 335, 341, 344

Aryeh family, 78

Ashkenazic Jews: Castel-Bloom on hegemony of, 24, 221, 222, 227, 240; Holocaust in identity construction of, 24; in pragmatics of Zionist narrative, 183

Assimilation, 82, 104, 224, 228, 245n. 19

Authenticity: fixed notion of, 159; and the Holocaust, 112, 128; and identity, 325–28

Avneri, Uri, 192

Azoulay, Ariella, 16, 31n. 24

Bakhtin, Mikhail, 225, 228

Ballas, Shimon, 212–13

Barthes, Roland, 89n. 12, 101–2, 119n. 8

"Bartleby the Scrivener" (Melville), 325, 348n. 17

"Bashert" (Klepfisz), 105–8; "Chicago, 1964: I am walking home alone at midnight," 106–8; Elza, 107; incorporation in, 105

Baumgarten, Albert, 278

Bearn, Gordon C. F., 25, 26–27

Beauvoir, Simone de, 26, 313–16, 322n. 36

Beilis, Mendel, 50, 60n. 22

355

tional allegory, 205–7, 209, 210, 214; "National Unity" slogan in, 195, 196; Netanyahu, 181; 1967 war, 179, 193, 208; peace process, 191, 194; peace treaty with Egypt, 234, 235; *tsabar* symbol of, 135; West Bank, 194, 234, 244n. 11. *See also* Israeli Jews; Israeli literature; Palestinians

Israeli Jews: and American Jews remembering the Holocaust differently, 23, 32n. 29; Castel-Bloom on identity of, 220, 222, 241; Hebrew literature in construction of, 201–2; the Holocaust in identity of, 23, 24, 178–79, 228–30; the "New Jew," 205; Palestinians in identity construction of, 12–13, 14, 23; post-Zionists on, 186; in pragmatics of Zionist narrative, 183; self-representation contrasted with that of American Jews, 135–36; Sephardic Jews, 224, 229, 240; on Spiegelman's *Maus*, 136, 139n. 6; victim position in identity of, 23, 178, 182–84, 191; violence in construction of identity of, 203–4. *See also* Ashkenazic Jews; Mizrahi Jews

Israeli literature: coherent narrative sought by, 23; ethnocentric Jewish narrative striving to dominate, 214; Hebrew literature becoming, 202, 203–4, 214, 217; maps in, 24, 209–15; oedipal model in, 211, 212, 216; space as fundamental to, 24, 203; territory and violence in, 201–19. *See also* Hebrew literature

Iterability, 327, 345n. 1

Jabès, Edmond, 37–39
Jakobsen, Janet, 78–79
Jerome, Saint, 273, 276, 294n. 35
Jerusalem, 208
Jesus: accused Christians required to curse, 276, 277; Bethlehem as birthplace of, 274; and Christian-Jewish continuum, 268; Rabbi Eliezer refusing to curse, 277, 289; and Galilean Jewish traditions about Joshuas, 291n. 11; as magician, 287, 297n. 62, 297n. 69; offer to heal Ben Dama in name of, 283, 284, 289; *Toledot Yeshu* literature, 291n. 11

Jewish American literature, 37–64; author-

ial self-inscription in, 38; and biblical imperative to remember, 43–44; cultural and religious grounding of, 41; Howe on, 40; Jewish hermeneutic heritage in, 43; poststructuralism as informing contemporary, 44; Roth, 19, 40, 42, 45, 127; traditional Jewish narratives rewritten in, 19, 39

Jewish American Short Stories (Howe), 40
Jewish Museum (New York City), 90n. 19
Jewish National Fund Forest, 203, 211
Jewish Theological Seminary (New York City), 163, 164
Jews: anti-Semitism, 85, 193, 315; blood libel accusation, 50, 60n. 21, 60n. 22; contradiction between Israeliness and Jewishness, 23, 203, 206–7; east-west split within, 138n. 3; as ethnic group, 31n. 14; Hasidic Jews in Spiegelman's *New Yorker* magazine cover, 21, 125–29; identifying, 84; Levinas on gender and Jewishness, 316–17; as "the People of the Book," 38; as religious group, 31n. 14; self-hatred alleged in, 127, 139n. 6. *See also* American Jews; Diaspora; Holocaust; Identity, Jewish; Israeli Jews; Judaism

Jews/America/A Representation (Brenner): Aryeh family image, 78; Brenner's *Marranes* contrasted with, 92n. 36; "Citizens Protesting Anti-Semitic Acts, Billings, Montana, 1994," 75, 77, 92n. 33; as concealing ambivalences of American Jewish life, 20, 87, 96n. 61; as ethnography, 76, 77–78, 92n. 35; "The Hebrew Academy, The Luxor, Las Vegas, Nevada, 1994," 75; "Icons," 79–80; images used in other Jewish contexts, 72; "Inventory june 1993–september 1995," 79, 80, 81, 94n. 47, 94n. 48; liberal pluralism of, 78–80, 87; marketing of, 72; "Marxists, New York City, 1994," 75; *New York Times* review of, 75–76; readings of, 76–81; stereotypical images in, 77, 78; Sultan's *Pictures from Home* compared with, 71–72, 87

Jews and Feminism: The Ambivalent Search for Home (Levitt), 89n. 9, 94n. 49, 94n. 50
"Joe, a Man from Cairo" (Castel-Bloom), 245n. 20